T0330330

Internal Control Audit and Compliance

Wiley Corporate F&A Series

The Wiley Corporate F&A series provides information, tools, and insights to corporate professionals responsible for issues affecting the profitability of their company, from accounting and finance to internal controls and performance management.

Founded in 1807, John Wiley & Sons is the oldest independent publishing company in the United States. With offices in North America, Europe, Asia, and Australia, Wiley is globally committed to developing and marketing print and electronic products and services for our customers' professional and personal knowledge and understanding.

Internal Control Audit and Compliance

Documentation and Testing Under the New COSO Framework

LYNFORD GRAHAM

WILEY

Library of Congress Cataloging-in-Publication Data:

Graham, Lynford.
  Internal control audit and compliance : documentation and testing under the new COSO framework / Lynford Graham.
     1 online resource. – (Wiley corporate F&A series)
  Includes index.
  Description based on print version record and CIP data provided by publisher; resource not viewed.
  ISBN 978-1-118-99621-8 (cloth); ISBN 978-1-118-99647-8 (ebk);
ISBN 978-1-118-99630-0 (ebk) 1. Auditing, Internal. I. Title.
  HF5668.25
  657'.458—dc 3
                                                                    2014035947

Contents

PREFACE

M UCH HAS BEEN learned in the decade since corporations, other entities, and auditors started re-reading the 1992 COSO Internal Controls Framework document to understand their mandates to document and assess internal controls. We have been through a version of the guidance targeted to smaller public companies (2006) and special guidance for unscrambling what is meant by Monitoring (2009). In 2013 we were presented with the updated Framework that will replace that prior COSO literature after December 15, 2014, and serve as our basis for going forward. Many entities that began the COSO process in 2002-2003 have not made major changes in their approach since that time. The revised Framework provides an excellent opportunity to re-examine past practices and seek improvements and efficiencies, since some level of change is likely to be necessary anyway.

It is likely that the COSO Internal Controls Framework will be around in some form throughout our working lives. Some still fail to embrace its goals and others work hard to find ways to try to change the laws and standards or short-cut the required assessment procedures. Still others are starting to recognize some of the benefits that can be realized from effective controls and more orderly and automated processes.

This book will look back on some of the "lessons learned" as experienced by entities and auditors. We will examine some of the academic and professional literature that provides wider insight than can be obtained from solely one entity's experience. As we face the new Framework, we will consider efficient approaches to migrate entities from current approaches to the new guidance with a minimum of disruption and effort. As with any process, the assessment benefits from periodic reconsideration and improvements, and this book can assist in implementing more effective solutions in that update process.

We are now into the second and for some the third round of staff and management changes over the controls documentation and assessment project. In the natural order of things, systems are known to deteriorate over time. From my observation, that is a real challenge to all entities – "how to keep the music playing." Internal control pioneers in the early 2000s period had a lot to learn and not much time to learn it. Many of those warriors have now moved on, up, or out. How do we properly train new team members in the use of our developed tools and also fully explain the concepts we are trying to achieve? If approached as a paint-by-numbers exercise, the end product may look acceptable (from a distance) but still not meet the main objective. Controls "101" remains a requested topic on the speaker circuit for the benefit of new project members and helps fill the gaps in understanding by those already involved in projects. This book will also try to provide some history and context from which to understand not just *how* to do the tasks, but to understand *why* they are being done and how to make the project more meaningful and valuable to the entity—and in that process, facilitate working with the independent auditors in an efficient and effective way.

This volume is meant to supplement, not replace, the COSO Framework documents. An investment in the actual Framework is worthwhile and undoubtedly at some point with some Principle or Point of Focus, you will need to dig as deep as possible into the Approaches and Examples to find a nugget you can use in crafting your assessment of how the Principle is being met. This volume cannot possibly (or legally) reproduce all the potential COSO reference material you may wish to refer to as your project proceeds.

Some suggestions, based on first readers' comments as to how to get the most out of this volume include:

- Use the material in this volume first to get the lay-of-the-land and understand the concepts underlying the revised Framework.
- Use the guidance here to make an initial mapping of the current state of your assessment to what COSO 2013 is seeking.
- Look at the suggested tools in this volume and in the illustrative templates in the COSO template materials and craft an initial idea of what you think your documentation might look like in a few areas.
- Take advantage of the unique guidance in this volume on crafting interviews and questionnaires, sampling and testing and deficiency assessment.
- Try your ideas out. Include IT assessments and walkthroughs and controls tests to give any revised approach a full trial.
- Revise the plan and flesh out the new directions.
- Provide a forum for discussion with all core team members to share observations and suggestions.
- Develop training material to ensure consistent application as you roll out the new direction.
- Utilize continuous improvement and other techniques to keep the project fresh and current.

This book updates and replaces two separate volumes previously published by John Wiley & Sons: *Internal Controls–Guidance for Private, Government, and Nonprofit Entities* (2007) and *Complying with Sarbanes Oxley Section 404: A Guide for Small Publicly Held Entities* (2010). Because of the common Framework these diverse applications now share, it makes sense to combine these volumes at this time. Many of the technical and operational issues are shared in these applications, albeit with different levels of importance and intensity to specific entities and audit environments.

The evolution of the COSO Framework is one of close personal association since I was a partner with Coopers & Lybrand as the 1992 Framework was first being drafted for COSO and introduced to (C&L) clients. I was responsible for the development and training at BDO in applying the Framework to SOX, was a member of a professional Firm 404 Implementation Task Force and was a member of the Auditing Standards Board as the COSO Framework was further integrated into Generally Accepted Auditing Standards. I was appointed as an AICPA representative in roundtable discussions with COSO developers leading up to the release of the 2006 enhanced guidance for smaller public entities and have worked with companies and auditors in implementation issues throughout this period and to date. I have developed several training courses for the AICPA and other associations in documenting internal controls. My sincere hope is that this work will make a difference for those seeking new insights and better approaches to the implementation of the Framework. I would like to thank my clients for all the learning opportunities along the way.

Acknowledgments

A S ALWAYS, SPECIAL THANKS go to my wife Barbara and to my family, who again tolerated my being sequestered in my office during the development and refinement of this work.

Thanks to my clients, both companies and auditors and peers, that provided the experiences and training grounds. Also to be acknowledged are the dedicated professionals of the various COSO development teams and the AICPA and PCAOB whose writings have been woven into this work.

A special thank you also goes to the many John Wiley and Sons production and editing professionals that have helped make this work and its predecessors along the way more readable and focused and to the Wiley leadership of John DeRemigis and Timothy Burgard who strongly supported the production of this volume.

Internal Control Audit and Compliance

CHAPTER ONE

What We All Share

REGARDLESS OF THE type of entity, all Committee of Sponsoring Organizations of the Treadway Commission (COSO) Framework users and auditors in the public and nonpublic sectors share a great deal in common. We broadly outline those shared characteristics here before plunging into the details of application and documentation. This will also help readers to target the specific goals they have in studying this material. Later these concepts are developed in more detail. For now they serve to overview the subject matter.

NEED FOR CONTROL CRITERIA

Early auditing literature talked about controls, primarily in terms of controls over more routine transactions, such as cash receipts and disbursements. Based on the analysis of business and accounting failures over decades of experience, it became clear that a broader view of controls was necessary to address the various management, information processing, or oversight weaknesses that so often contributed to these events. However, there was no broader framework or set of criteria against which to evaluate the effectiveness of the entity in controlling its risk of filing materially false financial information and preventing other types of fraud. The COSO Framework has filled that void.

A set of criteria is a standard against which a judgment can be made. In the United States, the internal control integrated framework published by COSO is just about the only overall controls criteria to assess the effectiveness of internal controls over financial reporting (ICFR). Choosing an appropriate control criteria is a Securities and Exchange

Commission (SEC) requirement for public companies when performing an assessment of the effectiveness of an entity's internal control. The American Institute of Certified Public Accountants (AICPA) auditing literature references COSO components in its guidance to auditors of nonpublic companies, so from a practical perspective, COSO is the only game in town. While there are other frameworks out there (e.g., the criteria of control (COCO) framework from Canada, the Turnbull Report in the United Kingdom, and SOX of Japan), these are not that dissimilar to COSO in overall concept and have not gained wide acceptance outside of their home countries.

OVERVIEW OF THE COSO INTERNAL CONTROL INTEGRATED FRAMEWORK

In 1985, COSO was formed to sponsor the National Commission on Fraudulent Financial Reporting, whose charge was to study and report on the factors that can lead to fraudulent financial reporting. It was motivated by yet another intense period of time when financial reporting fraud and alleged audit failures were prominent in the news. Since this initial undertaking, COSO has expanded its mission to improving the quality of financial reporting. A significant part of this mission is aimed at developing guidance on internal control. In 1992, COSO published *Internal Control—Integrated Framework*, which established a framework for internal control and provided evaluation tools that businesses and other entities could use to evaluate their control systems.[1]

The COSO internal control framework identifies five components of internal control:

1. Control environment
2. Risk assessment
3. Control procedures
4. Information and communication
5. Monitoring

Today these remain unchanged from the 1992 Framework. That is a testament to the fundamental correctness of the COSO Framework. However, the level of detailed guidance over the years has increased due to the more recent widespread implementation of the Framework in our business environment and a desire to have more consistency in the application of COSO principles.

---

[1] In 2003, COSO published a draft of a document, entitled *Enterprise Risk Management (ERM) Framework*, whose purpose was to provide guidance on the process used by management to identify and manage risk across the enterprise. This new framework is not intended to supersede or otherwise amend its earlier internal control framework guidance on internal control. Internal control is encompassed within and an integral part of enterprise risk management. Enterprise risk management is broader than internal control, expanding the discussion to form a more robust conceptualization of enterprise risk. *Internal Control–Integrated Framework* remains in place for entities and others looking at internal control over financial reporting by itself. Note: Entities using the *ERM Framework* will still need to make a pointed financial statement risk assessment, as detailed in the risk assessment component discussion.

HOLISTIC, INTEGRATED VIEW

The COSO Framework identifies five main components of internal control, and one of the keys of working with it is to understand how these components relate to and influence one another. COSO envisions these individual components as being tightly integrated in a nonlinear fashion. Each component has a relationship with and can influence the functioning of every other component, operating in an almost organic way.

The five interrelated components of the COSO Framework are, briefly:

1. *Control environment.* Senior management must set an appropriate tone at the top that positively influences the control consciousness of entity personnel. The control environment is the foundation for all other components of internal controls and provides discipline and structure.
2. *Risk assessment.* The entity must be aware of and deal with the financial reporting risks it faces. It must set objectives, integrated throughout its activities, so that the organization is operating in concert. Once these objectives are set, the entity is in a better position to identify the risks to achieving those objectives and to analyze and develop ways to manage them.
3. *Control activities.* Control policies and procedures must be established and executed to help ensure transactions being processed on a day-to-day basis, such as sales and expense transactions, or on a periodic basis, such as accruals and consolidations, are resulting in complete and accurate accounting recognition.
4. *Information and communication.* Surrounding the control activities are information and communication systems, including the accounting system. Whether manual or most likely today implemented using automated (computer) systems, they enable the entity's people to capture and exchange the information needed to conduct, manage, and control its operations. The information and communication component is comprised of both internal (e.g., management, governance) and external communications (e.g., shareholders, prospective investors, or creditors).
5. *Monitoring.* The COSO Framework identifies monitoring as the responsibility of management. The auditor is not a part of the entity's system of internal control. The entire company control process should be monitored on a regular basis by management, and issues that arise should be communicated appropriately within the organization. In this way, the system should be in a position to react dynamically, as changing as conditions warrant, and not require that special procedures or independent audit procedures detect these problems. The company is expected to be proactive in identifying and correcting control deficiencies.

Figure 1.1 is from the 1992 COSO *Integrated Framework* report. It depicts these five elements of internal control and their interrelationships in a 3-sided pyramid, with the control environment as the base.

Note that the information and communication component is positioned along the edge of the pyramid structure, indicating that this component has close linkages to the

FIGURE 1.1 COSO Framework

other components. It probably would be even more accurate if the component were depicted as affecting all other ones, including control environment and monitoring, as it is difficult to envision these components being effective without effective information and communication.

Historically, the auditing literature has pictorially described the COSO Framework in the shape of a cube (see Figure 1.2). This representation shows that controls can

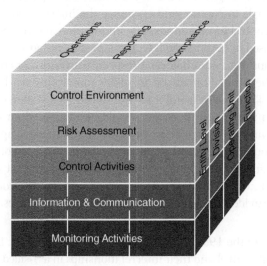

FIGURE 1.2 COSO Framework II

affect the entity either on an entity-wide basis or specifically on a divisional, regional or product line basis. The 2013 revision changed the "cube" and placed the control environment at the top of the cube. The strong hierarchical image of the pyramid and its strong base is somewhat lost in this representation, but for complex entities with multiple product lines or locations, the cube works well.

While both models have advantages, whatever the model used to communicate the Framework, it is helpful to have some physical representation of the Framework as a training tool and as a reminder of the components when initiating a project or bringing new personnel into an existing project. In the early days of Sarbanes-Oxley (SOX) implementation, some creative ways were developed to etch the components firmly in the auditor's mind. A unique product was a pen that revealed a new component each time the ballpoint pen point was retracted or extended.

A blessing of the COSO Framework is that together the five components seem to be satisfactory in describing the broad sources of internal control issues. The corresponding curse is that it is sometimes difficult to determine where specific facts and controls fall within the framework. While it would be nice if a one-to-one relationship existed between processes and controls and the Framework components, that is not the case. Entities can and did make their own decisions where controls belonged under the 1992 Framework. The focus and 17 Principles in the 2013 Framework will reduce the variability in classifying controls within the Framework going forward.

For example, the 1992 COSO Framework report contained only passing mention of information technology (IT). Can we cleanly assign IT to just one component? Clearly there is a linkage to the control activities component since automated accounting processes and controls depend on the IT being effective. In another sense, IT is important to information and communication, which relies on data in company databases being accurate and complete. And it is hard to imagine running a business or performing the governance function effectively without accurate and timely financial data, so failures of IT can also impact the control environment. The fact is that IT has a pervasive effect on many aspects of the controls assessment and does not fit neatly into only one of the component categories. However, IT General Controls are now a specific principle to be satisfied (Principle 11).

Another example is fraud risk. There is now a principle (Principle 8) of risk assessment directed to assessing management's implementation of antifraud programs and controls. However, fraud risk can also be associated with the control environment, because of the risk of management override of controls. Fraud can be associated with transaction processing (a control activity) such as cash disbursements. So, prior to the recent guidance, it was not so clearly assigned to one component.

The point here is that while some topical issues fall neatly within a COSO component, there are control issues that may potentially affect many other components. That is also a reason that the new guidance stresses the interrelationship of controls and control deficiencies. One deficiency can touch several principles and components.

REVISED COSO INTERNAL CONTROLS FRAMEWORK

The revised COSO Framework (2013) replaces the 1992 and 2006 Framework guidance and documents. Those prior publications will be considered superseded after December 15, 2014. Some key elements of the new guidance include:

- Retention of the five basic components: control environment, risk assessment, control activities, information and communication, and monitoring.
- Identification of 17 Principles that are deemed essential to the five components
- Clear expectations that the elements of internal control work together in an integrated way.

Indeed, unless these elements are satisfied, COSO would conclude the system of internal controls is not effective.

Internal controls are defined in the revised Framework, and similarly in literature of the Public Company Accounting Oversight Board (PCAOB)[2] and AICPA, as: "a process, effected by the entity's board of directors, management and other personnel, designed to provide reasonable assurance regarding the achievement of objectives relating to operations, reporting, and compliance."

This definition is consistent with the focus in the revised Framework on articulating the objectives in the three elements of operations, reporting, and compliance.

The COSO Framework retains these three elements of internal control. For purposes of this book, our focus is on the financial reporting element. However, as we discuss the issues surrounding this element, note that putting on blinders to issues from the other elements is not appropriate. Failures in operating controls can create increased allowances for returns and greater estimated warranty expenses, and failures in regulatory controls can cause liabilities for environmental issues or labor law violations with financial consequences. What may seem like a bright line in the diagrams is in reality a blurred line in practice.

In all cases, COSO and regulators expect the entity, and not the auditor, to be responsible for the design and implementation of the system of internal control. Likewise, all entities are expected to document and maintain updates to their internal processes and controls. In public companies, auditors are often impaired by independence rules from venturing very far into the design, assessment, and documentation process. In private companies, the auditor may be more helpful at present; however, future independence rules may limit auditor involvement in government and private engagements. Private companies should prepare to annually maintain and update the documentation of their controls systems. Auditors need to prepare their clients to do so.

Accompanying the Framework guidance are illustrative templates for documenting assessments, deficiencies, and aggregating issues from the detailed deficiency level to an overall conclusion. These templates may be structured as entities wish, but it

---

[2] For example, PCAOB Auditing Standard (AS) No. 5, paragraph A5.

may be worthwhile to note their suggested content in the development of proprietary approaches. Not published are forms, documents, and work programs to guide the entity or auditor when gathering information, performing assessments, and drawing conclusions. While various vendors may make such forms available to entities and auditors, the responsibility for ensuring the quality of those materials lies with the user, since COSO nor the auditing standards setters do not "certify" specific products.

The new guidance retains the much of the conceptual look and feel of the original 1992 Framework. In addition to guidance, there is a separate COSO volume with suggested approaches and examples of gathering evidence to support the principles, points of focus, and components. The COSO guidance should be accessible to the project leader or audit team, particularly in the initial period of implementation of the new guidance. In addition to purchasing the set of guidance at www.cpa2biz.com, various technical information vendors (e.g., Accounting Research Manager) have online versions for subscribers. Project leaders and audit team leaders should take the time to study these resources in some detail to ensure that the team is properly interpreting the principles and what sources of evidence might exist. Neither companies nor auditors are required to follow the suggested approaches or examples. They are presented simply as guidance; unlike the 17 Principles, they do not have to be satisfied or followed.

Although checklists are popular in auditing, users should resist creating checklists of controls in lieu of analyses, descriptions, and explanations of controls. COSO guidance seeks to ask the question "How do you accomplish this objective, or how do you satisfy this assertion?" and not whether a specific control exists or does not. In the identification of the points of focus articulated for each principle, it may be worthwhile to read these in connection with each principle and ensure that most are considered when assessing the effective implementation of the principle. While not a "checklist," the points are a helpful reminder of the scope of intended issues embodied in the principle. However, not all of these more than 80 points will apply to all entities.

Since 1992, business has changed in many ways. The 2013 Framework notably picks up two major trends and has implemented them widely in the new Framework. These trends include:

1. *Widespread use of outsourcing.* Today more and more business functions are being outsourced to third parties. Just because a function is outsourced does not remove it from the table when the function relates to ICFR. It should adhere to the same standards the entity is held to, including ethical standards of the entity. That includes outsourcing to far distant parts of the earth where cheaper wages may prevail. Outsourcing is mentioned in the discussions and examples of 12 of the 17 Principles. That does not preclude its application to other principles. Since 2003 the Securities and Exchange Commission (SEC) has required outsourcing entities to include a right-to-audit clause in agreements so that entities can ensure, if necessary, that controls are effective in the outsourced facility. Enhancements to the requirements for issuing Service Organization reports (e.g., Service Organization Control (SOC) Reports 1 and SOC 2) have also advanced the quality of these reports and their usefulness in placing reliance on outsourced functions.

2. *Widespread use of computer processing.* While the 1992 Framework gave limited mention of computer systems, the revised Framework weaves computer and network issues into the discussions of 14 of the 17 Principles.

Other changes brought about by the 2013 guidance will likely include:

- *More attention to areas other than control activities.* The 17 Principles and numerous points of focus will force many entities to gather more information than previously regarding the "softer" controls and assessments. It was perhaps easier for all to focus on transaction controls, but the new COSO guidance attempts to rebalance the efforts.
- *More focus on risk assessment.* Risk assessment is more carefully articulated, and more assessment is sought of the types of risk as well as the potential magnitude and likelihood of a risk occurring. In addition, the COSO introduces two new measures of the risk: *velocity* and *persistence.* Like a storm, the intensity of a risk and duration can have a very direct effect on the damage sustained. Hurricanes Sandy and Katrina and Midwest tornadoes provide evidence that some unlikely events can have devastating and long-lasting impacts. So also with some business risks. Risk assessment can be seen as a fundamental task that provides a framework for assessing the adequacy of the system of internal controls to prevent or detect material misstatement.

WHAT WE MUST DO

Entities should assess and document their internal controls. COSO and auditing standards agree that this is a responsibility of the entity. One often hears the concern voiced that entities have neither the expertise nor the manpower to perform this task. When such excuses are offered, the auditor often begins to question whether the lack of expertise might indicate a controls deficiency. An entity without the expertise to document controls might also lack the ability to design and monitor controls or to respond to issues that arise when controls fail. If the entity does not view internal control as a priority, then questions arise as to whether the control environment is lacking in some respect. The fact is that many entities would rather not bother with this responsibility, despite its overall value to society in adding integrity to investor reports and to the security and success of the entity itself. Attitude is important in shaping the quality of the controls and the quality of the oversight and continuous improvement that sustains and strengthens systems.

Entities and auditors should also have some evidence to support the fact that the descriptions of the internal controls relate to what is actually happening. That evidence may be through observation, examination of evidence, or reperformance of the control. Auditors are instructed to document their understanding of internal controls (and not the whole system of processes and activities). To the extent the entity has done the process and controls documentation well, the auditor can test that work and draw from it in lieu of reinventing the wheel.

All entities need to take a broad look at internal control over financial reporting (ICFR) and not ignore elements that are difficult to assess (the control environment, IT, or processes and controls that are outsourced). In some derivative applications of internal controls in other applications (SOX of Japan), only major processes are "in scope" for purposes of the assessment. There is no 80–20 rule or simple exclusions for U.S. generally accepted auditing standards (GAAS) applications. Materiality (alone or in aggregate) is the benchmark threshold for COSO assessments.

One message that rings clear in the 2013 COSO guidance is the need to articulate various management objectives in terms of operations, financial reporting, and regulatory compliance. These objectives are in turn the genesis for management to identify "risks" to their objectives. The risk assessment component in the Internal Controls Framework and in the COSO ERM relates risks to the stated objectives, answering the question: "Risks to what?" In reality, the objectives related to financial reporting might be fairly obvious. For example, "fair financial reporting in accordance with generally accepted accounting principles (GAAP)" would often be a high-level objective, and the presence of many estimates in the accounting process often presents risks to meeting that objective. An entity objective could also be to protect certain proprietary entity information from public disclosure and competitor scrutiny. The risks to that objective might be more meaningful to ponder and more specific to the entity. Entities should try to articulate their specific objectives, since meaningful risk assessments and the design and maintenance of controls to mitigate the risks follow from the objectives. While auditors may guess at the company-specific risks related to financial reporting and the assertions relating to financial reporting (completeness, existence, valuation, etc.) help structure the audit goals, auditors cannot possibly know all the nuances that management might be considering. Thus the assessment of risks associated with financial reporting is best performed by the entity and shared with the auditor. Too often it happens the other way around for many of the risks. Entities that fail to set objectives and identify risks are likely to exhibit and be assessed a material weakness in the risk assessment component of the Framework.

Transitioning to COSO 2013

Many entities will seek the quickest and easiest way to transition to COSO 2013. For many, there will be a significant number of additional control points to consider, since "2013" is more specific (using 17 Principles and numerous points of focus) than the original 1992 Framework. However, this challenge should also be viewed as an opportunity to reconsider any current documentation or approach and not to institutionalize past practices that may not be the most efficient and effective. The concept of "let's just get through this year" usually results in needed changes never being made and opportunities lost. While much of this book is devoted to providing the insight to assist in an effective and efficient assessment, there is a real issue of how to best take advantage of what has already been done and carry any best practices forward.

Those entities who adopted the 20 Principles outlined in the 2006 COSO guidance directed to smaller public entities will be farther down the road to converting to the 2013 guidance than those that by-passed this guidance and built their assessment process around the original Framework. As mentioned in the legacy versions of this work, that 2006 guidance was potentially useful to all entities and could be a real help in structuring effective assessment projects for any entity. And so it has come to pass. Where there was a change in the 2013 guidance from the 2006 version, this book also provides a road map of what has been added or reallocated to other principles. In addition, various hints are provided throughout the work to illustrate the potentially related principles when deficiencies are identified, in keeping with the integrated nature of controls as discussed in the 2013 guidance.

Mapping to the 2013 Guidance

One method used to map the 2013 guidance to the current project is to create a spreadsheet with the principles and relevant points of focus along one dimension and the previously identified controls along the other dimension. To be more effective, the matrix should also identify the relevant assertion(s) addressed by the controls (when assertions apply, such as for transaction controls) to ensure the coverage of the financial statements assertions and to identify any gaps. When identifying assertions, it may be appropriate to assign a numerical or letter value to the assertions you are using, so that the assertions covered can be sorted and gaps more easily identified. It may also be necessary to segregate the transaction- or disclosure-based controls by account or cycle so that the spreadsheet does not become unwieldy. Note that when considering cash controls, a deficiency might also indicate failure in a related principle, such as competence and training (Principle 4). It is a daunting task to pre-consider all the possible interactions between controls and principles and points of focus, so you may find some common linkages like the aforementioned example will be sufficient for mapping most controls. These linkages will not be automatic; they will depend on the specific root cause of the deficiency if it can be determined. A column or two could be allocated to identify potentially related principles. This task would be a new one, requiring familiarity with the 2013 approach and details of the principles and points of focus.

In total, the 2013 guidance notes 88 points of focus across the 17 Principles. However, a few of these points of focus are more closely related to operations and compliance objectives. Before discarding them from your analysis, note that such objectives often have a financial reporting implication in disclosure controls or for estimating allowance or reserve accounts. We discuss these issues further in connection with the risk assessment component itself.

Table 1.1 is an example template that maps identified entity controls to the 2013 guidance. You may wish to experiment with different approaches to this mapping before settling on one that makes the most sense for your organization, based on where you are and where you want to go. Depending on the component, subcomponent, and number of controls to be mapped, some matrices may be more effectively developed with the principles and points of focus across the top or down the side. While consistency in format is helpful, an unwieldy mapping format is not. Depending on the number of controls likely to be associated with a principle or related point of focus, it may be worthwhile to split the assessment into subsets (by component, by principles, or by other units, such as financial statement captions) that are more manageable. No one design will be perfect for all

TABLE 1.1 Mapping Controls to the 2013 COSO Framework

(a) Control Environment

Control ID	Primary Assertion	Secondary Assertion	P1 Ethical[3]	POF1	POF2	POF3 ...	P2 ...
CE1	NA	NA	X			X	
CE2	NA	NA	X	x			X

(b) Sales Cycle (P12)

Control ID	Primary Assertion	Secondary Assertion	Sales	POF1	POF2	POF3	POF4 ...
S 1	1	3	X			X	
S 2	3		X				X

entities and industries. The important thing is that all currently identified key controls are mapped and that all principles and points of focus are arrayed so that potential gaps can be identified.

While COSO clearly states that all the points of focus need not be met to be able to state that an effective system of ICFR exists, many are using the points of focus (and principles) to determine if there might be gaps in controls or yet-undocumented controls of importance that should be recognized. From a documentation standpoint, it is a short leap to expect that a point of focus (POF) considered irrelevant or not applicable will be supported with an explanation of why this is so.

A secondary benefit of this exercise is to assist the independent audit team in relating your assessment to their work paper tools and templates, which often are not customized to your entity approach. Auditors spend considerable time mapping entity approaches to audit requirements, time often better spent on more productive and useful activities or even reductions in seasonal workload.

BASIC SCOPING AND STRATEGIES FOR MAINTENANCE

All managements and auditors need to consider broadly the scope of ICFR. Just because a wide net is cast in examining controls does not mean that all of the controls under that net are key or critical; thus, testing and detailed analysis may not be required. However, managements were surprised in 2004 when controls over the hiring and use of specialists in determining fair values or allowances were declared by the PCAOB as in scope regarding ICFR. Current auditing standards require a specific assessment of the internal controls over the fair value estimation process. Nonpublic entity auditors are likewise directed by auditing standards to assess such controls over all estimates in the financial reporting process. Similarly managements and auditors were embarrassed when an academic, Professor Eric Lie, post-SOX, discovered that the values of stock options

---

[3] The notation P1 refers to Principle 1 and is noted this way throughout the text.

were being manipulated to benefit management in a number of large companies. This activity and process was not included in the early scoping of public company audits of internal control. A continuing conundrum is the issue of using service organizations for various accounting, IT, and data storage functions. A contemporary issue is the controls and security issue surrounding the use of cloud computing and cloud data storage. Outsourcing does not remove a function from the scope of internal controls assessment and analysis. Examples also exist of the failure to recognize the risks associated with trading or derivatives activities that may create exposures that exceed the apparent size of the operation; examples such as the Barings Bank collapse (currency trading) and Orange County, CA, bankruptcy (interest rate swaps) come quickly to mind.

The natural state of systems is for them to deteriorate over time. Managements, through monitoring and thoughtful annual reassessment, can keep a system in tune through an effective monitoring function. The absence or ineffectiveness of an effective monitoring function is likely to be a material weakness that would preclude an effective internal controls assertion or auditor reliance on controls to reduce other auditing procedures.

WHERE WE DEPART

Financial statement preparers of public, nonpublic, government, and nonprofit entities have the basic level of responsibility for assessing and documenting controls over financial reporting. While still responsible for the scoping, documentation, and verification that the described controls are implemented, nonpublic entities and their auditors may not need to test the controls as a basis for reliance on controls in setting the audit strategy. However, public companies have a specific requirement that they publicly assert the effectiveness of controls over financial reporting; doing that includes tests of the controls to be able to make that assertion. These various nonpublic entities and their auditors do have requirements that noted material weaknesses and/or significant deficiencies in controls (defined later) be reported to governance or to the overseeing regulator.

However, when auditors of any entity seeks to rely on the effectiveness of internal controls to reduce the scope of their other audit procedures, testing is necessary to confirm the assessment that the controls are designed and are operating effectively. Unlike in an attestation where high assurance is sought, the financial statement auditor may determine the right amount of testing and assurance to support the desired level of controls assurance from "low" (some) to "high." When high assurance is sought, the project scope and testing level is similar to that required for an attestation. However, the assurance sought for controls reliance usually covers the entire audit period, not just the status of internal controls on the date of the report.

Nonpublic entities may optionally report on the effectiveness of their internal controls. Auditors can attest to these assertions under the revised AICPA attestation standards (e.g., AT 501). Alternative attestations allow for attestations on only the design of the controls or an attestation on both the design and operating effectiveness of the controls over financial reporting. For example, a nonprofit entity may wish to report on internal controls to provide assurance to donors of its stewardship over the donated funds and as a competitive tool to attract new donors. It seems likely that some government entities may soon be required to publicly report on their internal controls as a demonstration of their stewardship of public funds.

For certain regulated program audits (e.g., Office of Management and Budget [OMB] A-133 program audits of federal awards and programs), there may be specific audit requirements to meet compliance (with laws and regulations) that require tests of specifically identified controls over compliance by auditors. A source of confusion among some auditors is the fact that there exists very different guidance for financial statement and compliance-oriented government program audits. The focus of this book is on the ICFR.

Public companies report publicly on the effectiveness of their ICFR. As a result, SEC regulations require these entities to test controls as a basis for their assertion. There are specific exemptions from this requirement for companies when they first become public. Auditors of smaller public companies do not have to specifically report to the public on the effectiveness of the auditee's internal controls in the SEC 10-K annual filing. (This relief is now permanent under the Dodd-Frank Act of 2010.) However, auditors of larger public companies, accelerated filers,[4] *do* have to report to the public on the effectiveness of the auditee's internal controls in the required SEC 10-K annual filing. Therefore, auditors would also have a requirement to test internal controls as a basis for their assertion. The auditors of newly registered companies (under the Jumpstart Our Business Startups [JOBS] Act) may qualify for an exemption to auditor reporting on internal controls, provided revenues are under a predefined threshold.

As noted later, auditor oversight and testing may be important to ensure the quality of management's assertion regarding the effectiveness of controls. This seems to be particularly true as management first becomes familiar with controls issues.

TRIANGLE OF EFFICIENCY

Everyone desires an efficient project. From experience, an important consideration in achieving an efficient implementation of a controls assessment project is an understanding of the tasks and the acquisition of the skills before beginning in earnest the documentation, assessment, and testing process. Time and again the failure of one of the three key elements in what I call the triangle of efficiency (see Figure 1.3) is the root cause of wasted time and energy, and more often than not it results in an incomplete or incorrect assessment. This is an issue worth mentioning at the start, because false steps will cost money to correct.

The three knowledge components are:

1. Knowledge of entity and/or auditor requirements.
2. Knowledge of COSO.
3. Knowledge of company controls and processes.

---

[4] Accelerated filers have a market capitalization of $75 million or more.

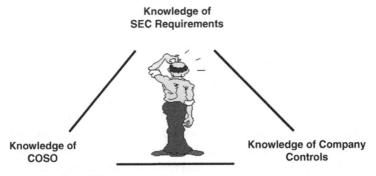

FIGURE 1.3 Triangle of Efficiency

In the case of public companies, their specific requirements are stated by the SEC. Private companies should look to COSO for guidance. While there is nothing contradictory about the SEC and COSO literatures, public companies should be familiar with the SEC-specific requirements, which may contain more detail regarding specific reporting and filing requirements. Public company auditors will be looking toward PCAOB Auditing Standard No. 5 for their requirements, which happen to be closely aligned with the SEC requirements, and ensuring public companies are following that guidance.

It often feels good just to get started on a project and begin to accumulate some evidence of progress. Indeed, that was a clear motivation in companies and auditors beginning to document the detailed activity-level controls over transactions before comprehending the scope of the requirements in 2004 when first reporting on controls under SOX. The resultant complaints about costs and time expended are intertwined with issues regarding failures to consider one or more of the three triangle components.

Experience says that if any of the three elements here is lacking, then there will be an impact on the efficiency and effectiveness of the overall project. Company consultants may be very competent in knowing COSO and knowing company and audit requirements, but they still have to learn the entity and its controls in order to perform their task. Close integration of company and consulting personnel can contribute greatly to efficiency of the company project over a strategy where the task is given primarily to the consultant. In the long run, the most efficient process is often one that is brought in-house and maintained by the entity. This controls focus in entity culture and auditing is not likely to go away. It is likely a part of our permanent business environment.

CONTROLS VERSUS PROCESSES

A good discussion to have before plunging into more subject matter here concerns the source of the surprisingly widespread misunderstanding regarding the distinction between controls and processes. COSO and the regulatory requirements for companies and auditors are directed at controls. The public company assertions about internal control effectiveness are directed at controls. So why is so much time and effort devoted to evaluating and documenting the business processes underlying the controls in company and auditor documentation? A significant potential source of efficiency and greater effectiveness in the controls documentation and assessment tasks is a clear distinction between controls and processes.

A simple example: A cash payment (cutting the check) is part of a process. A review of the support for the payment by someone other than the accountant is a control. A sale on credit initiates a process of shipment and recognition of a receivable. Checking the credit rating of the customer or checking that the customer is preapproved is a control over the validity or existence of the sale. The requirements are to document, assess, and test controls, not processes. But mountains of documentation are produced and retained in the name of controls documentation, which many times do not contain the description of a single real control.

If all the unnecessary documentation that has been produced magically evaporated from the hard drives and storage rooms of companies and auditors, some highly under-utilized storage capacity would be revealed. Please understand, I know we are fond of our flowcharts, narratives that go on and on, and creating a lot of detailed descriptions of how things work. There is nothing wrong with all that. But the focus here is controls. How do we ensure completeness, how do we ensure our ownership of the assets we claim, how do we ensure the transactions are recorded in the proper period? As long as all these considerations (and a lot more to be discussed later) are addressed, the only drawback to the volumes we create are the updating review and edit we have to apply when changes occur and the mountains of data that has to be reviewed by management and the independent auditors. It's only money.

A current trend is away from the beloved narratives toward more flowcharting to document the business process and control points. However, it may be more efficient to keep separate controls documents than to muddy up flowcharts with all the data necessary to describe, assess, and hold the tests of the controls. Flowcharts or narratives can still be referenced to specific controls documentation.

By careful adherence to the spirit of the COSO Framework, the documentation of controls can be concise and organized. Whether you are just beginning in this process now or are seeking ways out of the quagmire of documentation produced previously, there is a way to meet the requirements without producing excessive volumes of documentation.

Internal Control Has Limitations

The existence of undesirable outcomes like misstatements and omitted disclosures may indicate that the process itself was flawed. However, that direct connection may not always hold true. It is possible that an internal control failure can be attributed to something other than a flawed process.

Internal control provides reasonable but not absolute assurance that an entity will achieve its financial reporting objectives. Even an effective internal control system can experience a failure due to:

- *Human error*. The people who implement internal controls may make simple errors or mistakes that can lead to control failures.

- *Management override.* Even in an otherwise well-controlled entity, managers may be able to override internal controls for selfish purposes.
- *Collusion.* Two or more individuals may collude to circumvent what otherwise would be effective controls.

Objective-Driven Approach

The COSO Framework views internal control as built-in to an entity's overall business processes, as opposed to a separate added-on component that attaches itself to the company's real business. Building in internal control requires that management do four things:

1. *Establish business objectives.* For our purposes, the most relevant objectives relate to financial reporting.
2. *Identify the risks to achieving those objectives.*
3. *Determine how to manage the identified risks.* The establishment of internal controls is just one of several options.
4. *Where appropriate, establish controls as a way to manage certain risks.* Individual controls are designed and implemented to meet the stated risks.

Internal controls have limited value by themselves—they do not produce a product or service or generate revenue for the business. Controls have value to the degree in which they help the entity to achieve its objectives through providing complete, accurate, relevant, and reliable information for decision making and for the fair communication of financial results to third parties. The effectiveness of internal control is judged according to how well it aligns with and addresses the objectives of the company.

Flexible, Adaptable, No One-Size-Fits-All Approach

The COSO Framework is a conceptual and not a rigid, prescriptive approach to internal controls. Thus, a paint-by-numbers approach is not going to be effective in complying with the aims of COSO. COSO recognizes that different entities will make different choices about how to implement controls in their businesses. The key is not whether the company uses control A or control B but whether the controls in place meet the risks by proper design and effective operation. COSO is not a checklist of suggested controls. Furthermore, management will make certain cost–benefit judgments and trade-offs. For example, an elaborate control structure over cash disbursements may be warranted in a large and complex business, but simpler controls may be effective and efficient in smaller enterprises. The result: Internal control is not a one-size-fits-all proposition, and a checklist of "usual" controls is not an effective tool to satisfy the COSO Framework guidance.

What can sometimes be frustrating about COSO controls guidance and the auditing standards is that simplifying the assessment and testing process through the use of practice aids is not easy. To have a successful project, it requires thought and understanding to apply the objectives of the Framework to a specific company circumstance. It takes knowledge of the entity and its processes, the regulatory environment, and the COSO Framework to make sense of the assessment and testing process. Early in the implementation of SOX, an experienced audit partner noted that she obtained a much better knowledge of her clients and their risks after going through the controls assessment process with them. Companies seeking practice aids to take the work out of the assessment process eventually realize this is not an achievable goal. However, an assessment and testing project done right is much easier to maintain over time than one cobbled together to get through this year. Think long term. Practice aids can still have value, but they must be adapted to the application. There is no turn-key approach out there, despite any Web site or brochure claims.

Furthermore, circumstances change at the entity, and so its internal control must be designed in a way to adapt and remain effective in a dynamic business environment. In fact, one of the primary objectives of the monitoring component of internal control is to assess the quality of the system's performance over time, recognizing that circumstances will change. In the 2013 guidance, analyzing and responding to change is a Principle (9) to be satisfied.

Reasonable Assurance

COSO recognizes the limitations of internal control. No matter how well designed or operated, internal control can provide only reasonable assurance that objectives will be met. Reasonable assurance is a *high* threshold, but it stops short of absolute assurance. The presence of an isolated internal control failure (less than a material weakness) does not, in and of itself, mean that a system is ineffective. The COSO even states that "even an effective internal control system can experience failure."

However, to be able to report publicly that internal controls are effective or to rely on the effectiveness of internal controls in lieu of other audit procedures requires that material weaknesses are either not present or are limited to specific areas that can be identified and mitigated by other procedures. When reporting on controls, the public expects a correspondingly high level of audit assurance.

People Factor

COSO recognizes that internal control is implemented by people. Documentation of controls is important, but documentation is not all there is to internal control. The effectiveness of internal control depends on the people responsible for carrying out individual control elements—from the chief executive officer and board of directors, all the way to rank-and-file employees charged with performing day-to-day transaction processing and control-related tasks.

Thus, the design of internal control must take into account the human element and must consider the role of human nature. For example, people are greatly influenced by the actions taken by an entity's senior management, more so than they are by what these individuals say. Therefore, the relative strength of an entity's control environment depends in large part on the actions of the entity's leaders and how they are perceived by the rest of the organization. This factor is assessed as part of the control environment.

The ability of individuals to carry out their responsibilities also depends on their competencies and how well they understand what is required. This need for understanding requires that the entity's internal controls have an effective hiring, training, and communication element. This is also an element of the control environment.

THE DEBATE CONTINUES

Companies and regulators continue to debate the cost–benefit of the requirements to assess and report on internal controls. Detractors have been somewhat successful in resisting auditor attestation in smaller public companies in the Dodd-Frank Act of 2010 and the JOBS Act of 2012. However, history has shown that inattention to internal controls is at the root of many business failures and frauds, which weaken investor confidence in the capital and stock markets. In addition, in the period before the imposition of the SOX Act of 2002, an alarming increase in the number of restatements of previously issued financial statements was observed. A lack of ICFR was a likely root cause of many of these restatements. A spike of fraud and restatement in smaller public companies may indeed bring reconsideration of the need for auditor verification of managements' assertions regarding controls.

It has been observed that certain categories of losses due to fraud and the incidence of restatements have come down in the post-SOX period. Whether this is due to greater management awareness of and attention to internal controls or strengthened auditor requirements regarding fraud and internal controls effectiveness is not known. What is clear is that there have been some notable improvements and reversals of downward trends, and thus the "medicine" seems to be working. The revised COSO Framework is intended to keep the ball rolling and help us to take the updates that have been issued since the original 1992 report and codify them into basic principles we can carry into the future.

Some executives have spoken out in favor of the value that the current regulatory requirements bring to the business environment. A recent survey of the Financial Executives Institute relates a more positive shift in management opinion when compared to the early days of the imposed regulations.

ORGANIZATION OF THIS BOOK

The remainder of this book will go into more depth on the 5 components and 17 Principles of the COSO framework and provide examples of the issues that arise in the assessment and testing of the controls. Specific reporting requirements of public companies are also covered throughout the book. Since many entities already are performing some controls assessments, the section on project management is placed farther back in this book than in previous editions; however, those new to this process (e.g., new companies, new personnel, and new responsibilities) or those seeking to improve current processes may want to review this material sooner or even next.

As the material is covered, there will be opportunities to speak directly to specific audiences, such as auditors or management or assessment team members, on specific issues, and these sections will be identified by special headings.

COSO 17 Principles

Component	Summary Principle
Control Environment	1. Demonstrates commitment to integrity and ethical values 2. Exercises oversight responsibility 3. Establishes structure, authority, and responsibility 4. Demonstrates commitment to competence 5. Enforces accountability
Risk Assessment	6. Specifies clear objectives 7. Identifies and analyzes risk 8. Assesses fraud risk 9. Identifies and analyzes significant changes
Control Activities	10. Selects and develops control activities to mitigate risks 11. Selects and develops information technology general controls 12. Deploys controls through policies and procedures
Information and Communication	13. Uses relevant information 14. Communicates internally 15. Communicates externally
Monitoring	16. Conducts ongoing and/or separate evaluations 17. Evaluates and communicates deficiencies

CHAPTER TWO

Setting the Scope of Your Documentation Project

Identifying the Core

 START WITH BUSINESS OBJECTIVES

The essential starting point for determining the extent of documentation you should include in your project is a clear statement of your objectives. Regardless of whether you are formally reporting on your controls or not, you should initially cast a broad net across your entity and reduce the focus on the exclude accounts or transactions streams only as evidence concludes that risks are low. The new COSO guidance emphasizes this as a precursor to risk assessment since the identified risks relate to the objectives.

To meet the minimum documentation standards expected for any project, you probably can cut out the very minor (trivial) revenue streams and locations that individually are clearly insignificant in terms of assets, revenues, and income. Unfortunately, there is no consensus on where a bright-line minimum might be. Early on, auditors working with large public clients were bludgeoned into including just about everything with a dollar sign in the reporting on internal controls project because of the early interpretations of the guidance in Public Company Accounting Oversight Board (PCAOB) Auditing Standard (AS) No. 2. Now that that standard has been replaced (AS No. 5) with a more risk-based standard than the original. Nonpublic companies follow similar guidance regarding scoping, but there is no clear discernible demarcation between items that should be in scope or out of scope. The danger is that errors in this judgment that later result in material misstatements can create legal liabilities.

For example, the lack of known issues regarding revenue recognition is not sufficient evidence to deemphasize revenue recognition issues from the assessment in a business with clearly complex sales arrangements. The fact that a company's business is basically a cash business and there are no lingering revenue recognition or period-end cut-off issues is perhaps a more logical basis on which to deemphasize this common control issue in a company's analysis.

Even in its interpretative guidance on evaluating internal control, the Securities and Exchange Commission (SEC) makes it clear to public companies that management's evaluation need not encompass all the controls that have been implemented at the company. The objective of management's evaluation is to provide it with a reasonable basis for determining whether any material weaknesses in internal control exist at year-end, the date of the required report on internal controls.

In a risk-based approach, it is helpful for scoping and project management to identify and distinguish your "core." These are the main activities of your business and likely constitute the bulk of revenues, expenses, and transactions. While not the limits of your scope, the core helps define objectives and identify the key risks to achieving those objectives. It is likely that your internal control efforts will often be concentrated on your core business, and if your core is not well designed and operating effectively, then it is hard to see how the system as a whole can be effective.

You may be able to develop a practical guideline of your core by analyzing the financial statements and the segment/division/location contributions to the numbers flowing into the financial statements. You should be able to include in the scope of your documentation a significant portion of the revenues, expenses, account balances, and net income by selecting a reasonable number of accounts and locations and transaction types within the scope of your project. For example, suppose your municipal entity had several different revenue sources, such as income taxes, fees, fines and judgments, usage charges, and revenue sharing. (See Table 2.1.)

The amounts or the risks associated with a component of the financial statements will cause you to include those streams within your project scope. Based just on revenues, you might be able to cover 85% of the revenues by evaluating the controls related to the two main streams of revenue. But the next question is whether you have covered your identified risks with this scope. Because fees and fines are more volatile from year to year, are more difficult to predict and verify, and involve more human interaction and judgment and fraud risk than the other areas, they probably still require controls attention.

For example, if the receipt and recording of the revenue-sharing portion were easy to track because these revenues are allocated in a scheduled or known way from a larger pool of county revenues and transferred to you in an easy-to-audit transaction, the area

TABLE 2.1 Using Revenue to Set Scope

Revenue Source	Income Tax	Fees	Fines	Usage	Revenue Sharing
2007	$5,000,000	500,000	400,000	600,000	3,500,000
Percentage of Total[1]	50%	5%	4%	6%	35%

[1] Total = $10,000,000

may be considered a low risk and require only limited evidence to conclude the controls are effective. However, if the process over fees and their collection and recording is not as well controlled, and there is some risk of completeness (e.g., skimming, a type of fraud) and some risk of inaccurate processing when collecting these fees, then more effort may be placed on controls over these transactions than their sheer size might suggest.

You might take similar key measures of other financial statement accounts and, in profit-oriented entities, consider the contribution to profit. Thus, you may find a profile of revenues, expenses, and locations or segments emerging from your analysis that really define the core of your entity. That core can be a starting point to determine the main focus of your controls assessment project.

You may need some talking points to address the peripheral and trivial areas you do not identify as your core based on volume or risk. Auditors cannot reliably use size as a risk indicator when understatement is a risk. For example, a completeness risk could be that all the activity of a remote location might not be reported. Skimming is a fraudulent withholding of some of the revenue stream such that some revenues never get recorded.

One approach followed by some entities is to make a list of the main controls and procedures that are in place regarding those amounts that might be candidates for exclusion from the analysis. For example, numerous smaller entities may be part of the consolidated entity but individually and in the aggregate still make up only a small portion of the overall entity. If these entities adhere to a common accounting manual of procedures, use the approved company software, and perform monthly bank reconciliations and management or internal audit visits these locations periodically to audit the details, monitoring the key statistics and cash flows from these locations may be sufficient for management to detect a significant departure from expectations.

As a general guide, you might start with all the financial statement accounts and elements in your initial scope of documentation and assessment of controls. Often the financial statement caption items are larger than materiality or are separately presented for some reason. Your documentation and design assessments can be broader (and should be, for your own protection) than any testing plans need to be. In my view, too many entities and their auditors are too quick in using risk assessment judgments to exclude amounts completely from the scope of the examination. There will come a day of reckoning for those who incorrectly assess risk, as there was with those who thought there was little or no risk in auditing Enron, WorldCom, and Parmalat. Smaller entities suffer similar fates based on bad guesses regarding risk; you just do not hear about them. They just become empty storefronts at the local strip mall.

One quip attributed to Yogi Berra, the oft-quoted Hall of Fame catcher for the New York Yankees, applies here: "It's amazing what you see when you look." I am sure many misstatements and frauds are overlooked because of faulty risk assessments that do not indicate an observable risk. All the more reason not to shortcut the process of gathering evidence to support low-risk assessments and periodically reexamining decisions about risks. For example, in 2004 and 2005, few companies or auditors included the stock option granting process in their controls assessments. In the past it was not on the radar screen for substantive audit testing, either since it seemed to be a rather low-risk area or was subject to written corporate policies and clear accounting rules and was not generally noted as a risk area. There was no explicit exclusion of this process in the Sarbanes-Oxley (SOX) Act or any other guidance. Well, what followed was a discovery by an outsider academic (Dr. Eric Lie) of a widespread "fudging" of the stock option dating process to favor the executives receiving the options. Companies and their auditors were embarrassed by the discovery. For sure, this is not a forgotten process these days.

As you perform this analysis, you may wish to review your conclusions with your independent (external) auditor to see if your reasoning is on target with his or her expectations. Having to expand a project late in the year can be both annoying and expensive. In one case I can recall, a reluctant client with an attitude started with a proposed scope of coverage that was far less than any reasonable estimate of the required scope under the standards and kept coming back time and time again with proposed incremental increases, becoming angrier and angrier that the scope had to increase and never understanding that the better answer was to start at the other end and exclude trivial and low-risk aspects of the entity. In the end, the same result would have been achieved by starting with a broad scope, with the side benefit of decreased blood pressure for all involved.

AFTER THE INITIAL YEAR

It does not hurt to think longer term. The first year of documentation requires a significant commitment of time and effort. You may prioritize the core that needs to be included in year 1. However, in subsequent years, you should consider whether to expand the documentation process into a few other less significant areas. Additionally you should consider if your experience has offered a better way to document the core areas for more efficient update and assessment in the future. Once you have the internal experience in doing the documentation and assessment, you will find these procedures do not take long to perform, and you may conclude that unexpected benefits and efficiencies can be gained from digging into the business at this level. Many entities are today following the same documentation paths in some core areas that were established early on when first documenting processes and controls.

A frequent opportunity that is missed to reduce costs and attain some benefits of the controls focus is to adopt an attitude of "continuous improvement" in the process and testing. Taking good ideas back from conferences or even examining best practices from within the organization can result in significant benefits. Auditors sometimes fall into the trap called SALY (same as last year), which creates a false sense of efficiency when changes occur in the business.

Also frequently encountered and a contributor to higher-than-necessary costs is the lack of training and learning on the part of today's assessment teams. It might be shocking, but many new college accounting major graduates have not had significant exposure to COSO or any of the issues discussed in this book. In the early days of increased attention to internal controls, one could understand this. Today, more than a decade later, not all of the professors and the texts they use have caught up with this important and durable topic. Some professors claim there is no room for the subject in their curriculum. Also shocking are the number of company employees who are expected to learn on the job by following their predecessors' practices. Without some global understanding of this whole COSO process, how could one expect to figure it out from just following specific procedures? Since the approach is conceptual and not prescriptive, some level of conceptual understanding is essential to effective implementation. We are all familiar with the parlor game where a thought is shared around the room and morphs in meaning as the message is passed. Such is the nature of some on-the-job training unless supplemented by consistent, effective structured training.

 ## MAPPING THE ENTITY TO THE FINANCIAL STATEMENTS: INS AND OUTS

In the last section, we illustrated a technique for using revenues to identify the core of the entity for documentation and assessment. A further suggestion would be for the controls documentation project manager to make a template of accounts and balances based on the recent financial statements. Both the balance sheet and the income statement are relevant, so include them along the left column of a multicolumn spreadsheet. In most financial reports, the detailed accounts listed in the consolidated auditor's report are material in amount, or else they likely would have been summarized in some way. Enumerate them in the spreadsheet. Decide on some meaningful way of expressing the different parts of the business across the top rows: say, by segments/divisions/locations/types of revenues, and so on, that describe your entity. (I will call these "segments" for discussion purposes.) Leave a column between each segment. Now, using data relating to each of the identified segments, break out the aggregate consolidated numbers into the individual segments. In some commercial companies, there exist sales subsidiaries for which a sales activity is the only activity associated with the location; order fulfillment and other activities are accounted for elsewhere. In such entities, do not be surprised if some such segments only have one relevant or significant process or transaction cycle (sales to cash).

Have the spreadsheet compute for you the percentage of the consolidated total of each segment. What you should see emerging from this analysis is the ability for you to identify the central core of your entity. You may wish to give special consideration to the implications of transactions (or transfers of costs and revenues) between segments (if there are any) when they are present, even though they may be eliminated during the consolidation process.

In Table 2.2, the financial statement data is used to identify those accounts and cycles that are to be included in the scope of the documentation and assessment project.

This example shows summary financial data only as an illustration. The New York location is a headquarters and a first-stage manufacturing center; sales transactions are conducted out of the Connecticut facility, which finalizes the product to specifications for shipment. By including the assets and liabilities and expenses at corporate and the

TABLE 2.2 Using the Financial Statements to Set the Scope—Summary Categories

Accounts	Consolidated	Connecticut	Percentage	New York	Percentage
Revenues	1,000,000	800,000	80	200,000	20
Expenses	950,000	250,000	26	700,000	74
Income	50,000	300,000	150	(250,000)	—
Assets	4,000,000	1,000,000	25	3,000,000	75
Liabilities	3,500,000	0	0	3,500,000	100
Owners' Capital	500,000	1,000,000	200	(500,000)	—

revenues at the primary sales location, most of the core business can be covered. The income row is not a very meaningful one from which to make inclusion or exclusion decisions in this example; however, it may be in some situations. Note that in the Barings Bank implosion, the previously significant Singapore-based contributions to consolidated earnings from trading currencies originated from a tiny operation, one that would not be detectable if assets were used to determine scope. The same was true with Orange County, CA, where the profits (before the collapse) from interest rate derivative trades were far more significant than any associated fixed assets or even expenses. Even in the areas that are not identified as the core, a risk assessment, some documentation, and some analysis regarding key controls may need to be developed, since the amounts in the noncore areas are not often trivial.

Do not be surprised if the largest revenue and the largest cost contributors are not in the same segment or location. The key is to look at the entity as a whole and identify where the revenues and costs are accumulating. In some universities, revenues (e.g., day tuition, graduate tuition, night school tuition, fees, etc.) are meticulously segregated, but the costs of undergraduate, graduate, and distance learning faculty may be all accounted for in the aggregate and not separated. In a municipality, the budget may also be an excellent tool for risk assessment and scoping.

You may have to slice and dice your entity several different ways (e.g., product line, location, revenue type such as cash sales and Internet sales) in order to find a logical entity profile or use these different perspectives in ensuring all important areas and scoped into the assessment. However, this actually results in an excellent documentation of your thought process as to what portion of your entity is considered your core and why it is or is not included in the scope of your documentation project. Public companies should clearly document the rationale associated with decisions, particularly ones that limit or scope out certain areas from the assessment.

Plan to update this analysis annually going forward to have it respond to changes in the business. Along the way you may even need to reconsider the bases used to assess the entity. If location was a logical base to use for the assessment initially, product line may be a more logical and cost-effective base to use in future years. Don't get stuck in a rut. COSO has included in the risk assessment component a new principle that management should be updating the risk assessments for changes in the business environment (Principle 9).

CONSIDER RISKS, NOT JUST QUANTITATIVE MEASURES

I mentioned risk several times in conjunction with what to include in and what to exclude from your documentation project. As you can see by now, I am skittish about excluding accounts and processes because they are judged to be low risk, since if you exclude an item from the scope of your procedures, you may not identify until it is way too late that the item, account, or process is in fact not low risk. There are lots of examples of low-risk areas becoming major problems. Fraud has a tendency to migrate to the weakest links in the chain of controls. As Walter Matthau noted in the movie *The Fortune Cookie*, "Every time you build a better mousetrap, the mice get smarter."

No businessperson or auditor in their right mind starts out deliberately taking chances that a risky area will allow a material misstatement to occur that will cause the financial statements to be misstated. As skilled and as experienced as many managers and auditors are, the auditors of public entities, and the businesses they audit, have many painful reminders of the consequences of making bad judgments regarding risks. The reminders are in terms of income loss and reputation effects, and they stretch back over decades.

Nevertheless, risk judgments are made, and in order for audits and entity projects to be economical, they will continue to be. But very few financial statement elements are inherently and by their nature always low risk in all circumstances. Generalizing from experiences with other businesses or from other audit engagements gives a distorted view of risk, because the only risk that counts is the one specific to the entity and engagement right here and now. The probable low assessment of risk in the cash account did nothing to protect the shareholders and auditors of Parmalat, an Italian dairy company, from financial ruin when it was discovered that the auditors were served a bogus confirmation of a Bank of America account of over $3 billion. This led to the discovery that a significant portion ($13 billion) of the reported entity was bogus, and had been growing for years.

Go ahead, name some low-risk areas. Auditors generally pick fixed assets as a low inherent risk area for many businesses. Well, that was not the way it worked out at WorldCom, where major reclassifications of expenses were charged to fixed assets and doing so inflated reported income. In the previous decade the capitalization of garbage (literally) led to litigation and fines for the management and auditors of Waste Management. The poster child for audit skepticism and fixed assets risk was ZZZBest, a Wall Street darling start-up with interests in building restoration projects and all kinds of growth potential. In reality, the company was building files of fraudulent documents and misleading its auditors into thinking that it had interests in various buildings and fixed assets, when it did not.

Barings Bank and Orange County, CA, were stung some years ago when financial instruments and currency trading that in the past had been profitable went sour and what had been profitable ventures for the entities wound up creating huge losses and financial exposures that generated financial disaster, well beyond just the loss of income from these operations. Care needs to be taken to understand what risks various types of transactions and activities can expose the entity to; do not just look at the measure of revenue, asset, or income measurement in a "normal" year. Different thinking is required when derivative financial instruments are assessed.

It is hard to think of an inherently safe area in the financial statements and processes that does not deserve some level of consideration or scrutiny every once in a while. Consequently, it is helpful to rotate the emphasis and the areas in which management monitors and auditors audit. The nature, timing, and extent of monitoring and testing procedures should be varied such that the unpredictability of the oversight and the audit process helps ensure that those tempted to take risks and misstate or misappropriate realize that they are really taking a risk. All too often, management oversight and monitoring and the audit procedures applied become predictable and thus create an easy target for the fraudster.

 INHERENT AND CONTROL RISK

Following up on the risk discussion further, a concept that is difficult to communicate is that companies and auditors find it difficult to separate in their minds the underlying components of inherent risk and control risk (two distinctive risks identified in the audit literature) when making risk assessments. This sometimes leads to risk assessments that are low because of the *assumed* presence of effective controls, but without examining the design and operation of those controls, the basis of the low-risk assessment may not be valid. For example, in common conversation, the cash account may be considered low risk, but why? Is it not a sensitive asset and a frequent target of fraudsters? The answer may lie partly in the fact that the account is usually reconciled to the bank statement (a control), and extensive controls are in place over expenditures and over depositing cash receipts. If the reconciliation and other controls were not being performed or were improperly performed, would the low-risk assessment still be valid? Probably not. Therefore, one of the complexities in risk assessment is to identify the basis for the low-risk assessment and ensure that an otherwise high-risk area is not being given a pass in the scoping because of reliance on controls effectiveness, the very purpose of identifying the risks in the first place. At the scoping stage, the most relevant focus for the risk assessment is the inherent risk of the account and transactions stream.

 OVERSTATEMENT AND UNDERSTATEMENT

The risks of overstatement and understatement regarding internal controls over financial reporting are commonly misunderstood. Many auditors working in public company environments easily recognize the risk of an overstatement of income. However, in a private entity, minimization of taxes might motivate owners to want to understate accounting income to the extent it impacts tax liabilities. The assertion of *occurrence* often associated with income overstatement sometimes needs to take a backseat to the assertion of *completeness.*

Let's say you base your scoping of procedures on the recorded amounts of sales at various locations. If the sales at the Binghamton, NY, location are being systematically skimmed, then that location will seem to be less important for both controls assessment and monitoring—just the opposite of what should happen at that location. This sort of internal theft can be difficult to detect, which points out a common limitation of monitoring (or auditing) based on reported numbers (analytical procedures) that might not be accurate: It is harder to detect error in amounts that never enter the journals and accounts than it is to detect errors in amounts that are actually recorded. Suppose your entity is a church; do you have a record of how much loose cash is generally collected at a weekly service? Do you have statistics that relate the loose plate collections to the attendance? Is the amount recorded in the books what was put in the plate, or just the amount that was deposited in the bank account? How do you know? Is there opportunity for a disconnect to arise here?

A product line or location may appear to be poorly performing because someone has figured out a scheme to skim revenues from the organization. Restaurant license revenues of a municipality may be less than they should be because poor controls over the identification of licensed restaurants are keeping all restaurants from being properly identified in the database. For example, a standing database of licensed facilities should be updated when new licenses are issued or when businesses close, but in some organizations the two files are not related or reconciled. Unfortunately, businesses, governments, and auditors do not have a sterling track record of identifying all these businesses and financial reporting risks up front.

The lack of a consistent, reliable method for making such assessments may be part of the problem. In my view, when entities scope out locations, accounts, and business processes up front, before a careful analysis and some evidence that the area is truly low risk, they are just asking for trouble. To do the job right, I suggest first obtaining some evidence that all is well and that all the exposures have been considered, before concluding the process is indeed a low risk.

Additional Scoping Considerations

As you right-size the scope of your project, you will need to make sure you considered factors that contribute to the overall breadth and depth of the project. Those matters may be affected by one or more of these issues:

- Operations in multiple locations
- Internal controls that reside with third parties, such as service organizations (SOs)
- Recent internal audit and consulting projects
- Work performed by others
- Other technical scoping issues

Multiple Locations

Your evaluation of internal control should initially consider all the company's locations or business units. This does not mean that management is required to replicate its evaluation process at each location. Rather, you should make risk-based judgments about which locations should be scoped into the analysis and the nature, timing, and extent of procedures to be applied. To help you make those judgments, you may want to consider three types of risks:

1. *Risks subject to centralized controls.* Some companies may manage multiple locations or business units by using standard control procedures, the same software, and centralized controls. For example, consider the ABC Co., which owns and operates shopping malls. The company has developed its own information technology system, which stores and manages tenant leases and performs the basic accounting functions. The centralized processing and controls may adequately address many of the risks associated with ABC's financial reporting. In that case, it may be sufficient for management to consider the shared controls and processes as one system, barring reasons that might contribute to differences (e.g., differences in staffing quality or a local culture of questionable ethics).

2. *Specific risks at individual locations or business units.* In some cases, a risk may be related only to an individual location or business and therefore may not be adequately addressed by the common controls. For example, suppose that ABC acquired a very significant new mall during the year, and as of year-end it had not yet transitioned the new mall over to its central processing system. Or suppose that one of the malls was in a location that had a unique operating environment (e.g., the management and systems and policies were markedly different from other parts of the country).

   In those situations, management will want to consider the controls related to those location- or business unit–specific risks.

3. *Low-risk locations or business units.* Some of the controls that operate at an individual location or business unit may be related to risks that are relatively low, based on experience and prior testing. In addition, the relative size of some locations in terms of assets, liabilities, and contribution of profit may be very small and the locations pose no specific risks such as are sometimes identified when they are engaged in specific risk activities, such as currency trading or investing in derivative financial instruments. In those situations, management may determine that evidence about the operation of those controls gained through self-assessment and ongoing monitoring activities, when combined with the evidence derived from centralized controls, may be sufficient. However, recall the warning raised earlier regarding understated balances providing a false comfort about the insignificance of the account, balance, or location.

When making risk-based judgments about multiple locations or business units, keep in mind that the three types of risks and controls just described are not mutually exclusive. You should evaluate risk for each financial reporting element, not for the location or business unit as a whole.

The SEC, in Release 33-8810, provides specific warning about wholesale assessments in the context of evidence examination, but the implications are clear for all risk assessments by all entities:

Management should generally consider the risk characteristics of the controls for each financial reporting element, rather than making a single judgment for all controls at that location when deciding whether the nature and extent of evidence is sufficient. (p. 33)

Some implications:

- You probably should identify those business units where common controls can be considered as one population of entity level and activity level controls from which a common conclusion can be reached.
- For others you may need to assess risk by account and by process and use materiality as a guide in selecting what to examine and where. In those locations that (even in the aggregate) are insignificant, you may able initially to rely on effective company monitoring procedures, but you may want to explore some of these locations in future examinations to continue to have a basis for their low risk assessment.
- AS No. 2 for public companies had challenged auditors to examine entity-level and activity-level controls that would cover a "large portion" of the company. Of all the auditing and SEC guidelines, this was probably the most costly to comply with, and the risk-based nature of AS No. 5 guidance avoids the specificity of that original requirement. Nevertheless, in the absence of a solid risk and materiality basis for excluding locations, it is conservative and often wise to sweep more locations into the initial scoping and weed out or rotate emphasis for the low-risk ones in future periods.

Service Organizations and Outsourcing

An often-troublesome SOX issue for larger entities has been the extent to which the use of outside SOs such as payroll services and information technology network administration and maintenance services (and now cloud computing and cloud data storage) have grown in usage in recent years. Outsourcing was seen as a way to acquire lower-cost services by specialist providers. Sometimes entire accounting systems are outsourced to companies in third-world countries.

Outsourcing or using a SO does not necessarily remove the outsourced function from the controls assessment process if the function is relevant and important to financial accounting and reporting. How does one obtain assurance that the SO's controls exist and are effective in order to make a supportable assertion? COSO now adds that the entity should have evidence that that outsource company is aware of and subscribes to the ethical policies of the entity.

In addition, in recent years more and more statutory restrictions have been imposed on companies outsourcing manufacturing and processing activities in certain countries. This also can be troublesome to the entity.

Service organizations may provide a wide variety of services, ranging from performing a specific task under the direction of the entity to replacing entire business units or functions. The types of services such an organization may provide include:

- *Information processing.* Information processing is probably the most common type of SO service. An information-processing SO may provide standardized services, such as entering the company's manually recorded data and processing it with software that produces computer-generated journals, a general ledger, and financial statements. At the other end of the spectrum, the information-processing SO may design and execute customized applications. Examples include credit card charge processing and payroll processing.
- *Trust departments.* SOs, such as the trust department of a bank or an insurance company, may provide a wide range of services to user organizations, such as employee benefit plans. This type of SO could be given authority to make decisions about how a plan's assets are invested. It also may serve as custodian of the plan's assets, maintain records of each participant's account, allocate investment income to the participants based on a formula in the trust agreement, and make distributions to the participants.
- *Transfer agents, custodians, and record keepers for investment companies.* Transfer agents process purchases, sales, and other shareholder activity for investment companies. The custodian is responsible for the receipt, delivery, and safekeeping of the company's portfolio securities; the cash related to transactions in those securities; and the maintenance of records of the securities held for the investment company. Record keepers maintain the financial accounting records of the investment company based on information provided by the transfer agent and the custodian of the investment company's investments.
- *Other SOs* include:
  - Insurers that maintain the accounting for ceded reinsurance.
  - Mortgage servicers or depository institutions that service loans for others.
  - Value-added networks.
  - Third-party entities that act as a conduit for collecting amounts to be remitted in whole or in part to the company.

When an entity uses a SO to process transactions, the controls over that processing reside *outside the entity*, at the SO. When developing a strategy under these conditions, you will need to determine whether the scope of the engagement can be restricted to those controls that remain directly administered by the entity or if they need to extended to include the controls at the SO. In making that determination, you could consider:

- The significance of the processing activity.
- The functions performed by the SO.
- The degree of interaction between the entity and the SO.

When assessing the significance of the processing activity, some prefer to assess the risks as though the SO were a separate business unit or location and follow the guidance discussed previously. For example, you should consider the materiality of the transactions processed relative to the financial statements taken as a whole. In addition, you could consider whether the nonfinancial or operational information processed by the SO is significant to the entity and should be subject to disclosure controls and procedures.

AU 324 for public companies and AU-C Section 402 *Service Organizations* for others sets the rules as to how the auditor gathers sufficient evidence regarding these outsourced operations to be able to render an opinion on the financial statements. Entities may consider these standards when assessing these outside organizations. Some guidelines:

- If the services provided by the SO are limited to recording user organization transactions and processing the related data, and the user organization retains responsibility for authorizing the transactions and maintaining the related accountability, there will be a high degree of interaction. When there is a high degree of interaction between the user and SOs, you are more likely to be able to obtain the information necessary to evaluate internal control by focusing solely on the controls maintained by the user. In these situations, you would evaluate company controls over company provided inputs to and outputs of data to the SO.
- Unfortunately, if the procedures performed by the SO are complex, testing inputs and outputs of company data on a routine basis may result in company reperformance of the service the company is outsourcing to save money. Payroll is a good example. How would you know if the various tax and benefit deduction computations were processed properly without reperforming them?
- Alternatively, when the SO is authorized to initiate and execute transactions without prior authorization of each transaction by the user, there will be a lower degree of interaction. Under these arrangements, the user must record activity from information provided by the SO because the user has no means of independently generating a record of its transactions. In these situations, you will be more likely to *extend* the scope of your project to include an assessment of the SO's controls.

It is not uncommon for the SO to take action to help its customers gain a better understanding of the design and operating effectiveness of its controls. Another reason for SOs to take action is to avoid duplicative requests from various client managements and numerous auditors for access to its business processes in order to assess the controls and test their effectiveness.

For example, the SO might engage an auditor to review and report on the systems and controls it uses to process client transactions. The SO, to avoid direct requests from numerous clients regarding the same controls issues, often will make available an audit report describing the systems examined by the service auditor and his or her findings. In some cases, if timely, relevant, and sufficient in scope and opinion for reliance, this may be sufficient for management and auditor purposes.

The type of report sought that includes testing the effectiveness of controls is called a *Type II* report. These reports are generally written as of a specific date. That may work for public company reports or AT 501 reports on internal controls since those reports are issued "as of" a date. If the report conclusions indicate that relevant controls are effective in a time frame near the reporting date, then the report and perhaps an updating inquiry regarding recent changes or problems may provide sufficient evidence.

For audit purposes as a source of reliance on controls, the conclusions need to be applicable to the period on which the reliance is to be placed. This may be accomplished by more frequent Type II reports or through inquiry and examination of some evidence that the SO has maintained these controls through the period of reliance. The farther the SO report date from the reporting date, the more updating procedures are expected to be applied to be able to use the report. Many SOs have new reports issued every six months to obviate the issue.

Type I reports only address controls design and are not sufficient for reliance for high-assurance audit purposes (including SOX). They can be sufficient for nonpublic engagements where limited or no reliance is placed on controls and only an assessment of design is sought. Many former Type I reports have now been modified to be Type II reports, which are more useful to many clients. Managements and auditors need to make sure the report addresses the specific service of interest. A payroll SO might also perform other services relating to pensions and benefits administration. A report on one service has no value in concluding on the effectiveness of another service.

An early practical issue has been that, outside the United States, the concept of an SO report has not been established as a part of international auditing practice. Thus, when outsourced activities in remote locations are engaged, there may be difficulties in avoiding flotillas of auditors and managements seeking to directly test controls over important functions unless a service organization controls (SOC) report is provided. Since 2003, the SEC has expected companies to execute "right to audit" clauses in outsourcing contracts to avoid scope limitations that would preclude companies from asserting that controls are effective. There are no such regulations for private companies, but it is a good idea from a business as well as an audit efficiency perspective to include such clauses in outsourcing contracts.

When considering the implications that an outside SO has on your engagement, you may find the guidance contained in AU-C Section 402 and the related *Audit Guide* published by the American Institute of Certified Public Accountants (AICPA) to be helpful.

Internal Audit Activities

Professional standards are supportive in permitting independent (external) auditors leeway in placing reliance on the work of internal auditors, provided that they test that work for competence and assess that there is sufficient objectivity in the work that was performed. Before turning to planning the project, management and independent auditor scoping considerations should consider the work that has already been performed and will be performed by internal audit to avoid costly reperformance and duplicated effort. Close liaison between the controls documentation and assessment and IA teams will yield cost savings.

A fundamental objective of the internal audit function is to help the entity maintain effective operational and financial controls by evaluating their adequacy and effectiveness. Standards established by the Institute of Internal Auditors (IIA) state that this evaluation should include:

- Reliability and integrity of financial and operational information.
- Effectiveness and efficiency of operations.

- Safeguarding of assets.
- Compliance with laws, regulations, and contracts.

In planning the scope of your project, you will need to consider any findings of internal audit or any external regulator that reflect on the effectiveness of internal control over financial reporting. Keep in mind that the objectives of the engagements performed by others may not have been planned, documented, and performed primarily for the purpose of assessing internal control the way you want to do this. Therefore, when determining how the engagements and conclusions of others affect the scope of your engagement, you should consider:

- *The scope of the other projects and whether it is sufficient to meet some or all of the objectives of your project.* For example, an internal audit engagement may have evaluated one aspect of internal controls for only a limited number of business units as part of a rotational audit strategy. No recent evidence may have been gathered about accounts, assertions, and locations you consider significant. In that case, you would want to include an evaluation of the other significant business units in your scope.
- *The timing of the work and whether it is within a time frame that would permit you to draw a conclusion as to the effectiveness of the entity's internal control.* If a significant amount of time has elapsed since, say, the internal auditors performed their engagement, additional testing may be needed to determine whether the conclusions reached are still appropriate for your purpose.
- *The documentation of the procedures and whether it is sufficient for the independent auditor.* If you plan to have your auditors incorporate the work of others, you should evaluate the documentation of their work to ensure that you can rely on their conclusions. Did their work address all of the relevant assertions? Did they sufficiently test the higher-risk accounts and higher-risk assertions? Did they assess the design of the controls, or just the correctness of processing? Did they truly evaluate controls effectiveness or simply test the substantive correctness of the entries of the transactions in their sample?

    When considering an internal auditor's work in an audit of internal control, the independent auditors will refer to the auditing standards. The auditor will usually consider such factors as whether the internal auditor's:
    - Audit programs are adequate.
    - Working papers adequately document work performed, including evidence of supervision and review.
    - Conclusions are appropriate in the circumstances.
    - Reports are consistent with the results of the work performed.

Investment and Merger Scoping Considerations

Complex accounting issues create questions about what should be in scope. For public companies, the SEC staff's answers to frequently asked questions provide additional guidance on issues relating to the scope of the company's assessment process. Such guidance may be helpful to other entities in properly gauging the scope of internal controls over financial reporting.

- *Variable interest entities (VIEs) and proportional consolidations.* Ordinarily, the SEC would expect management's report on internal control to include all consolidated entities, including VIEs and those accounted for via proportional consolidation. However, these entities may be excluded from the scope of management's assessment if all of the next three conditions are met:
  1. The VIE was in existence before December 15, 2004.
  2. The VIE would not have been consolidated absent the application of Financial Accounting Standards Board (FASB) Interpretation No. 46.
  3. The company does not have the right or authority to assess the internal controls of the consolidated entity and also lacks the ability, in practice, to make that assessment.

If all of these conditions are met, the company does not have to include the VIE in its control assessment process. However, a public company should make these disclosures (not specifically required for nonpublic entities but may be considered if the company is reporting publicly on internal controls):

- A reference in the Form 10-K to the scope of management's report on internal control.
- A statement that the company has not evaluated the internal controls of the entity excluded from its scope and any conclusions regarding internal control do not extend to that entity.
- Key subtotals that result from consolidation of entities whose internal controls have not been assessed.
- A statement that the financial statements include the accounts of certain entities consolidated pursuant to FASB Interpretation Number (FIN) 46 or Emerging Issues Task Force (EITF) Consensus Position 00-1, but that management has been unable to assess the effectiveness of internal control at those entities because the registrant does not have the ability to dictate or modify the controls of the entities and does not have the ability, in practice, to assess those controls.
- For equity method investments, controls over the recording of transactions in the *investee's* accounts are not part of the investor company's internal control. That is, if the company has equity or cost-basis method investments, the controls that relate to the investee's transactions are considered outside the scope of the company's internal control. However, the investor company should have controls over the recording of income or loss and cash dividend or distribution amounts in its own financial statements. This is good guidance for all entities.
- For business combinations made during the year, ordinarily, public companies would be expected to include controls over the combinations process and of the business combination entities themselves. However, it is recognized that it might

not always be possible to conduct such an assessment between the consummation date of the acquisition and year-end. Thus, public companies may exclude such a business combination from its internal control assessment, provided that:

- The company identifies the acquired business and its relative significance to the financial statements and discloses that the acquired business has been excluded from the company's assessment of internal control.
- The company discloses any material change to its internal control due to the acquisition.
- The exclusion of the acquired business from the scope of the company's internal control assessment may not extend beyond one year from the date of acquisition.
- Anticipated discontinued operations are expected to be in the controls assessment until they are discontinued.

 ## DOES "IN SCOPE" IMPLY EXTENSIVE TESTING?

No. All in-scope assessments need not receive the same level of attention, since the highest levels of attention and testing should be given to higher-risk areas and controls over those areas. The application of effort is scalable and responds to the risk assessment. The all-or-nothing approach is potentially a source of significant inefficiency and possible ineffectiveness if some risk areas are inadvertently excluded from the analysis. In setting the scope, you should follow a reasoned process, such as follows:

- Any assessment may exclude certain areas, issues, and controls. However, you should provide a reasoned explanation for those decisions.
- In lower-risk areas, you may decide to document controls over the potential risks and examine some evidence that these controls are in operation but not fully test the controls due to the limited risk. In future periods you may decide to test these controls periodically.
- For moderate-risk accounts, you might document and test controls with a small sample.
- In risk areas and core accounts, you should document controls and test to support the level of assurance desired from the controls. For public companies, that level is a high level of assurance (low risk); for nonpublic entities, it can range from a walk-through or some evidence the control is in operation (low level of assurance) to high assurance, depending on the level of reliance to be placed on the controls.

Levels of tests are discussed later in this book. The point here is that "in scope" is not an attribute that implies documentation and testing to high levels of assurance. There is a sliding scale of required effort that can be applied to the COSO principle, account, balance, and disclosure. This helps auditors to right-size the effort and hopefully will encourage annually taking a look at a broader range of controls. The most dangerous situation is where, based on a risk judgment, a component, account, or control receives no attention whatsoever.

PCAOB guidance to public company auditors in AS No. 5, paragraph 11, gets to this point:

> A direct relationship exists between the degree of risk that a material weakness could exist in a particular area of the company's internal control over financial reporting and the amount of audit attention that should be devoted to that area. In addition, the risk that a company's internal control over financial reporting will fail to prevent or detect misstatement caused by fraud usually is higher than the risk of failure to prevent or detect error. The auditor should focus more of his or her attention on the areas of highest risk. On the other hand, it is not necessary to test controls that, even if deficient, would not present a reasonable possibility of material misstatement to the financial statements.

In the interest of overall efficiency and in the context of testing, it should be remembered that independent auditors can rely on most of the management control tests that are performed with demonstrated objectivity and competence. When management performs high-quality assessment and testing procedures, this can contribute to reductions in required auditor procedures. From big-picture and aggregate efficiency perspectives, doing more than the minimum level of assessment and testing may not raise company costs of compliance but may actually lower them.

However, there is a reason to be concerned that management assessments might not always meet the definition of high quality. Public company auditors sometimes choose to perform more extensive and expensive substantive procedures (direct tests of amounts in the financial statements) in lieu of testing and relying on management internal controls assessments because they do not deem those assessments or tests to be of a high quality. This is supported by research that shows in the early years of SOX nearly all engagements identified control deficiencies, and most of them were identified by the independent auditor and not by the company that had completed its assessment before the independent auditor. An academic study [1] of smaller accelerated filer public companies revealed that the auditors were aware of nearly 3,990 control deficiencies identified in 44 companies (76 audit units) over a two-year period, 2004 to 2005. A surprise was that these were public companies and auditors had been relying in some cases and to varying degrees on the effectiveness of internal controls, yet nearly 4,000 internal control deficiencies were identified for these engagements. While management assessed and tested controls before the auditors did their assessment and testing, auditors still identified over 70% of the control deficiencies eventually identified. In another surprising statistic, management underassessed the severity of its more serious deficiencies over 70% of the time. This calls into question the effectiveness of these management assessments and judgments. While some of this effect might be due to the issue of "marking your own paper"

---

[1] J. Bedard and L. Graham, "Detection and Severity Classifications of Sarbanes-Oxley Section 404 Internal Control Deficiencies," *Accounting Review* 86, no 3 (2011).

and some might be attributed to the newness of the regulatory requirements, some is and continues to be attributable to management performing minimal assessments and testing that is not breeding confidence in their auditors. Unfortunately, many companies do not seem to approach the assessment task with the mind to build confidence in their assessments or to save/reduce/control audit costs.

In entities where lesser auditor oversight is provided over the process, such as with smaller public companies [2] or nonpublic entities, the question remains as to the level of quality that entities are targeting for their COSO and any regulatory compliance. The SEC has recently raised the issue of whether a sufficient number of material weaknesses are being identified in current financial reports. PCAOB inspections will undoubtedly be looking at this issue as auditor engagement files are reviewed in future periods.

 ## A CONSOLATION

If, after your analysis, you are left with a depressingly long list of in-scope processes and accounts, remember that the documentation of the relevant controls is a one-time activity if it is performed with competence and that testing levels and monitoring levels for controls are set commensurate with the relative risks of misstatement and can be varied over time and from year to year to achieve an overall effective process to assesses controls effectiveness. Over time, more processes and accounts and even assertions within the processes and accounts of importance can be assessed as lower risk that warrants less testing as evidence is gathered regarding the effectiveness of these controls, and thus can provide support for these lower-risks assessments. Over time, policies and practices can be centralized in large, multi-location entities to reduce the number of individual assessments required.

Guidance to auditors by the PCAOB in AS No. 5, paragraph 59, mirrors this perspective.

> After taking into account the risk factors … the additional information available in subsequent years' audits might permit the auditor to assess the risk as lower than in the initial year. This, in turn, might permit the auditor to reduce testing in subsequent years.

This latter point is important, as it establishes the need to have a solid basis for a low-risk assessment. When that is obtained, future risk reductions and reductions of testing effort are warranted. This approach is helpful to all entities and not just public companies.

---

[2] For example, the auditors of nonaccelerated filers are not required to assess, test, and report publicly on internal controls. However, they are expected to review the validity of the assertions management makes regarding internal controls. While the precise extent of this review is not specified, it has been analogized to be similar to the audit attention and procedures applied to the management discussion and analysis (MD&A) section of the annual report. Both the SEC and PCAOB are relying on this level of oversight to management's assertion and basis for the assertion.

For Public Companies Only: Disclosure Committee

Subsequent to the passage of the SOX legislation, many companies have formed a disclosure committee for overseeing the process by which the extensive disclosures mandated by the SEC are created and reviewed. This function as a whole can be viewed as a control over regulatory compliance and financial disclosures.

When scoping your engagement, you should consider the policies and processes of the committee and the extent to which its work product can be used to support the entity's evaluation of its internal control. Policies and processes of the disclosure committee that may affect the planning of your project include:

- Areas of the entity's business that should be monitored for disclosure issues.
- Individuals identified within each monitored area who are best able to identify potential disclosure issues.
- Methods of communicating with the operating and accounting functions and reporting back the identified disclosure issues to the disclosure committee.
- Disclosure documents (in addition to Exchange Act filings) that are the responsibility of the disclosure committee. These documents may include:
  - Reports and letters to shareholders.
  - Earnings releases.
  - Presentations to analysts.
- Any comparisons of the entity's disclosures to those of its competitors that the committee may have done to benchmark the company's disclosures.
- Sources and quality of disclosure checklists used in ensuring the completeness of the required disclosures.
- If applicable, the impact on the entity's disclosure controls and procedures of any significant changes to the entity, for example:
  - New information systems.
  - Significant acquisitions or dispositions.
  - Changes in lines of business.
  - Geographic expansion.
  - Changes in personnel with significant control responsibilities.

 BE CAREFUL OUT THERE!

Okay, you have gone through this analysis and assessment process, and you have identified your core business and other operations for documentation and assessment. That is not the end of it. Fires rarely occur next door to firehouses. You have put controls and monitoring in place, but stuff happens. You will need to pay attention to all kinds of possible signals and unexpected test results. If complaints and calls indicate that shipments are not being fulfilled or billed accurately, then controls over that process need to be examined more closely. Identified substantive misstatements in drafted financial statement amounts generally imply some sort of control failures. You may need, based on an alarm signal, to assess the risk of misstatement as higher in an area that did not initially attract a lot of attention because it was not that significant. If the area is teeming with risk, the dollar exposure might be proportionally greater than the size of the process or account might indicate. Leverage your past experience, both good and bad. And don't forget to periodically revisit even the low-risk areas and look at them with fresh eyes.

Summary of Scoping Inquiries

Identifying the Core

This appendix summarizes some of the inquiries and checks you might make when scoping your project to assess the effectiveness of a company's internal control. The second column provides guidance on how the answers to the questions might be used for planning and scoping purposes. The third column offers suggestions on some sources for obtaining the information.

Planning Questions to Consider	Relevance for Engagement Performance	Information Sources
Company Operations and Industry Characteristics		
What are the primary characteristics of the entity's industry? Consider the effect of: Financial reporting practices Economic conditions Laws and regulations Technological changes	Determine significant business and internal control objectives. Establish materiality thresholds. Understand business and financial reporting risks.	SEC Form 10-K and other filings, or financial statements and disclosures of nonpublic entities Inquiries of management or auditors Industry trends in trade publications News reports and press releases Analyst reports Company and close competitor Web sites Industry benchmark statistics
What are the fundamental operating characteristics of the entity?	Develop a preliminary understanding of the entity's significant transactions and business processes.	Same as above

Planning Questions to Consider	Relevance for Engagement Performance	Information Sources
Which financial statement accounts, balances, or disclosures are affected by one or more of these attributes? Subjective in nature Complex accounting issues Accounting rules subject to interpretation Dependent on external information Related party transactions	Make judgments about inherent risks, which will help identify those areas where strong controls are important.	Financial statement captions and footnotes Analysis of related entities Unusual transactions and transactions with a material effect on the metrics of the financial statement Inquiries regarding transactions with related entities Confirmations of significant agreements and commitments
Engagement Scope		
Which business activities or locations: Are financially most significant? Are operationally most significant? Have the potential to expose the entity to significant risk or obligation? Lack adequate available information?	Determine scope of engagement.	SEC Form 10-K and other filings or annual report and footnotes Multiple criteria analyses of segments, product lines, and locations Management and auditor brainstorming to identify scenarios of risk and exposure
Does the entity use a service organization to process significant information?	Determine scope of engagement.	Inquiries of management Examination of significant contracts Service organizations in common functions, such as payroll
What is the nature and extent of the entity's: Internal audit function? Regulatory audits and audit results? Disclosure committee (public)?	Determine if internal control assessments of engagement can be leveraged.	Inquiries of management Knowledge of the industry SOX team structure and organizational charts
Internal Control Considerations		
What processes does the entity currently have in place to perform an assessment of its internal control?	Determine scope of engagement. Plan the nature of the procedures to be performed. Could be a deficiency itself, if inadequate.	Inquiries of management and those responsible for internal controls Review of documentation or any work papers of others. Annual report and other filings
What have been the most significant recent changes to the company and its internal controls?	Identify potential problem areas and set the focus for the engagement. Determine significant controls.	Inquiries of management and auditors Form 8-K disclosures (public) Review of 302 certifications Trade publications Analytical procedures on draft financial statements Expanded or new disclosures for this year

(continued)

Planning Questions to Consider	Relevance for Engagement Performance	Information Sources
What is the nature and extent of the entity's existing documentation of its internal control?	Determine scope of the engagement. Assess needs.	Inquiries of management and assessment team members Examination of documentation
What are management's current views regarding: The most important policies, procedures, and practices it uses to control the business? Areas of potential weakness in internal control?	Help determine significant controls. Help focus the engagement on risk areas (also see the Risk Assessment component discussion).	Inquiries of management Any written documentation of risk analysis Any reports of others or incidents indicating a risk
Has management responded to deficiencies reported internally and from the independent auditor or other regulators regarding control deficiencies observed?	Help identify significant controls. Help determine the scope of the engagement.	Inquiries of management Reports to internal governance groups Replies to regulators Any written reports available Examination of evidence that deficiencies have been remediated
Existence of a Significant Deficiency and Possible Material Weakness		
In the past year, has there been a restatement of a previously issued financial statement to reflect the correction of a misstatement?	Identify a significant deficiency and material weakness.	Inquiry of management Review of reports and filings
In the past year, have the independent auditors identified a material misstatement in the financial statements that was not initially identified by the company's internal control?	Identify a new significant deficiency and material weakness. Setting scope based of risk.	Inquiry of management Review of letter/communication from independent auditors or regulators
Are there any significant deficiencies that have been communicated to management that remain uncorrected after a reasonable time?	Identify a significant deficiency and material weakness. A potential control environment issue. Setting scope.	Inquiry of management Auditor or regulator communications Evidence of correction Comparison of internally reported incidents to resolutions
Is the board aware of a fraud of any magnitude on the part of senior management?	Identify a significant deficiency and material weakness. Setting scope. Fraud risk awareness.	Inquiry of board of directors, audit committee and/or select management News reports Examination of turnover in key positions

3

The Risk Assessment Component

A MONG THE FIVE components in the COSO Framework, the one most often discussed first is the control environment (CE) component. This is because from a controls performance perspective, if this component is ineffective, most of the other components could be negatively affected. For example, if the entity operates in an environment devoid of ethical values and honesty and management has a tendency to override controls, it is unlikely that specific controls over transactions can be considered as effective. An ineffective control environment effectively trumps the lower-level controls. However, we explore the CE component in the next chapter.

A reason to discuss the risk assessment (RA) component first is because the task of scoping the assessment project and the RA component have so much in common. Indeed, from a planning and project perspective, the other components, including the CE, drive off of the identification and assessment of risks. From a project *process*, and not a hierarchical controls perspective, the RA tasks need to precede much of the other controls assessment and testing since the object is to do three things:

1. Identify risks to achieving organizational (and financial reporting) objectives.
2. Assess the design of controls that mitigate these risks.
3. Assess whether the controls are effective.

While these three objectives are all important to the entity, the second and third points rely on the effective identification and assessment of the importance of the risks.

RISK ASSESSMENT PRINCIPLES IN COSO

COSO identifies four basic principles that should be satisfied in relation to the RA component. The concept of principles was first introduced with the 2006 smaller public company guidance but is now proposed for all entities. Specifically, these principles should be assessed as "functioning" in the entity. In addition to the principles, points of focus (PoF) are articulated to help users identify the characteristics and attributes embodied in the principles. There are 88 of these points of focus, but not all may relate to internal controls over financial reporting. If material weaknesses are identified in one of the principles, then the overall system of internal control cannot be assessed as effective. The principles help the entity to focus on the detailed elements of internal control related to the more general component (e.g., RA). At the end of this chapter, guidance is be provided for transitioning from the 2006 RA principles to the 2013 Principles if you have been following the 2006 COSO guidance. Those who have been following the 1992 Framework will need to consider if your assessment has addressed these principles or if you need to expand your project to encompass them.

In sum, the four RA principles are:

1. The specification of clear, suitable financial reporting objectives.
2. The identification and analysis of risks to achieving the objectives.
3. The assessment of fraud risk.
4. The identification and assessment of significant change.

While not asserted to encompass all the issues that might affect this component, the principles help identify its key elements. This approach facilitates documentation and assessment that is more standardized to help both preparers and reviewers in their roles and create a more level playing field for all participants using the Framework.

 COST CONTROL

One issue that has contributed to excessive costs of compliance is the diversity of documentation approaches between and sometimes within entities, leading to unnecessary complexity. Public company regulators and standard setters (Securities and Exchange Commission [SEC] and Public Company Accounting Oversight Board [PCAOB]) note that auditors cannot dictate the details of the approaches to be taken by companies in performing their assessment, but the more reconcilable the company and auditor assessment tools are to each other (reducing the time to map one assessment tool to the other), the more efficient review can be made, and at a lower audit cost. Thus, some up-front conversation and discussion with the auditors of public and nonpublic entities may still be useful in reducing review costs if entities are beginning anew or now revising their COSO project documentation. Some issues it may be helpful to discuss approaches are listed next.

- Documentation formats—matrices, narratives, or flowcharts.
- Views on the segments, locations, and product lines and how they are determined, documented, and assessed from a controls perspective.
- Those controls that will be considered entity-level controls with commonality across the entity.
- Assertions to be used—the 13 in the American Institute of Certified Public Accountants (AICPA) auditing literature, those proposed by the PCAOB, or a lesser set.
- Approaches to testing and extent of desired testing.
- Methods to assess the severity of deficiencies that are identified.

Mindful of the independence requirements, particularly for public companies, entities still determine how they set up their COSO documentation. However, the auditor needs to follow whatever interpretation of the Framework is adopted by the entity in making any required assessments of the project effectiveness in supporting management's assertions. If, in 2014 and beyond, the Framework applied is the 1992 or 2006 Framework, then the auditor needs to use that in the assessment. The SEC has noted that public companies must disclose the Framework version they are following and that questions *may* be raised if entities do not evolve to the 2013 Framework in annual reports issued after December 15, 2014.

Regulated businesses and government engagements should be alert to any specific guidance provided in this matter, to ensure that their projects meet that guidance. For example, "single audits" (under Office of Management and Budget [OMB] A-133) may need separate controls assessments for some programs, when they differ from program to program. Carefully strategized documentation is necessary to avoid unnecessary documentation and testing when common controls are shared by different programs, but still meet the "by-program" assessment requirement. Industry and trade groups may also be a source of guidance and best practices, but to date they have not been a major force in driving company practices.

BASICS

Since RA is the filter for determining the specifics of the scope of the processes included in the assessment and extent of procedures performed, it pays to devote some attention here to the basics. While the rules of COSO are not highly prescriptive in the methods to be used, a text such as this one is expected to provide some additional perspective from which you can develop an approach you can be comfortable with and defend, if need be.

While the audit requirements are directed at auditors, companies wishing to align their thinking with the audit requirements to create a more efficient audit process should be mindful of how the auditors will be viewing the engagement and should try to minimize differences in approach. There are a large number of variant practices in the "real world," but the defensibility of some of these approaches is debatable if they were to be examined closely. The perspective from which this book is written is one of conservatism and defensibility. It is *a* way to view risk, not *the* way. For example, the PCAOB Auditing Standard (AS) No. 5, paragraph 10, speaks to the importance of the RA component:

> Risk assessment underlies the entire audit process described by this standard, including the determination of significant accounts and disclosures and relevant assertions, the selection of controls to test, and the determination of the evidence necessary for a given control.

First we should clarify what we mean by risk. The risk in question is that the controls in place (or the lack of controls) *could* allow a material misstatement in the financial statements (or a failure in one of the other elements of the Framework, such as operations or compliance[1]). It also covers the failure to disclose a required or material fact.

Risk emanates from business (e.g., financial reporting) objectives that need to be articulated. Once articulated, the risks are identified that might interfere with achieving the objective. An easy financial reporting objective to understand is the presentation of the financial statements in accordance with generally accepted accounting principles (GAAP) (or other framework). The risks then become the potential impediments to achieving that, say the use of estimates or development of fair values used in the accounts.

LIKELIHOOD, MAGNITUDE, VELOCITY, AND PERSISTENCE

Risk is composed of two principal elements:

1. The likelihood that such a misstatement might occur.
2. The potential magnitude of the misstatement if the control did fail.

The concepts of likelihood and magnitude as discussed in the COSO guidance have parallels in the auditing standards as measures of entity risk. Likelihood is a probability concept: How likely is the occurrence of a misstatement? Magnitude is associated with materiality: How big *could* the misstatement be? The importance of the word *could* in this discussion is discussed further below. Sometimes these concepts are represented in a chart like Figure 3.1.

When there is an assessed low likelihood and low magnitude associated with a risk, then the controls surrounding the risk are of lesser importance. When either the magnitude or likelihood is greater, the controls deserve more attention. When likelihood and magnitude are both greater, the issue should be a priority.

How do we assess likelihood? It should an informed judgment based on the situation, but with consideration of past experience and present circumstances. At the time

---

[1] While our primary focus is financial reporting controls, there is a blurred line between compliance and operational control failures, as such often lead to financial statement required disclosures or financial consequences. It is best to be broadly generous at the early stage in defining risk.

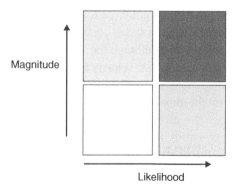

FIGURE 3.1   Measuring Risk using Likelihood and Magnitude

of this writing, a hot issue is the criminal breach of corporate computer systems for the theft of personal information. Widely publicized security breaches such as the one at Target Stores in December 2013 had a chilling effect on the general public's willingness to trust their information with vendors. After that, many entities raised their assessments of the likelihood that such an attack might occur. The magnitude of the issue is related to the potential size of the loss. In terms of the security breach, the liability to customers and likely fines under federal and state laws and the loss of future customers and sales could be very substantial. The magnitude of a control requiring dual signatures on larger checks might be measured by the value of checks with this attribute that should have been controlled with dual signatures. If assessing the potential magnitude of loss associated with a petty cash or low-value inventory item theft, the magnitude is likely to be assessed as low.

A point that needs emphasis is that a risk does not have to result in an actual misstatement to be considered a risk. The issue is whether the risk *could* lead to a material misstatement. However, the existence of some misstatement is an indicator that a risk and deficiency in controls exists. The more significant the misstatement, the more likely the risk is a material risk that resulted from a material weakness. I aver that the relationship between misstatement and risks and control weaknesses might be thought of this way: the amount of the misstatement means that the deficiency is at least as severe as that relationship to materiality implies, but the deficiency could be much more severe than the amount of the misstatement indicates.[2]

This is why an auditor cannot conclude that a lack of observed current or past misstatement is sufficient evidence that the process, account, or class of transactions is low risk. Some evidence relating to the controls design and operation or some inherent factors would have to be gathered and considered in the low-risk assessment. Research has shown that the existence of a misstatement makes it easier to rate a control deficiency as more severe (a significant deficiency or a material weakness).[3] This tendency does not

---

[2] For more information see Bedard, J., and L. Graham. 2011. Detection and severity classification of Sarbanes-Oxley Section 404 internal control deficiencies. *The Accounting Review* 86 (3): 825–855.

[3] Bedard and Graham, 2011 previously cited.

match with the requirements but is a potential source of bias that entities and auditors need to be aware of and try to avoid.

In addition to magnitude and likelihood, the 2013 COSO guidance has introduced two additional criteria for assessing risk: velocity and persistence. *Velocity* relates to the swiftness that an event might occur. *Persistence* relates to how long the situation might continue and how that might impact the magnitude of the risk. An analogy might be made to a weather event. The greater its velocity and the longer its persistence, the more damage the risk can cause. Hurricane Sandy is a good example. While at best classified as a Category 1 hurricane (and in many areas just a tropical storm, by definition), its persistence along the New Jersey shore created significant damage beyond what might be expected. The "perfect storm" of the landfall, high tide, and a full moon created havoc that is still being addressed. The unexpected is hard to predict, but following Hurricane Katrina, it was noted that for a long time, the levies protecting the shore were not sufficient to hold back a storm of its magnitude. Disaster was a matter of time. If you live in hurricane alley or in tornado territory, you need to understand the risks and protections. While being hit by a tornado is unlikely, the intensity of one can obliterate houses, neighborhoods, and towns. Its swiftness in appearance can cost lives. In the business situation, natural disasters, terrorism, and unmonitored legislation can change the course of business in an instant. In the 1970s, the Federal Communications Commission (FCC) made an unexpected rule requiring all citizens band (CB) radios to carry 40 channels. In an instant, 23-channel CB radios were obsolete. I was an auditor of an electrical components manufacturer then, and we had an interesting time assessing the impact of the rule on the existing parts inventories. In an instant, that line of business changed. Between the Environmental Protection Agency (EPA), Food and Drug Administration (FDA), and myriad of other agencies issuing rules and restrictions today, and the lack of calm in weather systems, the RA should consider velocity and persistence as additional dimensions of risk assessment.

SEPARATE ASSESSMENTS OF INHERENT AND CONTROL RISKS

In the prior chapter we discussed the difference between inherent risk and control risk when assessing "risk." To clarify, in RA our initial focus is on the inherent risk (before the consideration of the effect of any internal controls) associated with an account, balance, or disclosure. This distinction becomes very important when identifying risk since it is precisely the inherent risk that controls are supposed to be designed to mitigate. Later on, we consider the design and functioning of the nature of the internal controls that are in place to prevent misstatement.

A common misunderstanding occurs when inherent and control risk are assessed together as low when the inherent risk might be high, and it is really the assumed excellent controls that make the risk low. For example, payroll, as an expense, is usually very significant to an entity. If there were really no controls over payroll, most would agree that the inherent risk would be high that errors and fraud could occur. As such, the account would usually be in the most serious quadrant in the graph. Failing to separate these assessments by inherent and control components could erroneously place this account in the low likelihood category, and the importance of its controls to achieving the low risk not fully considered. This is an area that needs to be explained and even trained, as it is not clear to even experienced managers and auditors.

ROLE OF ASSERTIONS

The COSO Framework is much more oriented today to entities working with the financial statement assertions than evident in previous guidance. All auditing literature today requires the use of assertions when identifying and responding the risks. However, despite the reemphasis on assertions in the audit standards more than a decade ago, entities and auditors still struggle to associate risks and procedures with assertions. The long-range implications are clear. The use of assertions is here to stay. It is an integral piece in the fabric of risk and controls assessment. While no specific set of assertions is required, professional standards for auditors and entities recite similar assertions for accounts, balances, and disclosures. Entities would be wise to adopt an assertions mentality when developing their COSO documentation.

In the new COSO guidance, the use of assertions is frequently illustrated for documenting and assessing controls effectiveness. A related but different approach was prevalent in prior literature—the use of control objectives for each account or balance. Control objectives are still acceptable and indeed serve as reminders to consider the types of errors often found in these accounts. For example, a detailed control objective related to inventory might be: Physical counts are taken periodically to verify the amounts on hand. This control objective relates to the *existence* of the inventory. A feature of COSO that has been consistent over the years is the desire to offset the natural tendency for entities and auditors to create checklists of controls (yes-no lists) and instead turn around the question to become: How does your entity ensure (*insert the assertion or control objective here*) is satisfied? Either control objectives or assertions can be used to complete your documentation.

An issue here is that a complete inventory of control objectives for specific accounts has not been published by an authoritative source. Each entity and auditor has been on its own to develop specific objectives. However, a sample listing of financial statement assertions has been published by regulators and in the auditing standards. Therefore, it is more likely that the use of assertions will create a more common language within organizations and between entities and their auditors.

If you are considering a reexamination or an overhaul of your COSO approach and documentation, I would suggest consideration of the assertions as a basis for (or as an addition to) that documentation. Appendix 5A titled "Linking Common Control Activities and Assertions" is provided to Chapter 5, which relates some common control objectives, by account, to related assertions they address.

If you have not worked with assertions before, a caution. Control objectives often could be tied to specific account-based risks on a one-to-one basis. This is why most accounts had so many associated control objectives. However, it may take two or more different control procedures to fully satisfy the assertion of, say, *completeness* of expenses. So, mapping controls and the assertions might require more thought in the initial setup. This is balanced by the fact that instead of focusing on potentially hundreds of control objectives that may differ from account to account, the same limited set of assertions can be utilized in most accounts, simplifying the application. Even though sometimes an assertion might not apply to a specific account (e.g., if all currency is in the same denomination, then translation measurement and valuation risks would not be relevant), the simplification and standardization may be worthwhile and may sharpen thinking about controls and how they address the identified inherent risks.

 ## ASSERTIONS

Assertions are used to ensure that the web of controls over the financial statement assertion risks is complete. While assertions have been cited in the professional auditing literature for a long time, they have had varying effects on the audit approaches of different independent auditing firms. They are now being integrated more fully into the COSO Framework discussion. Starting back in 2004 for audits of public companies and in 2007 for all other audited entities, auditors were expected to use assertions extensively in the documentation of the audit process to provide linkage between assessed risks, controls, and further audit procedures. Before that, the assertions were viewed as a "suggestion" and were not used universally in the audit process. Assertions are particularly relevant to the COSO control activities (CA) component.

The long period in which the assertions have been part of the COSO literature and the auditing standards literature gives us some comfort that they are a solid basis on which to classify risks and procedures. Because they can be used by both entities and auditors, they will also facilitate communication. Documenting your work by assertion may save you the extra auditor service time and fees.

The assertions that follow were adapted from the AICPA/PCAOB literature. There are other assertion schemes out there, and you may use them for documenting your controls. However, if these schemes are not coordinated with your auditor's methodology, the auditor will have to map your assertions to those used in his or her audit process. You may wish to ask your auditor in advance which assertions he or she is using, unless you have a strong preference.

As mentioned, for some accounts, an assertion may be unimportant, and that can be explained as part of the documentation.

Income Statement and Current-Period Transactions

1. *Occurrence*. Recorded transactions reflect events that relate to the entity and actually occurred.
2. *Completeness*. All transactions that should have been recorded have been recorded.
3. *Accuracy*. Amounts and other key data relating to recorded transactions were appropriately recorded.

4. *Cutoff.* Transactions were recorded in the correct accounting period.
5. *Classification.* Transactions were accounted for in the proper accounts.

Balance Sheet Accounts at Period-End

6. *Existence.* Assets, liabilities, and equity interests that are recorded actually exist.
7. *Rights and obligations.* The entity owns the assets, and the liabilities are obligations of the entity.
8. *Completeness.* All assets, liabilities, and equity interests that should have been recorded have been recorded.
9. *Valuation and allocation.* Assets, liabilities, and equity interests are accurately reflected in the financial statement. Any accounts requiring valuation assessments (e.g., allowances for uncollectible accounts, product warranty costs, etc.) or cost allocation adjustments (e.g., variances assigned to inventory, shared costs of separately reported product lines) are appropriately recorded.

Presentation and Disclosure in the Financial Statements

10. *Occurrence and rights and obligations.* Transactions that were disclosed actually pertain to the entity.
11. *Completeness.* All required disclosures are made in the financial statements.
12. *Classification and understandability.* These assertions, derived from the Financial Accounting Standards Board (FASB) Concept Statements, note that the presented financial information (including the footnotes) are appropriately described and that the disclosures are clearly expressed.
13. *Accuracy and valuation.* Information in the financial statements is disclosed at appropriate amounts.

Some entities and auditors simplify these 13 assertions into fewer. For example, the cutoff assertion is used to make sure that sales and costs are recorded in the proper period. The concept of the "thirty-fifth of December" is leaving the books open to advance transactions into an earlier period. In other cases, the transaction cutoff date occurs before it should, pushing transactions from the current period to the next. Some of the risks to be considered when considering the importance of cutoff include:

- Business objectives to maximize reported income.
- Business objectives to minimize taxes.
- Sales commission plans that create incentives to move sales from period to period to maximize sales person's income.
- Management bonus plans based on achieving certain targets in certain periods.
- Expenditures to be made in a specific period to avoid loss of budget authorization.

In any case, the cutoff assertion relates to either a completeness or an occurrence problem. Some entities and auditors do not use it but instead apply the two related assertions to the related transactions stream around the period-end.

While stated a little differently, the PCAOB guidance seems to arrive at the same place, but some words may resonate differently with different individuals. According to AS No. 5, paragraph 28:

> The auditor should identify significant accounts and disclosures and their relevant assertions. Relevant assertions are those financial statement assertions that have a reasonable possibility of containing a misstatement that would cause the financial statements to be materially misstated. The financial statement assertions include—
>
> - Existence or occurrence
> - Completeness
> - Valuation or allocation
> - Rights and obligations
> - Presentation and disclosure

Other entities and auditors may use only four assertions for the balance sheet, income statement, cash flow statement, and disclosure applications. For example:

1. Completeness
2. Existence
3. Accuracy
4. Valuation

The concepts behind the 13 assertions can be shoehorned into these 4, so these simplified assertions may be an alternative for documenting controls. When using such an abbreviated version, you may need to be aware that more controls will be encompassed by an assertion, but the simplification may still make it worth considering this approach. With fewer assertions, there are more types of risks that may need to be considered when mapping the risks and assertions. Again, I suggest that entity and auditor documentation be designed to facilitate an efficient audit and promote good communication.

Include Information Technology Issues in Your Risk Assessment

One risk area that causes the eyes of many managers to glaze over is the role and importance of information technology (IT) to the entity and how IT is integrated into business strategies and risk assessments. Most Internet-based businesses have some appreciation for technology and its risks, but few entities understand how really dependent they have become on communications, networks, and software and on the security of electronically stored data, customer lists, and intellectual property. RA needs to consider IT-related risks.

In the COSO Framework, the effectiveness of IT general controls (ITGCs) is a separate principle (Principle 11) listed under the CA component. However, because IT deficiencies can have pervasive effects on all components, IT risks should be considered early and reconsidered if new facts arise.

Auditors are reminded in professional standards about their responsibilities to understand internal controls, including IT. Thus IT-based controls are in scope for even the minimum procedures of controls documentation required in a nonpublic entity audit, and auditors need to assess the design and implementation of IT application and general controls. All entities need to consider access and security issues and the risks that relate to IT, in part because of legal and regulatory exposure. Under various federal and state privacy act laws, certain personal information of employees is to be protected, and an entity is subject to severe fines for exposing or making public such data. Many institutions and smaller medical offices are now required under the Affordable Care Act to digitize patient records and certain information currently protected under the privacy laws. With new requirements for businesses such as medical offices less attuned to information security issues comes opportunity for data-mining thieves and cybercriminals to access and exploit such information. With the explosive expansion of identity theft, facilitated by technology and social media sites, the most mundane entity needs to consider its procedures for protecting not just proprietary entity data but the sensitive personal data of its employees.

General computer controls are generally considered to include:

- Access and security
- System changes
- New systems development
- Operations—including backup and disaster recovery

In some writings, a fifth component of ITGCs is identified: IT organization and environment.

Application controls are those controls applied at the accounting software level, often including password protections, data accuracy, and sometimes data reasonableness checks.

While IT specialist assistance is often necessary to get into the nuts and bolts of complex systems and make detailed assessments of security, the accountant and auditor generalist can often gather a lot of the basic information and be alert to some obvious security and access issues and potential conflicting segregation of duties issues that can provide an early warning regarding reliance on the system controls.

In early implementations of Sarbanes-Oxley (SOX) documentation and testing, information systems were sometimes reviewed and tested very late in the year. In some cases, this resulted in hurried fixes to access, security, and password issues, and sometimes issues could not be remediated and retested before the year-end date deadline, resulting in adverse internal controls opinions. What it also meant was that auditors could not rely on the automated systems to perform properly during the year, and thus reliance on costly substantive audit procedures was necessary, adding insult to injury.

It is valuable to monitor systems issues continuously and to identify, test, and correct any systems issues as soon as practical to reduce entity exposure to financial consequences and to maximize auditor reliance on automated controls.

PRINCIPLES 6 AND 7: SPECIFY SUITABLE OBJECTIVES; IDENTIFY AND ANALYZE RISK

Principles 6 and 7 go hand in hand since our focus is financial reporting. They are closely related and are likely to be viewed holistically by some. But they are identified in COSO as two separate principles. Objectives can be suitably articulated; however, the risks of not achieving the objectives may not be well defined. Yet it is hard to say if all the relevant risks have been identified if the objectives have not been clearly stated. Thus, in one sense, the effectiveness of the risk identification is conditional on stating the objectives effectively. In the case of quality financial reporting objectives, certain entities may have very specific objectives, but financial statement objectives can be thought of broadly as:

- Fair presentation of the financial statements.
- The application of the concept of materiality.
- Adherence to GAAP and regulatory requirements.
- Completeness and understandability of amounts and disclosures.
- Timeliness of reporting.

In addition, the FASB Concepts statements can be helpful in articulating additional desirable characteristics of elements of the financial statements. For example, in addition to the previous concepts, add:

- Faithful representation.
- Verifiability.

In the old world of historical cost accounting, the objectives were a challenge; in the new world of fair value accounting, the challenges are increased. More subjectivity and less objectivity in fair value estimates may present more relevant data to financial statement users but present challenges in verifiability.

Objective setting becomes more interesting when specific entity objectives start to be important and are more precisely articulated. For example:

- To comply with required financial and nonfinancial disclosures with the desire to not disclose proprietary or competitive information
- To reflect our stewardship and prudence in expending public funds/foundation resources
- To attract new contributors to a foundation by highlighting the quality of responsible spending and internal controls
- To emphasize certain programs and investments that highlight green values, social consciousness, and social responsibility

The articulation of entity-specific objectives should aid in the RA process. The use of simple, generic objectives is less helpful when identifying associated risks that are specific to the entity. Objectives should help articulate the entity's mission and can help identify the risks that challenge these objectives and help guide the presentation of the data to the intended audience. Unstated, they can result in confusion or inefficiencies or missed risks.

Operating objectives might also have financial statement implications and thus should not be ignored. For example, management's tolerance for risk in operations can have implications for allowances and warranty estimates. It can clearly be seen how the financial meltdown of 2008–2009 was precipitated by excessive risk tolerance by certain institutions (whether fully understood or not). Similarly, compliance objectives often create real or contingent liabilities or disclosures, so they must be considered, even though we are focusing on the slice of the COSO Framework that addresses financial reporting. Failure to adhere to many new foreign trade restrictions, such as trading with rogue states or dealing in manufacturing with conflict-minerals countries, can lead to hefty fines and other punishments. Even failing to protect personal data of employees from disclosure due to an accident or cybercrime can lead to significant financial consequences.

For setting objectives (Principle 6), the new guidance provides 15 points of focus. Points of focus are just that—considerations to clarify what the principle is seeking to achieve. COSO makes clear that not all points of focus need to be satisfied. In some cases they will simply not apply to the entity. Some have suggested that the points of focus be used as a sort of checklist to prompt ideas of how to document that the principle is achieved. However, it may be best practice when a point of focus is not addressed or when it does not apply to also provide an explanation as to the reasoning behind that judgment. This is because future project people may not understand the rationale that seemed so clear when it was carefully thought through. It is likely that after two to three years, the project team will include new members and may not include those who made these initial decisions. Another reason to do this is to clarify for reviewers, auditors, and maybe third parties the support for your judgments. It is not at all common for future team members to be unable to explain past judgments that were poorly documented. Time and distance from the issues cloud memories. Documentation can actually be your friend.

The 15 points of focus associated with Principle 6 are presented next. Note that six of these are classified as operational and compliance objectives. This does not mean they are irrelevant to financial reporting. For example, high risk tolerance in the preparation of estimates may suggest additional disclosures are appropriate in the financial statements. Failure to meet regulatory or legal requirements might create financial contingencies and trigger additional disclosures.

Operations Objectives

1. *Reflect management's choices.* Operations objectives reflect management's choices about structure, industry considerations, and performance of the entity.
2. *Consider tolerances for risk.* Management considers the acceptable levels of risk relative to the achievement of its operations goals and objectives.
3. *Include operations and financial performance goals.* The organization reflects the desired level of operations and financial performance for the entity within operations objectives.

4. *Form a basis for committing of resources.* Management uses operations objectives as a basis for budgeting and prioritization needed to attain desired operations and financial performance.

External Financial Reporting Objectives

5. *Comply with applicable accounting standards.* Financial reporting objectives are consistent with accounting principles suitable and available for that entity. The accounting principles selected are appropriate in the circumstances.
6. *Consider materiality.* Management considers materiality in financial statement presentation. Materiality as a concept is rooted in user needs.
7. *Reflect entity activities.* External reporting reflects the underlying transactions and events to show qualitative characteristics and assertions.

External Nonfinancial Reporting Objectives

8. *Comply with externally established standards and frameworks.* Management establishes objectives consistent with laws and regulations, or standards and frameworks of recognized external organizations.
9. *Consider the required level of precision.* Management reflects the required level of precision and accuracy suitable for user needs and as based on criteria established by third parties in nonfinancial reporting.
10. *Reflect entity activities.* External reporting reflects the underlying transactions and events within a range of acceptable limits.

Internal Reporting Objectives

11. *Reflect management's choices.* Internal reporting provides management with accurate and complete information regarding and consistent with management's choices and information needed in managing the entity.
12. *Consider the required level of precision.* Management reflects the required level of precision and accuracy suitable for user needs in nonfinancial reporting objectives and materiality within financial reporting objectives.
13. *Reflect entity activities.* Internal reporting reflects the underlying transactions and events within a range of acceptable limits.

Compliance Objectives

14. *Reflect external laws and regulations.* Laws and regulations establish minimum standards of conduct that the entity integrates into compliance objectives.
15. *Consider tolerance for risk.* Management considers the acceptable levels of risk relative to the achievement of various compliance objectives.

Since some of these points of focus are related, they might be satisfied by similar controls and observations. All the more reason to carefully study the points of focus and related principles (e.g., information and communication) before venturing to gain evidence to support them. There may be fewer pieces to the real puzzle than there might first appear to be.

**IDENTIFYING RISKS**

Principle 7 is all about identifying the risks to not achieving the objectives articulated under Principle 6. These risks will then be the basis for assessing how well the actual controls under the CA component (Principle 10) mitigate risks. Sometimes it is difficult for entities to directly articulate their objectives. In some cases, an objective can be reverse-engineered by observing the risks and controls that have grown to be in place and asking: Why is this being done? What is the purpose of this procedure? What objective is this risk related to?

The five points of focus for Principle 7 highlight important characteristics relating to it:

1. *Include entity, subsidiary, division, operating unit, and functional levels.* The organization identifies and assesses risks at all the levels relevant to the achievement of objectives.
2. *Analyze internal and external factors.* Risk identification considers both internal and external factors and their impact on the achievement of objectives.
3. *Involve appropriate levels of management.* The organization puts into place effective RA mechanisms that involve appropriate levels of management.
4. *Estimate significance of risks identified.* Identified risks are analyzed through a lens that includes estimating the potential significance of the risk. Likelihood, magnitude, velocity, and persistence concepts can be used to assess the potential severity of a risk.
5. *Determine how to respond to risks.* RA includes considering how the risk should be managed and whether to accept, avoid, reduce, or share the risk.

COSO asks that entities identity specific potential risks to the achievement of the objectives. One approach for doing so within the entity is a currently required auditing procedure—a brainstorming session where appropriate levels of personnel are involved in identifying potential risks.

However, to cast a broad net over the issue and in the interest of completeness, auditors might want to also look from the other direction at some sources of risk and trace them back to the objectives. For example, from the get-go, certain account situations suggest a higher risk:

- The presence of a number of financial statement estimates, such as warranty reserves and allowances for uncollectible accounts.
- The presence and importance of fair value estimates.
- Transactions that involve related parties.

In addition, the SEC and PCAOB identify some risk considerations of relevance to a broad number of entities. According to AS No. 5, paragraph 29:

> To identify significant accounts and disclosures and their relevant assertions, the auditor should evaluate the qualitative and quantitative risk factors related

to the financial statement line items and disclosures. **Risk factors relevant to the identification of significant accounts and disclosures and their relevant assertions include—**

- Size and composition of the account.
- Susceptibility to misstatement due to errors or fraud.
- Volume of activity, complexity, and homogeneity of the individual transactions processed through the account or reflected in the disclosure.
- Nature of the account or disclosure.
- Accounting and reporting complexities associated with the account or disclosure.
- Exposure to losses in the account.
- Possibility of significant contingent liabilities arising from the activities reflected in the account or disclosure.
- Existence of related party transactions in the account.
- Changes from the prior period in account or disclosure characteristics.

EXTERNAL SOURCES OF RISK INFORMATION

A variety of external sources of risk information might be consulted and updated periodically to ensure that your RA is current and thorough. While some of these resources may be more easily identified for public companies, parallels may exist to help nonpublic entities become informed. For example, as more experience is gained in seeking formal financial statement opinions on federal agencies, it can be helpful to seek out issues that have been faced by similar entities (e.g., initial balance sheet issues) to anticipate and plan for such issues in advance. Some sources of such types of information include:

- Financial statement trends and disclosures, and management discussion and analysis (MD&A) discussions of similar entities.
- News releases from industry or trade publication sources or from similar entities.
- General news sources regarding the entity.
- SEC 8-K filings of public companies or from comparable entities.
- Web sites of your entity and comparable entities.
- Releases by regulators.
- AICPA audit risk alerts.
- AICPA accounting and audit guides.
- Analyst reports.
- Conference presentations.

Unfortunately, no simple boundaries can be drawn that will ensure only the relevant possible sources are consulted. Industry awareness and expertise by the entity's internal controls team and the audit team are invaluable assets in targeting information sources.

The more effective and thorough the entity's documented RA process is, the more potential reliance the auditor can take from that assessment. This reduces audit cost and reduces redundancy in performing procedures. While the auditor will still have to make some independent inquiries of various information sources, the quality of an entity's documented assessment can reduce time-consuming audit procedures.

INTERNAL AND EXTERNAL REPORTING RISKS

While also very much related to the Information and Communication component of the Framework (Principles 13–15), RA should consider any known risks associated with internal and external communications up front. For example, do weaknesses in the integrity of the databases of financial or nonfinancial information impair the ability of management to identify or communicate issues on a timely basis or the ability of the entity to provide reliable alerts to regulators or investors?

The integrated nature of the Framework implies that there will be overlaps in the assessments from various components. Entities and auditors have choices as to whether to address these issues in one or more of the components. An efficient approach to such choices is to recognize up front the interrelationship of some points of the controls analysis by deciding that the details of the analysis will reside in one of the components and in the related areas the issues will be cross-referenced. For example, internal and external reporting risks might emanate from the Information and Communication component and any perceived risks to the financial-statement close process or Monitoring component functions cross-referenced there, and vice versa. This will be particularly important when considering computer information systems and their implications, which can have pervasive implications across all five components. Redundant and sometimes conflicting documentation can result from multiple assessments of the same control attribute from different perspectives and for different purposes, so an integrated perspective on the components of internal control needs to be maintained and be made part of the documentation and review process. The tendency is to want to chop up the big project (COSO) into smaller self-contained projects, but the integrated nature of internal controls argues against this being an appropriate or effective approach unless carefully done.

COMPLIANCE RISKS

Of particular concern at the moment to international commerce is the significant number of laws recently enacted to support international, political, and environmental initiatives and that carry significant penalties and sanctions for violating the law. While legislation is ever-changing, the next lists specify just a few of the issues in play as of 2013–2014.

Legislation

- H.R. 850: Nuclear Iran Prevention Act of 2013
- S. 960: Syria Transition Support Act of 2013
- S. 298: North Korea Nonproliferation and Accountability Act of 2013
- S. 892: Iran Sanctions Loophole Elimination Act of 2013

Executive Orders

- ▪ 13645: Implementation of Certain Sanctions Set Forth in the Iran Freedom and Counter-Proliferation Act of 2012

Regulations

- ▪ Amendment of Iranian Financial Sanctions Regulations to Implement Sections 503 and 504 of Threat Reduction Act and Provisions of Executive Order 13622

Agency Guidance

- ▪ Advisory on the Use of Exchange Houses and Trading Companies to Evade U.S. Economic Sanctions Against Iran
- ▪ Guidance re: Iran Threat Reduction and Syria Human Rights Act of 2012
- ▪ Release of 2012 Terrorist Assets Report

In early 2014, various sanctions were being put in place as a response to perceived Russian aggression in Crimea and the Ukraine. Entities need to consult with legal advisors to identify any potential operations affected by the various laws or regulations and, if relevant, to establish controls over the risks of noncompliance. Auditors are expected to consider these controls as part of their audit responsibility but generally do not need to design specific procedures to test for noncompliance unless there are other indications of noncompliance.

Various sources report an increased incidence of investigations and prosecutions under the Foreign Corrupt Practices Act in 2012 and thereafter. Entities are reminded that the overarching provisions of that act relate to corruption in its many forms.

 ## DISCLOSED MATERIAL WEAKNESSES IN RISK ASSESSMENT

Based on public company disclosures under Section 404 of SOX, there have been relatively few material weaknesses disclosed as sourced in the RA component of public companies. Perhaps the reason is that RA as a component is somewhat conceptual in nature, and the sufficiency of the RA process is difficult to measure. Every entity to some extent does some risk assessment, whether fully documented or not. In a practical sense, it may be difficult to classify an RA deficiency as from one source or another. For example, a failure in the RA process might result in a financial statement misstatement (e.g., the allowance for uncollectible receivables is too low). This deficiency might be more easily classified as a Control Activities component weakness (e.g., the process for computing the allowance is not adequately controlled). However, a failure of the entity to consider fraud risk (Principle 8) is more objective, given that there are benchmarks, so entities need to be alert to demonstrating that adequate attention is given to the fraud risk assessment.

 ## PRINCIPLE 8: ASSESS FRAUD RISK

Much of the current focus on internal controls in public companies, private companies, and government has been motivated by instances of fraud, as analyzed over many years, leading to the conclusions that the root facilitator of fraud was weak internal control. It seems only natural that fraud RA be identified as a specific principle. To be clear, COSO (and auditing literature) identifies the responsibility for this assessment and for establishing controls to lie with management.

The following points of focus for Principle 8 highlight important characteristics that should be considered when assessing achievement of this principle. Entities should:

- *Consider various types of fraud.* The assessment of fraud considers fraudulent reporting, possible loss of assets, and corruption resulting from the various ways that fraud and misconduct can occur.
- *Assess incentives and pressures.* The assessment of fraud risk considers incentives and pressures.
- *Assess opportunities.* The assessment of fraud risk considers opportunities for unauthorized acquisition, use, or disposal of assets, altering of the entity's reporting records, or committing other inappropriate acts.
- *Assess attitudes and rationalizations.* The assessment of fraud risk considers how management and other personnel might engage in or justify inappropriate actions.

The "fraud triangle"[4] was formally introduced into the auditing standards literature in Statement on Auditing Standards (SAS) No. 99 in 2002.[5] The last three points of focus here are the three points in the triangle.

Some Statistics

While definitive conclusions cannot be reached yet, the SOX focus on controls over the last decade does seem to have had a positive effect on statistics of fraud loss (and reducing the number of financial statement restatements) for public companies. The Association of Certified Fraud Examiners (ACFE) publishes a semiannual survey of reported frauds. This study has consistently estimated that approximately 5% of all revenues are lost to frauds. The 2014 survey shows strong improvements in reducing the median[6] size of financial statement frauds from a previously high of $8 million to $1 million. Most recently strong improvements have been shown in the reduction in private company frauds from a $231 thousand median in 2010 to $160 thousand now. While the metrics for government entities ($90 thousand) are roughly similar to the median 2006 loss amounts, for public companies the median loss has declined somewhat from the 2006 survey, but had been reported as significantly lower in the 2012 survey ($200,000 versus $220,000 in 2006, but in the 2012 survey the public company median was $127,000). Nonprofit median losses are at $108,000 currently and smaller private companies with less than 100 employees are at a disturbing $154,000.

---

[4] Donald R. Cressey, *Other People's Money* (Montclair, NJ: Patterson Smith, 1973) p. 30.

[5] AICPA, Statement of Auditing Standards No. 99, *Consideration of Fraud in a Financial Statement Audit,* 2002.

[6] The median indicates that half the reported frauds were larger than this number and half were smaller. The median can be a useful measure of trends in controls effectiveness, since the use of the average amount can be highly influenced by a single or a few large or small amounts. No single statistical measure is universally useful for all purposes.

Hopefully, reductions can continue as we find more effective and efficient antifraud measures and strengthen controls awareness in organizations of all sizes and natures.

While asset theft still ranks as the most common type of reported fraud (85%) and the first one to come to mind by the general public, it does not lead in financial consequences. Asset theft median losses were $130,000. Financial statement fraud is less common (less than 9% of the reported frauds), but it leads in median dollar impact at $1 million. Corruption (e.g., bribes, pay-to-play, etc.) accounts for 37% of the reported losses and the median reported corruption losses were $200,000.[7]

Corruption is an emerging issue today for all entities. Those entities doing business in various countries need to pay close attention to the differing ethical environments around the world. The Corruptions Transparency Index, published by Transparency International (www.transparency.org), ranks various countries in a relative perceived corruption scale. To examine the potential exposure of operations, auditors can relate the index to entity business locations and transactions sources. At the top of the 2014 index are Denmark and, New Zealand. Tied for last place at the bottom of the 2014 index were Afghanistan, North Korea, and Somalia. The United States rates at country position index number 19, and below Canada (position 9). These ratings have been remarkably consistent over the last few years. Anyone operating in countries with a high index should consider having special controls in place to address these issues as there has been an increase in SEC initiated litigations under the Foreign Corrupt Practices Act in recent years.

Corruption can be difficult to identify and address across cultures since special terms may be used in communications that obscure the real purpose of the payment. For example, in China, "red" cards or gift cards may indicate a payment or bribe. In India, the terms *tea and water* may be an invitation to make a bribe or "facilitating" payment, and in Brazil, the terms inviting a bribe may include *chocolate* or *flowers*. Clearly the environment poses a challenge to entities in complying with the 1977 Foreign Corrupt Practices Act as well as SOX.

Some antifraud measures have been shown to be successful in reducing the amounts of losses from fraud. Entities that adopted the following antifraud controls experienced the following *reductions* in median fraud losses compared to entities not adopting these measures:[8]

- Data monitoring – 60% less loss
- Employee support programs – 55% less loss
- Management review – 52%
- Internal audits and surprise audits – 44%
- Fraud reporting hotline: 41% less loss

Additional measures shown to be effective include offering whistleblower rewards and enforcing mandatory vacations and job rotations, when feasible.

---

[7] The percentages add to more than 100% since some entities experienced multiple types of frauds.
[8] Per the 2014, Association of Certified Fraud Examiners. *Report to the Nations on Occupational Fraud and Abuse*, ACFE. (www.acfe.com).

Also notable in the 2014 survey is the significant reduction in the proportion and median value of frauds attributed to executive and upper management. Hopefully the focus on the CE component is one reason for this change.

Disturbingly, in 58% of the identified frauds, there is no recovery from the perpetrator. The implications of that for smaller entities and nonprofits can be devastating. The very entities most at risk are those most resistant to implementing controls and fraud prevention.

AUDITOR RESPONSIBILITY TO DETECT FRAUD

While entities may still believe that external, independent auditors are seeking to identify fraud and thus management can be less vigilant in its fraud risk assessment, statistics do not warrant this reliance. As of 2014, only 3% of the reported frauds are detected by the auditor's procedures. Most frauds (42%) are still detected by tips from employees or suppliers or customers. Management and internal auditors each find about 14 to 16%. Of course, these statistics may not be totally fair, since if the fraud is detected in advance of auditor procedures, it is no longer a fraud that can be detected by the auditor. However, anecdotal evidence suggests that the auditor may miss fraudulent financial amounts that were present during the last audit performed. What can be said is that entities need to take primary and proactive responsibility for assessing the fraud risks and establishing the controls to prevent fraud.

Auditing standards (public and nonpublic entities) indicate that it is the responsibility of the auditor to plan to detect material misstatement whether caused by error or fraud. This is a change from historical audit thought that sought to say the auditor might not be able to detect a collusive fraud. As a defense, when a fraud was missed in the audit, that excuse never held any sway with jurors. Auditors today are directed to use brainstorming among the engagement team members to identify fraud vulnerabilities as well as nonfraud financial risks. Entities can also use this brainstorming strategy to consider their vulnerabilities and identify how those can be mitigated or detected.

In this area, as in others, a quality fraud assessment by the entity and the demonstration of in-place antifraud controls can go a long way to reducing unnecessary or redundant auditor procedures and reducing audit costs.

SAS No. 99, *Consideration of Fraud in a Financial Statement Audit* (2002), established a new enhanced model of audit risk in the auditing literature that is now widely recognized. The fraud triangle adds the element of rationalization (the ability of the perpetrator to find a justification for his or her actions) to the previously recognized motivation and opportunity characteristics. Sometimes it is the rationalization and attitudes of management and personnel (e.g., it's *my* business anyway, it compensates me for my low wage, etc.) that can provide an entryway into identifying a potential fraud risk. Discussions with employees and management can sometimes trigger these warning signs. Disturbing is the statistic that 80% of the identified perpetrators do not have any prior record or indication of charges against them.

ANTIFRAUD CONTROLS FOR MANAGEMENT TO CONSIDER

Some of the aforementioned antifraud controls are discussed in more detail in a jointly produced AICPA document directed specifically at management: *Management Antifraud Programs and Controls* (2002).[9] A search should enable entities to find this document, which is not scheduled to be republished in the revised AICPA "clarified standards" literature.[10] Originally issued as a companion to SAS No. 99, *Considerations of Fraud in a Financial Statement Audit*, this document has been widely used by all types of entities in designing and implementing effective antifraud controls.

Another AICPA fraud publication that is available for free download at this time is *Management Override of Internal Controls: The Achilles' Heel of Fraud Detection* (2005).[11] While neither document is a turn-key program on how to implement effective antifraud controls, both present practical suggestions on implementation. These reports are also very readable.

TIES TO OTHER PRINCIPLES AND COMPONENTS

Like many principles, fraud assessment is related to other principles and components in the COSO Framework. The CE is related since the CE constitutes the tone at the top in which the fraud risks may be cultivated or shunted. Individual principles can be related when specific fraud issues are identified. Monitoring is also related since the presence or absence of monitoring is important to fraud prevention and detection. How management responds to reported internal incidents is also important for setting the tone of compliance and entity values (CE). Where many see the linkage most clearly is in the transactional controls: CA where payroll, purchasing, and cash management issues and deficiencies arise.

In the revised COSO guidance, new weight is placed on relating deficiencies in controls that affect one component and principle and in identifying the impacts on related components and principles and considering relationships between the deficiencies when assessing their combined severity (see Chapter 10).

PRINCIPLE 9: IDENTIFY AND ASSESS SIGNIFICANT CHANGE

While always inherent in RA, the direction to formally include identifying and assessing significant change as a separate principle is indicative of how importantly this practice is

---

[9] This document is reproduced in Appendix 3A with permission.

[10] http://www.sox-expert.com/uploads/files/Management%20Antifraud%20Programs%20and%20Controls %20(SAS%2099%20Exhibit).pdf. This Appendix has now been reproduced in the 2014 edition of the AICPA Audit Guide: *Assessing and responding to audit risk in a financial statement audit*.

[11] http://www.aicpa.org/ForThePublic/AuditCommitteeEffectiveness/DownloadableDocuments/achilles_ heel.pdf

now viewed and evidence that some failed to consider it when it was not an articulated principle. Now that we are passing down our initial assessments to new leadership and staff, sometimes it is very easy to fall into a trap independent auditors term *SALY*—same as last year. The dynamics of business today do not support the SALY principle in COSO assessments. (The concept did not serve auditors very well either, as noted in peer review, inspection, and litigation outcomes.)

Change can come from anywhere at any time. Internal business strategies change. The external business and compliance environment is ever-changing, and new management brings new skills and sometimes new risks to the table. While it is difficult to justify a clean-sheet-of-paper approach each year, some freshness of thinking needs to be inserted into the process. One way audit firms try to keep the risk perspective fresh is to insert a specialist (e.g., a certified fraud examiner (CFE) or a management consultant) into the risk and fraud brainstorming sessions. Another way is to involve a senior audit or systems person not previously familiar with the client in the discussions to try to challenge the assessments and discussions. Entities may also borrow from these techniques to keep their analysis from becoming stale.

In general, the aforementioned sources for risk information are the same ones that can provide the hints to changes that are important. It should be obvious from many sources when management takes a new strategic direction for the business (e.g., moving to commercial lending from residential lending). Less obvious might be the business changes that will accompany the implementation of laws like the Affordable Care Act and the Dodd-Frank Act of 2010, for which the rules are still being written as of 2014.

One failing in documentation I have seen too often is vague descriptions of risks and issues. When coupled with changes in personnel, the documentation itself becomes a source of risk to the entity. An example I have used is the assessment of interest rate risk on the financial viability and financial performance of an entity. Changes in prevailing interest rates can have dramatically different impacts on entities if their interest-sensitive assets are, say, long term and fixed in value and liabilities mostly are short term and variable with market interest rates. Depending on the mix of exposed assets and liabilities, there can be risks associated with rising (or falling) interest rates. When the documentation simply says the interest rate risk is low, is that because the entity is not "at risk" if the interest rates change up or down, or is it because interest rates were announced by the Treasury Secretary not to be likely to change? In late June 2013, stock and bond markets were upset when interest rates unexpectedly rose moderately after repeated announcements to the contrary by the Treasury Department earlier in the year. In the absence of clarity in the documentation for the basis of the assessment, how could the reviewer of the documentation or the person doing the task in the following year measure the change? I am sure the original author of the documentation knew the basis considered when the assessment was made, but to everyone else it could just be a guess as to what low risk meant and the basis for that assessment.

Change cannot be assessed effectively if the current risk assessments are vague and not supported by the evidence considered in reaching them.

GATHERING INFORMATION TO SUPPORT THE RISK ASSESSMENT AND CONSIDER CHANGE

RA is not an armchair exercise. In the absence of some framework for considering risk, it is easy to conclude that "Nothing comes to mind." Various business RA frameworks have been proposed over the years and many are being developed today. These matrices, approaches, and their accompanying scoring systems, color charts, and decision rules are often overengineered and difficult to use consistently within an enterprise. Others propose to identify all the possible "controls" that could exist, and by completing the checklist, the "no" responses become asserted fertile soil for identifying gaps in controls.

COSO, in contrast, asks the question: How does the entity achieve the stated principle, objective, or assertion? The issue is not whether a specific control is present or absent. Therefore, the highly structured or checklist approaches may not serve the purpose; quite the opposite, they may detract from thoughtful assessments. While we may seek to routinize and dumb down many tasks to drive efficiency, the RA is a poor place to apply that thinking.

However, there is a balance here, and an outline of some of the factors to be systematically evaluated for risks and change can be helpful in the process of RA. Clearly internal and external factors need to be routinely discussed and considered. Internal factors will likely include:

- Personnel changes.
- Management organization and operating philosophy and changes.
- Infrastructure.
- The sensitivity of the business to fraud risks and the types of risks.
- Issues related to the main business processes.
- Previous financial reporting issues and their status/resolution.

From an external perspective, assessments are likely to include some discussion of:

- Competitive issues.
- Regulatory environment.
- General and local economic demand and supply factors.
- Technological risks, opportunities and trends.
- Social trends and demographics.
- Political and world developments.

While perhaps not evident on first blush, these factors can have a profound effect on entities in the private, government, and public sectors. Entities may wish to experiment with what is most effective and efficient form them, adapting a generic form such as illustrated in Table 3.1 for entity use.

Issues can be analyzed as to how they may impact the entity objectives and create challenges for proposed business directions. To do this task effectively, some evidence may need to be gathered as a basis for the assessment. This evidence is worthwhile noting in the documentation to clarify the perspective from which the assessment is made.

TABLE 3.1 Consideration of Risks and Changes

Economic Factors	Weak local economic growth
Perceived Risk	Sales goals not met
Objectives Impact	To grow by 8–10% in sales per year in local markets
Likelihood/Probability	50% (moderate)
Velocity/Persistence	Foreseeable and not long lasting
Severity/Materiality	85% (high)
Components and Principles Affected	CA inventory (potential excess production and possible write-downs)
Assertions Affected	Valuation
Specific Controls in Place	CA 3.121; CA 3.124
Evidence Examined and Reference	Chamber of Commerce business statistics (file document 1A1), competitor financial information (10-K of Micron Tech)
Changes in the Past Year	Local growth even slower than prior year
Cross-Reference to Monitoring Program*	Covered in management step 17
Comments on Basis for Assessment	C of C report is the primary basis for the assessment

*Note: Cross-reference to how addressed in audit plan. For auditor use, this reference is usually helpful

For example, to assess the competitive situation, the auditor might review trade journals and news articles, read public company financial statements (including the MD&A and Risks section in the 10-K), monitor benchmark data regarding industry statistics (e.g., in real estate: a benchmark is cost per square foot and trends; in wholesale and retail: inventory turnover statistics and number of days credit sales are outstanding).

A well-documented and -referenced entity project can yield dividends in:

- Identifying important issues for management and governance.
- Providing support for auditor reliance on the entity assessment process, reducing redundant or unnecessary procedures.
- Assisting reviewers and future teams understand the basis for the judgments.

There is no magic to the format here, as a matrix could be designed with columns rather than rows, but the content is the issue. Matrices and forms may help keep the documentation succinct, to the point, and consistent. Matrices and forms reduce the navigation overhead associated with narratives, which often are difficult to use to quickly extract salient points.

I am not a fan of terms like "high–medium–low" when making risk assessments. It has been my experience that unless these terms are very well defined in terms of illustrative scenarios or detailed examples or even discrete probability assessments or ranges of probability (e.g., less than 20% likelihood) for the users of the tool, even those with similar views on risks find it hard to reach consistent judgments and communicate. The words become yet another judgment on top of the assessment that was made of the risk. Nevertheless, many RA tools use these terms. My preference is to estimate risks in terms of percentages or ranges of percentages that are less ambiguous in communication, even if they are judgments and not precise calculations.

Inquiries and Corroboration

Auditors historically relied on management inquiries and explanations as part of their auditing procedures. Today auditors are asked to find corroborating evidence (e.g., observation, gathering physical evidence, or reperforming procedures) to support as many management representations as possible. Entities may also utilize inquiry of management and staff as part of their RA procedures. However, they are also challenged to support their assessments and document that support. For example: Management may represent that the early repayment of mortgages is expected to be the same as in prior years. Is that supported by industry statistics? Is there any contradictory evidence? Can management point to the basis for its views? If the board, audit committee, or governance asserts financial competence, is it observable in the meetings or minutes of meetings, or in other communications? While this can get out of hand, it is important to scratch deeper than the surface to support assessments to distinguish them from cursory procedures. More guidance is given to inquiry techniques in Chapter 8 (Evidence and Testing).

Transitioning to the 2013 Principles

When revising an existing project to reflect the 2013 COSO Framework guidance, the best process is to map the existing controls in your project to the 2013 principles. If your project reflects the 2006 guidance, you already have some principles to work with and the mapping may be simpler. (See Table 3.2.)

The new 2013 principle of identifying and assessing change makes very explicit the need to regularly reassess risk and scope as business conditions change. Business environments today change faster than ever before, and risk and scoping need to keep pace. As mentioned previously, the longer a system is in place, the greater the likelihood it will deteriorate, so a fresh infusion of brainstorming and reexamination of the importance and risk associated with the balances and disclosure is necessary.

The place in your project where this new principle might have been assessed previously might already be in the RA component section. Also, some entities assessed this new RA principle as part of the CE component under the theory that it reflected on the overall attitudes of top management toward controls and compliance. This principle also may not have been explicitly covered in prior analyses, and so it now becomes an addition to the existing project.

TABLE 3.2 Risk Assessment Principles: 2013 versus 2006

2006 Principles	2013 Principles
Specifies relevant objectives	Specifies relevant objectives
Identifies and assesses risk	Identifies and assesses risk
Assesses fraud risk	Assesses fraud risk
	Identifies and assesses significant change

The more complex task is the mapping of entity projects that were developed under the 1992 Framework that did not contain principles. Here it may be simpler to first grasp all the principles of the component and then seek the existing documentation that falls under these headings, recognizing there may be gaps in the prior analysis relative to the principles. In addition, previous controls and assessments may relate to more than one principle. The earlier this is recognized and considered in the project plan, the less likely will be surprises when aggregating deficiencies later or when conflicting conclusions arise. Obviously, more detailed guidance such as the addition of principles in the recent revision is designed to help identify and fill in any gaps.

SAS No. 99 Exhibit: Management Antifraud Programs and Controls

T HE *GUIDANCE TO Help Prevent, Deter, and Detect Fraud* was published with State-ment of Auditing Standards (SAS) No. 99, *The Auditor's Consideration of Fraud in an Audit of Financial Statements*, and is reproduced with the permission of the American Institute of Certified Public Accountants (AICPA). It is not part of the auditing standards, but it is a statement of best practices and is endorsed by a number of profes-sional and business organizations. The author of this book was a member of the Auditing Standards Board that approved SAS No. 99.

Fraud risk is included in the COSO controls framework as a principle in the risk assessment component but has potential affects touching each of the five components of internal control over financial reporting. An element that often relates to entity-level controls is a company's antifraud program. Many organizations have implemented for-mal programs in recent years, and professional organizations have assisted companies in establishing controls, training programs, and reporting mechanisms to deter and detect fraud. Most likely, the recent implementation of such a program means that documen-tation is readily available, and the company may have recent monitoring data that can assist you in understanding management's basis for their assessment of effectiveness.

Nevertheless, the auditor must base his or her assessment of the program on the procedures applied by the entity.

In reading the program documentation, the auditor considers:

- Is the program sufficiently comprehensive in scope for the type of business con-ducted by the company?
- Does it apply to the entire company or to a portion of the company?
- How is the program implemented?

- Is it reaching all of the right people?
- Are employees aware of program and the toll-free tip line?
- Are tips actively investigated and resolved?
- Have there been any disciplinary or legal actions taken based on findings?

In interviews with employees and management in different locations, awareness of the program and its goals can be confirmed and information about the program's effectiveness may be obtained.

Reading and understanding the accompanying exhibit can be a resource and a benchmark for your understanding the elements of an antifraud program.

The exhibit discusses the following:

- Creating a culture of honesty and high ethics—preventive procedures.
- Evaluating antifraud processes and controls—detective procedures.
- Developing an appropriate oversight process—the role of management and others.
- A sample code of conduct.
- A sample ethics statement.

GUIDANCE TO HELP PREVENT, DETER, AND DETECT FRAUD

[Note: This exhibit is reprinted for the reader's convenience but is not an integral part of SAS No. 99.]

This document is being issued jointly by the following organizations:

American Institute of Certified Public Accountants
Association of Certified Fraud Examiners
Financial Executives International
Information Systems Audit and Control Association
The Institute of Internal Auditors
Institute of Management Accountants
Society for Human Resource Management

In addition, we would also like to acknowledge the American Accounting Association, the Defense Industry Initiative, and the National Association of Corporate Directors for their review of the document and helpful comments and materials.

We gratefully acknowledge the valuable contribution provided by the Anti-Fraud Detection Subgroup:

Daniel D. Montgomery, *Chair*	David L. Landsittel
Toby J.F. Bishop	Carol A. Langelier
Dennis H. Chookaszian	Joseph T. Wells
Susan A. Finn	Janice Wilkins
Dana Hermanson	

Finally, we thank the staff of the American Institute of Certified Public Accountants for their support on this project:

Charles E. Landes	Kim M. Gibson
Director	*Technical Manager*
Audit and Attest Standards	*Audit and Attest Standards*
Richard Lanza	Hugh Kelsey
Senior Program Manager	*Program Manager*
Chief Operating Office	*Knowledge Management*

This document was commissioned by the Fraud Task Force of the AICPA's Auditing Standards Board. This document has not been adopted, approved, disapproved, or otherwise acted upon by a board, committee, governing body, or membership of the above issuing organizations.

 ## PREFACE

Some organizations have significantly lower levels of misappropriation of assets and are less susceptible to fraudulent financial reporting than other organizations because these organizations take proactive steps to prevent or deter fraud. It is only those organizations that seriously consider fraud risks and take proactive steps to create the right kind of climate to reduce its occurrence that have success in preventing fraud. This document identifies the key participants in this antifraud effort, including the board of directors, management, internal and independent auditors, and certified fraud examiners.

Management may develop and implement some of these programs and controls in response to specific identified risks of material misstatement of financial statements due to fraud. In other cases, these programs and controls may be a part of the entity's enterprise-wide risk management activities.

Management is responsible for designing and implementing systems and procedures for the prevention and detection of fraud and, along with the board of directors, for ensuring a culture and environment that promotes honesty and ethical behavior. However, because of the characteristics of fraud, a material misstatement of financial statements due to fraud may occur notwithstanding the presence of programs and controls such as those described in this document.

 ## INTRODUCTION

Fraud can range from minor employee theft and unproductive behavior to misappropriation of assets and fraudulent financial reporting. Material financial statement fraud can have a significant adverse effect on an entity's market value, reputation, and ability to achieve its strategic objectives. A number of highly publicized cases have heightened the awareness of the effects of fraudulent financial reporting and have led many organizations to be more proactive in taking steps to prevent or deter its occurrence. Misappropriation of assets, though often not material to the financial statements, can nonetheless result in substantial losses to an entity if a dishonest employee has the incentive and opportunity to commit fraud.

The risk of fraud can be reduced through a combination of prevention, deterrence, and detection measures. However, fraud can be difficult to detect because it often involves concealment through falsification of documents or collusion among management, employees, or third parties. Therefore, it is important to place a strong emphasis on fraud prevention, which may reduce opportunities for fraud to take place, and fraud deterrence, which could persuade individuals that they should not commit fraud because of the likelihood of detection and punishment. Moreover, prevention and deterrence measures are much less costly than the time and expense required for fraud detection and investigation.

An entity's management has both the responsibility and the means to implement measures to reduce the incidence of fraud. The measures an organization takes to prevent and deter fraud also can help create a positive workplace environment that can enhance the entity's ability to recruit and retain high-quality employees.

Research suggests that the most effective way to implement measures to reduce wrongdoing is to base them on a set of core values that are embraced by the entity. These values provide an overarching message about the key principles guiding all employees' actions. This provides a platform upon which a more detailed code of conduct can be constructed, giving more specific guidance about permitted and prohibited behavior, based on applicable laws and the organization's values. Management needs to clearly articulate that all employees will be held accountable to act within the organization's code of conduct.

This document identifies measures entities can implement to prevent, deter, and detect fraud. It discusses these measures in the context of three fundamental elements. Broadly stated, these fundamental elements are (1) create and maintain a *culture* of honesty and high ethics; (2) *evaluate* the risks of fraud and implement the processes, procedures, and controls needed to mitigate the risks and reduce the opportunities for fraud; and (3) develop an appropriate *oversight* process. Although the entire management team shares the responsibility for implementing and monitoring these activities, with oversight from the board of directors, the entity's chief executive officer (CEO) should initiate and support such measures. Without the CEO's active support, these measures are less likely to be effective.

The information presented in this document generally is applicable to entities of all sizes. However, the degree to which certain programs and controls are applied in smaller, less complex entities and the formality of their application are likely to differ from larger organizations. For example, management of a smaller entity (or the owner of an owner-managed entity), along with those charged with governance of the financial reporting process, are responsible for creating a culture of honesty and high ethics. Management also is responsible for implementing a system of internal controls commensurate with the nature and size of the organization, but smaller entities may find that certain types of control activities are not relevant because of the involvement of and controls applied by management. However, all entities must make it clear that unethical or dishonest behavior will not be tolerated.

 ## CREATING A CULTURE OF HONESTY AND HIGH ETHICS

It is the organization's responsibility to create a culture of honesty and high ethics and to clearly communicate acceptable behavior and expectations of each employee. Such a culture is rooted in a strong set of core values (or value system) that provides the foundation for employees as to how the organization conducts its business. It also allows an entity to develop an ethical framework that covers (1) fraudulent financial reporting, (2) misappropriation of assets, and (3) corruption as well as other issues.[1]

Creating a culture of honesty and high ethics should include the following.

Setting the Tone at the Top

Directors and officers of corporations set the "tone at the top" for ethical behavior within any organization. Research in moral development strongly suggests that honesty can best be reinforced when a proper example is set—sometimes referred to as the tone at the top. The management of an entity cannot act one way and expect others in the entity to behave differently.

In many cases, particularly in larger organizations, it is necessary for management to both behave ethically and openly communicate its expectations for ethical behavior because most employees are not in a position to observe management's actions. Management must show employees through its words and actions that dishonest or unethical behavior will not be tolerated, even if the result of the action benefits the entity. Moreover, it should be evident that all employees will be treated equally, regardless of their position.

For example, statements by management regarding the absolute need to meet operating and financial targets can create undue pressures that may lead employees to commit fraud to achieve them. Setting unachievable goals for employees can give them two unattractive choices: fail or cheat. In contrast, a statement from management that says, "We are aggressive in pursuing our targets, while requiring truthful financial reporting at all times," clearly indicates to employees that integrity is a requirement. This message also conveys that the entity has "zero tolerance" for unethical behavior, including fraudulent financial reporting.

The cornerstone of an effective antifraud environment is a culture with a strong value system founded on integrity. This value system often is reflected in a code of conduct.[2] The code of conduct should reflect the core values of the entity and guide employees in making appropriate decisions during their workday. The code of conduct might include such topics as ethics, confidentiality, conflicts of interest, intellectual

---

[1] Corruption includes bribery and other illegal acts.
[2] An entity's value system also could be reflected in an ethics policy, a statement of business principles, or some other concise summary of guiding principles.

property, sexual harassment, and fraud.[3] For a code of conduct to be effective, it should be communicated to all personnel in an understandable fashion. It also should be developed in a participatory and positive manner that will result in both management and employees taking ownership of its content. Finally, the code of conduct should be included in an employee handbook or policy manual, or in some other formal document or location (for example, the entity's intranet) so it can be referred to when needed.

Senior financial officers hold an important and elevated role in corporate governance. While members of the management team, they are uniquely capable and empowered to ensure that all stakeholders' interests are appropriately balanced, protected, and preserved. For examples of codes of conduct, see Attachment 1, "AICPA 'CPA's Handbook of Fraud and Commercial Crime Prevention,' An Organizational Code of Conduct," and Attachment 2, "Financial Executives International Code of Ethics Statement," provided by Financial Executives International. In addition, visit the Institute of Management Accountant's Ethics Center at www.imanet.org/ethics for their members' standards of ethical conduct.

Creating a Positive Workplace Environment

Research results indicate that wrongdoing occurs less frequently when employees have positive feelings about an entity than when they feel abused, threatened, or ignored. Without a positive workplace environment, there are more opportunities for poor employee morale, which can affect an employee's attitude about committing fraud against an entity. Factors that detract from a positive work environment and may increase the risk of fraud include:

- Top management that does not seem to care about or reward appropriate behavior
- Negative feedback and lack of recognition for job performance
- Perceived inequities in the organization
- Autocratic rather than participative management
- Low organizational loyalty or feelings of ownership
- Unreasonable budget expectations or other financial targets
- Fear of delivering "bad news" to supervisors and/or management
- Less-than-competitive compensation
- Poor training and promotion opportunities
- Lack of clear organizational responsibilities
- Poor communication practices or methods within the organization

The entity's human resources department often is instrumental in helping to build a corporate culture and a positive work environment. Human resource professionals are responsible for implementing specific programs and initiatives, consistent with

---

[3] Although the discussion in this document focuses on fraud, the subject of fraud often is considered in the context of a broader set of principles that govern an organization. Some organizations, however, may elect to develop a fraud policy separate from an ethics policy. Specific examples of topics in a fraud policy might include a requirement to comply with all laws and regulations and explicit guidance regarding making payments to obtain contracts, holding pricing discussions with competitors, environmental discharges, relationships with vendors, and maintenance of accurate books and records.

management's strategies, which can help to mitigate many of the detractors mentioned above. Mitigating factors that help create a positive work environment and reduce the risk of fraud may include:

- Recognition and reward systems that are in tandem with goals and results
- Equal employment opportunities
- Team-oriented, collaborative decision-making policies
- Professionally administered compensation programs
- Professionally administered training programs and an organizational priority of career development

Employees should be empowered to help create a positive workplace environment and support the entity's values and code of conduct. They should be given the opportunity to provide input to the development and updating of the entity's code of conduct, to ensure that it is relevant, clear, and fair. Involving employees in this fashion also may effectively contribute to the oversight of the entity's code of conduct and an environment of ethical behavior (see the section titled "Developing an Appropriate Oversight Process").

Employees should be given the means to obtain advice internally before making decisions that appear to have significant legal or ethical implications. They should also be encouraged and given the means to communicate concerns, anonymously if preferred, about potential violations of the entity's code of conduct, without fear of retribution. Many organizations have implemented a process for employees to report on a confidential basis any actual or suspected wrongdoing, or potential violations of the code of conduct or ethics policy. For example, some organizations use a telephone "hotline" that is directed to or monitored by an ethics officer, fraud officer, general counsel, internal audit director, or another trusted individual responsible for investigating and reporting incidents of fraud or illegal acts.

Hiring and Promoting Appropriate Employees

Each employee has a unique set of values and personal code of ethics. When faced with sufficient pressure and a perceived opportunity, some employees will behave dishonestly rather than face the negative consequences of honest behavior. The threshold at which dishonest behavior starts, however, will vary among individuals. If an entity is to be successful in preventing fraud, it must have effective policies that minimize the chance of hiring or promoting individuals with low levels of honesty, especially for positions of trust.

Proactive hiring and promotion procedures may include:

- Conducting background investigations on individuals being considered for employment or for promotion to a position of trust[4]
- Thoroughly checking a candidate's education, employment history, and personal references

---

[4] Some organizations also have considered follow-up investigations, particularly for employees in positions of trust, on a periodic basis (for example, every five years) or as circumstances dictate.

- Periodic training of all employees about the entity's values and code of conduct (training is addressed in the following section)
- Incorporating into regular performance reviews an evaluation of how each individual has contributed to creating an appropriate workplace environment in line with the entity's values and code of conduct
- Continuous objective evaluation of compliance with the entity's values and code of conduct, with violations being addressed immediately

Training

New employees should be trained at the time of hiring about the entity's values and its code of conduct. This training should explicitly cover expectations of all employees regarding (1) their duty to communicate certain matters; (2) a list of the types of matters, including actual or suspected fraud, to be communicated along with specific examples; and (3) information on how to communicate those matters. There also should be an affirmation from senior management regarding employee expectations and communication responsibilities. Such training should include an element of "fraud awareness," the tone of which should be positive but nonetheless stress that fraud can be costly (and detrimental in other ways) to the entity and its employees.

In addition to training at the time of hiring, employees should receive refresher training periodically thereafter. Some organizations may consider ongoing training for certain positions, such as purchasing agents or employees with financial reporting responsibilities. Training should be specific to an employee's level within the organization, geographic location, and assigned responsibilities. For example, training for senior manager level personnel would normally be different from that of nonsupervisory employees, and training for purchasing agents would be different from that of sales representatives.

Confirmation

Management needs to clearly articulate that all employees will be held accountable to act within the entity's code of conduct. All employees within senior management and the finance function, as well as other employees in areas that might be exposed to unethical behavior (for example, procurement, sales and marketing) should be required to sign a code of conduct statement annually, at a minimum.

Requiring periodic confirmation by employees of their responsibilities will not only reinforce the policy but may also deter individuals from committing fraud and other violations and might identify problems before they become significant. Such confirmation may include statements that the individual understands the entity's expectations, has complied with the code of conduct, and is not aware of any violations of the code of conduct other than those the individual lists in his or her response. Although people with low integrity may not hesitate to sign a false confirmation, most people will want to avoid making a false statement in writing. Honest individuals are more likely to return their confirmations and to disclose what they know (including any conflicts of interest or other personal exceptions to the code of conduct). Thorough follow-up by internal auditors or others regarding nonreplies may uncover significant issues.

Discipline

The way an entity reacts to incidents of alleged or suspected fraud will send a strong deterrent message throughout the entity, helping to reduce the number of future occurrences. The following actions should be taken in response to an alleged incident of fraud:

- A thorough investigation of the incident should be conducted.[5]
- Appropriate and consistent actions should be taken against violators.
- Relevant controls should be assessed and improved.
- Communication and training should occur to reinforce the entity's values, code of conduct, and expectations.

Expectations about the consequences of committing fraud must be clearly communicated throughout the entity. For example, a strong statement from management that dishonest actions will not be tolerated, and that violators may be terminated and referred to the appropriate authorities, clearly establishes consequences and can be a valuable deterrent to wrongdoing. If wrongdoing occurs and an employee is disciplined, it can be helpful to communicate that fact, on a no-name basis, in an employee newsletter or other regular communication to employees. Seeing that other people have been disciplined for wrongdoing can be an effective deterrent, increasing the perceived likelihood of violators being caught and punished. It also can demonstrate that the entity is committed to an environment of high ethical standards and integrity.

Evaluating Antifraud Processes and Controls

Neither fraudulent financial reporting nor misappropriation of assets can occur without a perceived opportunity to commit and conceal the act. Organizations should be proactive in reducing fraud opportunities by (1) identifying and measuring fraud risks, (2) taking steps to mitigate identified risks, and (3) implementing and monitoring appropriate preventive and detective internal controls and other deterrent measures.

Identifying and Measuring Fraud Risks

Management has primary responsibility for establishing and monitoring all aspects of the entity's fraud risk-assessment and prevention activities.[6] Fraud risks often are considered as part of an enterprise-wide risk management program, though they

---

[5] Many entities of sufficient size are employing antifraud professionals, such as certified fraud examiners, who are responsible for resolving allegations of fraud within the organization and who also assist in the detection and deterrence of fraud. These individuals typically report their findings internally to the corporate security, legal, or internal audit departments. In other instances, such individuals may be empowered directly by the board of directors or its audit committee.

[6] Management may elect to have internal audit play an active role in the development, monitoring, and ongoing assessment of the entity's fraud risk-management program. This may include an active role in the development and communication of the entity's code of conduct or ethics policy, as well as in investigating actual or alleged instances of noncompliance.

may be addressed separately.[7] The fraud risk-assessment process should consider the vulnerability of the entity to fraudulent activity (fraudulent financial reporting, misappropriation of assets, and corruption) and whether any of those exposures could result in a material misstatement of the financial statements or material loss to the organization. In identifying fraud risks, organizations should consider organizational, industry, and country-specific characteristics that influence the risk of fraud.

The nature and extent of management's risk assessment activities should be commensurate with the size of the entity and complexity of its operations. For example, the risk assessment process is likely to be less formal and less structured in smaller entities. However, management should recognize that fraud can occur in organizations of any size or type, and that almost any employee may be capable of committing fraud given the right set of circumstances. Accordingly, management should develop a heightened "fraud awareness" and an appropriate fraud risk-management program, with oversight from the board of directors or audit committee.

Mitigating Fraud Risks

It may be possible to reduce or eliminate certain fraud risks by making changes to the entity's activities and processes. An entity may choose to sell certain segments of its operations, cease doing business in certain locations, or reorganize its business processes to eliminate unacceptable risks. For example, the risk of misappropriation of funds may be reduced by implementing a central lockbox at a bank to receive payments instead of receiving money at the entity's various locations. The risk of corruption may be reduced by closely monitoring the entity's procurement process. The risk of financial statement fraud may be reduced by implementing shared services centers to provide accounting services to multiple segments, affiliates, or geographic locations of an entity's operations. A shared services center may be less vulnerable to influence by local operations managers and may be able to implement more extensive fraud detection measures cost-effectively.

Implementing and Monitoring Appropriate Internal Controls

Some risks are inherent in the environment of the entity, but most can be addressed with an appropriate system of internal control. Once fraud risk assessment has taken place, the entity can identify the processes, controls, and other procedures that are needed to mitigate the identified risks. Effective internal control will include a well-developed control environment, an effective and secure information system, and appropriate control and monitoring activities.[8] Because of the importance of information technology

---

[7] Some organizations may perform a periodic self-assessment using questionnaires or other techniques to identify and measure risks. Self-assessment may be less reliable in identifying the risk of fraud due to a lack of experience with fraud (although many organizations experience some form of fraud and abuse, material financial statement fraud or misappropriation of assets is a rare event for most) and because management may be unwilling to acknowledge openly that they might commit fraud given sufficient pressure and opportunity.
[8] The report of the Committee of Sponsoring Organizations of the Treadway Commission, *Internal Control—Integrated Framework*, provides reasonable criteria for management to use in evaluating the effectiveness of the entity's system of internal control.

in supporting operations and the processing of transactions, management also needs to implement and maintain appropriate controls, whether automated or manual, over computer-generated information.

In particular, management should evaluate whether appropriate internal controls have been implemented in any areas management has identified as posing a higher risk of fraudulent activity, as well as controls over the entity's financial reporting process. Because fraudulent financial reporting may begin in an interim period, management also should evaluate the appropriateness of internal controls over interim financial reporting.

Fraudulent financial reporting by upper-level management typically involves override of internal controls within the financial reporting process. Because management has the ability to override controls, or to influence others to perpetrate or conceal fraud, the need for a strong value system and a culture of ethical financial reporting becomes increasingly important. This helps create an environment in which other employees will decline to participate in committing a fraud and will use established communication procedures to report any requests to commit wrongdoing. The potential for management override also increases the need for appropriate oversight measures by the board of directors or audit committee, as discussed in the following section.

Fraudulent financial reporting by lower levels of management and employees may be deterred or detected by appropriate monitoring controls, such as having higher-level managers review and evaluate the financial results reported by individual operating units or subsidiaries. Unusual fluctuations in results of particular reporting units, or the lack of expected fluctuations, may indicate potential manipulation by departmental or operating unit managers or staff.

Developing an Appropriate Oversight Process

To effectively prevent or deter fraud, an entity should have an appropriate oversight function in place. Oversight can take many forms and can be performed by many within and outside the entity, under the overall oversight of the audit committee (or board of directors where no audit committee exists).

Audit Committee or Board of Directors

The audit committee (or the board of directors where no audit committee exists) should evaluate management's identification of fraud risks, implementation of antifraud measures, and creation of the appropriate "tone at the top." Active oversight by the audit committee can help to reinforce management's commitment to creating a culture with "zero tolerance" for fraud. An entity's audit committee also should ensure that senior management (in particular, the CEO) implements appropriate fraud deterrence and prevention measures to better protect investors, employees, and other stakeholders. The audit committee's evaluation and oversight not only helps make sure that senior management fulfills its responsibility, but also can serve as a deterrent to senior management engaging in fraudulent activity (that is, by ensuring an environment is created whereby any attempt by senior management to involve employees in committing or concealing fraud would lead promptly to reports from such employees to appropriate persons, including the audit committee).

The audit committee also plays an important role in helping the board of directors fulfill its oversight responsibilities with respect to the entity's financial reporting process and the system of internal control.[9] In exercising this oversight responsibility, the audit committee should consider the potential for management override of controls or other inappropriate influence over the financial reporting process. For example, the audit committee may obtain from the internal auditors and independent auditors their views on management's involvement in the financial reporting process and, in particular, the ability of management to override information processed by the entity's financial reporting system (for example, the ability for management or others to initiate or record non-standard journal entries). The audit committee also may consider reviewing the entity's reported information for reasonableness compared with prior or forecasted results, as well as with peers or industry averages. In addition, information received in communications from the independent auditors[10] can assist the audit committee in assessing the strength of the entity's internal control and the potential for fraudulent financial reporting.

As part of its oversight responsibilities, the audit committee should encourage management to provide a mechanism for employees to report concerns about unethical behavior, actual or suspected fraud, or violations of the entity's code of conduct or ethics policy. The committee should then receive periodic reports describing the nature, status, and eventual disposition of any fraud or unethical conduct. A summary of the activity, follow-up and disposition also should be provided to the full board of directors.

If senior management is involved in fraud, the next layer of management may be the most likely to be aware of it. As a result, the audit committee (and other directors) should consider establishing an open line of communication with members of management one or two levels below senior management to assist in identifying fraud at the highest levels of the organization or investigating any fraudulent activity that might occur.[11] The audit committee typically has the ability and authority to investigate any alleged or suspected wrongdoing brought to its attention. Most audit committee charters empower the committee to investigate any matters within the scope of its responsibilities, and to retain legal, accounting, and other professional advisers as needed to advise the committee and assist in its investigation.

---

[9] See the report of the National Association of Corporate Directors (NACD) Blue Ribbon Commission on the Audit Committee, (Washington, D.C.: National Association of Corporate Directors, 2000). For the board's role in the oversight of risk management, see report of the NACD Blue Ribbon Commission on Risk Oversight, (Washington, D.C.: National Association of Corporate Directors, 2002).

[10] See AU-C section 265, *Communicating Internal Control Matters Identified in an Audit* (AICPA, *Professional Standards*), and AU-C section 260, *The Auditor's Communication With Those Charged With Governance* (AICPA, *Professional Standards*).

[11] The *Report of the NACD Best Practices Council: Coping with Fraud and Other Illegal Activity, A Guide for Directors, CEOs, and Senior Managers* (1998) sets forth "basic principles" and "implementation approaches" for dealing with fraud and other illegal activity.

All audit committee members should be financially literate, and each committee should have at least one financial expert. The financial expert should possess:

* An understanding of generally accepted accounting principles and audits of financial statements prepared under those principles. Such understanding may have been obtained either through education or experience. It is important for someone on the audit committee to have a working knowledge of those principles and standards.
* Experience in the preparation and/or the auditing of financial statements of an entity of similar size, scope and complexity as the entity on whose board the committee member serves. The experience would generally be as a chief financial officer, chief accounting officer, controller, or auditor of a similar entity. This background will provide a necessary understanding of the transactional and operational environment that produces the issuer's financial statements. It will also bring an understanding of what is involved in, for example, appropriate accounting estimates, accruals, and reserve provisions, and an appreciation of what is necessary to maintain a good internal control environment.
* Experience in internal governance and procedures of audit committees, obtained either as an audit committee member, a senior corporate manager responsible for answering to the audit committee, or an external auditor responsible for reporting on the execution and results of annual audits.

Management

Management is responsible for overseeing the activities carried out by employees, and typically does so by implementing and monitoring processes and controls such as those discussed previously. However, management also may initiate, participate in, or direct the commission and concealment of a fraudulent act. Accordingly, the audit committee (or the board of directors where no audit committee exists) has the responsibility to oversee the activities of senior management and to consider the risk of fraudulent financial reporting involving the override of internal controls or collusion (see discussion on the audit committee and board of directors above).

Public companies should include a statement in the annual report acknowledging management's responsibility for the preparation of the financial statements and for establishing and maintaining an effective system of internal control. This will help improve the public's understanding of the respective roles of management and the auditor. This statement has also been generally referred to as a "Management Report" or "Management Certificate." Such a statement can provide a convenient vehicle for management to describe the nature and manner of preparation of the financial information and the adequacy of the internal accounting controls. Logically, the statement should be presented in close proximity to the formal financial statements. For example, it could appear near the independent auditor's report, or in the financial review or management analysis section.

Internal Auditors

An effective internal audit team can be extremely helpful in performing aspects of the oversight function. Their knowledge about the entity may enable them to identify indicators that suggest fraud has been committed. The *Standards for the Professional Practice of Internal Auditing* (IIA Standards), issued by the Institute of Internal Auditors, state, "The internal auditor should have sufficient knowledge to identify the indicators of fraud but is not expected to have the expertise of a person whose primary responsibility is detecting and investigating fraud." Internal auditors also have the opportunity to evaluate fraud risks and controls and to recommend action to mitigate risks and improve controls. Specifically, the IIA Standards require internal auditors to assess risks facing their organizations. This risk assessment is to serve as the basis from which audit plans are devised and against which internal controls are tested. The IIA Standards require the audit plan to be presented to and approved by the audit committee (or board of directors where no audit committee exists). The work completed as a result of the audit plan provides assurance on which management's assertion about controls can be made.

Internal audits can be both a detection and a deterrence measure. Internal auditors can assist in the deterrence of fraud by examining and evaluating the adequacy and the effectiveness of the system of internal control, commensurate with the extent of the potential exposure or risk in the various segments of the organization's operations. In carrying out this responsibility, internal auditors should, for example, determine whether:

- The organizational environment fosters control consciousness.
- Realistic organizational goals and objectives are set.
- Written policies (for example, a code of conduct) exist that describe prohibited activities and the action required whenever violations are discovered.
- Appropriate authorization policies for transactions are established and maintained.
- Policies, practices, procedures, reports, and other mechanisms are developed to monitor activities and safeguard assets, particularly in high-risk areas.
- Communication channels provide management with adequate and reliable information.
- Recommendations need to be made for the establishment or enhancement of cost-effective controls to help deter fraud.

Internal auditors may conduct proactive auditing to search for corruption, misappropriation of assets, and financial statement fraud. This may include the use of computer-assisted audit techniques to detect particular types of fraud. Internal auditors also can employ analytical and other procedures to isolate anomalies and perform detailed reviews of high-risk accounts and transactions to identify potential financial statement fraud. The internal auditors should have an independent reporting line directly to the audit committee, to enable them to express any concerns about management's commitment to appropriate internal controls or to report suspicions or allegations of fraud involving senior management.

Independent Auditors

Independent auditors can assist management and the board of directors (or audit committee) by providing an assessment of the entity's process for identifying, assessing, and responding to the risks of fraud. Those charged with governance, such as the board of directors or audit committee, should have an open and candid dialogue with the independent auditors regarding management's risk assessment process and the system of internal control. Such a dialogue should include a discussion of the susceptibility of the entity to fraudulent financial reporting and the entity's exposure to misappropriation of assets.

Certified Fraud Examiners

Certified fraud examiners may assist the audit committee and board of directors with aspects of the oversight process either directly or as part of a team of internal auditors or independent auditors. Certified fraud examiners can provide extensive knowledge and experience about fraud that may not be available within a corporation. They can provide more objective input into management's evaluation of the risk of fraud (especially fraud involving senior management, such as financial statement fraud) and the development of appropriate antifraud controls that are less vulnerable to management override. They can assist the audit committee and board of directors in evaluating the fraud risk assessment and fraud prevention measures implemented by management. Certified fraud examiners also conduct examinations to resolve allegations or suspicions of fraud, reporting either to an appropriate level of management or to the audit committee or board of directors, depending upon the nature of the issue and the level of personnel involved.

Other Information

To obtain more information on fraud and implementing antifraud programs and controls, please go to the following Web sites where additional materials, guidance, and tools can be found.

American Institute of Certified Public Accountants	www.aicpa.org
Association of Certified Fraud Examiners	www.cfenet.com
Financial Executives International	www.fei.org
Information Systems Audit and Control Association	www.isaca.org
The Institute of Internal Auditors	www.theiia.org
Institute of Management Accountants	www.imanet.org
National Association of Corporate Directors	www.nacdonline.org
Society for Human Resource Management	www.shrm.org

ATTACHMENT 1: AICPA "CPA'S HANDBOOK OF FRAUD AND COMMERCIAL CRIME PREVENTION" CODE OF CONDUCT

The following is an example of an organizational code of conduct, which includes definitions of what is considered unacceptable, and the consequences of any breaches thereof. The specific content and areas addressed in an entity's code of conduct should be specific to that entity.

Organizational Code of Conduct

The Organization and its employees must, at all times, comply with all applicable laws and regulations. The Organization will not condone the activities of employees who achieve results through violation of the law or unethical business dealings. This includes any payments for illegal acts, indirect contributions, rebates, and bribery. The Organization does not permit any activity that fails to stand the closest possible public scrutiny.

All business conduct should be well above the minimum standards required by law. Accordingly, employees must ensure that their actions cannot be interpreted as being, in any way, in contravention of the laws and regulations governing the Organization's worldwide operations.

Employees uncertain about the application or interpretation of any legal requirements should refer the matter to their superior, who, if necessary, should seek the advice of the legal department.

General Employee Conduct

The Organization expects its employees to conduct themselves in a businesslike manner. Drinking, gambling, fighting, swearing, and similar unprofessional activities are strictly prohibited while on the job.

Employees must not engage in sexual harassment, or conduct themselves in a way that could be construed as such, for example, by using inappropriate language, keeping or posting inappropriate materials in their work area, or accessing inappropriate materials on their computer.

Conflicts of Interest

The Organization expects that employees will perform their duties conscientiously, honestly, and in accordance with the best interests of the Organization. Employees must not use their position or the knowledge gained as a result of their position for private or personal advantage. Regardless of the circumstances, if employees sense that a course of action they have pursued, are presently pursuing, or are contemplating pursuing may involve them in a conflict of interest with their employer, they should immediately communicate all the facts to their superior.

Outside Activities, Employment, and Directorships

All employees share a serious responsibility for the Organization's good public relations, especially at the community level. Their readiness to help with religious, charitable, educational, and civic activities brings credit to the Organization and is encouraged. Employees must, however, avoid acquiring any business interest or participating in any other activity outside the Organization that would, or would appear to:

- Create an excessive demand upon their time and attention, thus depriving the Organization of their best efforts on the job.
- Create a conflict of interest—an obligation, interest, or distraction—that may interfere with the independent exercise of judgment in the Organization's best interest.

Relationships with Clients and Suppliers

Employees should avoid investing in or acquiring a financial interest for their own accounts in any business organization that has a contractual relationship with the Organization, or that provides goods or services, or both to the Organization, if such investment or interest could influence or create the impression of influencing their decisions in the performance of their duties on behalf of the Organization.

Gifts, Entertainment, and Favors

Employees must not accept entertainment, gifts, or personal favors that could, in any way, influence, or appear to influence, business decisions in favor of any person or organization with whom or with which the Organization has, or is likely to have, business dealings. Similarly, employees must not accept any other preferential treatment under these circumstances because their position with the Organization might be inclined to, or be perceived to, place them under obligation.

Kickbacks and Secret Commissions

Regarding the Organization's business activities, employees may not receive payment or compensation of any kind, except as authorized under the Organization's remuneration policies. In particular, the Organization strictly prohibits the acceptance of kickbacks and secret commissions from suppliers or others. Any breach of this rule will result in immediate termination and prosecution to the fullest extent of the law.

Organization Funds and Other Assets

Employees who have access to Organization funds in any form must follow the prescribed procedures for recording, handling, and protecting money as detailed in the Organization's instructional manuals or other explanatory materials, or both. The Organization imposes strict standards to prevent fraud and dishonesty. If employees become aware of any evidence of fraud and dishonesty, they should immediately advise their superior or the Law Department so that the Organization can promptly investigate further.

When an employee's position requires spending Organization funds or incurring any reimbursable personal expenses, that individual must use good judgment on the Organization's behalf to ensure that good value is received for every expenditure.

Organization funds and all other assets of the Organization are for Organization purposes only and not for personal benefit. This includes the personal use of organizational assets, such as computers.

Organization Records and Communications

Accurate and reliable records of many kinds are necessary to meet the Organization's legal and financial obligations and to manage the affairs of the Organization. The Organization's books and records must reflect in an accurate and timely manner all business transactions. The employees responsible for accounting and recordkeeping must fully disclose and record all assets, liabilities, or both, and must exercise diligence in enforcing these requirements.

Employees must not make or engage in any false record or communication of any kind, whether internal or external, including but not limited to:

- False expense, attendance, production, financial, or similar reports and statements
- False advertising, deceptive marketing practices, or other misleading representations

Dealing with Outside People and Organizations

Employees must take care to separate their personal roles from their Organization positions when communicating on matters not involving Organization business. Employees must not use organization identification, stationery, supplies, and equipment for personal or political matters.

When communicating publicly on matters that involve Organization business, employees must not presume to speak for the Organization on any topic, unless they are certain that the views they express are those of the Organization, and it is the Organization's desire that such views be publicly disseminated.

When dealing with anyone outside the Organization, including public officials, employees must take care not to compromise the integrity or damage the reputation of either the Organization, or any outside individual, business, or government body.

Prompt Communications

In all matters relevant to customers, suppliers, government authorities, the public and others in the Organization, all employees must make every effort to achieve complete, accurate, and timely communications—responding promptly and courteously to all proper requests for information and to all complaints.

Privacy and Confidentiality

When handling financial and personal information about customers or others with whom the Organization has dealings, observe the following principles:

1. Collect, use, and retain only the personal information necessary for the Organization's business. Whenever possible, obtain any relevant information directly from the person concerned. Use only reputable and reliable sources to supplement this information.
2. Retain information only for as long as necessary or as required by law. Protect the physical security of this information.
3. Limit internal access to personal information to those with a legitimate business reason for seeking that information. Use only personal information for the purposes for which it was originally obtained. Obtain the consent of the person concerned before externally disclosing any personal information, unless legal process or contractual obligation provides otherwise.

ATTACHMENT 2: FINANCIAL EXECUTIVES INTERNATIONAL CODE OF ETHICS STATEMENT

The mission of Financial Executives International (FEI) includes significant efforts to promote ethical conduct in the practice of financial management throughout the world. Senior financial officers hold an important and elevated role in corporate governance. While members of the management team, they are uniquely capable and empowered to ensure that all stakeholders' interests are appropriately balanced, protected, and preserved. This code provides principles that members are expected to adhere to and advocate. They embody rules regarding individual and peer responsibilities, as well as responsibilities to employers, the public, and other stakeholders.

All members of FEI will:

1. Act with honesty and integrity, avoiding actual or apparent conflicts of interest in personal and professional relationships.
2. Provide constituents with information that is accurate, complete, objective, relevant, timely, and understandable.
3. Comply with rules and regulations of federal, state, provincial, and local governments, and other appropriate private and public regulatory agencies.
4. Act in good faith; responsibly; and with due care, competence, and diligence, without misrepresenting material facts or allowing one's independent judgment to be subordinated.
5. Respect the confidentiality of information acquired in the course of one's work except when authorized or otherwise legally obligated to disclose. Confidential

information acquired in the course of one's work will not be used for personal advantage.

6. Share knowledge and maintain skills important and relevant to constituents' needs.
7. Proactively promote ethical behavior as a responsible partner among peers, in the work environment, and in the community.
8. Achieve responsible use of and control over all assets and resources employed or entrusted. [Revised, April 2007, to reflect confirming changes necessary due to the issuance of Statement on Auditing Standards No. 114.]

Understanding Fraud Risk Assessment

S OME THINK OF fraud as a rare event, but it is really not that rare. Almost every long-lived organization has a tale of woe based on a past incident. They are the lucky ones, as many businesses no longer exist because they were drained by fraudsters. In groups of auditors to whom I have asked the question, almost every experienced auditor indicated that they have had a client impacted by fraud, and some of the stories are incredible.

Underlying the researched cases of fraud, misstated financial statements, and alleged audit failures lay discovered weaknesses in internal control. This linkage led to the current SOX requirements to publicly report on internal controls after the massive frauds and rise in restatements in the early 2000s.

SOX project members and auditors may benefit from reviewing some common fraud scenarios when sharpening their awareness of fraud risks, leading to more contributions to risk and fraud brainstorming sessions during the SOX scoping phase.

SOME COMMON FRAUD RISK AREAS AND SCHEMES

This is certainly not an exhaustive list of risk areas to consider, but in the self-defense of the entity, these are a few of the areas you might think through, particularly as you are reviewing the controls in these areas. Such considerations can also be introduced into the suggested brainstorming sessions for entities and the required auditor brainstorming sessions.

Sales and Cash Receipts

The following points describe some common revenue- and cash-based schemes:

- Common risks can include not even recording certain sales and funneling the money outside the entity. Such "skimming" can be hard to detect, but declining profit margins can be a sign. "Under-ringing" sales also allows the siphoning off of a part of the sale money. Directly skimming cash receipts is not uncommon (and frightfully hard to detect).
- In some cases, sales are actually diverted to another supplier by a sales person, and a kickback greater than the usual ("skimpy") commission comes back to the salesperson for the referral.
- The deliberate underpricing of sales can lead to a kickback for those authorizing the order.
- Lapping of receipts can occur when cash customer receipts are taken and the sales to those customers are "covered" on the books by later receipts from other customers that are credited to the stolen cash customer accounts. Watch for mismatched cash payments (over- and underpayments of amount due).
- Bogus credit memoranda can be issued or returns and allowances can be diverted for personal gain. In one case, cash deposits on rental furniture were diverted and never deposited, but refunds of "deposits" were expended from company funds on presentation of the deposit receipt.

Purchasing and Cash Disbursements

A myriad of possibilities in purchasing and cash can go on here.

- Purchasing departments are notorious breeding grounds for kickback schemes, where suppliers reward "faithful" purchasers of their product.
- Kickback schemes can also exist where other services (e.g., landscaping, painting, driveway paving, etc.) are contracted for at higher-than-competitive rates and the monies diverted back to the inside contracting person. Sometimes the billed-for work is not even performed (are you an electrical inspector?). Overpriced janitorial supplies are practically legendary in fraud annals.
- Goods that are "under spec" can be substituted for ordered items, resulting in defective goods. Consider the liability when airplane engine bolts are defective.
- Merchandise can sometimes be ordered through the entity but delivered or diverted to an employee's personal use.
- Unreasonable expense reimbursement requests can divert company funds.
- Legitimate purchase rebates for business purchases can be able to be diverted to personal gain when the rebate form is completed in the employee's name.
- Petty cash (it may not be petty to someone) used to be an area of audit interest but is generally ignored in the financial audit today. It is still a great source of fictional writing. The petty cash (and cash advance) teller for a large CPA firm was fired and prosecuted after 20 years of service for theft. While the auditor payout limit was

$100, there were thousands of dollars behind the window. Pay attention to anything that is cash.

Payroll

The following points describe some common payroll-based schemes:

- In smaller businesses, it is usual to recognize when a bogus employee is being paid, but in a large organization, how is this risk addressed?
- Is there anything wrong with giving yourself, as the payroll clerk, a raise for a few weeks or months during the year? Just make sure to put the correct payroll amount in the period before the auditors show up, since they usually test the latest payroll.
- Another opportunity is to have other employees pay part of your (the payroll clerk's) taxes for you, and make sure to give yourself full credit on your payroll tax forms. Uncle Sam himself will send you the payoff check in the form of a refund.
- Expense reimbursements are a notorious area for creative writing. Let's generate some expenses! Got a sure thing in the eighth race.

Equipment, Inventory, and Anything Not Bolted Down

While employees might covet a painting or a vase, the loss of office equipment, particularly computers, is common and potentially disastrous to a business or entity. In office buildings, these thefts often occur at night or over the weekend. Some brazenly occur during office hours. An "insider" leaving the outside back door open (or taping the lock so that the lock will not latch) or a complicit cleaning staff person may set this up. Having not made timely data backups all of a sudden becomes a big issue, as all your records are somewhere but not in your office. Now, do not think that the fact that you have a password on the computer renders it useless. Au contraire—many computers wind up being disassembled and partitioned for parts. In other cases, skilled hackers can usually get data off the hard drive if they want it and/or can wipe the disk clean and reinstall software. Such thefts also carry the risk that personal information about employees might be exposed, in violation of federal or state privacy acts and subjecting the entity to significant fines.

Personal Information Risks

What makes the laws protecting personal data really bad news for you is that state and federal laws now hold entities responsible if an individual's unencrypted personal data (e.g., Social Security number, driver's license, access information to a financial account) is lost.

For example, in 2003, California passed a law dealing with identity theft, privacy, and security issues. Under this law, a state agency, person, or business that conducts business in California that owns or licenses computerized data that includes personal information must disclose any breach of the security of the data to the data owner. For more details of the law's requirements, see California Civil Code Sections 1798.82 and 1798.29. In similar legislation in December 2005, the New York State Information

Security Breach and Notification Act became effective with similar provisions. The law was prompted by high number of information security breaches that occurred in 2005 as well as the information breach at ChoicePoint. The time to start considering the risks of information loss and having unencrypted data is not the day after the equipment and data take a walk.

Consult with your business advisor regarding such risks. A lot of commerce in the United States goes on in California and New York.

If privacy issues are important to you, you might want to visit www.business.ftc .gov/privacy-and-security/data-security.

Inventory Mischief

In some cases, inventory frauds have taken on massive proportions, such as the Great Salad Oil Swindle, where storage tanks of "oil" were filled with water and a skim of oil floated on top to "coat" the measuring rods. While auditors worked through the maze of seemingly similar (and in actuality the same) storage tanks, workers were also busy renumbering them so that "new" ones could be tested. This stuff is too good even to make up.

In other cases, inventory was deliberately moved to where the inventory counts were going to happen so that the counts would agree with the accounting records in those locations. This hides shortages in those locations. This scam has happened in the retail industry and in trailer leasing businesses. Sure, announce to the entity when and where the counts are going to happen well in advance.

Most inventory frauds "fall over" at some point and get discovered. I would pick a better fraud than this type if I had such intentions.

 FRAUD TRIANGLE

The general concept of the fraud triangle was introduced in earlier literature but refined in SAS No. 99, *Consideration of Fraud in a Financial Statement Audit* (2002).[12] The concept is that many frauds share common characteristics, including:

- Motivation.
- Opportunity.
- Rationalization.

The first is easy to understand when money is involved, but there can be other motivations of equal or greater force. Some frauds can also be motivated by a person's need for power, ego, or revenge. If the money was not worth the crime, look for the other motivations, as they are probably the key.

---

[12] In 2012, the AICPA began implementation of its revised "clarified" standards. This fraud standard is now re-codified in AU-C Section 240. The PCAOB continues to codify SAS No. 99 with revisions in its interim standards, AU Section 316.

Opportunity is, of course, a major contributor. In an environment of well-designed controls, adequate management oversight, and employee ethical standards, the opportunities are greatly reduced. At least the simple, stupid schemes that will make you ashamed you did not detect them in the first place will not haunt you. Better to be defrauded with pride by a clever scheme than be shammed by ineptness. Make them work at it!

A new wrinkle in the equation that was enumerated in this recent auditing standard seems to be how people doing these sorts of things seem to find a rationale for their actions and get up and look themselves in the mirror every day. Some of these rationalizations are time-worn, but they do creep into the picture when needed to "justify" the fraud:

- I always intended it be a loan.
- As soon as I hit the lottery, I was going to repay the monies (the gambler's promise).
- I could not help myself.
- I am underpaid, and this just balances things out more. (Earth to fraudster: We are all underpaid, except maybe for a few guys on Wall Street, who think they are too.)
- Nobody seemed to care or notice, so I thought it was okay.
- They have plenty.
- I really needed the money (for the boat, house, boathouse, fur coat, jewelry, vacation home, face-lift, etc.).
- I could not let [insert family relation or close personal friend's name here] see me in this situation.
- My [insert family relation here, also] was going to [leave/shame/kill me] if I was not able to get them a [insert name of worldly good here].

As you can see, motivation and rationalization can be tied together, with some factors providing two legs of the three-legged stool. Once in a while we read stories about family medical bills, personal tragedies, and other issues in life that can be devastating, motivating fraud. Often it is pride and shame that keep people from seeking help that is available in our society to get though these issues. An open and compassionate management or human resources function can be a great support to those in need and often can help employees find solutions within the law. Imagine how difficult things will be when fraudsters are incarcerated or are unable to find any work because of a criminal record. How much help will they be to their family and those in true need from that position?

DETECTING FRAUD

As an auditor by profession, I find it embarrassing how few frauds are actually detected during independent audits. While management stares dumbfounded at frauds that are found by accident and says, "That's what I hired you for," the reality is that financial statement audits are not "forensic," and management would not be willing (or perhaps able) to pay for a true forensic audit every year. The auditor plans the audit to find material misstatement of the financial statements from error or fraud, but many frauds are clever enough to escape detection until they are quite large—and by that time, they often stand out like a sore thumb.

Most frauds that involve numbers in the financial statements eventually fall over of their own weight. For example, inventory frauds often need to keep increasing each year to keep the ball rolling, and they grow so large that detection is just a matter of time. Non-accountants sometimes do not realize that an overstatement of ending inventory in year 1 winds up as additional "costs of sales" in year 2, depressing profits by the amount that last year they were raised. Double-entry bookkeeping can be the demise of many a fraudster.

More frauds are detected because of a tip—someone says something—than by any other means. The majority of frauds today are detected either by tips or by accident. In small businesses, accidental discovery actually exceeds tips slightly as the source of detection.

Better internal controls, more auditor attention to controls design, and more fraud awareness should change these statistics over time.

4

Control Environment

THE CONTROL ENVIRONMENT sets the overall tone of the entity. It influences the control consciousness of the people within the organization and is the foundation for all other components of internal control. Various writings have stated the critical importance of this component in the overall Framework. Indeed, it holds a trump card role in the overall assessment, as it is difficult to imagine an effective system of internal control with a defective control environment. Management override of controls, a common element in many frauds, shows how controls over transactions and policies and procedures can be defeated by the willful action of executives and senior management. Additional tools have been encouraged to mitigate allowing such actions to go unnoticed or unchallenged; these include the antifraud controls of hotline reporting and the implementation of whistleblowing laws meant to protect employees who report issues.

While a superior control environment may go a long way toward an assessment of effective controls, it cannot carry the weight of the whole assessment, as all the various components need to be working in an integrated fashion to be able to conclude the controls over financial reporting are effective. In addition, the principles in this component ask for subjective judgments, reducing the precision with which these assessments are made.

Following is a discussion of the principles highlighted in the revised Framework that contribute to an effective control environment.

PRINCIPLE 1: COMMITMENT TO INTEGRITY AND ETHICAL VALUES

The effectiveness of internal control cannot rise above the integrity and ethical values of the senior management and their expectations for the rest of the company and in the company's business practices. Integrity and ethical values are essential elements of the control environment because they affect the design, administration, and monitoring of other internal control components.

Management may *tell you* a great deal about their integrity and ethical values. They may even commit their *words* to a *written document*. Responses to inquiries and written policies are good, but the COSO report makes it clear that the effectiveness of an entity's control environment depends primarily on management's *actions* and how these actions affect the entity on a day-to-day basis. In general, the more specific the code or guideline is in defining ethical or unethical behavior, the more helpful it is in guiding actions, but when it is too narrowly worded, it can encourage abuses by individuals focusing just on the words rather than the concept.

Subsets of the principle (points of focus) help define the boundaries of the principle and help provide direction to obtaining evidence that would support the effectiveness of the principle. These points include:

- Tone at the top.
- Standards of conduct.
- Evaluates adherence to the standards.
- Addresses deviations in a timely manner.

In order for management's integrity and ethical values to have a positive impact on the entity:

- The business owner of executives and management must personally have high ethical and behavioral standards.
- These standards must be communicated to company personnel and understood. In a small business, this communication is often less formal.
- The standards must be reinforced. Over time, messages tend to lose their desired effect. They must be brought to the forefront again and again to have a lasting impact. Different delivery mechanisms can be used (e.g., direct one-to-one communication, broadcast e-mails, training, and meeting discussions) to vary the delivery, but not the message.

Through its actions, management can demonstrate its ethical values in a number of ways, including these:

- Ensuring that management adheres to the same principles it expects from its employees.

- Dealing with actual problems in a professional and serious way. Consider how management deals with signs that problems exist, particularly when the cost of identifying and solving the problem could be high. For example, suppose that senior management became aware of a possible environmental contamination on the premises. How would they react? Would they try to hide it, deny its existence, or act evasively if asked about it? Or would they actively seek advice on how to best handle the situation?
- Removal or reduction of unproductive incentives and temptations. Individuals may engage in dishonest, illegal, or unethical acts simply because the owner-manager gives them strong incentives to do so, such as oversize bonuses or other rewards or temptations. Removing or reducing these incentives and temptations can go a long way toward diminishing undesirable behavior.

> An entity provided a very generous commission for sales of a highly aggressive tax shelter to high-worth individuals and corporations. The commissions paid were enough to encourage the employee to retire from the entity shortly after the commissions were paid.
>
> Might such an incentive be counterproductive to the entity? What does it say about the care that is needed in designing the incentive program?

The overemphasis on accounting *results*, particularly in the short term, fosters an environment in which the price of failure becomes very high. *Incentives* for engaging in fraudulent or questionable financial reporting practices include:

- Pressure to meet unrealistic performance targets, particularly for short-term results.
- Intimidation and threats of job loss.
- Rewards dependent on high performance.
- Overly generous rewards for meeting specific targets.
- Upper and lower cutoffs on bonus plans, focusing attention on meeting the threshold issue and encouraging the manipulating of the timing of transactions.

Temptations for management and employees to engage in improper practices include:

- Nonexistent or ineffective controls, such as poor segregation of duties in sensitive areas that offer temptations to steal or conceal questionable financial reporting practices. As another example, the issuance of company business credit cards with insufficient guidelines for use and poor enforcement of the policies for use.
- Senior management that is unconcerned with details of the business operations, allowing exceptions to business policies. Some entities are led by technical subject experts (e.g., doctors, chemists, clergy) who have mission-specific interests but no specific business experience, acumen, or even interest.

- Penalties for improper behavior that are insignificant or unpublicized and thus lose their value as deterrents.
- Management intervention. There are certain situations in which it is appropriate for management to intervene and override prescribed policies or procedures for legitimate purposes. For example, management intervention is usually necessary to deal with nonrecurring and time-sensitive transactions or events that otherwise might not be handled timely by the accounting system. COSO guidance recommends that management provide discussion on the situations and frequency with which intervention of established controls is appropriate. Post-review and approval by a level higher than the authorizing person can be an effective solution that still facilitates meeting business goals. Occurrences of management intervention should be documented and explained. "Silent" overrides connote a different environment.

Management's philosophy and operating style encompass a broad range of characteristics. Such characteristics may include:

- Senior management's approach to taking and monitoring business risks. See Principle 7, Identifies and Assesses Risk.
- Attitudes and actions toward financial reporting and tax matters (e.g., pushing aggressive accounting or tax positions).
- Excessive emphasis on meeting budget, profit, and other financial and operating goals.

Management's philosophy and operating style, elements of this component, have a significant influence on the control environment, regardless of the consideration given to the other control environment factors.

While this may be a judgment call, signs of problems can often be discerned in:

- Frequent turnover in key management accounting positions (especially finance- and accounting-related positions).
- Long-vacant key accounting or finance-related positions.
- Overall personal attitudes and work ethic of personnel.
- Complaints regarding the actions of senior executives.

Do service organizations that the entity relies on for important functions have a satisfactory commitment to integrity and ethical values? As an extension of the entity, actions of the service organization can reflect on the entity and not only cause reputational harm but lead to financial misstatements affecting reporting quality. The revised Framework brings this issue to the forefront. It will be a new concept for many entities to consider.

Obtaining evidence of meeting this principle usually involves several procedures, as well as being generally observant and sensitive to these issues on a regular basis. To assess the tone at the top, attitudes of a wide variety of entity personnel, perhaps gathered through observation and/or survey questions, may provide important input. The choice of written or oral input and the approach to asking the questions (e.g., a special-purpose survey or adding some questions in conjunction with walk-throughs, control tests, or other activities) is a matter for judgment, and some mixture of approaches may be used. Variation in the techniques and approaches over time may help ensure representative and valid inputs. Developing questionnaires and forming inquiries are addressed in more detail in Chapters 8 and 9.

While one should read any mission statement, code of conduct, or ethics policy for content, as the mere existence of these documents is not sufficient. Are the policies understood and read? Are there procedures in place to make sure that these statements are periodically reviewed? Larger organizations may require an annual signed employee statement regarding reading and agreeing with such policies. If so, a census (all) or sampling of the compliance records can be an objective source of evidence. Smaller entities may discuss these policies in meetings, and thus meeting minutes may provide some evidence supporting the assertion. Surveys and interviews can be designed to test for the awareness and attitudes toward the policies.

Enforcement of the standards established is important to their effective implementation. Is there a record of reports and dispositions regarding ethical and human resource (HR) complaints that involve management and employees? If so, can it be tested for completeness and accuracy? Understanding the resolutions to some or all of the identified issues, you will also gain evidence about the timeliness of the response, another point of focus. Interviews can also be conducted to confirm the accuracy and completeness of the reported incidents and their resolution. Inquiries regarding any related legal challenges in process may reveal issues handled outside the normal processes. Major issues should be identified by management proactively, and failure to be forthright in such circumstances also reflects on management and the tone at the top.

A corporate entity fired its controller because he had overstated business expenses to finance his gambling habit. The auditing standards (e.g., those of the Public Company Accounting Oversight Board [PCAOB] and American Institute of Certified Public Accountants [AICPA]) define fraud of any magnitude on the part of senior personnel to be an indicator of a material weakness. So far, so good.

A lesser-qualified employee with limited experience was promoted into the position, and the fired controller was hired back as a paid consultant to support some aspects of the accounting function.

What kind of signal does this send to other personnel about misconduct? Does the promotion of the marginally qualified employee send another message regarding Principle 4, Commitment to Competence?

Later, errors in judgment as a result of the controller's competence deficiencies allowed accounting errors that led to misstated financial statements and contributed to the woes of the entity as it eventually headed into bankruptcy.

PRINCIPLE 2: BOARD OF DIRECTORS (GOVERNANCE) DEMONSTRATES INDEPENDENCE FROM MANAGEMENT AND EXERCISES OVERSIGHT OF THE DEVELOPMENT AND PERFORMANCE OF INTERNAL CONTROL

When organizational leadership extends beyond a single business owner, the role that leadership plays is of critical importance. The COSO guidance is mostly written from the perspective of the usual corporate structure of a board and audit committee. When adapting that guidance to other entities, it can be difficult to identify parallel structures in other situations. For example, what is the board and audit committee equivalent in a municipality or in a proprietorship or in a church? In some cases, an elected municipal township committee might provide certain oversight; in other cases, the business manager serves in all these roles. Some church structures concentrate responsibility in the minister; in other denominations, the congregation is supposed to provide oversight and take responsibility for the operations of the entity. The term *governance* is used in the AICPA auditing standards because of these different structures in the noncorporate world. It is sometimes necessary to evaluate the organization to identify who is responsible for the governance function before tackling this principle. As organizations change over time, the governance function may indeed change. In any case, the term *governance* (in its different forms) is the focal point here.

The points of focus here help direct the gathering of evidence to support the principle:

- Establishes oversight responsibilities.
- Applies relevant expertise.
- Operates independent from management.
- Provides oversight for the system of internal control.

Granted, it will be difficult or impossible in some simpler business circumstances to separate governance from management and find evidence of independence unless the owner has a split personality. In such cases, are there any mechanisms that help provide some independent oversight to the business operations? If not, that might indicate a material weakness that is hard to correct without imposition of another business structure. The point here is that although the weakness is inherent in the business structure, it still counts as a weakness from a COSO or auditing standards perspective.

Although principles are intended to be applicable to every type of entity, there is an opportunity to provide an explanation as to why a particular point of focus might not be relevant to an entity. That may indeed be the case here with some entities like small proprietorships. However, even in such cases, the proprietor should be concerned about internal control, and the last point of focus is still relevant. Considering the expertise of the proprietor and how it is brought to bear on entity management might also be relevant to even smaller entities. One should not be too quick to dismiss a point of focus just because the wording of the concept does not appear to apply to the entity.

The structure of the audit committee and board of directors in a corporate structure is sometimes emulated in larger private enterprises or not-for-profit foundations.

Independent (and objective) oversight is considered a key element in an entity's control environment and the monitoring component of internal control. Because of the importance of the audit committee and the board of directors to a public company, the auditing standard requires external auditors to assess the effectiveness of the audit committee and the board *in the context* of obtaining an understanding about the company's control environment and the monitoring of its internal control.

The effectiveness of boards varies widely, and some companies are notorious for selecting board members based not on business acumen but on their likelihood to support the objectives of senior executives. Some boards have been accused of being puppets of management and ineffective as a check and balance on management. This is not surprising, considering that in the past the chief executive appointed loyal friends and supporters as board members or discharged board members who question or oppose the owner's plans.

There is a body of academic accounting research going back 20 years on the effectiveness and characteristics of members of the board. The need for independent directors who are not part of management is today recognized in the rules of the Securities and Exchange Commission (SEC) and exchanges that list stocks and in some state laws. Change has been slow in coming, but there is a clear trend toward including more independent directors and directors with financial accounting expertise on boards and audit committees. As a result, entities are expected to model their boards after, and be fully compliant with, the SEC listing exchange requirements that now incorporate many of the recommendations of the Blue Ribbon Commission on audit committees (see Figure 4.1). The Web sites of the larger certified public accounting firms as well as resources available through the AICPA provide more detail on enhancing the effectiveness of audit committees and boards of directors. Using the general search term "audit committee effectiveness" will return many examples of publications, academic studies, and checklists on this important subject.

During the public comment period for its internal control auditing standard, the requirement relating to the audit committee and board effectiveness drew many requests for clarification. The PCAOB thus took great pains to note its intention that the requirement does *not*:

- Transfer the responsibility for maintaining internal control from management to the audit committee. Management retains the responsibility for the company's internal control.
- Require the auditor to make a stand-alone evaluation of all aspects of the audit committee effectiveness. The auditor's evaluation of the audit committee is solely in the context of understanding the control environment and the effectiveness of the governance function over financial reporting and the monitoring components of internal control. In this particular area, strengths in the board may compensate for some deficiencies in the audit committee since they together form the "effective governance" function identified as a control objective in COSO. As with defining governance, differences in the operation of the boards and audit committees need to be considered. As long as the principle is satisfied, it is of less consequence how it is satisfied, provided it does not violate any mandate or regulation.

Recommendation 1 The committee recommended that both the New York Stock Exchange (NYSE) and the National Association of Securities Dealers (NASD) adopt the following definition of independence for purposes of service on the audit committee for listed companies with a market capitalization above $200 million.

Members of the audit committee shall be considered independent if they have no relationship to the corporation that may interfere with the exercise of their independence from management and the corporation. Examples of relationships that impair independence include:

- A director being employed by the corporation or any of its affiliates for the current year or any of the past five years
- A director accepting any compensation from the corporation or any of its affiliates other than compensation for board service or benefits under a tax-qualified retirement plan
- A director being a member of the immediate family of an individual who is, or has been in any of the past five years, employed by the corporation or any of its affiliates as an executive officer
- A director being a partner in, or a controlling shareholder or an executive officer of, any for-profit business organization to which the corporation made, or from which the corporation received, payments that are or have been significant* to the corporation or business organization in any of the past five years
- A director being employed as an executive of another company where any of the corporation's executives serves on that company's compensation committee
- A director who has one or more of these relationships may be appointed to the audit committee if the board, under exceptional and limited circumstances, determines that membership on the committee by the individual is required by the best interests of the corporation and its shareholders, and the board discloses, in the next annual proxy statement subsequent to such determination, the nature of the relationship and the reasons for that determination.

Recommendation 2 The committee further recommended that the NYSE and the NASD require that listed companies with a market capitalization above $200 million have an audit committee comprised of only independent directors.

The committee recommends that the NYSE and the NASD maintain their respective current audit committee independence requirements as well as their respective definitions of independence for listed companies with a market capitalization of $200 million or below (or a more appropriate measure for identifying smaller-sized companies as determined jointly by the NYSE and the NASD).

FIGURE 4.1 Blue Ribbon Commission—Independence Recommendations

*The committee views the term "significant" in the spirit of section 1.34(a)(4) of the American Law Institute's Principles of Corporate Governance and the accompanying commentary to that section.

The structure of governance needs to be appropriate for the entity. One could hardly imagine a Fortune 500 company with a governance structure consisting only of a chief executive officer. However talented and benevolent the person, would this structure instill trust that the shareholder, employee, and other stakeholder interests are being looked after and that financial reports and other communications are free of bias? Similarly, it would be overkill to establish a complex structure for a simple and small business. So one action step here for all could be an assessment that the governance structure appears appropriate for the entity and does not concentrate the governance function in a few hands (or one hand) when many hands are part of the official organization chart of the governance function. When there is a board and audit committee, they should perform duties consistent with those structures, as defined by best practices or by the appropriate regulating overseer.

While simple or small business entities might not have governing boards, consider whether trusted legal and tax advisors or a group of family members might constitute an advisory group that might emulate some of the formal structures in corporations. If so, are there some guidelines established on how these advisors relate to the entity that can be leveraged to support the principle to achieve a passing grade? Remember that the COSO Principles are not a checklist of characteristics or controls; rather, they ask you to identify *how* the entity satisfies the principle. There is no universal answer to support achievement of the principles.

Various guidelines are available to help define best practices for corporate boards and audit committees. The AICPA, various industry trade groups, and the stock exchanges establish regulations that address expected duties and independence of board and audit committee members.[1] Corporations need to comply with the regulations of their exchanges in order to be permitted to have their shares traded on the exchange. For example, the Blue Ribbon Commission[2] specifically made recommendations on the independence issue. These recommendations may help noncorporate structures adapt their practices.

Factors you might consider when evaluating the audit committee include:

- The independence of the audit committee (or alternative governance) members from management.
- The clarity with which the audit committee's responsibilities are articulated (e.g., in the audit committee's charter).
- How well the audit committee and management understand those responsibilities.
- The audit committee's involvement and interaction with the external auditor and with internal auditors as well as interaction with key members of financial management, including the chief financial officer and chief accounting officer.

---

[1] For example, see www.nyse.com/pdfs/finalcorpgovrules.pdf for the New York Stock Exchange governance rules.

[2] From the Report and Recommendations of the Blue Ribbon Committee on Improving the Effectiveness of Corporate Audit Committees (1999). Each year, the National Association of Corporate Directors (NACD) convenes a Blue Ribbon Commission comprising experienced board members and leading issue experts to study a critical area of board practice where clear guidance is needed. As the environment changes rapidly, commissions help identify and disseminate leading practices among all boards.

▪ Whether the right questions are raised and pursued with management and the external auditor, including questions that indicate an understanding of the critical accounting policies and judgmental accounting estimates and responsiveness to issues raised by the external auditor.

Independence is a state of mind, but it has specific definitions for specific purposes. In auditing and financial reporting, independence includes a lack of a financial interest in the entity or its success. That makes no sense in a sole proprietorship. So for the most part, independence might be satisfied if the actions taken by governance appear to be objective and not clouded by total conflicts of interest—an extension of Principle 1. Looking at all the other attributes of the control environment, does it appear that the proprietor has a reasonable interest in and approach to addressing any issues that may arise and resolving them? Such a conclusion can help in assessing whether this principle is met. Governance is also about the organizational structure—not just the physical chart with the lines and names, but how it works—and it can either strengthen the organization or allow it to become crippled.

In all cases, this principle asks if governance is involved in oversight of the internal control. Is there an interest in designing controls where possible and in ensuring that they are followed? While some entities complain they are too small to have controls, we are not speaking of lemonade stands on a street corner. Any business of some size has the capacity to design procedures that can ensure (all) cash gets to the bank, merchandise is protected from theft, inventories can be taken, and fixed assets depreciated. Maybe the controls of a multinational cannot be applied the same way in smaller entities, but key controls over the business processes can be designed and implemented. I have done this exercise with some clients. In my experience, the perceived problem is also often associated with laziness. Sometime later that attitude can be accompanied by anger when bad things happen that probably could have been prevented. Because they are dealing with "good causes," religious institution and not-for-profit entities can make the hardest sell that governance should care about internal controls. The number and size of frauds in these entities serve as a testament to the folly of those beliefs. The control environment of COSO may not extend skyward.

A public company was faced with reporting on internal controls, but there were only three full-time employees. The company was in the investment business and was large (an accelerated filer public company) because of the size of the investments it managed. The company volunteered to wave the white flag of surrender and just not evaluate controls, but when faced with sanctions for not asserting the effectiveness of controls, it started looking for solutions. It found a way through computer and manual control processes and some expert outside assistance (not the auditor) to assert controls effectiveness. The company's toughest problem was preparing financial statements, and that was resolved by hiring a retired certified public accountant to prepare its drafts and footnotes.

PRINCIPLE 3: MANAGEMENT ESTABLISHES, WITH BOARD OVERSIGHT, STRUCTURES, REPORTING LINES, AND APPROPRIATE AUTHORITIES AND RESPONSIBILITIES IN THE PURSUIT OF OBJECTIVES

An entity's organizational structure provides the framework within which its activities for achieving entity-wide objectives are planned, executed, controlled, and monitored. Poorly organized entities can create more opportunities for fraud and error to affect the financial health and quality of financial reporting by the entity.

Significant aspects of establishing an organizational structure include considering key areas of authority and responsibility and appropriate lines of reporting. What is considered appropriate will vary according to the size, complexity, and needs of the business. Small business entities usually have fairly simple organizational structures. A highly structured organization with formal reporting lines and responsibilities may be appropriate for large entities, but for a small business, this type of structure may impede effective operations and the necessary flow of information. A key issue is to right-size the organizational structure.

The points of focus noted for this principle include:

- Considering all components (lines of business, administrative functions, locations, and use of service organizations) of the entity.
- Establishing reporting lines and flows of information.
- Defines authorities and responsibilities and limits.

When an organization is unnecessarily complex, with multiple subsidiaries, many related party linkages, and loose management and controls, this environment is ripe for fraud and inappropriate management override and self-dealing. Questions from third parties, such as SEC comments or regulators, regarding organizational structure, management roles, and possible conflicts of interest are warning signs that these conditions may be evidence of or may lead to fraud or malfeasance.

> Prior to a large corporate bankruptcy, the SEC inquired as to why the structure of the business included numerous subsidiaries that seemingly served no purpose. The comment letter was still unaddressed when the company declared bankruptcy. After the bankruptcy, it was determined that related party transactions were improperly accounted for in recent and prior periods; and provided false comfort to users of the financial reports about the viability of the business. It was also determined that management override reduced the effectiveness of existing controls.

The assignment of authority and responsibility may include:

- The establishment of reporting relationships and authorization procedures.
- The degree to which individuals and groups are encouraged to use initiative in addressing issues and solving problems.

- The establishment of limits of authority.
- The maintenance of job descriptions and terms of service for externally sourced personnel (e.g., agreements with service organizations). This could also relate to Principle 4, Competence.
- Policies describing appropriate business practices (see also Control Activities Principle 10 and Control Environment Principle 1).
- Resources provided for carrying out duties.
- The definition of the role of internal auditors and monitoring this to ensure implementation.

Whatever the size of the entity, these considerations are relevant to the entity.

Alignment of authority and accountability is often designed to encourage individual initiative, within limits. While delegation of authority means surrendering central control of certain business decisions to lower levels of management, those are the people who are closest to everyday business transactions. With proper oversight and monitoring, this can be an effective organizational structure. Monitoring is more critical when authority and responsibility for day-to-day transactions are widely delegated within the organization.

A critical challenge is to delegate only to the extent required to achieve objectives. Doing this requires ensuring that risk acceptance is based on sound practices for identifying and minimizing risk, including sizing risks and weighing potential losses versus gains in arriving at good business decisions.

Another challenge is encouraging all personnel to understand the entity's objectives. It is desirable that each individual knows how his or her actions interrelate and contribute to achievement of the objectives. Without such understanding, issues and problems that should be identified and addressed in a timely manner can be overlooked.

The control environment is greatly influenced by the extent to which individuals recognize that they will be held accountable. This holds true all the way to the chief executive officer, who should be accountable to the board of directors and who has the ultimate responsibility for all activities within the organization, including the internal control system. This element has cross relationships with Principles 16 and 17, Monitoring, as well as Control Environment Principle 1.

PRINCIPLE 4: COMMITMENT TO ATTRACT, DEVELOP, AND RETAIN COMPETENT INDIVIDUALS IN ALIGNMENT WITH OBJECTIVES

Competence should relate to the knowledge and skills necessary to accomplish tasks that define an individual's job. Commitment to competence includes management's consideration of the competence levels for particular jobs and how those levels translate into requisite skills and knowledge.

Competence is an attribute that is assessed based on the company and its operating environment. The controller of a small company with a simple operating environment may be fully capable of meeting the accounting and reporting needs of that business, but the person's experience and training might not support his or her serving in that role in a large, complex SEC reporting business environment.

The points of focus regarding this principle include:

- Establishing competence policies and practices.
- Evaluating competence and addressing deficiencies.
- Attracting, developing, and retaining competent employees (and contract workers from outsourcing companies).
- Planning for succession.

While this may be a judgment call, signs of competence problems are usually visible if they are looked for. In the context of the controller position, problems include:

- Frequent or significant corrections in accounting and reporting matters.
- Auditors discover significant adjustments to accounting records.
- Failure to obtain or maintain professional licenses and meet continuing professional education (CPE) requirements.
- Frequent reliance on consultants and auditors to address somewhat routine accounting issues.

A small public company hired a controller with industry but not SEC experience. To support the controller, additional resources were brought on board to address SEC reporting issues, and a training program involving an outside vendor was put in place to help the controller become proficient with the reporting requirements and SEC literature.

What could have been rated a severe deficiency due to a competence issue was mitigated by the additional resources and the implemented training program.

HR policies and practices affect an entity's ability to employ sufficient competent personnel to accomplish its goals and objectives. HR policies and practices include an entity's policies and procedures for hiring, orienting, training, evaluating, counseling, promoting, compensating, and taking remedial action. In some entities, the policies may not be extensive, but they should nevertheless exist and be communicated. For example, in a smaller entity, senior management may make explicit his or her expectations about the type of person to be hired to fill a particular job and may even be active in the hiring process. Unfortunately, some form of formal documentation is expected when regulations or audit standards seek documentary evidence that a policy is in place and operating effectively. While COSO originally did not require written documentation, the 2013 revisions made a clarification to address audit and Sarbanes-Oxley (SOX) concerns. Therefore, entities that wish to be able to demonstrate controls assessments to third parties (or auditors) need to consider documentation of competencies sought in such situations.

Standards for hiring the most qualified individuals, with emphasis on educational background, prior work experience, past accomplishments, and evidence of integrity and ethical behavior, demonstrate an entity's commitment to competent and trustworthy people. Hiring practices that include formal, in-depth employment interviews and informative and insightful presentations on the company's history, culture, and operating style send a message that the company is committed to its people.

Personnel policies that communicate prospective roles and responsibilities and that provide training opportunities indicate expected levels of performance and behavior. Rotation of personnel and promotions driven by periodic performance appraisals demonstrate the entity's commitment to advancement of qualified personnel to higher levels of responsibility. Competitive compensation programs that include bonus incentives serve to motivate and reinforce outstanding performance. Disciplinary actions send a message that violations of expected behavior will not be tolerated.

Some issues involving competence may also involve HR issues (hiring, training, etc.), and an issue identified may be a competence issue and may also involve a control environment issue. For example, deliberately seeking lesser levels of competence than required for the position and salary may be a way for management to control or intimidate employees. Consequently, such issues may be assigned to more than one category in your assessment. In the COSO Framework, issues often may not neatly fall into only one principle, but the important thing is that they be assessed and considered. In some cases it may be appropriate when using a formatted tool to cross reference an issue that could be assessed in one place or another in your documentation to where it is actually addressed to avoid repeating the assessment and to help reviewers and auditors follow the documentation better and identify the relationships.

Common sources of evidence regarding this principle include a full review of HR policies and procedures and seeking some evidence that the policies and documented procedures are actually in place. Seeking more evidence, such as when high reliance on controls is sought, would perhaps lead to interviews or group discussions. The absence of contrary evidence is also a consideration. Lawsuits and allegations from the hotline or from active or settled cases could belie the effective implementation of policies. Accountants are likely to be particularly sensitive to indications that accounting supervisory and clerical staff might not be properly trained or of the proper background for their assigned responsibilities.

Auditors and corporate project team members may be reluctant to criticize the quantity or quality of accounting resources and leadership, even when called for, since auditors have to work with these individuals in the audit process. However, not addressing the issue usually does not lead to a resolution and often just delays the inevitable. Failing to note such deficiencies can be a source of business risk to the auditor since professional standards require communication of deficiencies that are significant or material. In addition, ignoring the issue leads to continuing risk that a problem will arise that may not be detected in a timely manner. Concrete examples of delays in processing or errors discovered can help support observations and judgments. Research has shown that deficiencies are rated more severely when there is an accompanying misstatement of some magnitude,[3] although theory states that a misstatement need not be present for a deficiency to be rated as severe (significant deficiency or material weakness). In most cases the communication can be accompanied with some remediation suggestions that can make the communication less of a pure criticism. Some auditing vendor products provide sample deficiency citations that can be modified for the particular circumstances.

PRINCIPLE 5: THE ORGANIZATION HOLDS INDIVIDUALS ACCOUNTABLE FOR THEIR INTERNAL CONTROL RESPONSIBILITIES IN THE PURSUIT OF OBJECTIVES

When viewed as a whole, the control environment is highly dependent on every key person having controls awareness. Controls are not likely to be effective if thought of as the controller's problem. Every individual in an organization has some role in implementing internal control, and these roles and responsibilities will vary.

Points of focus for this principle are that the entity:

- Enforces accountability.
- Establishes performance benchmarks and rewards based on performance.
- Actively reconsiders the performance and rewards structure.
- Looks for excessive pressures that may deteriorate performance or encourage fraud.
- Rewards or disciplines individuals.

Some of these points may also relate to the flawed implementation of incentives associated with fraud risk (Principle 8).

Management and governance need to follow through when controls significantly fail or employees perform very poorly. An organization that fails to set a tone that shows there will be consequences when performance fails to meet expectations in essence neuters the stated policies and creates a paper-tiger mentality despite all the bluster that the policies and management may imply. Others in the organization are often affected when obvious problems are ignored. Subordinates and peers can become complacent or cynical, and their work may also be affected.

---

[3] Bedard, J., and L. Graham. 2011. Detection and severity classification of Sarbanes-Oxley Section 404 internal control deficiencies. *The Accounting Review* 86 (3): 825–855.

An entity hired an information technology (IT) specialist into a leadership role. She had not worked in the practice end of IT in some years. After the initial honeymoon period, she began to fail to deliver promised project output, became visibly absent when on business trips, and submitted some questionable expense reports. Questions also were raised about her competence regarding current technology and whether she was growing in that knowledge over time. She became abusive and defensive when questioned about her poor work habits and other concerns. She generously spread around blame to others.

Because IT is often a difficult area to assess for general management, problems went on for a relatively long period. The consequence was that she drove capable IT subordinates and peers to become demoralized and angry and to seek positions with other companies or transfers to other positions in the organization. Eventually, the real source of the problems was crystal clear, and she was fired. The weakened department then required a complete overhaul to ensure the proper skill sets were able to meet the organizational needs.

Better oversight and early identification of the competence issues (maybe during or shortly after the hiring process) could have resulted in a much less disruptive and costly process to the organization.

Sources of evidence to support or refute adherence to this principle can be management files and records regarding disciplinary actions, issues reported via the hotline, patterns of excessive turnover in specific business functions, and issues raised in interviews or focus group discussions. Has the entity found a way to communicate that actions, and not just words, are behind the policies and procedures? What monitoring steps are taken to ensure that problems do not go on without internal identification? In that sense, Monitoring Principle 17 on evaluating and communicating deficiencies can be related to this issue of accountability.

Appendix 4A summarizes guidance on the responsibilities of those in the organization who often contribute most significantly to the effectiveness of internal control.

Important Interactions with Other Components and Principles

More than in other iterations of the COSO guidance, the interrelationship of the components and principles is stressed in this update to the Framework guidance. When analyzing deficiencies, it will be necessary to try to identify a possible root cause in order to identify relevant interactions. It does not seem possible to hard-code linkages between specific principles such that, in all cases, the linkage will hold. It really requires analysis of the deficiency to see where the linkage might be.

Suppose management was not timely in resolving an alleged ethical breach. Ethical considerations and effective implementation issues are a Principle 1 issue. If the employee did not know or understand the ethical guidelines, that is one potential principle affected. Holding individuals accountable is Principle 5, so the delay, if management was able to resolve the issue, may relate also to that issue. Did analysis of the breach indicate that management did not receive important information on a timely basis? If the information came in via the hotline, management's hotline antifraud controls (perhaps evaluated with Principle 8, Fraud Risk) might be affected. If the deficiency seemed to be a failure to receive timely information, that might imply the root of the deficiency was related to Principle 14, Internal Communication. Without careful analysis, how could you identify related components and principles?

Because this is a complex analysis and involves judgment, it may not be an effective task for junior staff to address. Knowledge of COSO as well as knowledge of the entity and ability to reason through to a conclusion may require several skills. If a dispersed responsibility, then controls and training (including review) may need to surround implementation. In all fairness, it may also be a process that not everyone will go about in the same way and/or reach the same conclusions. As with deficiencies when first studied under the AICPA guidance or the SEC/PCAOB guidance, some information sharing and team group discussion may be necessary to train individuals to be more consistent in the performance of the task. Training can follow when some limited experience is developed. I suspect this will initially be an unstructured exercise for companies and auditors alike. Disputes can be costly in terms of time and reaching correct conclusions, so there is value in developing a process and examples that can be communicated to the team. If you knew the root cause would be important, staff might be able to gather some information toward that end when the deficiency is first identified. This issue is pervasive and holds importance for every principle and component in the Framework.

Sample templates distributed with the 2013 Framework make special note of cross referencing and relating other principles and components impacted by documented deficiencies. We discuss these templates and propose other approaches in Chapter 14.

Transition to 2013 Principles

Those transitioning directly from then 1992 Framework will need to link existing documentation and controls testing to the principles and components in the new Framework. The new principles and points of focus can then be used to identify any obvious holes in the analyses conducted to date. In earlier guidance, control objectives or assertions may have been used to classify controls within components. Generally, the most accurate mapping of controls to the new guidance usually starts with the more granular descriptions and tests of the controls and then associates them with the components, then the principles, then the points of focus in the 2013 guidance. Since control objectives and assertions are often related, either may be used to ensure that all the relevant financial statement assertions are being addressed in the new documentation. My personal preference would be to use the financial statement assertions in the control activities area for the validation of the mappings and identification of any gaps. This will also help synchronize company and auditor assessments regarding the mapping and the resulting documentation, since the auditor is likely to use assertions in the auditing process.

Those transitioning from the 2006 guidance for smaller public companies (and nonpublic companies that also used that guidance to structure their assessments) will find some reshuffling of the former 20 Principles to the new 17 Principles. Presumably the fewer categories will be simpler to work with. In the control environment area, two former stand-alone principles have disappeared and been merged into other principles. The new principles have been reworded, so be careful to identify the new principles as they are now worded, with the assistance of the points of focus. The 2006 Principles that were merged are:

- *Management Philosophy and Operating Style.* This principle seems mostly encapsulated in new Principle 1, but some deficiencies can have a relation to accountability (Principle 5).
- *Human Resources.* This principle seems mostly encapsulated in the new competence principle (Principle 4).

Understanding and Awareness of Control Responsibilities

E VERY INDIVIDUAL IN an organization has some role in effecting internal control, and these roles and responsibilities will vary. Controls awareness and controls consciousness are a respected attribute of an effective control environment. This appendix summarizes guidance on the more common responsibilities of those in the organization who contribute most significantly to the effectiveness of internal control. They may also be helpful when benchmarking roles and responsibilities.

Individual	Control-Related Responsibility
Chief Executive	▪ Sets the overall tone at the top.
	▪ Establishes a management philosophy and operating style.
	▪ Oversees the selection of the board of directors without dictating the selection.
	▪ Provides leadership and direction to senior management that shapes the corporate culture.
	▪ Participates in identifying business and financial reporting risks.
	▪ Meets with senior managers to review control-related responsibilities and gains knowledge of controls and their effectiveness.
	▪ Shares with governance the responsibility for internal controls: ensures that all components of internal control are in place. With governance, ensures monitoring is in place with respect to key controls.
	▪ Serve as a role model for following ethical guidelines.

(continued)

Individual	Control-Related Responsibility
Management	■ Establishes more specific internal control procedures.
	■ Monitors and reports on effectiveness of controls.
	■ May perform some control procedures themselves as part of the monitoring function.
	■ Identify changes and risks that may affect internal control design.
	■ Serve as a role model for following ethical guidelines.
Finance Officers	■ Have primary responsibility for the design, implementation, and monitoring of the entity's financial reporting system.
	■ Provide input to the establishment of entity-wide objectives and risk assessment.
	■ Oversee liquidity and financing issues that may require financial statement disclosures.
	■ Serve as a role model for following ethical guidelines.
Board of Directors	■ Exercises oversight of top management.
	■ Understands and watches over various stakeholder interests.
	■ Is responsible for overseeing the implementation of system of internal controls.
	■ Provides guidance and oversight to management.
	■ Through oversight of the selection of management, helps define expectations for integrity and ethical values.
	■ Performs high-level objectives setting and strategic planning. Identifies impediments and risks to achieving company goals.
	■ Investigates any finance-related issues board members deem important.
	■ Defines and coordinates responsibilities with the audit committee.
	■ Exhibits independence from management and freedom from conflicts of interests.
	■ Serves as a role model for following ethical guidelines.
Audit Committee	■ Has primary responsibility for selection and retention of the independent auditors.
	■ Holds principal interactions with the independent auditors on accounting and reporting matters.
	■ Oversees how top management is carrying out its financial reporting responsibilities.
	■ Requires corrective action for internal control and financial reporting deficiencies.
	■ May investigate allegations involving management misconduct or deficiencies in competence.
	■ Identifies and takes action when top management overrides internal controls or otherwise seeks to misrepresent reported financial results.
	■ Communicates and coordinates with the board of directors.

Individual	Control-Related Responsibility
Internal Auditors	<ul><li>May document and test internal controls over financial reporting as a basis for a management assertion. When their work can be assessed as objective and competent, the independent auditor may place reliance on their work in some areas.</li><li>Directly examine internal control design and analyze deficiencies and recommend improvements.</li><li>Perform a number of monitoring functions throughout the year.</li><li>In public companies, may also identify control deficiencies that should be communicated to the independent auditor under SEC regulations.</li></ul>
Other Entity Personnel	<ul><li>Know and follow the codes of conduct, ethics policies, etc., in carrying out their responsibilities.</li><li>Perform control-related activities with due care.</li><li>Suggest improvements in the efficiency and effectiveness of controls that they are responsible for.</li><li>Communicate to a higher organizational level problems in operations, noncompliance with the code of conduct, or other violations of policy or illegal actions.</li></ul>

CHAPTER FIVE

Control Activities

I N THIS CHAPTER we examine the type of internal controls that well predated the Framework. Here we examine the controls over transactions and accounting processes. Here also is where experienced accountants and auditors feel the most comfortable—testing the operation of specific transaction controls to establish a basis for reliance. The Framework expands thinking to consider whether the risks identified that relate to stated business and financial reporting objectives have been mitigated by controls (Principle 10). In Principle 11 the important role played by information technology general controls (ITGCs) is assigned its own principle, Principle 12. Finally the transaction controls, including the financial statement close process and final accruals, are examined through Principle 13. This latter principle is comprised of numerous assessments and tests of accounts, estimates, and valuations, and that belies the assignment of just one principle to this characteristic. A great deal of time will be spent with Principle 13, so careful planning and consideration of the best way to define, walk through, and test each element will pay dividends. For those previously using the earlier frameworks, it is likely that Principle 12 will map well to the past controls assessments and tests.

 PRINCIPLE 10: SELECTS AND DEVELOPS CONTROL ACTIVITIES TO MITIGATE RISK AND ACHIEVE OBJECTIVES

The points of focus for this principle include:

- Integrate with risk assessment.
- Consider entity-specific facts.

- Determine relevant business processes—for example, assertions.
- Evaluate the mix of control activity types.
- Consider the level the control activities are applied.
- Assess the segregation of duties.

Genesis: Risk Assessment

In Chapter 2 we focused on risk assessment because it is the starting point for understanding what controls *should be* in place. The risks discussed in that chapter drive the need for controls. They may even influence your assessment of the adequacy of management's structure and organization to meet business needs and address risks, the competence of the governance function, and the competence of employees to perform their functions (control environment). Not wanting to overthrow the hierarchy of COSO or diminish the importance of the control environment, looking at risks first (early and often) can give you a better perspective for viewing all the components.

The short story for this point of focus is: How well do the entity financial reporting risks that have been identified map to the control activities? The risks should drive the implementation of controls.

A variety of methods might be used to link risks and controls. One approach includes management and staff brainstorming sessions with documentation of the linkages identified. A distinction might be made between transactional risks (e.g., purchasing, payments, cash receipts, etc.), periodic estimation, and fair valuation risks and special transaction risks (e.g., business combination, divestitures, etc.). In the transactional risks, assertions can often be the driver in linking risks and controls. Some information that might be included in a schedule or matrix of such documentation includes:

- An enumeration of the risk and reference to the risk identification source.
- Identification of what could go wrong if the control failed.
- The relevant assertion(s).
- Control description.
- Frequency of transactions.
- Magnitude of transaction values.
- Whether the control is manual, automated (computer), preventive, or detective.
- Any past issues with the control or other related controls.
- Any information systems aspects (e.g., application software and security and segregation of duties) of the transactions and controls.

Some risks that might arise from unusual transactions (e.g., business combination) or estimation of fair valuation procedures might result in special processes and controls that are separate from the usual transaction controls, but the same assertions might apply. However, some risks that might arise relating to the control environment might not be able to be tied to specific assertions, such as the risk of management override or the risks associated with a low level of governance financial expertise. These risks may require individual analysis as to what controls do or do not mitigate them and how it might be detected if an issue occurred. As an example, an engagement team made an assessment that management fraud (in some form—override, accounting policy, misclassification of accounts, etc.) was a risk due to terms in a soon-to-be-renewed debt covenant and weak financial results in the latter part of the year. Unable to tie that risk to a specific account and control, the team decided to be sure all team members were particularly alert to findings that might suggest this risk with some more attention to the accounts comprising the numerator and denominator of the current ratio, which was an important metric in the covenant. More experienced personnel were assigned to perform and oversee the work in some of the areas where this risk could be realized (e.g., comparison of lending terms to underwriting policies, estimations and allowances, and fair valuations). In addition, additional inquiries were made of employees regarding management requests that were outside normal written policy. While the transaction processing controls appeared to be effective, override circumvents the controls, which otherwise may still be effective for most routine transactions. It was also reasoned that certain normal monitoring procedures and analytics would likely identify material anomalies.

If you identify a risk related to financial reporting over which there is no control, you have a gap that needs to be filled (remediated) or the deficiency needs to be recognized and rated. There are day-to-day transactions that need to be controlled, but unusual transactions such as a merger, unique financial instrument, or a separation of a business segment for sale also should receive oversight for, say, valuation issues, which are often a source of risk in such transactions.

One other reason that generic checklists of possible controls are not effective is that each entity faces a different set of risks with different levels of associated potential magnitude and likelihood of occurrence. Industry-specific checklists may help get at the root industry-level risks, but even they are not a reliable tool for all entities. Entities in the same industry, while they may share certain broad risks, such as market demand and limited skilled pool of workers, manufacturing problems, and such, still experience different risk profiles because of policies (e.g., customer acceptance and business terms), geography, and financing structures (e.g., debt versus equity). Because of the configuration of sales locations, the accrual of tax amounts may be much more complicated and prone to risk in estimation than for other entities. For example: Location is very strong determinant of demand. In times of general real estate contraction from 2010 to 2012, some localities were simultaneously experiencing a spike in demand and house prices, often selling homes at more than the asking price. As the old real estate adage goes, it is "location, location, location!"

Plugging a gap is not necessarily difficult. If you have a weak internal tax function, you may support that function with hiring a consultant to help you accrue the taxes and determine liabilities. Just because you hired a consultant to help with a task does not mean the gap is filled. You should have some oversight and monitoring in place to ensure that the task output is appropriate (e.g., complete, accurate, etc.) for financial reporting purposes. If you do not have any way of knowing whether the work was competently performed, then you may have a competence deficiency that needs to be recognized.

Some gaps are filled by service organizations that perform functions that entities find more efficient to outsource (e.g., payroll). Even here the processes of the service organization may need to be analyzed and monitored. Even if a Standards for Attestation Engagements No. 16 (SSAE 16 or SOC 1, *Attestation of Controls Design and Implementation*) report is available from the service organization, it may not be sufficient to satisfy the assessment needs. Some issues to consider:

- Does the report just address design (Type 1) effectiveness or design and testing operating effectiveness (Type 2)? A Type 2 report is necessary to *rely* on the controls. A Type 2 report is expected for public company use.
- Does the report address the relevant ITGCs of the service organization?
- Does the report cover the required time period? Update procedures may often be necessary.
- Are issues identified in the report that might affect reliance? Reading the report and any findings is a necessary procedure, and consideration of any deficiencies cited in the report conclusions is also expected. Just obtaining a report and slapping it in the file is not sufficient.
- What are the boundaries of the report? There is usually a handoff of some sort between the entity and the service organization, and there may also be a handback to the entity of the processed data. The activities leading up to and following the handoffs to and from the service organization are the responsibility of the entity and are not covered by the service auditor's report.

Public companies for a decade now have been advised by the Securities and Exchange Commission (SEC) to include a right-to-audit clause in their contracts with service organizations. Such organizations are often reluctant to allow outsiders to review and test their systems, so it may be difficult due to distance or resistance to apply procedures to get the required assurance if a SOC report is not available. Difficulty is not an excuse. It may be that there will be insufficient evidence to support reliance on or an attestation on controls. There are no "except-for" provisions in COSO or in the auditing standards regarding internal control.

Care needs to be taken that independent auditors do not become too involved in assisting in the financial accounting process, or their independence can be impaired and can cause a recall of the opinion. Public companies have wrestled with heightened independence restrictions since the Sarbanes-Oxley (SOX) Act of 2002 was implemented. No longer can tax professionals from the independent audit firm perform or closely collaborate in the preparation of the financial statement tax accrual in public companies. Nonpublic engagements need to consider their independence restrictions on drafting financials and footnotes, preparing estimates, and making cash-to-accrual adjustments. As of this writing, an American Institute of Certified Public Accountants (AICPA) ethics rule would establish in 2015 that cash-to-accrual adjustments and preparing the financial statements and footnotes are considered nonattest services that would need to be considered when assessing independence. Independence violations are serious and may cause the reaudit of financial statements by another auditor.

Prior to the issuance in 2009 of the additional monitoring guidance by COSO,[1] an unfortunate trend was developing wherein deficiencies in controls identified at the transaction level were being dismissed or downgraded in severity because of the assumed effectiveness of monitoring ("management would catch that when they reviewed the sales reports"). In reality, this was probably not the case. This potential get-out-of-jail card excuse was played often enough to be a problem. While monitoring controls, depending on their design, can be very powerful, contemporaneous controls at the transaction level (often preventive controls) are more desirable and more likely to be effective in reducing risks. Supervisory review and monitoring are supposed to be above the transactional level of controls to ensure the controls are being applied throughout the year. Otherwise, the monitoring becomes the detailed control, and some other procedure would have to be the monitor. While a lot of words were expended in further defining what was and was not likely to be effective monitoring in the COSO 2009 release, that guidance contains a lot of good defining examples and suggestions.

Role of Assertions

Assertions have been used in financial statement auditing at the account balance and class of transactions (and disclosure) level for decades to ensure that the web of audit assurance regarding the amounts and disclosures is a complete one. While not new, assertions have been incorporated differently and sometimes not at all into the audit approaches of different independent auditing firms. Starting in 2004 for audits of public companies and in 2007 for all other nonpublic audited entities, auditors have had to use assertions extensively in the documentation of the audit process to provide linkage between assessed risks, controls, and further audit procedures. Assertions are particularly relevant to assessing controls related to the control activities component.

The value of assertions is that they can be a useful tool from which to consider the risks in accounts, transactions, and disclosures that are required in financial reporting. They were also very useful when faced with accounts where a predefined set of control objectives had not been developed, such as when a particular entity activity is not in the "classical" activities normally undertaken by retail or manufacturing entities. For example, control objectives relating to the securitization of a pool of mortgages of a mortgage lender were not easy to come by. Control objectives for manufactured inventory and purchases were more commonly available.

Assertions are used the same way control objectives are: to answer the question "How does the entity ensure that … ?" A blessing about the assertions approach applied to specific account or balance control activities is that it:

---

[1] Committee of Sponsoring Organizations. *Internal Control—Integrated Framework: Guidance on Monitoring Internal Control Systems*, three volumes. COSO, 2009.

- Will help you identify the most important controls related to the processes.
- Is the same for each category of transaction—balances, income items, and disclosures, so those working on the project will become familiar with these assertions, since they will be using them all the time.
- Is more likely to be easily related to the audit approach followed by the independent auditor, since the auditor uses these concepts in the audit of the financial statements.

Home grown assertions and objectives may be more difficult to relate to the auditor's approach, but the SEC makes clear that companies do not have to follow any direction from the auditor as to what approach they should use for their assessment project. Nevertheless, using assertions can save you the extra service time and fees for the auditor to link your approach to the auditor's tools.

The assertions in Figure 5.1 were adapted from the recently implemented AICPA literature. There are other assertion schema out there, and you may also use them for documenting your controls, but if they are not coordinated with your auditor's methodology, the auditor will have to map your assertions to those used in his or her audit process. You may wish to ask your auditor in advance which assertions are used unless you have a strong preference.

For some accounts, an assertion may be unimportant, such as the *valuation* assertion over cash when cash is denominated in a single currency. In this case, the valuation assertion is generally not relevant, and it can be explained as part of the documentation and scoped out of the assessment. When the translation of currencies is necessary to prepare financial statements, the valuation assertion would be relevant.

Some entities and auditors simplify these 13 assertions into a smaller set. For example, the cut-off assertion is used to make sure that sales and costs are recorded in the proper period. The concept of the "thirty-fifth of December" is leaving the books open to advance transactions into the prior period. In other cases, the transaction cutoff date occurs before it should, pushing transactions forward from this period to the next. Some of the risks to be considered when considering the importance of cutoff include:

- Objectives to maximize reported income or shift the period of expense recognition to a later date: perhaps the current period shows a "gusher" of profit.
- Owner objectives to minimize taxes and understate taxable income.
- Sales commission plans that create incentives to move sales from period to period to maximize a salesperson's income.
- Management bonus plans based on achieving certain income-related targets.

In any case, the cutoff assertion relates to either a completeness or an occurrence problem regarding the periods involved; thus some entities and auditors do not use it, but instead reach the same place by including the cutoff issue into the two assertions when they are applied to the accounts and balances.

The Public Company Accounting Oversight Board (PCAOB) identifies five key assertions. Rights and obligations could be a subset of existence since, without ownership, the item or account would not "exist" in the context of the entity.

AICPA: AU-C 315: *Understanding the Entity and Its Environment and Assessing the Risks of Material Misstatement.*

Income Statement and Current Period Transactions

- **Occurrence.** Recorded transactions reflect events that relate to the entity and actually occurred.
- **Completeness.** All transactions that should have been recorded have been recorded.
- **Accuracy.** Amounts and other key data relating to recorded transactions were appropriately recorded.
- **Cutoff.** Transactions were recorded in the correct accounting period.
- **Classification.** Transactions were accounted for in the proper accounts.

Balance Sheet Accounts at Period End

- **Existence.** Assets, liabilities, and equity interests that are recorded actually exist.
- **Rights and obligations.** The entity owns the assets, and the liabilities are obligations of the entity.
- **Completeness.** All assets, liabilities, and equity interests that should have been recorded have been recorded.
- **Valuation and allocation.** Assets, liabilities, and equity interests are accurately reflected in the financial statement. Any accounts requiring valuation assessments (e.g., allowances for uncollectible accounts, product warranty costs, etc.) or cost allocation adjustments (e.g., variances assigned to inventory, shared costs of separately reported product lines) are appropriately recorded.

Presentation and Disclosure in the Financial Statements

- **Occurrence and rights and obligations.** Transactions that were disclosed actually pertain to the entity.
- **Completeness.** All required disclosures are made in the financial statements
- **Classification and understandability.** These assertions are derived from the FASB Concepts Statements, and note that the presented financial information (including the footnotes) are appropriately described, and that the disclosures are clearly expressed.
- **Accuracy and valuation.** Information in the financial statements is disclosed at appropriate amounts.

PCAOB: Auditing Standard No 15. *Audit Evidence*

- **Existence or occurrence** – Assets or liabilities of the company exist at a given date, and recorded transactions have occurred during a given period.
- **Completeness** – All transactions and accounts that should be presented in the financial statements are so included.
- **Valuation or allocation** – Asset, liability, equity, revenue, and expense components have been included in the financial statements at appropriate amounts.
- **Rights and obligations** – The company holds or controls rights to the assets, and liabilities are obligations of the company at a given date.
- **Presentation and disclosure** – The components of the financial statements are properly classified, described, and disclosed.

FIGURE 5.1 Assertions adopted by the AICPA and PCAOB

A few entities and their auditors may further simplify the assertion schema and use the next four assertions for all the balance sheet, income statement, and disclosure applications:

1. Completeness.
2. Existence.
3. Accuracy.
4. Valuation.

As long as the concepts behind the 13 assertions can be mapped into any proposed subset, alternative approaches with fewer assertions may be an efficient and effective alternative for documenting controls. You may need to be alert that when using such an abbreviated set of assertions, the terms may be applied slightly differently in each of the areas, but the overall simplification may still make it worth considering fewer assertions. Note that as the assertions are collapsed, the processes and controls relevant to each assertion can increase. In the cutoff example, the controls over year-end cut off may now be assigned to one or to two of the related assertions. That can increase the volume and complexity of documentation under each assertion. Again, I suggest that the approach of the client and the auditor be as much in sync as possible to facilitate an efficient audit.

Assertions versus Control Objectives

Important to the discussions regarding controls documentation and assessment is the driving force in the COSO Framework that defines the direction of the documentation and assessment. COSO documentation is driven by answering the questions "How does the entity achieve the control objective?" or "How does the entity ensure that the assertions of completeness, accuracy, and so on are achieved?"

As such, simply checking off boxes relating to descriptions of controls that are in place is not likely to result in an effective compliance with COSO unless those controls are also linked to the assertions underlying the accounts and processes and the controls demonstrate adequately meeting all those assertions. Extensive narratives of the whole accounting process from soup to nuts is nice but may result in a lot of unnecessary documentation that will need to be maintained annually, and the control aspects included in such documentation often get lost in the large files. Having an inventory of controls or risks is not inherently bad, so long as the list is used as a completeness check on your entity assessment and not as a census of controls or risks.

The 1992 COSO Framework introduced the concept of using *control objectives* to focus attention on the effective operation of the controls and not just the process itself. Control objectives prompt the respondent to answer *how* the entity processes and procedures achieve the framework-defined control objectives. For example, this is a sample control objective related to cash disbursements:

How do you ensure that disbursements are approved and accurately made out to the correct payee or vendor?

This approach was a revolutionary concept. Instead of starting with a checklist of controls, the COSO approach started with asking *how* this entity achieved the objective. The approach acknowledges that there are many ways to accomplish the objective and realizes that no complete checklist of required or suggested controls would ever be sufficient to meet all business situations. It also forced the assessor to think about the controls the company had in place and how they related to the objective. In the 1992 Framework, some control objectives related to purchasing and expenses were illustrated. In the 2006 COSO guidance for smaller companies, the control objectives (called *attributes* in this document) for another major cycle, revenues, were illustrated.

However, this approach required that the control objectives for an account, balance, or class of transactions or disclosure needed to be stated. A weakness of the concept is that there was no complete and recognized inventory of control objectives for every process and account.

The revised 2013 Framework shifts emphasis to the financial statement assertions. That does not negate the use of assertions but focuses more attention on an approach that has wide acceptance and current use in business practice and when all the assertions are considered together pretty much cover the waterfront of possible risks. To the assertions you would need to add the consideration of segregation of duties, and you would then have a pretty consistent and limited set of criteria to apply to each process, account, or disclosure. Sometimes an assertion might not be relevant to a particular business process, but that can then be put to the side with an explanation. A common example would be the currency valuation assertion in the cash account when all transactions are denominated in a single currency. Multinational businesses would have to consider the valuation assertion because of transactions in different currencies.

In this book we will make the conversion to assertions. If you wish to continue to use control objectives, then it may be helpful to link them to the assertions in your documentation as a check that you have addressed all the relevant assertions in your control activities assessment.

There is also a cost associated with primarily using assertions. The cost is that in thinking through how your controls ensure the population is complete, there may not be a one-to-one correspondence between an assertion and a control. Therefore, the assertion of completeness may be associated with a number of control procedures along the way of transaction processing. When ensuring that all cash received is posted and deposited and is reflected in the bank statements, a number of controls and reconciliations are often involved. In a sense the control objectives approach sometimes had a similar issue, but because more control objectives often were defined than there are assertions, sometimes there were fewer multiple controls underlying many of the control objectives. In some cases more than one assertion may have been contained in a control objective, as in the previously noted objective: How do you ensure that disbursements are approved and accurately made out to the correct payee or vendor? On balance, the focus on assertions is often simpler since it is consistently applied to each account or balance or disclosure and more likely to reveal any gaps in controls that could lead to a misstatement.

The focus on principles and points of focus in the 2013 Framework may also obviate the need to create detailed control objectives directed at the control environment, risk assessment, and monitoring. The assertions seem most applicable to the types of controls described in the control activities (transactions) and information and communication components.

If converting to assertions or adding assertion indications to current documentation, a sample of some control objectives by account and cycle and their linkage to assertions is provided in Appendix 5A. As stated, you may continue to use control objectives for assessment and documentation so long as you assess there are no gaps in the objectives. Some governmental financial reporting audit objectives are cited by the Government Accountability Office (GAO) in the *Financial Auditing Manual*, which is posted at www.gao.gov. That publication contains Specific Control Evaluation (SCE) forms and Account Risk Analysis (ARA) forms. Some examples are included at the end of the 300 Section in that document.

Accounts versus Transaction Cycles

There are two basic approaches that are used to organize the documentation and assessment of transaction-based control activities: by financial statement account or by transaction cycles (business process activity). A financial statement approach defines the work unit according to the individual financial statement account (e.g., cash, accounts receivable, accounts payable, etc.). Under that organization, one person on the team might be responsible for the controls relating to cash, a second would take on accounts receivable, and so forth. This approach is how some auditors organize their financial statement audits.

The second approach defines the work unit according to the transaction cycle (e.g., Sales > Receivables > Cash Collections, or Purchasing > Accounts Payable > Cash Disbursements). Under this approach, a team may take responsibility for a whole cycle. Often the best way to organize an assessment of internal control is by cycles for the simple reason that this is the way companies organize themselves. Companies don't organize themselves according to the balance sheet—you won't find a vice president of fixed assets or accrued expenses. Companies organize themselves around their business activities, so you will likely find a person in charge of purchasing, for example, or sales. In addition, the cycle approach allows for a more integrated understanding of the processes and controls surrounding related accounts and balances. This minimizes the risk that some control aspects or risks will fall between the chairs since one person is looking at the related parts and how the controls and software relate to each other through the cycle. It also facilitates walk-throughs to confirm the control descriptions, as they often are most efficiently performed when they follow a transaction through a number of controls.

Be aware that the *business process owner* (sales manager, purchase department manager, etc.) will be a key contact person during your engagement, and your project may be much simpler for everyone to understand and execute if you organize your control activities documentation around the company's cycles and business processes.

Mix of Controls Types and Levels of Application

COSO has always made the distinction between *preventive* controls and *detective* controls, and expressed the view that a combination of these types of controls are often more effective than utilizing just one type of control. A simple illustration of the difference in these controls is a department store inventory. A preventive control against shrink (theft or loss) is the use of tags that need to be deactivated at the register before merchandise leaves the premises. Devices monitor the exits and sound an alarm when an active tag passes the exit point. How totally effective this is may not be clear (you have all seen the employees waving people through), but it is a deterrent. A detective control would be the taking of a physical inventory, which can identify losses when compared to the perpetual inventory records that are maintained. For many items of inventory, both types of controls are common.

There are trade-offs for each approach. *Preventive* controls help ensure that errors never enter the accounting records to begin with. However, to design and perform fully effective preventive controls at each step in the processing stream may be very costly. *Detective* controls may sometimes be cheaper to design and perform. For example, performing a reconciliation once a month between the general ledger and a subsidiary ledger may be more efficient than performing preventive controls on each transaction at each step in the process. However, the drawback to detective controls is that they are performed after the fact, and sometimes well after the fact. The lack of timely performance of a detective control could mean that errors remain in the accounting records for extended periods of time, and may distort interim reporting or management reports. Most systems rely on a combination of preventive and detective controls, and it is common to build some redundancy into the system, in which more than one control meets the same objective.

Neither COSO nor auditing standards mandate the proportion of preventive and detective controls. That decision rests with the entity based on efficiency and effectiveness. Presumably, the nature and potential magnitude of the underlying risk issue the control is meant to address influence the design. To continue in the department store example, the high-value jewelry department might be subject to more frequent physical inventory counts than the garden tools department due to the higher potential magnitude and risk of loss.

Preventive and detective controls do share one important point in common. Both types of controls need to have both an error detection and a correction component to be effective. The fact that a control procedure can identify an error does not make the control effective. It is the process of communicating identified errors to individuals who can then make corrections that makes the control complete.

It may not be reassuring, but there are few, if any, examples of companies or auditors being strongly criticized because entity controls design was not both "belt and suspenders." While not a worrisome entity issue, analysis of the risks and exposures will often suggest the most effective and efficient approach to addressing the risk—whether it be a *preventive* or *detective* control, or both in some combination.

Since the 1992 Framework, the existence of automated controls and edit routines as a part of transaction processing has become pervasive. Many entities subject to SOX that have sophisticated software systems assisting with transaction processing have actively sought to build controls, exception reports, automated reconciliations, and monitoring features into the systems and decrease the number of manual control procedures. As discussed further under Principle 11, automated controls have the advantage of consistent operation (provided they were implemented correctly) when IT general controls (e.g., security and access, and system change controls) are operating effectively. This reduces the number of tests required to ensure such controls and control exception reports are operating reliably because human error is taken out of the equation. Even some basic programs can identify transactions outside certain normal ranges of amounts or transactions that do not balance or involve illogical accounts or subsidiary and general ledger amounts that do not reconcile. While the motivation of public companies may have been cost reductions, there are benefits to all entities to have systems apply logic to identify anomalous issues for follow-up. Since computers can rarely resolve anomalies, human involvement is often still needed to make sure the identified issues are properly resolved. More discussion on this point and the implications for testing automated controls is under the testing of controls in Chapter 8.

Segregation of Duties

The assessment of potential segregation of duties issues is a critical part of the controls assessment process. In a sense, it is akin to another assertion. It needs to be considered throughout the assessment of the various processes and controls, as well as at the management level and even for the various IT positions. Here the focus is not on the control itself but on who is performing that control and what other responsibilities that person has that might create a risk. Note that there is nothing that grants IT specialists special dispensation from the temptations of self-benefit that we associate with other personnel.

The intent of assigning different people the responsibilities of authorizing transactions, recording transactions, and maintaining custody of assets is to reduce the opportunities for any person to be in a position to both initiate transactions and approve them or to conceal errors or irregularities in the normal course of his or her duties. Designing an appropriate segregation of duties is often a challenge for smaller business entities with few personnel. The issue often arises surrounding any account involving cash or asset controls (protecting the list of payables from theft is not a common risk). The concept also extends to the IT environment, where IT professionals are often given broad powers of system access for periods of time (sometimes without limitation) and where the absence of systems logs might make it difficult to identify if unauthorized changes were made to system databases or transaction processing.

While some vendors and auditing firms have developed proprietary automated tools and approaches designed to identify potential segregation of duties issues in entities, a healthy internal review of what could go wrong as well as an analysis of who has access to what as it relates to company assets is likely to identify the main conflicts. Seeking to understand who can initiate and approve a transaction or authorize a payment may provide an initial assessment of potential conflicts. Even when segregation of duties could be a problem, there are often some easy fixes to reduce the risk. Significant and frequent oversight of the bookkeeper's actions can mitigate many of the risks in small organizations.

Sometimes smaller entities feel helpless to resolve segregation of duties problems because of the lack of a large staff. Experience shows that a careful analysis and some willingness for executive involvement and more frequent oversight in the controls process can resolve many of the seemingly impossible situations. Companies are also instituting more automated controls (e.g., vendors must be in the preapproved vendor database before the transaction is processed) to reduce the human error factor and to better control the processes.

PRINCIPLE 11: SELECTS AND DEVELOPS GENERAL CONTROLS OVER TECHNOLOGY

Principle 11 brings to the forefront the significant role computer processing plays in today's environment. The 1992 Framework had but a single section devoted to information technology. Now IT is pervasively associated with 14 of the 17 Principles. General controls are distinguished from application controls. The latter are associated with specific pieces of software that process the accounting data. General controls are those that operate at the level above specific application (software specific) controls. It is usual to assess the application controls in conjunction with the associated transaction or account controls. General controls can be examined apart from application controls (except for security and access which can be implemented at either level). However, general control failures are likely to cast concern over the underlying application controls and can undermine the reliance on a control to continuously perform as described and tested in the same way over time.

The points of focus for this principle include:

- Determines the dependency between use of technology in business process technologies and ITGCs.
- Establishes relevant technology infrastructure controls.
- Establishes relevant security management controls.
- Establishes relevant technology acquisition, development and maintenance.

Determining Dependency

A characteristic of the 2013 Framework is the integration of computer systems, programs, and technology-based controls throughout the principles. Most of the principles mention some aspect of computer processing or computer controls in their discussions of examples and approaches relevant to meeting the various principles. Noteworthy is the identification of a specific principle related to ITGCs.

You need to map how the various accounting functions and information feeds for the disclosures interface with various entity computer programs, standing data files, and other aspects of the systems. It is difficult to envision an entity of any real size that does not place significant dependency on its programs, networks, and systems for generating and storing important accounting information and for transmitting that information to individuals who will use it in performing their duties. This task can be done as a systems or an accounting project.

The documentation also needs to be maintained and updated as new software, spreadsheets, and software versions are added or changed over time. While performing this mapping, the auditor should think carefully about whether some of the production systems also provide financial information or management reports and may need to be scoped into the assessment. For example, quality control data that might influence warranty accruals or returns and allowances estimates may have a tangential accounting role. Data management uses to manage the business, if unreliable, can expose the entity to risks (Principles 13 and 14: relevant information and internal communication). Flowcharts and diagrams can often provide the needed mappings in a concise and efficient manner. Even without a specific flowcharting tool, PowerPoint may serve the needs of many smaller entities.

A frequently overlooked risk is that some accounting functions are performed outside the main systems and software. In many entities, users develop financial information using spreadsheets. Not often thought of as software, the spreadsheets can serve in that capacity and should be inventoried and evaluated as to risk and controls as would any other software function. A few horror stories are usually sufficient to convince all concerned that important uses of such "software" should be properly controlled and documented and protected against accidental or deliberate unauthorized change. Scott Adams, the *Dilbert* cartoon creator, has published quite a few cartoons around this topic. A good motivational resource for getting the attention of all concerned about spreadsheets is the Web site of the European Spreadsheet Risks Interest Group dedicated to documenting spreadsheet anomalies and dangers: www.eusprig.org/index.htm. Further, academic research has documented the high proportion of spreadsheet applications that contain errors of one sort or another (see http://panko.shidler.hawaii.edu/SSR/Mypapers/whatknow.htm). As mentioned in Chapter 8, PricewaterhouseCoopers in 2004 released a whitepaper on spreadsheet applications as used in accounting. It is recommended that project leaders download this helpful guide and heed its guidance.

Spreadsheets that are integral in financial reporting should have:

- Specifications and documentation explaining the spreadsheet.
- Controls over development.
- Tests of the spreadsheet functions and calculations before use.
- A version designation to track changes and identify the latest version.
- Protected cells, when appropriate.
- Controls over access and controls over changes to the functions.

Once the detail linkages between programs and accounting functions are made, the relationships between the application software and controls and the ITGCs also need to be established.

The purpose of ITGCs is not to process data but to ensure the integrity of the overall system of programs and applications. As such, weaknesses in the ITGCs may not themselves cause errors and misstatements but may allow them to happen or go undetected. While we discuss these ITGCs in more detail in the next section, a simple example here would be the need to assess how access and security (e.g., passwords, permissions), which are important ITGCs, protect standing data from unauthorized changes and restrict access to accounting programs to those individuals who need to access them to perform their duties. If security and access controls are poor, that does not mean errors will occur in the system, but the poor design or implementation *could* allow errors to occur. An analogy here is the proverbial horse and barn door. If the door is open and the horse is free to leave, that does not mean the horse will venture out, but there is no barn door impediment to prevent that from happening. The risk is the same, regardless of the actions of the horse.

What Are ITGCs?

There exists a framework for considering IT-related controls that groups these controls into two types: general computer controls and application-specific controls. This framework has been adopted in the auditing literature.

1. *General controls* include controls over:
   - Access and security.
   - Systems development and modification.
   - Operations (e.g., maintenance, job scheduling, backup, and disaster recovery procedures).
2. *Application controls* are designed to control data processing and help ensure the completeness and accuracy of transaction processing, authorization, and validity. Application controls also encompass the way in which different applications interface with each other and exchange data. Examples of applications include a fixed asset depreciation program, and an application control could be an edit check to ensure certain anomalies are identified in the processing of data or in making computations. Application controls are those that directly relate to the software used to process transactions and the standing data (such as price lists, payroll data, and product cost data) that the software applications use. In simple systems such as QuickBooks and in higher-end systems such as SAP, the controls (e.g., edit checks, permitted functions, requirement to enter debits and credits of equal sums) that are inherent in the software or are implemented optional features fall under this term.

COSO does not mandate any specific procedure or approach when assessing the effectiveness of these internal controls but states that this is one set of groupings of IT-related control activities that can be used. The significance of the IT component to the overall process will drive the level of inquiry and testing necessary to be satisfied that the applications are processing data correctly and that general controls create an environment of integrity and control for these applications.

Technology has implications for most framework components and principles. In control activities, for example, the individual controls may be automated controls, such as when software is used to record and classify financial transactions and some control features are part of the software, such as matching purchase order, invoice, and proposed cash disbursement amounts. Another aspect that relates to communications is the use of networks and standing data files (e.g., sales records, payroll records, inventory records) to generate and distribute reports to those that need the information to perform their duties. Monitoring is usually dependent on IT to provide management access to information and data that are needed to perform this function. It is hard to imagine the effective management and governance of a company without effective systems and software and timely, accurate, and relevant reports.

An argument can be made that this topic is so broad in influence that it cannot be uniquely assigned to any single COSO component. Nevertheless, it needs to be resident somewhere, and the close association of ITGCs with transaction processing leads to the area of control activities as a logical resting point. Wherever its position, the important point is that its influence in some entities is critical and pervasive and in others it takes a more passive, lesser role. One-size-fits-all is not appropriate as an approach to documenting and assessing IT application or general controls.

In the 1992 COSO Framework guidance, relatively little was said about IT, but by 2006 many questions were raised with the prerelease COSO working group about how to assess IT controls and by what set of standards IT should be assessed. The final 2006 COSO guidance provided expanded guidance in this area and a sample template to assist the documentation and assessment of IT issues.

General controls say something about the overall IT environment in which the applications lie. These aspects of IT controls have a "control environment" component that has its own tone at the top—this time focused on the IT function and its specific environment. The four components of ITGC commonly mentioned in the auditing literature are:

1. Security and access.
2. Change controls.
3. System development controls.
4. Operations and maintenance.

Some of these elements had more relevance and importance in older IT systems, but the auditor has to gauge to what extent these elements have application in the circumstances. For example, scheduling was an important part of operations in mainframe computing days because certain batch-processed files, such as the sales file, had to be updated before other files, such as the cash receipts file, could be run, and thus batch-file updates were scheduled to occur in a particular order. In today's environment, the hardware processing speeds and availability and access to data entry and processing power have made this process unnecessary. However, in some locations and situations, the old hardware and software continue to chug along.

An anomaly about ITGCs and control deficiencies is that severe ITGC deficiencies do not always give rise to significant deficiency (SD) and material weakness (MW) ratings for SOX purposes. This is because ITGCs are thought of as overarching controls over the computer software applications rather than controls over transactions and transaction processing. Only if it is observed that severe deficiencies appear in the underlying applications as a result of failed ITGCs would the ITGCs also be cited as having severe deficiencies. While the logic of this assessment anomaly might be creditable for change controls and new systems development, in my view it fails to make much sense for weaknesses in security and access controls. Security and access weaknesses would meet the recognition test in deficiency assessment if they "could" permit or allow material misstatements to occur. Some auditors believe the exception to the general rules was developed to avoid generating too many MWs early in the SOX assessment implementation period. Because the new COSO Framework has now identified general controls as a principle that must be satisfied, the prior guidance regarding ITGCs may be obsolete. Should this issue be important to a project or audit, it would be prudent to review any new interpretive guidance on this point or seek confirmation that prior guidance still holds. Anecdotal evidence exists of more instances appearing of weak ITGCs generating a severe weakness even in the absence of an identified weakness in a related application control.

Again, outsourcing functions involving IT does not excuse the entity from ensuring the service organization exercises proper ITGC in its operations. A service organization report on an outsourced computer process (e.g., SOC No. 1) should include a review of the general controls at the vendor site.

Security and Access

The security and access component is probably the most critical for the entity and for SOX. It is also the IT element most likely to reveal weaknesses. It was high on the list of identified deficiency areas (even when compared to the control activities component) in the early years of implementing audits of internal control—and that was for the largest and presumably best-controlled commercial entities. As noted in Chapter 10, deficiencies tend to be of the same nature when examined over time. The good news is that it is often one of the easiest deficiencies to overcome, provided it is identified in time to make remediation.

Security and access are what they say: They involve permitting individuals to access all the information and only the information needed to do their jobs, or as authorized by the entity. Sure, let whomever view and edit your payroll data records—no problem. Better yet, give someone access to your whole system and let them initiate transactions, create employees, or change payroll data and schedule payments. Not only are there state and federal privacy laws that can expose your entity to significant fines for revealing certain personal identifying information (PII) that may be in these files, but the risk of fraud and misstatement soars as access and security deficiencies increase. The simple use of effective passwords, the securing of the computer hardware in a restricted access location, and the maintenance of information in protected files can go a long way to reducing the risks in a smaller entity. It is amazing to see the number of instances where passwords are placed on sticky notes pasted to the side of the screen or on the pull-out writing shelf on the desk, have gathered dust from being passed down from bookkeeper to the next bookkeeper, or are set to the word *password*. Don't be so sure that insiders and outsiders are not interested in your data. For example, foundation's list of contributors and their contact information can have value in the marketplace to other similar organizations. In any case, deficiencies are often easy to fix here without heroic costs or efforts. Passwords can be set up to better ensure a segregation of duties and to meet published standards (e.g., see ISO/IEC 27001 and 27002) commensurate with the risks associated with the data.

Change Controls

In entities that use today's simple packaged systems, the idea that users will request program changes of IT department programmers, based on past home-grown computer programs, is not as relevant as when entities built and maintained their software. There can still be features and controls that can be enabled or disabled, but the options are often limited. But in custom-built systems, such changes are still relevant and may be important. This element of ITGCs focuses on the initiation, approval, programming, testing, and user acceptance of changes to systems. In the absence of such controls, unanticipated changes may be introduced into the system that adversely affect other parts of the software, may result in data loss, or may result in changes that increase the risk of fraud. A related concept that is relevant for smaller entities is the upgrade of the application software or migration to a new operating system or platform. How do you ensure that the new program will perform as well as the old version and that any data incompatibilities are resolved? When users in smaller entities skip numerous updates to the software, simple transitions may not be possible. Imagine trying to transfer the data from a decades-old DOS version of accounting software to a current Windows version. Will it work? Do you know? How can you be sure?

This element of ITGCs is only relevant when there are changes in the programs and systems during the period. Unlike security and access controls, which are always and continuously relevant, the controls over the change process can be observed and assessed only when changes occur. Thus, it is important to be able to identify when and where the change process occurs. For entities where program changes and new systems implementations are common, well-documented controls and monitoring plans should be in place to guide the modification process.

I recall the unfortunate experience of advancing *hardware* making an old home-grown, but still useful, software program obsolete. A statistical sampling program, developed in the 1970s and updated in the 1980s, started to offer challenges because modern printers could not print the data output. Unfortunately, the program code was not properly documented during the development or updating (or the documentation was never found) and would have been expensive to re-create. No programmers capable of reading its language were readily available—a situation not uncommon with legacy software. In 1999 a search was performed for a Windows-based replacement for the product; it did not exist, and so a plea was made to the "Y2K police" to approve the application if it passed the Y2K tests. Once it passed the applied Y2K tests, the expectation was that the Firm was home free. They were willing to limp through the printer issue, only to be confronted a short time thereafter with an inability of the program to *find* external data because the processor speed of the new hardware program was too fast. The solution was then to retard the speed of the processor when running this program, an illogical but the only solution until an alternative software solution could be identified. The lesson: Do not wait too long to upgrade software.

The concept here is to place controls around the processes related to the modifications so that the changes:

- Accomplish the requested (and approved) change in the software operation.
- Generate documentation (e.g., a log) of the changes made to the code.
- Avoid business interruption during the modifications.
- Mitigate the risk of data loss or problems interfacing with related data and systems.
- Ensure the function is operating effectively before going live with the revised software.

A custom testing plan that involves testing related software functions is an important step in ensuring the program is working effectively.

New Systems Development

Many large entities change their computer systems, accounting software, and so on from time to time. The idea is to make the transition safely, without a loss of data or function. An effective systems development element will have a methodology in place to handle new systems projects that will include a needs assessment, an assessment of hardware and software options, an implementation approach with backups and "undo" points to safely migrate data, and a testing function to ensure all systems are "go." In some cases, the old and new systems will be run in parallel for some time before reliance is placed on the new system.

Like change controls, this element of ITGCs is relevant only when new systems development and implementation occurs during the period, as the process can be observed and assessed only when systems development and implementation occur. Thus, it is important to be able to identify when and where this attribute applies. In some entities, such major changes are uncommon. Larger, more complex entities are continuously making changes.

A current trend in corporate and government practice is to replace older (home-grown) legacy software with commercial software that can be adapted to meet entity needs. This minimizes the need to have a small army of programmers on hand to make modifications and keep the software humming along. It puts the onus back on the vendors to continually adapt and upgrade their software to meet the continually changing hardware configurations and operating systems. In the aggregate it is cheaper to have these adaptations done centrally by the vendor rather than each entity try to make them.

Another true story concerns the large service and equipment rental business that intended to install an enterprise software solution as a Y2K-compliant replacement to a company-developed (legacy) system. A significant location's operations were targeted as the first place for the conversion. The company decided its current IT team would be up to the task of making the conversion with a minimum of training. Somewhere along the way, the receivables and customer data from the old system were lost in the conversion process near the time of the fiscal year-end. This caused fits, since by the time of releasing the financials, the system still had not been restored, and the entity had to decide if it needed to make an extra allowance for some of the tens of millions of dollars of receivables for which it could not get detailed information. The auditors were assured by the company and an outside consultant that the company at least could restore the old system. IT professionals were sure of that. Incredibly, that never happened, unfortunately, and the company had to use very expensive and time-consuming procedures to re-create some of the data. In a later period the company realized financial losses due in part to data losses.

A competent plan for implementation should include a back-out plan in case the project is unsuccessful. Tests can be performed to verify the conceptual plan will work and to tweak any details before putting the entity at risk. While sometimes viewed as unproductive and time wasting, the downside risk here is sometimes too great to ignore such a step.

Systems development is not a do-it-yourself project, and even when competent systems people are involved, there are usually surprises and "learning opportunities." If you have an important project, make sure you have the technical assistance you need.

A structured process for planning, creating, testing, and implementing an information system called the systems development life cycle (SDLC) came into vogue in the 1960s as a methodical way to build information systems. The concept applied to hardware and/or software configurations. Since that time variants of the SDLC methodology have evolved to meet the evolving IT environment and advances in programming. For example, in the late 1980s, Coopers & Lybrand Consulting developed an adaption that focused on developing expert systems. However, the important point is that structured methodologies exist that can safely guide entities through a development project.

New systems issues are similar in some ways to the aforementioned changes in existing programs, but on a grander scale. Since more data and more software are involved, the risks are usually higher than for changes to existing programs.

Sources of evidence regarding this element (and change controls) are inquiry; review of the documented, structured approach to be followed; evidence the plan was adhered to during the development, testing and implementation phases; and the presence or absence of postimplementation adjustments or complaints.

Operations and Maintenance

Operations and maintenance cover a number of subject areas. This element encompasses the analysis and diagnosis of customer, supplier, or user IT complaints or annoyances to identify system problems of any nature. An effective function reports significant issues to management and enables the entity to take remedial actions to address the immediate situation. Another dimension covered by this element relates to backup and disaster planning functions. The incidence of deficient backup policies is very high in many businesses. The problem here is akin to the leaky roof—when it is raining, the roof cannot be fixed, and when it is not raining, there is no problem. Backups should be regularly scheduled and the backup data safely secured.

You should make a risk assessment of how critical your systems and associated data are to your entity and the accounting function (usually critical today), and use that assessment in developing some sort of disaster and recovery plan. Fires and floods happen (consider Hurricanes Katrina and Sandy), and when they do, there is no time to develop a plan. Systems and electronic data are becoming the lifeblood of many entities.

A simple plan might need only to secure a copy of the backup data and processing software off site. More elaborate plans may have hardware backup and battery capacity to address the critical entity needs.

One disaster story is about a thriving company that maintained leased equipment and software records for financial services businesses as a "service" to facilitate keeping these records updated and licenses "current." Computerized customer records and details of the key dates relating to the software *were* "the business," so fairly elaborate plans were established to make regular backups and retain them off site. In addition, backup hardware and supplies were also maintained at the secure site, to make the system as bulletproof as practical. The company's main office was destroyed in one of the buildings of the World Trade Center in the terrorist attacks of 9/11. Unfortunately, the backups were stored in the second tower of the World Trade Center. Similarly, in a broad flooding situation like Hurricane Katrina, off-site storage anywhere in the area, even miles away, can be a risk. You cannot anticipate all the possible circumstances, but you can cover the more likely disaster scenarios. IT professionals can help you develop policies and procedures for your company that are reasonable and affordable.

In the unusual case where transactions are still run in batches on mainframes (more often encountered in government applications), the order of running file updates (e.g., sales before cash receipts) may be important, and so glitches in running updates to various files would occasionally fall under this topic.

Information Systems Assessment Frameworks: COBIT and the IT Governance Institute

For the reader interested in a deeper understanding of the application of control objectives to the IT area, COBIT (Control Objectives for Information and related Technology), now in its fifth edition (www.isaca.org/cobit), was developed by the Information Systems Audit and Control Association's (ISACA). COBIT enumerates a detailed set of control objectives (over 300) tailored to the information systems environment. The COBIT framework is similar to COSO in that it puts controls within the context of specific objectives and the risks the company faces towards their achievement. Among IT audit professionals, COBIT is widely accepted as a framework for IT development, maintenance, and operations.

In defining the goals of IT governance and control, COBIT takes a rather broad brush and does not limit itself to the financial reporting process. COBIT describes three high-level goals for IT governance:

1. IT is aligned with the business, enables the business, and maximizes the benefits to the entity.
2. IT resources are used responsibly.
3. IT-related risks are managed appropriately.

For SOX purposes, which relate to the reliability of financial reporting, the third COBIT objective is most relevant. For the purposes of assessing the effectiveness of internal control over financial reporting, you typically will limit your consideration of IT-related controls to those that have a direct effect on the reliability of financial reporting and financial data.

Since COBIT is broader in scope than the focus of SOX, and many of its attributes overlap with COSO (e.g., delivery of relevant management information timely and accurately), extensive tailoring is required to efficiently use COBIT in the context of SOX requirements or to apply its concepts to nonpublic audit environments. However, if COBIT already is the benchmark to assess systems in an entity, a recent COBIT review may be used in full or part in lieu of a separate evaluation for COSO purposes.

Motivated by the need for more practical guidance to public companies in complying with the requirements to assess and report on the effectiveness of internal controls under the SOX, the IT Governance Institute issued *IT Control Objectives for Sarbanes-Oxley*, 2nd edition (2006). Many IT professionals find the guidance in COBIT to be directed to a broad IT mission and a high standard, and not as practical as the more focused guidance in the IT Governance Institute publication. Nevertheless, even the IT Governance Institute guidance contains nearly 100 control objectives. Some IT professionals believe that even this is overkill with respect to the need to assess IT as part of the SOX assessment of the effectiveness of internal controls. While readable by the non-IT specialist, to implement and assess the IT systems in a complex environment some specialist training and experience are likely to be necessary. That does not mean that you should just hand the responsibility to the IT specialist, as risks, IT issues, and control activities are so intertwined that these assessment tasks should not be sharply divided. A team approach with significant interaction and communication generally is the best one.

PRINCIPLE 12: DEPLOYS THROUGH POLICIES AND PROCEDURES

Principle 12 is where we finally get to assessing the important controls over the daily transactions and periodic accruals and the close process.

The points of focus for this principle include:

- Establish policies and procedures to support deployment of management's directives.

- Establish responsibility and accountability for executing policies and procedures.
- Perform activities in a timely manner.
- Take corrective action.
- Use competent personnel.
- Reassess policies and procedures.

Smaller entities that are simpler in structure with a simpler business model may have less documentation on policies and procedures. But adequate documentation is still expected. Often a general procedures manual will serve their purpose outlining the accounting treatment of special situations, say, advance pledge receipts, nonmonetary transactions and gifts, asset versus expense recordings, determining useful asset lives, and so on. More complex entities may have more sophisticated and detailed descriptions of procedures covering in more detail and how to address day-to-day transactions and exceptions.

Not to be forgotten here is the need to document the *controls* over processing and how they should operate, including the controls over developing estimates, determining accruals and the period-end close procedures. While these two purposes can be included in a single document, some entities with extensive process documentation in place may choose to create specific-purpose documentation separately, and tie the processes and controls together with cross references. In electronic documents, links can be developed to efficiently accomplish the cross references. There are no required formats for such documentation. Many entities find flowcharts and narratives work particularly well for documenting policies and procedures, and many also find that matrix templates are very efficient for documenting controls and how they address the relevant assertions for the accounts, balances, streams of transactions, and disclosures. In general, flowcharts are gaining in popularity for describing processes over narrative approaches, which are often criticized for being too difficult to read, comprehend, and update.

In Principle 3 we established that structure, authority, and responsibility were important elements in the control environment. To follow through, management needs to drive those elements down to the detailed transaction processing and control levels so that expectations regarding processing can be fulfilled and individuals held responsible for the timely and effective performance of their tasks. In addition, the lines of responsibility and authority need to be understood by all so that any necessary exceptions to policy or undefined situations can be properly channeled through the system for resolution. In this principle we are ensuring that the fundamental elements in Principle 3 (structure, authority, responsibility) are driven down to the level of the more detailed processes and controls. Weaknesses identified in Principle 11 could have implications for Principle 3, depending on the root causes and pervasiveness of the weakness discovered.

Mechanisms need to be in place to detect when timely and accurate processing is not occurring. These mechanisms can be as simple as ensuring that lines of communication between employees and between employees and management are kept open (e.g., access to management and proactive inquiry of management to employees about status, periodic staff meetings and forums, etc.). Analytical procedures may also alert management when unexpected variations in production or processing occur. These may be the result of programmed flags in the systems that signal events for further review and may also be a part of the monitoring function. Through continuous improvement, issues that in the past have caused problems can be monitored so that timely identification of issues is made.

At the detailed control activity level, issues that may arise may indicate that an employee is not adequately prepared to perform a task. Tracing the root issue of performance deficiencies here could result in a competency question (Principle 4) and that might also reflect on whether the human resources process used to staff the function was adequate, whether there was an improper or inadequate management specification of the position and required competencies, or whether the employee is just not able to meet the expectations of the position. Too often, new employees are thrust into a (vacant) position with a minimum of direction as to what they do and how it relates to other functions. If policies and procedures are properly written and accessible to the employee, much of the pain of learning experiences can be avoided. One thing should be clear at this point in the discussion: An incident involving Principle 12 could involve issues that involve other principles. Only in the analysis of the issue can the potential tentacles be identified.

Over time, the processes and controls may need to be modified to meet the evolving needs of the entity. The question becomes: How does the entity consider when to reconsider existing policies and controls? Feedback from issues that may arise in operations, employee suggestions, and changes in the business (e.g., a formerly insignificant line of business becomes a major line of business) will often provide clues as to when changes may be necessary. The careful attention to the issues raised in the risk assessment phase can also signal the need to change or clarify policies and practices.

SUMMING UP

Regardless of the approach you choose to follow when documenting controls, there will be a time, after scoping, after planning, and after considering the tools you intend to use, where you will be seeking either the financial statement assertions or control objectives to guide you through the COSO approach for each of the five components and 17 Principles and points of focus. Particularly in the 2006 and 2009 COSO releases and in the 2013 revision to the Framework, a significant number of approaches, examples, scenarios, points of focus, and suggestions can be helpful in designing the most efficient and effective tailored approach. In this regard, these resources together provide a rich set of guidance that can help clarify the kinds of issues that need to be addressed when assessing the principles.

Trade organizations and industry groups may publish guidance on the application of some of the Framework concepts to their unique industry characteristics, but it may take some time for that guidance to be specific to the 2013 Framework. Going forward, using financial statement assertions may have significant value in linking the Framework to unique accounts and disclosures. Assertions have proven valuable in achieving the breadth to cover the different risks that any process might face and also are relevant to the broad number of financial elements and disclosures in the project scope. Since the assertions are limited in number, they can be efficient to work with, but since they are few in number, they may prompt the documentation of numerous controls for each assertion in order to fully satisfy the assertion. For example, a number of risks could affect the valuation of inventory (e.g., obsolescence, regulation, change in demand), and the controls to address each of those risks can differ.

If you are already documenting controls using controls objectives, you may wish to continue to do so but to add the assertions to your documentation to better ensure there are no gaps. If you are "zero-basing" a revised project now that you need to integrate the 17 Principles into your assessment, you may want to experiment to see what sort of approach works best and will work best into the future. However, be aware that there is a natural bias toward retaining control objectives if the project team is not familiar with working with the assertions. Since assertions are likely to be a durable concept in the future, teams should be alert to this bias when choosing a direction. In addition, most auditors will align their assessment tools by the assertions, so it may be desirable to be on the same page to minimize the differences.

Appendix 5A provides some sample control objectives and assertions often associated with them. If you have existing control objectives, you will need to confirm the linkages with the assertions. Standardization of control objectives did not occur from previous releases, as there was never a generally accepted list of control objectives widely circulated for each account or disclosure.

Transitioning to the New Framework

Those entities following the five components under the 1992 guidance will find the control activities component here too. If control objectives and/or assertions were previously used, those elements can be mapped to the three principles by considering the various points of focus. It is possible that a full consideration of the 2013 Framework will identify some previously unaddressed control points that now need to be addressed going forward.

The 2006 COSO guidance identified four specific attributes that could be used for assessing the component:

1. *Integration with risk assessment.* Actions are taken to address risks to the achievement of financial reporting objectives.
2. *Policies and procedures.* Policies related to reliable financial reporting are established and communicated throughout the company, with corresponding procedures resulting in management directives being carried out.
3. *Information technology.* IT controls, where applicable, are designed and implemented to support the achievement of financial reporting objectives.
4. *Information needs.* Information is identified, captured, and used at all levels of a company to support the achievement of financial reporting objectives.

These attributes have now been collapsed into three principles, and the underlying control objectives and/or assertions may be the most reliable way to link the previous structure to the 2013 Framework. Attribute 1 and 2013 Principle 10 are similar. Attribute 2 and 2013 Principle 12 may address similar controls. Attribute 3 and 2013 Principle 11 may be similar. Attribute 4 may map to some controls now more associated with information and communication (Principles 13 and 14). Note that in transition, you may identify some previously unaddressed control points that may now need to be addressed going forward.

Examples of Controls

There are a variety of procedures that could be used to satisfy an attribute or control objective. While the use of checklists (yes/no) of controls is generally not an effective approach to evaluating whether a principle is being met, illustrations and examples of controls are often helpful in triggering a better understanding of how the concept works and can also be helpful as a completeness check that controls that are actually in place were documented.

Appendix 5A illustrates the linkage of sample control objectives/activities to assertions. The controls are the ones the entity asserts fully or partially satisfy the objective or principle.

Appendix 5B illustrates some of the more common interrelationships between the principles. Specific facts and circumstances will determine whether these linkages or other linkages might apply in a specific situation.

Linking Common Control Activities and Assertions

T HE 1992 *INTERNAL CONTROLS—Integrated Framework* document and the 2006 *Internal Controls over Financial Reporting—Guidance for Smaller Public Companies* document by the COSO presented sample control objectives for four of the five components (control environment, monitoring, information and communication, and risk assessment) of the COSO Framework. Control activities objectives for the cash disbursements function and for the revenues function are also illustrated in these documents.

The attached practice aid materials are provided to assist you in working with control objectives and relating them to assertions for your entity. Clearly, customization to specific industries and business circumstances is often necessary.

Readers are urged to review and consider edits and modifications to any illustrative control objectives/assertions before beginning the completion of any forms or matrices. Different assertions may be used by different entities, and a clear indication of the ones to be used in the documentation process needs to be established up front. Consider the circumstances of your application and processes first to ensure proper detail is captured without redundancy. In the examples that follow, the Public Company Accounting Oversight Board (PCAOB) assertions are illustrated. Consider:

- Completeness
- Redundancy
- Appropriate level/amount of detail

General Format

Area and Category	Control Objective	Assertions
Revenues		
Segregation of Duties	Functions with potential conflicts such as customer approval, sales, and cash receipts are segregated.	All
Sales	Prices used in recorded sales are accurate.	Valuation
Sales	Only valid sales orders are fulfilled.	Occurrence
Sales	All valid orders are processed and recorded and filled.	Completeness
Sales: Posting	Relevant information is captured and reported accurately and promptly.	Occurrence, Valuation
Sales:	A sales invoice is generated for every shipment or completed work order.	Completeness
Sales: Period	Invoices (sales) are recorded in the appropriate period.	Valuation (cutoff)
Allowances	An allowance for doubtful accounts is properly estimated.	Valuation
Shipments	Correct goods are shipped and accurately recorded.	Valuation
Shipments: Period	Deliveries are recorded and recorded in the proper period.	Valuation (cutoff)
Ownership	Recorded inventory is owned by the company.	Rights and Obligations
Cash Receipts	Cash receipts are accurately recorded.	Completeness, Existence, Valuation
Balances	The company has ownership rights to recorded cash and accounts receivable.	Rights and Obligations
Credits Issued	Credits issued are authorized and properly recorded.	Occurrence, Valuation
Credits Recorded	Credits (to accounts receivable) are accurately calculated.	Valuation
Credits Complete	All credit notes and proper adjustments to accounts receivable are recorded.	Completeness
Physical Safeguards	Physical controls over cash limit the risk of misappropriation.	Occurrence, Rights and Obligations
Financial Reporting	Postings to the general ledger are timely and accurate. Cash, receivables and related information is properly disclosed in the financial statements.	Completeness, Valuation, Disclosure
Data Files	Access to data files is restricted to authorized personnel.	All
Data Files	Approved changes to data files are recorded accurately and timely. Standing data are complete and accurate.	All

(continued)

Area and Category	Control Objective	Assertions
Purchasing and Cash Disbursements		
Segregation of Duties	Functions with potential conflicts such as vendor approval, purchasing, and payment processing are segregated.	All
Purchasing	Purchase orders and service requests are authorized, complete, timely and accurate.	Occurrence, Valuation
Receiving	All goods and services received were ordered and were processed accurately and recorded timely.	Occurrence, Valuation
Returns and Allowances	All returns and allowances are authorized, and were processed accurately and recorded timely.	Occurrence, Valuation
Invoice Processing	All invoices are promptly and accurately processed. Duplicate processing is prevented.	Occurrence, Valuation, Existence
Cash Disbursements	Payments were authorized, and associated goods or services were received and recorded in the proper period. Foreign currencies are properly recorded. Duplicate payments are prevented. Long-outstanding payments (e.g., uncashed checks) are investigated.	Rights and Obligations, Valuation Completeness
Electronic Funds Transfers	EFT authorized in advance as to amount and payee and controlled.	Valuation Existence Completeness
Physical Controls	Physical controls over cash limit the risk of misappropriation. Physical access to unsigned checks and check signature stamps or machine is controlled.	Completeness Valuation Rights and obligations
Financial Reporting	Postings to the general ledger are timely and accurate.	Valuation Presentation/Disclosure
Data Files	Access to data files is restricted to authorized personnel.	All
Data Files	Approved changes to data files are recorded accurately and timely.	All
Inventory		
Segregation of Duties	Purchasing, inventory record keeping, and physical inventory counting and physical access are segregated.	All
Transfers of Inventory	Transfers between locations or between accounting categories (raw materials, work-in-process, and finished goods) are authorized, accurate and complete. Only authorized shipments of finished goods are made.	Valuation Completeness Existence

Area and Category	Control Objective	Assertions
Quantity Verification	Physical counts are periodically taken to ensure accuracy and completeness.	Completeness Valuation
Inventory Costs	Complete and accurate records are maintained regarding product costs, including costs of each element (materials, labor, overhead) added at each stage (RM, WIP, FG) of the inventory process.	Allocation (Valuation)
Accounting Period	Proper cutoff is maintained on all goods entering or leaving the inventory system around period-end.	Completeness Existence
Accounting	Methods for assigning/allocating costs and inventory methods (LIFO, FIFO, WAM, etc.) are in accordance with GAAP and are consistently applied.	Allocation (Valuation)
Inventory Costs: *Standard Costing*	Standard costs products are updated and maintained.	Allocation (Valuation)
Inventory Costs: *Standard Costing*	Changes to standard costs are approved before implemented. Basis for the change to standard cost is documented.	Allocation (Valuation)
Inventory Costs: *Standard Costing*	Variances from standard costs and overhead charges (as applicable) are updated and applied to inventory and cost of sales in accordance with GAAP.	Allocation
Reserves and Lower of Cost or Market	Assessments are made of obsolete inventory as per GAAP and write-downs made on a timely basis. All adjustments are authorized.	Valuation
Physical Controls	Inventory is protected from loss due to theft, misuse, or physical damage.	Existence Completeness
Financial Reporting	Postings to the general ledger are timely and accurate.	Valuation Completeness
Data Files	Access to data files is restricted to authorized personnel.	All
Data Files	Approved changes to data files are recorded accurately and in a timely manner.	All
Payroll and Benefits		
Segregation of Duties	Hiring (human resources) and payroll functions are segregated. Time report approval is segregated from other payroll functions.	All
Basis for Payroll Amounts	Payroll is authorized only in accordance with time records or contractual agreements.	Occurrence Valuation

(continued)

Area and Category	Control Objective	Assertions
Payroll	Payroll is complete and accurate (including to the proper person) and in the proper period, including proper health and benefits deductions.	Completeness Valuation
Benefits	Benefits data and payroll deductions are accurately processed from the payroll records to the files for other benefits records for each employee in accordance with the plans.	Valuation
Follow-up	Missing, duplicate, or long-outstanding checks are investigated.	Completeness Valuation
Physical Controls	Checks, signature stamps, and the like are secured against unauthorized use.	All
Financial Reporting	Postings to the general ledger are timely and accurate.	Valuation
Data Files	Access to data files is restricted to authorized personnel. Personal data is protected from disclosure.	All
Data Files	Approved changes to data files (including withholding tables) are recorded accurately and in a timely manner.	All
Fixed Assets		
Segregation of Duties	Asset record maintenance and physical asset disposition or oversight are segregated.	All
Approved Capital Expenditures	Capital expenditures are approved and documented before acquisition.	Occurrence Valuation
All Fixed Assets Recorded	All fixed assets of the entity are recorded. New fixed assets are recorded accurately and in a timely manner.	Completeness Rights and Obligations Valuation
Expensed or Cap per Policy	Assets are capitalized (expensed) per GAAP and company policy.	Valuation
Ownership	Assets recorded are owned by the entity, and are not otherwise sold or represent rented facilities.	Rights and Obligations
Depreciation Methods	Depreciation methods for book and tax purposes are in accordance with GAAP, regulatory, or tax principles, as appropriate, and are accurately accounted for on a timely basis.	Valuation
Physical Controls	Protection of relevant assets from loss due to theft, misuse, lack of maintenance, or physical damage.	Completeness Valuation
Impairment	Fixed assets (including idle assets) are regularly reviewed for impairment.	Valuation
Self-Constructed Assets	Interest, costs, payroll, and overhead are accounted for as per GAAP, and costs are accumulated on a timely basis.	Valuation Completeness

Area and Category	Control Objective	Assertions
Disposals	Disposals are preapproved and recorded per GAAP on a timely basis.	Existence Disclosure
Financial Reporting	Postings to the general ledger are timely and accurate.	Valuation
Data Files	Access to data files is restricted to authorized personnel.	All
Data Files	Approved changes to data files are recorded accurately and in a timely manner.	All
Goodwill and Intangibles		
Segregation of Duties	Those responsible for accounting and physical controls over assets or records do not have duties that are incompatible with maintaining effective internal control.	All
Recorded Values	Amounts at which goodwill and other intangible asset balances are carried remain valid. Impairment considered.	Valuation
Amortization	Amortization of intangible assets is recorded in the appropriate period.	Valuation
Data Files	Access to data files is restricted to authorized personnel.	All
Data Files	Approved changes to data files are recorded accurately and in a timely manner.	All
Tax Accrual and Compliance		
Tax-Related Transactions	All related transactions or economic events are recorded completely, accurately, and in a timely manner. Tax issues are identified and resolved on a timely basis. Records support the recorded transactions and estimates.	All
Tax Compliance	Accurately process, prepare, and file required tax documents on a timely basis. Remit tax payments on a timely basis, including any sales taxes collected.	All
Tax Accrual	Accurately reflect deferred taxes per GAAP (FASB ASC 740), including the realization of any deferred tax assets and tax positions. Include local, state, and foreign commitments. Appropriate support and schedules underlie the calculations.	Valuation Disclosure

(continued)

Area and Category	Control Objective	Assertions
Tax Planning	Recognized tax positions meet GAAP criteria for recognition	Valuation
Recognized Deferred Tax Assets	Recoverability reviewed. Supporting, corroborating evidence obtained regarding realization.	Valuation
Consistency with Entity Goals	Tax strategies and tax positions are consistent with entity goals and strategies.	Valuation
Financial Reporting	Postings to the general ledger are timely and accurate.	Valuation
Disclosure	Management/those charged with governance are aware of significant tax-related issues and risks. Required disclosure of tax-related issues.	Presentation and Disclosure
Data Files	Access to data files or worksheets is restricted to authorized personnel.	All
Data Files	Approved changes to data files or worksheets are recorded accurately and timely.	All
Commitments and Contingencies		
Segregation of Duties	Those responsible for these functions do not have duties that are incompatible with maintaining effective internal control.	All
Contracts	Contractual liabilities are authorized and disclosed as required.	Completeness Disclosure
Commitments and Contingencies	Commitments and contingencies are estimated and identified in a timely manner.	Completeness Valuation
Litigation	Pending litigation is identified, estimated, and disclosed in a timely manner.	Completeness Valuation Disclosure
Regulation	Regulatory actions or exposures are assessed as to potential financial accounting consequences and estimated and disclosed as required by GAAP.	Valuation Disclosure
Product Recalls	Product recalls are properly authorized, estimated, communicated, and recorded in a timely manner.	Completeness Accuracy Disclosure
Derivatives: Reporting	Derivative financial instruments are identified, categorized, and classified. They are accounted for accurately and in a timely manner. When derivatives are common, company policies are in place covering authorization and permitted practices.	All

Area and Category	Control Objective	Assertions
Derivatives: *Information*	Company information systems are adequate to maintain the records necessary to account for derivative financial instruments.	Valuation
Financial Reporting	Postings to the general ledger are timely and accurate.	Valuation
Data Files	Access to data files is restricted to authorized personnel. Personal data is protected from disclosure.	All
Data Files	Approved changes to data files (including withholding tables) are recorded accurately an timely.	All
Equity		
Segregation of Duties	Those responsible for these functions do not have duties that are incompatible with maintaining effective internal control.	All
Equity: *Authorized*	Only authorized changes in the number of outstanding shares or amounts of partner equities are recorded. All transactions are recorded accurately and in the proper period.	Existence Rights and Obligations Valuation
Treasury Stock, Distributions	Stock buy-backs or distributions are authorized and recorded accurately in the proper period.	Completeness Valuation
Stock Options: *Granting*	Options are granted in accordance with a board-approved option plan. Controls prevent backdating or spring-lading.	Completeness Occurrence Valuation
Stock Options: *Accounting*	Valuations of options are made to record compensation, as appropriate. Appropriate disclosure information is retained in the information system. Authorized valid stock options (issued) are recorded completely, accurately, and in the proper periods. Authorized valid exercises, retirements, terminations, and modifications and cancellations of stock options are recorded completely, accurately, and in the proper period.	Completeness Existence Valuation Disclosure
Dividends or Distributions	Dividends or distributions are authorized, and recorded accurately in the proper period.	Valuation
Financial Reporting	Postings to the general ledger are timely and accurate.	Valuation

(*continued*)

Area and Category	Control Objective	Assertions
Data Files	Access to data files is restricted to authorized personnel.	All
Data Files	Approved changes to data files are recorded accurately and in a timely manner.	All
Investments		
Segregation of Duties	Cash management, investments, and debt management functions are properly segregated.	All
Cash Transactions	The execution of cash-related transactions is limited to authorized individuals.	Occurrence Rights and Obligations
Investments	Only authorized valid investment transactions are recorded completely, accurately, and in the proper period. Transactions are approved at an appropriate management level. Transactions are executed only with approved counterparties.	All
Investments: *Information*	Sufficient backup information is available to assist in the proper classification of securities (held, available for sale, trading) for reporting purposes and to fair value financial assets and investments accounted for by fair values.	Valuation Disclosure
Securities Pricing	Make a timely valuation of securities. Method of valuation is per GAAP. Examine related SOC No. 1 (SAS No. 70) report of service organization (if used).	Valuation
Follow-up	Long-outstanding or unusual trades in terms of amount, parties, nature of the investment, and so on are identified and reviewed.	Existence Valuation
Physical Controls	Physical controls over investments are maintained to reduce the risk of theft or unauthorized use.	Completeness Existence
Financial Reporting	Postings to the general ledger are timely and accurate.	Valuation
Data Files	Access to data files is restricted to authorized personnel.	All
Data Files	Approved changes to data files are recorded accurately and in a timely manner.	All
Treasury		
Segregation of Duties	Cash management, investments, and debt management functions are properly segregated.	All

Area and Category	Control Objective	Assertions
Bank Accounts	Accounts are properly authorized to open or close.	Completeness
		Valuation (Accuracy)
	Accounts are periodically and timely reconciled.	
	Activity is reviewed/monitored for unusual patterns.	
Currency	Cash is denominated in appropriate currency.	Valuation
		Disclosure
Policies	Monitor compliance with any loan covenant policies regarding balances.	Rights and Obligations
		Disclosure
Cash Transfers	Wire transfer transactions are limited to authorized individuals and purposes and controlled as to amount and timing.	Existence
		Completeness
		Valuation
Cash Transactions	The execution of other cash-related transactions is limited to authorized individuals.	Rights and Obligations
Derivatives	Debt contracts and agreements are routinely reviewed to identify possible imbedded derivative provisions.	Completeness
		Accuracy
	Derivatives are accounted for appropriately and in accordance with US GAAP.	
Borrowings: *Third Party*	Third-party debt obligations and related interest are complete, properly authorized, accurate, and recorded in the proper period.	All
	Appropriate disclosures are made.	
	Hybrid debt with equity features (and vice versa) is accurately classified and disclosed in financial statements.	
Borrowings: *Related Parties*	Intercompany borrowing and related interest are complete, properly authorized, accurate, and recorded in the proper period.	Completeness
		Existence
		Valuation
	Appropriate eliminations are scheduled for consolidation.	
Fair Value	Apply fair value measurements to any related debt as required by GAAP.	Valuation
Off-Balance Sheet	Off-balance sheet arrangements are identified and accounted for appropriately and in compliance with GAAP.	Completeness
		Existence
		Valuation
Physical Controls	Physical controls over cash and negotiable instruments are maintained to reduce the risk of theft or unauthorized use.	Completeness
		Existence
Financial Reporting	Postings to the general ledger are timely and accurate.	Valuation

(*continued*)

Area and Category	Control Objective	Assertions
Data Files	Access to data files is restricted to authorized personnel.	All
Data Files	Approved changes to data files are recorded accurately and in a timely manner.	All
Additional Objectives re: Period End (Quarterly and/or Annual) Process		
Related Party Transactions	All such transactions are identified. Amounts, entities, and timing are accurate. Examine transactions for required disclosure and GAAP treatment.	All
Fair Valuation of Relevant Assets and Liabilities	All relevant accounts/processes are identified. Quality appraisals obtained are timely and relevant. Consider: Financial Assets and Liabilities Investments	Completeness Valuation
Accruals	The accurate preparation of all accruals and adjustments are made	Completeness Valuation
Consolidation and Translation	All entities consolidated or equity pickup and eliminations are made. Translate per GAAP.	Completeness Valuation
Tax Accrual	Tax expense and accrual are reviewed for accuracy and completeness. Identify tax positions.	Valuation Disclosure
Data Files	Access to related data files is restricted to authorized personnel.	All
Data Files	Approved changes to related data files are recorded accurately and in a timely manner.	All
Loans (Financial Institutions)		
Segregation of Duties	Loan setup, processing, collections, and accounting for the loans are properly segregated.	All
Policy	All loans are processed in accordance with company policies and applicable rules and regulations.	Rights and Obligations Completeness Valuation
Loan Origination	Only accurate, complete, and valid loan applications are accepted.	Completeness Existence Valuation
Loan Origination	All loans are properly authorized, processed accurately, and recorded in a timely manner.	Valuation
Loan Payments	Payments for authorized/approved loans are recorded completely, accurately, and timely.	Valuation Completeness

Area and Category	Control Objective	Assertions
Sale of Loans	Loan sales are properly authorized. Loans held for sale are properly classified. Authorized loan sales are recorded accurately and in a timely manner.	Occurrence Rights and Obligations Valuation
Servicing Loans	All cash receipts/payments are deposited and recorded completely, accurately, and in a timely manner	Completeness Valuation
Servicing Loans	Delinquent accounts are monitored, and allowances are established.	Valuation
Loan Repayments	Loan repayments are accurate and properly recorded.	Completeness Existence Valuation
Loan and Related Asset Valuations	Allowances for loan loss reserves and charge-offs are accurate.	Valuation
Foreclosed Assets and Real Estate Investments	Acquisitions and sales of foreclosed assets are authorized and properly recorded.	Occurrence Existence Valuation
Physical Safeguards	Adequate physical controls over loan files and collateral are maintained.	All
Financial Reporting	Postings to the general ledger are timely and accurate.	Valuation
Data Files	Access to data files is restricted to authorized personnel.	All
Data Files	Approved changes to data files (e.g., loan master files and interest calculations) are recorded accurately and in a timely manner.	All
Generic Cycle		
Segregation of Duties	Those responsible for accounting and physical controls over assets or records do not have duties that are incompatible with maintaining effective internal control.	All
Process	Transactions are authorized and recorded completely, accurately, and in a timely manner.	Completeness Existence Valuation
Physical Controls	Protection of relevant assets or information from loss due to theft, misuse, or physical damage.	All
Financial Reporting	Postings to the general ledger are timely and accurate.	Valuation
Data Files	Access to data files is restricted to authorized personnel.	All
Data Files	Approved changes to data files are recorded accurately and in a timely manner.	All

Linkage of Principles to Controls, Policies, and Procedures

THIS APPENDIX ILLUSTRATES the COSO components and principles linked to some example controls, policies, procedures, and considerations. The examples and considerations are not an exhaustive list and are generic in the sense that they are intended only to illustrate the linkage. This appendix may give you a starting point for documenting the controls and gathering evidence of their operation, but ultimately your documentation should be modified to fit the unique facts and circumstances of the entity. In addition, some controls may address more than one principle, and some of those relationships are also illustrated below. Depending on the control and how it is applied, the relative strength of that control to address a specific assertion may differ. Guidance suggests considering related controls and principles when assessing control deficiencies. Additional examples of controls are in *A Compendium of Approaches and Examples*, a 158-page volume accompanying the May 2013 *Internal Control–Integrated Framework*.

Component/Principle	Example Control, Policy, or Procedure
Control Environment **Demonstrate commitment to integrity and ethical values (Principle 1).**	▪ Comprehensive codes of conduct are developed and maintained and are periodically acknowledged by all employees.[1] ▪ The board of directors sets the example for the tone at the top. ▪ The entity's code of conduct and ethical standards are communicated to outside parties such as vendors and customers (also Principle 15). ▪ Feedback mechanisms with outside parties exist that allow them to report concerns about corporate culture and ethical behavior (also Principle 15). ▪ Management and/or the board respond to reported policy violations (also Principle 5). ▪ Creates policies that contribute to a positive workplace environment (also Principle 12).

Component/Principle	Example Control, Policy, or Procedure

Exercise oversight responsibility (Principle 2).	▪ Governance provides an appropriate level of oversight with regard to:
	  ▪ Management's identification of fraud risks.
	  ▪ Implementation of antifraud measures.
	  ▪ Creation of an appropriate culture and tone at the top.
	  ▪ Establishment of appropriate controls and monitoring. (See Principle 8.)
	▪ The choice of accounting principles is reviewed and approved by the board of directors (also see Principle 10).
	▪ Takes an independent view from management.
	▪ Actively supports and oversees internal controls project (also see Principle 12).

Establish structure, authority and responsibility (Principle 3).	▪ Organizational structure is designed to facilitate the flow of information upstream, downstream, and across all business activities (also see Principles 13 and 14). ▪ Considers service organization and outsourcing in its oversight responsibilities (also see Principle 7). ▪ Authority, responsibility, and accountability are linked and delegated logically and together (also see Principle 12). ▪ Boundaries of authority are established and communicated. ▪ The delegation of responsibilities considers the need to segregate incompatible activities (also see Principle 10 and P12). ▪ Management periodically evaluates the entity's organizational structure to assess its continued effectiveness (also see Principle 16).
Commitment to competence (Principle 4).	▪ Policies and procedures are consistent with objectives (also see Principle 10). ▪ Senior management comprises individuals from several functional areas, not just a few. ▪ Senior management, the board of directors, and the audit committee stay current on financial accounting and reporting matters. ▪ Recruiting and hiring policies ensure that only competent individuals are hired (also see Principle 5). ▪ Training needs are evaluated and appropriate training provided to all entity personnel (possibly including the board of directors). ▪ Management evaluates the adequacy of the workforce—both in numbers and experience—necessary to carry out company objectives. ▪ Supervisory personnel provide timely performance evaluation feedback and suggestions for improvement to subordinates (also see Principles 5 and 16). ▪ Senior management, the board of directors, and the audit committee include individuals with appropriate levels of financial expertise. ▪ When the entity is structuring nonsystematic, nonroutine transactions, accounting personnel are consulted early in the process. ▪ Training on the proper application on company accounting policies is provided as necessary ▪ Contingency plans exist for management development and succession.

(continued)

Component/Principle	Example Control, Policy, or Procedure
Establish accountability (Principle 5).	▪ Responsibilities and expectations are communicated clearly to individuals, especially those in supervisory positions and new personnel (see also Principle 12). ▪ Incentives and target goals are congruent with performance objectives (see also Principle 7). ▪ Job descriptions are developed and maintained and contain specific references to control-related responsibilities (see also Principle 4). ▪ Periodic re-examination of the existing job descriptions and structure for effectiveness and efficiency (see also Principle 12). ▪ The disclosure committee, audit committee, and board of directors review all control issues and material weaknesses identified, and they take appropriate action (see also Principle 17).

Risk Assessment
Specify relevant objectives (Principle 6).
	▪ Through inquiry and corroborating evidence (notes, minutes of meetings, etc.), verify management's development of objectives.
	▪ Management articulates its risk tolerance as well as its objectives.
	▪ Financial commitment to GAAP and regulatory-compliant financial statements:
	  ▪ Financial objectives are consistent with operating objectives and practical realities.
	  ▪ Commitment to qualitative characteristics of financial reporting.
	  ▪ Materiality considerations in reporting and disclosure.
	▪ Resource commitment is consistent with objectives.

Identify and assess risk (Principle 7).	▪ Risks are identified and addressed at sufficiently high levels in the organization so their full implications are identified and appropriate action plans considered (see also Principle 10. If risk assessment is not successfully accomplished, that may preclude Principle 10 from being effective). ▪ Management identifies reporting risks arising from both external (economy, technology, foreign operations) and internal sources (technology, personnel issues, production issues) at all levels of business operations (see also Principle 10). ▪ Risk identification is included in the entity's strategic planning process (see also Principle 2). ▪ Assessment considers the potential velocity (speed of occurrence) and persistence (potential duration) of risks as well as their likelihood and magnitude (severity) of the risks (see also Principle 10). ▪ Board of directors or governance group oversees and monitors the risk identification and assessment process (see also Principle 2). ▪ Identify plans to preempt risk and/or respond to issues if they arise (also see Principles 10 and 12).
Assess fraud risk (Principle 8).	▪ Implement antifraud procedures and controls. ▪ Periodic brainstorming of risks. ▪ Study of fraud patterns identified in similar businesses or operating in similar environments. ▪ Management actively identifies and assesses fraud risk. A reporting hotline is in operation (see also Principle 17).

Component/Principle	Example Control, Policy, or Procedure
	▪ Procedures are established that allow employees to take appropriate action to report unacceptable behavior they observe (see also Principle 12).
	▪ Management identifies compensation policies and other incentives that can motivate unethical behavior (also Principle 7).
	▪ Actions in response to unacceptable behavior are communicated to employees as a means of providing an effective deterrent (see Principle 14).
	▪ Promotion, retention, and compensation criteria consider the individual's adherence to behavioral standards and standards of performance (see Principle 1).
	▪ Personnel policies minimize the chance of hiring or promoting individuals with low levels of honesty (see also Principle 4).
	▪ Alleged incidents of fraud are investigated appropriately, and disciplinary action is taken (see also Principle 5).
Identify and assess significant change (Principle 9).	▪ Risks related to significant change are identified, including those relating to:
	▫ Changed operating environment.
	▫ New personnel.
	▫ New or redesigned information systems.
	▫ Rapid growth.
	▫ New technology.
	▫ New lines, products, activities, and acquisitions.
	▫ Corporate restructuring.
	▫ Foreign operations.
	▫ Changes in accounting principles.
	▪ Changes to internal control are captured and communicated to management (see Principle 14). Public companies have special responsibilities regarding quarterly (Section 302) reporting (Principle 15).
	▪ Management reviews all changes to internal control and discloses these changes when appropriate (see also Principle 12).
	▪ Consider operating and regulatory or legal changes and effects on financial reporting.
	▪ Consider the risks associated with changes in key employees or management.
Control Activities **Select and develop control activities (Principle 10).**	▪ Internal controls, policies and procedures are designed specifically to address identified financial reporting and fraud risks (see Principle 7).
	▪ Special attention is given to designing controls around difficult accounting areas, such as:
	▫ Fair values.
	▫ Estimates.
	▫ Complex transactions.
	▫ Revenue recognition.
	▫ Contingencies.
	▪ Controls are established over period-end procedures and approvals of reclassifications and adjusting entries (see Principle 7).

(*continued*)

Component/Principle	Example Control, Policy, or Procedure
	■ Management makes changes to the entity's activities and business processes to mitigate identified fraud risks. (see Principle 9).
	■ Controls design is mindful of the appropriate segregation of duties in all facets of controls and monitoring.
	■ Management develops and maintains a process and related controls for closing the books and preparing financial statements at the end of an accounting reporting period, including authorizations/approvals of reclassifications and adjusting entries (see Principles 13 and 15).
	■ Nonroutine, nonsystematic transactions and journal entries are identified and given special attention (see Principles 7 and 8).
	■ Entity seeks advice from consulting experts or independent auditors on significant accounting issues (see Principle 4).
	■ Entity utilizes control objectives or financial statement assertions to link risks and controls.
	■ A mixture of preventive and detective controls are designed for effectiveness, as appropriate for the risk.
	■ Controls are designed at the appropriate level of detail to prevent or detect misstatements or fraud.
	■ Automated controls are implemented when practical and when general controls are assessed as effective.
Select and develop general controls over technology (Principle 11).	■ Executive management supports and adequately funds technology and support that is integral to operations and accounting (see Principles 2 and 7).
	■ Directed attention is given to the quality of information technology (IT) general controls:
	■ Organization of IT function
	■ Access and security issues
	■ System change controls
	■ New systems development
	■ Operations and recovery
	■ Change management controls operate over changes to:
	■ Applications.
	■ Database schemas.
	■ How the database presents data to the application.
	■ The operating system, including updates and patches.
	■ Entity limits and documents who has access to which applications and is mindful of segregation of duties issues (also see Principle 10).
	■ Incidents where an application does not run as intended are identified and reported (also see Principle 17).
	■ System incidents are logged for analysis and tracking. Systems breaches are analyzed, damages are assessed, and preventive measures are developed (also see Principle 17).
	■ Processing errors and exceptions are resolved in a timely fashion.
	■ Network penetration tests are periodically performed and analyzed for potential improvements.

Component/Principle	Example Control, Policy, or Procedure
Deploys through policies and procedures (Principle 12).	▪ Policy and procedures manual is maintained and followed (also Principle 5) ▪ Adherence and reference to the policy manual is part of entity culture (also see Principles 1 and 5).

Information and Communication

Generate relevant information (Principle 13).	▪ Management determines the information needs of personnel and the board of directors.
	▪ Management considers information from both external and internal sources that may affect:
	  ▫ Assumptions underlying significant accounting estimates.
	  ▫ Valuation of assets.
	  ▫ Recognition of liabilities.
	  ▫ Information used to make estimates and consider the recognition and measurement of assets and liabilities is consistent with industry conditions, entity plans, budgets, and its past performance.
	▪ Information gathering and communication processes are reviewed and updated to reflect changed accounting and reporting needs (also see Principle 9).
	▪ Data is organized and presented in a logical and useful format.
	▪ Data integrity is maintained as data is processed and communicated (valid, accurate, secure, retained, sufficient, timely).
	▪ Surveys and interviews indicate that employees and management are satisfied that relevant information is provided.
	▪ Requests for more or less information are assessed and acted on in a timely manner.
	▪ Absence of concerns that too much information is being generated.
	▪ Balances costs and benefits through analysis and oversight.

Communicate internally (Principle 14).	▪ Information is provided to the right people in sufficient detail and in a timely manner to enable them to carry out their responsibilities efficiently and effectively (see also Principles 2 and 4). ▪ Senior management has lines of communication with operating and financial management, particularly those operating from geographically remote locations (see also Principle 3). ▪ Company accounting policies are documented and communicated to all those who may affect their proper implementation (also Principle 12). ▪ Appropriate technologies are used to deliver information. ▪ Changes to policies are communicated on a timely basis. (also Principle 12). ▪ Mechanisms are established to encourage confidential reporting of violations of policy or laws, or fraud (also Principles 8 and 17).
Communicate externally (Principle 15).	▪ Management assesses the clarity and transparency of the entity's financial statements and disclosures (see also Principle 7). ▪ Nonfinancial communications (press releases, news articles, advertising, etc.) are previewed and approved as consistent with entity values and objectives.

(continued)

Component/Principle	Example Control, Policy, or Procedure
	▪ Required public disclosures (e.g., 8K) are timely and reviewed for accuracy and understandability.
	▪ Management regularly reviews its significant accounting policies and considers:
	▫ User needs.
	▫ Accounting principles applied by the entity for which acceptable alternative principles are available.
	▫ Judgments and estimates that affect the financial statements.
	▫ Evolving business and accounting issues and choices that affect financial reporting
	▫ Accounting for unusual arrangements. (Also see Principle 10.)
	▪ Management considers input from auditors, regulators, and similar entities when choosing or reconsidering its communications. Based on this input, it takes appropriate action.
Monitoring **Conduct ongoing and separate evaluations (Principle 16).**	▪ Management monitors key business metrics and identifies anomalies that could indicate that financial information could be materially misstated (also see Principles 3 and 5).
	▪ Monitoring is an established program involving internal audit and management.
	▪ Knowledgeable personnel are assigned to monitoring and analysis (also see Principle 4).
	▪ Management and the audit committee identify key controls that should be closely monitored and evaluated for deficiencies (also see Principles 7 and 10).
	▪ Elements of unpredictability (e.g., scope, frequency, extent) are introduced into the program.
	▪ Management and the board of directors monitor identified incentives and motivations (including compensation) to identify unintended consequences (e.g., possible violation of codes of conduct) (see also Principles 1, 7, and 8).
	▪ Monitoring is adapted to address anomalous transactions or unexpected patterns based on analyses (see also Principle 9).
Evaluate and communicate deficiencies (Principle 17).	▪ Management establishes policies for the timely communication of nontrivial control deficiencies and material weaknesses to the audit committee, disclosure committee, and the chief executive officer and chief financial officer and to independent auditors. (The Securities and Exchange Commission requires public companies to share control deficiency findings with their auditors) (see also Principles 12 and 14).
	▪ Timely communications of identified deficiencies.
	▪ Controls exist over the assessment of the severity of control deficiencies (see also Principle 10).
	▪ Monitor remediations of control deficiencies.

[1]The Center for the Study of Ethics in the Professions (www.iit.edu/departments/csep) has compiled a library of codes of conduct and ethics from a wide variety of entities. This is an excellent resource if you would like to compare your company's or client's code of conduct to other similar entities.

6

Information and Communication

T HE RELATIVELY EASY-TO-COMPREHEND component of Information and Communication has important tentacles throughout all of the principles and components. Data can be used to enlighten as well as to obscure. A strategy to hide information "in plain sight" is to flood the inquiry with so much data that the relevant information becomes a needle in the haystack. Forensic investigators and data analysis experts have developed sifting programs to signal potentially relevant information from the noise of masses of data. Computerized information makes possible the communication of masses of data at a minimum of cost, but if a human processor is at the end of the communication, the issue becomes one of delivering useful information.

In the infamous ENRON audit failure and management fraud, it was noted that literally rooms full of data were provided to the auditors. At the time the fraud was asserted, much of that information had not been reviewed by the auditors. It is not clear if that information would have contained any clues to the shenanigans that were happening, but by flooding the auditors with information, the distraction factor was well at work.

Assuming employees and stakeholders do not want to become forensic investigators to perform their responsibilities and tasks, it is important for the entity to provide the information needed to:

- Serve the purpose of the recipient.
- Avoid flooding the communication lines with data that numbs the senses and obscures rather than reveals.
- Make decisions based on reliable and timely information.

The auditing literature[1] describes the necessary elements of an information system for financial reporting, which include the methods and records that:

- Identify and record all valid transactions.
- Describe on a timely basis the transactions in sufficient detail to permit proper classification of transactions for financial reporting.
- Measure the value of transactions in a manner that permits recording of their proper monetary value in the financial statements.
- Determine the time period in which transactions occurred to permit recording of transactions in the proper accounting period.
- Present properly the transactions and related disclosures in the financial statements.

This guidance from the auditing literature is consistent with the Security and Exchange Commission's (SEC's) definition of internal control.

So many of the information- and communication-related issues today relate to computer systems, security, and data integrity issues, it is often difficult to identify a unique principle where they belong. In reality, most of the systems deficiencies impact several principles. As reinforced in the revised Framework, the interrelationships and multiple principles should be noted in the assessment and considered in the overall controls effectiveness assertion. For example, inaccurate sales data could imply deficiencies that could be pervasive with respect to gathering or summarizing other financial information; could weaken management's ability to effectively manage or monitor; and may imply weaknesses in security and access, testing new systems, or system changes.

In the absence of the need to relate deficiencies to multiple principles, important implications of deficiencies might not be identified because they would perhaps fail to aggregate with other deficiencies. By connecting all the linkages, more severe deficiencies can be identified.

PRINCIPLE 13: GENERATES RELEVANT INFORMATION

The general direction in Principle 13 is to identify the controls over those processes that ensure that complete, accurate, timely, and cost-effective information is directed to those individuals that need that information. If effective controls are established and documented (Principles 10 and 12), the information requirements to service these control points should naturally fall out of that process. Nevertheless, a simple question or two during the walk-throughs can provide evidence that the owner of the control assess that he or she receives the necessary information.

The points of focus for this principle are for the entity to:

- Identify information requirements.
- Capture internal and external data.

---

[1] For example, see American Institute of Certified Public Accountants, AU-C No. 315, *Understanding the Entity and Its Environment and Assessing the Risks of Material Misstatement.* 2012.

- Process relevant data into information.
- Maintain quality throughout processing.
- Consider costs and benefits.

How does the entity ensure that individuals are receiving the information they want and need? What *process* does management use to identify relevant and irrelevant or unnecessary information? What information does management say it needs to perform its management functions? What controls are present to ensure employees are not given sensitive information that by law or intellectual property rights or competitive concerns cannot be shared? Are segregation of duties issues considered when approving information requests?

At the end of the day, governance, management, and employees need to be satisfied that they are receiving the right information. Some companies have a centralized inventory of reports, including to whom and when they are made. No flowchart, diagram, or narrative by itself can measure sufficiency or adequacy. Individuals need to provide this feedback in interviews, surveys, and observation of whatever internal process there might be for requesting various reports or other information, and follow-up to assess the response to the request.

IMPORTANCE OF INFORMATION

In a retail business with numerous stores and lines of merchandise, management closely monitors activity by location and by product line on a regular basis to identify anomalies or required shifts in marketing strategies.

In a regular weekly meeting involving middle and top management, statistics about sales, turnover, and other performance measures are closely monitored, and anomalies and unresolved issues are followed up on by internal audit as directed by management. Management over time has added new measures and data sources, including benchmark information from outside the entity, to refine the analyses.

The reliance on timely, accurate information is critical to management's operating style. It is sometimes noted that data need to be corrected after the reports are generated and sometimes after the meeting is held. These glitches are taken seriously and investigated, and a program of continuous improvement in the data reporting (e.g., direct downloads into the report writer, automated edit checks for reasonableness) was put in place. Internal audit now regularly tests the data in the system and the reports because of their importance to management.

Timing is important. It is not enough to capture and communicate information. The communication must be done in a timely manner that allows it to be useful in controlling the entity's activities and reporting financial results. While there may be trade-offs among cost, timing, and absolute accuracy, these trade-offs need to be prioritized and accepted.

The information system captures relevant data from internal and external sources with implications for financial, operational, and regulatory issues that impact the entity and particularly any accruals and disclosures. The information needed to prepare reliable financial reports and to manage a business is not limited to financial information; nonfinancial information also is important. For example, the information needed to determine an allowance for inventory obsolescence may include an assessment of current and future market conditions and technology shifts. Assessing the reasons for anomalies in sales, regional or local economic data may need to be considered. Frequently, the assumptions underlying significant accounting estimates and fair valuations rely to some degree or another on nonfinancial markets information. The company's process in estimating allowances and reserves should demonstrate considerations of various sources of information, and that information should be reliable as cited and recorded.

Additionally, information received from external sources may indicate control weaknesses. For example, external auditors are required to report significant deficiency and material weakness internal control deficiencies to governance (e.g., the audit committee and the board of directors). Regulators (e.g., banking, insurance, and the SEC) report the results of their examinations, which may highlight control weaknesses or issues of the application of accounting principles. Auditors are asked to inquire regarding such comments and ensure governance (particularly the audit committee, if there is one) is aware of these issues. Complaints or inquiries from customers, vendors, competitors, or other third parties often point to operating problems that can affect financial accruals, estimates, or disclosures. Information from blogs, analyst reports, trade publications, and other sources may not always directly relate to the entity but can provide input regarding industry issues and a perspective on future directs that can shape shareholder and potential shareholder views. It behooves most companies to keep an eye on such sources for risks and forthcoming changes.

An entity's information system is *not* limited to merely capturing the company's recurring, routine transactions and events but also must include a means for identifying, capturing, and communicating information that is outside the normal course of business. For example, an entity may form a variable interest entity (formerly known as a special-purpose entity). The formation of such an entity has important accounting ramifications, and the company should have a mechanism to identify the information needed to properly account for the entity, and present it properly in the generally accepted accounting principles (GAAP) financial statements. Recent discussions of other accounting frameworks that might replace U.S. GAAP may require significant historical information be retained to be able to retroactively restate past financial results.

PRINCIPLE 14: COMMUNICATES INTERNALLY

It should be recognized that an entity's information and communication system includes *informal* communications, such as conversations with customers, vendors, other third parties, and between and among employees, as well as formal, documented lines of communication. Various forms of communication including e-mail, posters in common facilities, group meetings, and phone conversations can make up a complicated set of communication vehicles. Depending on the communication, these vehicles may not be appropriate alternatives for effective communication. Simple etiquette today dictates that text messages may not be appropriate in certain circumstances.[2] Important issues need to be documented to better ensure understanding and establish follow-up responsibility. If there is a separate accounting mission statement, is it communicated, understood, and effective? Memories dim quickly, and even more quickly after problems arise.

The points of focus for Principle 14 are for the entity to:

- Communicate internal control information.
- Communicate with governance.
- Provide separate communication lines.
- Select relevant methods of communication.

Ineffective communications are a good cover for hiding information that could be used to identify issues, problems, and fraud. Monitoring is particularly reliant on effective communication. The two- and three-way communication channels among management, governance, and employees need to be assessed to ensure that effective financial and business communications are achieved. This aspect of this principle has some overlapping goals with control activities, and in the 2006 COSO guidance, this point was partially covered under that component. It has now been moved to Principle 14. The entity's information and communication systems should be closely integrated with its control activities to support their proper functioning and the need to identify anomalies and problems as early as practical (see also Principle 12). In order for control activities to be effective, any controls-related issues must be communicated clearly to individuals who perform management and control functions:

- Specific control activity–related duties (including monitoring).
- Relevant aspects of the internal control system, how they work, and each person's role and responsibility in the system.
- How their activities relate to the work of others. This knowledge will help employees recognize a problem or help motivate them to determine its cause and propose a corrective action.
- Expected behavior: what is acceptable and unacceptable.
- The notion that whenever the unexpected occurs, attention should be given not only to the event itself but also to its cause.

All these points of communication are infinitely harder to assess in the absence of effective policy and procedures documentation.

As described previously, change management is an integral part of an entity's risk management process. To be effective, an information system must be flexible and

---

[2] As this book is being written, the media are reporting the outrage of affected Malaysian families concerning a text message from the airline regarding the fate of Flight 370. The vehicle of communication seemed inappropriate for that communication.

responsive to the constantly evolving needs of the business. How does the entity keep a finger on the pulse of change to identify information gaps that might occur (Principle 9)? Are there examples of effective or ineffective responsiveness in the information system to business change?

The establishment of an anonymous hotline for reporting various business and ethical issues is an important separate line of communication that needs to be assessed for effectiveness. If an outside service is responsible for maintaining this service, how well is it working from management and the service's point of view? How do employees feel about the hotline?

Are the views of production and sales and administrative personnel in alignment with others in the organization? The auditor's fraud standards include required inquiries to individuals outside the accounting and finance groups. Chapter 8 reminds project personnel to include other employees in questionnaires, surveys, and group discussions regarding entity issues such as integrity and ethics. Are these employees getting the information they need and have requested?

The information necessary for monitoring and effective governance needs to be available to the right persons on a timely basis. This includes some evidence that the feedback process on problems and issues encountered is also effective.

 ## PRINCIPLE 15: COMMUNICATES EXTERNALLY

External communications include financial reporting and disclosures. As with internal communications, there may be formal and informal aspects to the communication, but an assessment of the formal mechanisms between the entity and customers, vendors, regulators, taxing authorities, shareholders, and the general public is expected. Many of the financial reporting responsibilities are well defined for public companies. Nonpublic companies may look toward loan agreements and agreements with private equity providers and others for periodic reports on operations.

The points of focus for Principle 15 are for the entity to:

- Communicate with external parties.
- Enable inbound communications.
- Communicate with governance.
- Provide separate communication lines.
- Select relevant methods of communication.

Traditional business practices maintain records of complaints regarding billing, shipments, business practices, and other issues. These can be a significant external source of information regarding internal issues that should be addressed. What is the process for assessing and deciding which issues need to be communicated to management and/or governance? Is there evidence that judgments in accordance with the policy are being made? What is the evidence that issues are addressed in an effective and timely manner?

Regulatory agency or internal auditor reports citing deficiencies in practices or controls may not automatically be transmitted to the governance group. What is the process for assessing and transmitting this information and ensuring controls-related issues are communicated appropriately? Independent auditors are expected to inquire regarding any such reports and ensure they are appropriately communicated. Better that an internal process be in place to ensure this on a regular basis than have it appear on an auditor deficiency list.

Governance may have a claim against auditors who fail to communicate to them regulatory and/or internal control issues and fail to ensure they are properly reported to them. In one such case that arose before the auditor requirement regarding outside regulatory reports, top executive management blocked awareness or discussion of such reports with the board and audit committee. Top management was found to be engaging in a fraud on several dimensions, one of which related to the weak controls criticized in the regulatory report.

With the emergence and popularity of various social media, clear policies need to be stated regarding discussing any aspect of company business in these forums. In public companies, prosecution and penalties can be imposed against individuals and the entity by the SEC for revealing information that is not "public." A note that you will be seeking a new residence to staff a position in an unannounced business combination can be enough to set off a firestorm. Based on e-mail discoveries in litigation cases, it is amazing to me how seamless personal and business communications can become. In many situations, cases are actually decided because of evidence found in e-mails. For some entities, the advice to not write anything you would not want printed on the front page of the *Wall Street Journal* seems to get the message across. In some situations, external communication is *not* a good thing.

Transitioning to the New Framework

Those entities following only the five components under the 1992 guidance will find information and communication is still here. If control objectives and /or assertions were previously used, those elements can be mapped to the three principles by considering the various points of focus. It is possible that a full consideration of the 2013 Framework will identify some previously unaddressed control points that need to be addressed going forward.

The 2006 COSO guidance identified four specific attributes that could be used for classifying the component:

1. Financial reporting information is identified, captured, used, and distributed.
2. Internal control information is identified, captured, used, and distributed.
3. Internal communication supports the execution of internal control.
4. Matters affecting the achievement of the objectives are communicated.

These attributes have now been collapsed into three principles and the underlying points of focus, control objectives and/or assertions may be the most reliable way to link the previous structure to the 2013 Framework, as a simple matching of the 2006 attributes and principles is difficult. While inherent in the attributes discussed, the specification of relevance (Principle 13) as a principle may create more focus on this issue. Note that in transition, you may identify some previously unaddressed control points that now need to be addressed going forward.

CHAPTER SEVEN

Monitoring

M ONITORING IS A process carried out by the entity that assesses and ensures the quality of internal control performance over time. It is an entity responsibility to monitor controls implementation and effectiveness, and that role cannot be assumed by the independent auditor, even when the independent auditor is charged with evaluating and testing controls as a basis for an opinion on internal controls effectiveness or if auditor tests controls to reduce other audit tests as part of the audit strategy. Monitoring involves assessing the design and operation of controls on a timely and periodic basis and taking necessary corrective actions. Monitoring may be done on both an ongoing, routine basis and as part of a separate evaluation. A basic principle of effective auditing applies to monitoring: A highly predictable process will not yield reliable results over time.

As mentioned previously, in 2009, COSO published a report specifically directed at monitoring, describing what it is and is not and some examples of how to design and assess monitoring effectiveness. In the initial implementation of this concept, it became apparent that a broad number of companies and auditors had differing views on this component. One particularly difficult issue was the extent to which monitoring could provide fully adequate compensating control over transaction controls that were determined to be ineffective. Powerful detection capabilities were sometimes being ascribed to infrequently performed oversight procedures and rather high-level management reviews of aggregate financial data, without any real proof of their precision or effectiveness. While in some readers' view the 2009 document is more long-winded and complex than necessary to meet its mission, there are many worthwhile examples and illustrations of monitoring therein, and guidance on how the precision of a monitoring process might be assessed and how it might realistically relate to the assessment of the effectiveness of individual controls over transactions. The 2009 monitoring guidance is not set aside by the revised Framework, and COSO clarifies that any elements in the revised Framework guidance takes precedence, should there be any perceived conflict between it and the 2009 report. For example, the revised Framework places significant attention on the interrelationships between principles and components, and thus this emphasis should prevail going forward. It does not seem that there are obvious contradictions or conflicts between the documents. The 2009 report is worthwhile reading, at least for the leader of the entity controls project and the lead audit team member. The relative thinness of the content of the discussion, approaches, and examples (relative to other components) in the revised 2013 Framework may make it valuable to give further consideration to this earlier document.

 PRINCIPLE 16: SELECT, DEVELOP, AND PERFORM ONGOING AND/OR SEPARATE EVALUATIONS

The points of focus for Principle 16 are:

- Consider a mix of ongoing and separate evaluations.
- Consider rate of change (see also Principle 9).
- Establish baseline understanding.
- Use knowledgeable personnel (see also Principle 4).
- Evaluations integrate with business processes (see also Principle 7).
- Adjust scope and frequency.
- Objective evaluation.

Some examples of ongoing monitoring activities include:

- The regular management and supervisory activities carried out in the normal course of business. Is there an inventory listing of the regular monitoring activities? What is the evidence that these activities were performed?
- Communications to and from external parties, which can corroborate internally generated information or indicate problems, can be a source for monitoring. For example, customers implicitly corroborate billing data by paying their invoices. Conversely, customer complaints about billings could indicate system deficiencies in the processing of sales transactions or posting cash receipts. How does the entity ensure that feedback from this source is assessed for potential control deficiencies and elevated to the appropriate levels of management and governance?
- External auditors regularly provide recommendations on the way internal controls can be strengthened. These are called management letter comments. Auditors should identify to management and the audit committee potential significant deficiencies and material weaknesses in a separate communication from the management letter. Those recommendations often indicate the need for corrective action. What evidence is there that management has addressed auditor communications regarding serious control deficiencies?

▪ Employees may be required to sign off to indicate they have performed the control activity. The sign-off allows management to monitor the performance of these control functions. How does management monitor control performance?

Separate evaluations are of a slightly different nature. They may be initiated to focus on controls where deficiencies or potential deficiencies have previously been identified. Separate evaluations can also be triggered by analyses of data, results of regular monitoring procedures, or by new or old risks inherent in the entity's current operations or even the random selection of a process, location, or product line for deeper review. An occasional random check is helpful to keep oversight procedures from becoming too predictable. To paraphrase a line from the movie *The Fortune Cookie*, "Every time you build a better mousetrap, the mice get smarter." Varying the mix of how controls are monitored may serve as a deterrent to gaming.

Independent auditors often visit a few remote locations (including small locations) each year to verify the baseline of any analytical monitoring that is usually applied to these operations. In coordination with internal audit, the visitation of locations on some basis (e.g., random selection, weighted to consider location size and time since the last visitation) can be an effective audit process with value to the entity.

To be effective, monitoring that depends on data and trends analysis requires a reliable baseline from which to make comparisons if it is to identify anomalies. For example, if analytical procedures such as trends in sales and key financial ratios are used to assess the operations of a remote location facility, then the assumption is that the base data is a reliable benchmark. How does the entity ensure the base data used to measure the operations is correct? Even if the data transmitted is faithfully gathered, is it possible the data from the location does not tie to the books and records of the entity? One possible reason for this could be for the location to misstate the data to appear normal and escape attention. In an unusual situation, a location was found to consistently only report a part of its operations (understated sales, etc.). The unreported part of the business generated profits directly to the local managers while using the company's business software, brand name, and other business assets. Only through a chance visit by internal auditors was the fraud discovered. Nearly from the initial operations, the baseline for measurement of changes was unreliable. Analytical procedures applied without a periodic verification of the underlying data are subject to this risk.

In the use of analytical procedures and various metrics of production and operations, the recent term *dashboard* has evolved. Like the dashboard of a car, the term describes an array of analytical and metric data, periodically or continuously updated, that is presented in various ways, such as graphs, charts, or comparative numerics. Properly developed, a dashboard can be an effective tool for directing management attention to issues. However, if the points monitored are not continuously reassessed and updated to meet changing business structures, a dashboard can provide a false sense of security that the key points and data are on the radar screen. The dashboard is most effective as one ongoing aspect of a multiple-aspect monitoring program that also includes an element of unpredictability in which processes, locations, or product lines will receive deeper dive-in oversight during a period.

One area that monitoring needs to keep tabs on is outsourced processing and data services. Since the implementation of the Sarbanes-Oxley (SOX) Act of 2002 and the more recent trend to outsource many accounting and data storage functions, service organizations have increased the frequency and quality (from Type 1 to Type 2) of reports. Annual or even six-month updates of these reports might not be sufficient for critical functions, and so the entity may need to take additional steps (inquiry "plus") to extend report results to meet the fiscal year-end of the entity. Keeping tabs on the updates and ensuring that service organization controls being relied on are still reliable is a task that may fall under Principle 10, Selects Control Activities, but still needs oversight to make sure that the inventory of reports is complete and reviewed and that any relevant issues are communicated to management. A special type of service organization report exists for data centers and cloud-computing services. SOC No. 2 reports are appropriate for these activities. In their absence, entities may have difficulty gathering sufficient evidence to support reliance on the functions performed because of the technological and specialist nature of some aspects of this service. Because of the recent implementation of cloud processing and cloud data storage, a careful pulse needs to be kept on trends, issues arising, and related security issues.

So the broad questions become: What monitoring processes are in place to ensure service organization reports are received and reviewed and that any issues are properly communicated on a timely basis? How are emerging issues, such as security and access issues associated with service organization data processing and data storage, monitored to ensure current entity awareness?

 ## PRINCIPLE 17: EVALUATE AND COMMUNICATE DEFICIENCIES AS APPROPRIATE

The points of focus for Principle 17 are:

- Assess results.
- Communicate deficiencies (see also Principles 14, 3, and 5).
- Monitor corrective actions (see also Principle 5).

COSO uses the term *deficiency* broadly to mean any condition of an internal control system worthy of attention. Severe deficiencies are called *major* deficiencies in COSO lingo, although the Securities and Exchange Commission (SEC) and auditing standards recognize the distinctions between "significant deficiency" and "material weakness." The definitions surrounding these classifications are not predicated on how large a misstatement was generated by the deficiency, or even if there was a misstatement, but on whether it was "reasonably possible" that a misstatement *could* occur. These nuanced issues make it imperative that individuals responsible for assessing severity and having reporting responsibility to governance within the organization, or classifying these items for disclosure outside the organization (e.g., SOX Section 302 and Section 404 reporting, or reporting to regulatory bodies) have an excellent awareness of the definitions, requirements, and rationale for classifying control deficiencies and an objectivity in the assessment. In a study of accelerated filer audits from the 2004 and 2005 periods, it was found that 70% of management assessments of major deficiencies were overridden by even higher severity assessments when auditors looked at those deficiencies.[1]

Certainly all deficiencies that can affect the entity's ability to produce reliable financial information should be identified and reported. However, even seemingly simple problems with relatively simple, obvious solutions should be considered carefully because they might have far-reaching implications. A simple, small, misdirected payment could be the tip of an iceberg of fraud. When errors and deficiencies are identified, their underlying causes should be investigated. Monitoring requires judgment. It is not a mechanical task that can easily be pushed down to inexperienced personnel.

As an aspect of monitoring, providing information regarding internal control deficiencies to the right people is critical if the internal control system is to continue to function effectively. For this reason, the monitoring component of internal controls should include a mechanism for reporting internal control deficiencies and taking appropriate action. Findings of internal control deficiencies should be reported to the individuals who are in the best position to take action as well as following the chain to governance, as outlined in the responsibilities of the governance group (see also Principles 3 and 5). This may include reporting not only the person responsible for the activity involved but also to at least one level of management above the directly responsible person.

Obviously, potential deliberate misstatement and suspected fraud are worthy of heighted attention and sensitivity. Care needs to be taken that such discoveries are not handled as routine but that special attention is given to right way to report such issues to the appropriate organizational level. When alerted to discovery, some perpetrators have taken great steps to hide their deeds, such as by destroying systems and data. There also may be regulatory and legal requirements to publicly disclose or report violations of laws or regulations outside the organization. If the entity has an identified in-house or consulting legal counsel, these people may be helpful in determining next steps when sensitive issues arise. Again, this is an indication that oversight and monitoring may require significant experience, judgment and sensitivity, and clear guidelines as to how to handle special situations.

Transitioning to the Revised Framework

Inasmuch as the new Framework continues to recognize the two monitoring principles from the attributes in the 2006 smaller public company guidance, those transitioning from that guidance will have an easier time. Nevertheless, it is worthwhile for everyone to look at the points of focus, approaches, and examples to ensure that there are no gaps in the past analysis that need to be addressed going forward. Here are the 2006 Principles and some words used to describe them.

---

[1] J. Bedard and L. Graham, *Accounting Review*, 2011. It was noted in this study that the rate of underassessment was even greater for deficiencies later upgraded to material weaknesses.

- *Ongoing and separate evaluations.* Ongoing and/or separate evaluations enable management to determine whether internal control over financial reporting is present and functioning.
- *Reporting deficiencies.* Internal control deficiencies are identified and communicated in a timely manner to those parties responsible for taking corrective action and to management and the board as appropriate.

CHAPTER EIGHT

Evidence and Testing

G IVEN THE IMPORTANCE of testing in supporting assertions and objectives for controls, one would expect significant official guidance on such matters as the nature, timing, and extent of evidence gathering to meet the needs of the engagement or COSO project. However, the official guidance is somewhat scarce. COSO provides little concrete guidance on testing specifics, and while the Securities and Exchange Commission (SEC) and Public Company Accounting Oversight Board (PCAOB) identify some factors for scoping the assessment and testing, little concrete guidance is provided. The American Institute of Certified Public Accountants (AICPA) Audit and Accounting Guide *Audit Sampling* (AAG-S)[1] does provide some guidance on sample sizes and benchmarks that are in use in current audit practice. While not officially authoritative for public company audits, the AAG was crafted to consider Sarbanes-Oxley (SOX) applications, public company practice and corporate needs for sample size guidance.

SUFFICIENT EVIDENCE

A common inspection and peer review criticism of auditors is whether sufficient, appropriate evidence was obtained to support the degree of asserted reliance on the controls or on the overall assertions and accounts when considering all tests and procedures. This criticism can apply to all audits, public company or otherwise. While not publicly

---

[1] American Institute of Certified Public Accountants. Accounting and Auditing Guide: *Audit Sampling*, AICPA. 2014. 184 pages.

disclosed, the issue can extend to companies that cut corners on their internal controls testing without adequate documentation for the basis of their testing.

In some tests of controls, sampling is a logical procedure. For example, in testing the control activities, drawing samples of purchase orders or checks or payroll transactions to check for control operations are common sampling applications. However, some practitioner and internal auditor thinking is still rooted in the historical position that a sample size is a judgment and therefore not questionable. Not true today. Sample sizes should be comparable to what statistical sample sizes would be, given the same parameters of risk, expected deviations or misstatements, tolerable deviations or tolerable misstatement, and in some cases certain population characteristics (e.g., size, diversity, differential risks, etc.).[2] Thus, tables and charts are often suggested to aid decisions about sample size. Use of such tools also has the advantage of revealing the parameters used in reaching the sample size. This aids documentation and facilitates third-party review of the work performed. For auditors, it reduces the risk of challenges to the sample size, and for company project people, it helps auditors to assess the adequacy of the work performed and better assess their ability to rely on the work performed.

Several times now I have heard the story that upon inquiring of the engagement team of the assurance desired from a test, the inspector would pull out a chart and calculate a sample size for an assurance (confidence) level. In such an environment, the argument of using audit judgment to determine a sample size no longer holds much water. However, it is true that auditors still have to use judgment in setting the parameters (risk, tolerable, etc.) of the sample, but after those judgments are made, the resulting sample size should relate to some basis like a table or computation consistent with those parameters. I sometimes joke at seminars or with company clients that I can "divine" sample sizes in my head from parameters or situations. However, my estimates are really based on working with tables, formulas, and computations over a 40-year period, and not from any innate sense I was born with.

Even more complex than sample size is the extent of testing necessary when sampling is not an appropriate procedure. For example, when assessing the financial savvy of governance or audit committee members, it is difficult to envision a sampling methodology that would apply. The auditor might seek a few or many pieces of evidence, depending on the level of assurance needed for the task, to assess this characteristic. Observations of meetings, interactions when the auditors are present, verified resume credentials, minutes from the meetings, and the like might be candidate sources of evidence regarding this issue. In other cases, surveys and focus groups might be used to collect "opinions" of employees on specific topics (e.g., tone at the top, company follow-up on reported issues, etc.). Just because a sample is not appropriate does not mean the extent of evidence gathered is not relevant. One clearly expects more evidence to be gathered when publicly attesting to the effectiveness of internal controls. The issue

---

[2] This position is clearly taken in AU-C No. 530, *Audit Sampling*, and was added to the body of the American Institute of Certified Public Accountants (AICPA) authoritative literature in 2007 in SAS No. 107, *Consideration of Materiality and Risk in a financial statement audit*. Prior to that, the concept was stated in the AICPA Audit and Accounting Guide (AAG) *Audit Sampling* from the inception of the publication in 1983. Today that guidance is in the "clarified" AICPA Standards in the current AAG *Audit Sampling* (2008, 2012, and 2014 eds.).

becomes: Does the evidence support high reliance on the effectiveness (functioning) of this control?

Your Objective

Before venturing into how to set sample size and the extent of evidence that needs to be gathered, it is important to again recall the purpose of your engagement or project. The nonpublic company engagement (AICPA Standards) allow the auditor to place a continuum of reliance on internal controls when strategizing the audit to be able to conclude with a clean audit opinion that there is a low risk of material misstatement in the financial statements. Thus, the auditor might place no reliance, some reliance, or high reliance on controls as part of that strategy. And that strategy can be varied in the engagement, so perhaps fixed assets, revenue generally accepted accounting principles (GAAP) compliance, and payroll will be heavily reliant on controls testing, but other audit areas, not so much so. There is no requirement that the AICPA auditor test controls (or rely on them) beyond ascertaining that the controls design appears appropriate and the controls described actually exist. Testing for reliance is an option. Public company attestations of control effectiveness assume a high level of evidence was gathered to support that assertion.

Nevertheless, all auditors (public, private, government) today need to assess the design (presence) of the controls and gather some evidence that the described controls are operating as described in the documentation (aka *implemented* or *functioning*). This latter requirement can be satisfied with a controls walk-through,[3] observation, or examining documents as evidence. Inquiry alone is considered by auditing standards not sufficient to establish the control actually exists.

EFFICIENCY **TIP**

Private companies and governments can improve the efficiency of their audits by undertaking and atleast maintaining for themselves the documentation of controls and performing adequate tests of the controls to show effectiveness. This improves audit efficiency by demonstrating to the auditors the control effectiveness and encouraging audit leverage of this information in planning the audit. Audits that successfully incorporate reliance on controls are generally more efficient. This is because the sample sizes to establish high control reliance are usually smaller than sample sizes of details that establish substantive correctness. Auditors can directly use competently and objectively performed controls testing by entities as evidence to reduce the extent of other procedures.

---

[3] In such a procedure, the control points are identified and the procedure involves following a transaction through the system to see that all the controls were applied to the transaction from inception through summarization in the journals and ledgers. AICPA standards also allow for tracing transactions from summarization back to the inception of the activity (aka grave to cradle.). Generally a walk-through might count as a sample of **one** item in terms of the controls examined and is hardly a basis for placing much reliance on the control tested.

In addition, it is anticipated that tougher independence rules in the near future will lessen the level of assistance auditors of nonpublic entities can give clients in documenting their internal controls. It is a best practice to prepare entities as soon as possible to prepare and maintain their controls documentation.

Note, however, that for public company audits, auditors are cautioned that for sensitive and highly judgmental control areas (e.g., fraud risks and management financial competence assessments and fair valuations), auditors need to gain assurance themselves on these issues and cannot not just rely on internal company assessments.

For public companies and their auditors reporting on the effectiveness of internal controls (accelerated filers), the extent of evidence and testing is clearly established. In such situations, the assertion of effectiveness implies a *high* level of assurance that the internal controls are operating as described. Under PCAOB Auditing Standard (AS) No. 5, auditors can take assurance from competently and objectively performed tests of controls performed by management or internal audit. The extent of assurance taken is predicated on certain factors. For example, in highly judgmental areas such as controls over developing estimates, auditors should gain more evidence for themselves that the controls are effective. Some elements of the control environment, such as the tone at the top or the competence of accounting resources, are best objectively judged by a third party like the auditor rather than self-assessed by entities. Auditors seek to identify the sensitive audit areas and gather sufficient information for themselves to be satisfied that the controls are effective. That in no way diminishes the powerful effect of having reliable company assessment and testing as a basis for auditors' work. By the time auditors test and evaluate the controls, it may not be practical for companies to remediate or retest controls. Research has established that late-in-the-year testing is an important characteristic associated with unremediated material weaknesses and significant deficiencies.[4]

Smaller public companies (nonaccelerated filers) are not required to have a separate auditors' attestation regarding controls effectiveness.[5] However, the entity still needs to assert publicly to the effectiveness of its internal controls. The downside of this arrangement is the lack of an independent auditor check on the internal controls. If the auditor places reliance of the company's procedures, and those management assessments were too optimistic, then the audit could be deficient and not identify the errors that might be present. It is known that in the early days of SOX implementation, the *auditor* independent assessment and testing caught over 70% of the identified control deficiencies. Thus, a large portion of the deficiencies were not identified by the required company procedures to assess and test their own controls. In light of this, the procedures and tests performed by public entities to support their assertion become more important.[6]

---

[4] Bedard, J., and L. Graham. 2011. Detection and severity classification of Sarbanes-Oxley Section 404 internal control deficiencies. *The Accounting Review 86* (3): 825–855.

[5] This exemption from the separate auditor report requirements of SOX was made permanent by the Dodd-Frank Wall Street Reform and Consumer Protection Act of 2010 in response to smaller companies pleas for relief from the SOX requirements.

[6] Bedard and Graham, previously cited.

AUDITOR **CAUTION**

While auditors need not separately report on internal controls effectiveness for nonaccelerated companies, the SEC and PCAOB have stated that they expect auditors to review the client projects supporting their assertions and ensure that they provide an adequate basis for their assertions.[7] Supposedly, this feature was to force some auditor involvement in the process, without the onerous requirement to separately test and report. Audit firms have taken different positions as to how much oversight this requirement really implies. My view is that at some point this will become the focus of a PCAOB or SEC enforcement issue, likely prompted by a high-profile controls failure and traced to an optimistic or inadequate management assessment not challenged by the auditor.

Nonaccelerated filers report (assert) publicly on the effectiveness of their controls. However, auditors of these entities still have strategy choices regarding the reliance on controls in structuring the audit of the financial statements. This means that even though the entity may report that controls are effective, auditors may still design audits primarily based on analytical procedures tests and direct tests of the correctness of transactions and balances in the financial statement. In the view of some regulators, this approach is a "disconnect" since the theory is that reliance on effective controls should reduce the cost of the audit. However, in other minds, the testing of transactions and balances give direct evidence of the fairness of the financial statements, while controls provide indirect evidence and thus are less convincing. While accepted as more costly, the substantive strategy is more "fulfilling" to some and as a result will continue to be a favored audit approach.

When auditors of nonaccelerated filers wish to rely on controls they will need to gather sufficient evidence supporting that strategy. Simply relying on the assertion of management will be insufficient, even though auditors can place some reliance on competent and objective management assessments and tests of controls. The auditor placing some or a lot of reliance on internal controls will still need to carefully scrutinize the work performed by the entity as well as supplement that with sufficient independent auditor tests in areas where judgment is a major factor (e.g., control environment, estimates, and fair value determinations).

---

[7] For example: "Despite the fact that the revised rules no longer require the auditor to separately express an opinion concerning management's assessment of the effectiveness of the company's ICFR [internal control over financial reporting], auditors currently are required … and would continue to be required under the Proposed Auditing Standard [AS No. 5], to evaluate whether management has included in its annual ICFR assessment report all of the disclosures required by Item 308 of Regulations S-B and S-K. Both AS No. 2 and the Proposed Auditing Standard would require the auditor to modify its audit report on the effectiveness of ICFR if the auditor determines that management's assessment of ICFR is not fairly stated. Consequently, the revisions are fully consistent with, and will continue to achieve, the objectives of Section 404(b) of Sarbanes-Oxley." Source: Securities And Exchange Commission 17 CFR Parts 210, 228, 229 and 240 [Release Nos. 33-8809; 34-55928; FR-76; File No. S7-24-06], 2007. See also PCAOB. AS No. 5, C16.

Evidence

Understanding the nature, extent, and timing of tests should be a natural element of audit judgment. However, judgment is not a result of heredity, the name of the firm on the door, or the office or the position you hold. Solid judgment is built over time by exposure to a variety of situations, thinking those issues through in light of surrounding issues, and the development of internal guiding principles that aid in decision making. Judgment is a process, not just a decision. While we sometimes judge a person who makes snap judgments in a positive way, often those judgments do not consider the related issues and implications and might not result in favorable outcomes.

When the evidence gathered does not clearly lead to the conclusion the company or auditor reached, this can be considered to be an exposure where after-the-fact questioning may result in unpleasant outcomes (e.g., litigation exposure or comments on the quality of audit work). Sometimes this appearance is just due to insufficient documentation, as be discussed in the next topical area.

Documentation

To meet professional standards and possible later scrutiny, the basis of judgments should be discernible from the evidence considered. Auditors and companies are challenged to document the evidence that was obtained in their work papers. Common peer review and inspection comments criticize auditor documentation for failing to document the thought process leading to audit decisions and the considerations that went into forming audit judgments. In all fairness, reviewers are often not able to reconstruct various thought processes from different parts of the audit to support the judgments reached. If not documented clearly, do not expect a third party to give you credit for all the work that led up to your judgment.

A few times I have seen the "stovepipe" application of criticism applied to question the adequacy of auditor testing. Stovepipe thinking is when only a narrow focus is applied to the test performed, without thinking about related areas and other procedures that support the test. Good documentation practice prevents this on the part of third-party reviewers. Here is one example. A company has a very simple GAAP revenue recognition policy, but the auditor decides to take a small sample of sales anyway for the purpose of supporting primarily the existence assertion. The criticism of the procedure cites the sample as inadequate because high assurance on the assertion of existence would have required many times the sample size tested. Had the auditor explained in the documentation that controls over both cash receipts and accounts receivable (including confirmations) at year-end were extensively tested and found effective, and that the existence risk was therefore minimal, the sample size that was used could have been easily supported. The logic here is that third parties are not mind-readers and may not search for other sections of the audit to support the work performed. Sometimes even the auditors performing this work do not recall the test well enough after the passage of time to provide all the contemporary considerations that entered into the judgment. The lesson is that if you want to support your work, provide the reasoning that led to your decision or conclusion in the documentation. The documentation should be compelling in supporting the work performed and conclusions reached.

Likewise, companies should be careful to document their work so that auditors can provide full credit for the work they performed. On a test of 15 items in a sample of cash disbursements for management approval, the auditor might conclude that high assurance could not be attained with that level of testing. But if there are other tests (e.g., redundant controls, complementary controls, monitoring controls) that are performed elsewhere to that same objective that are not mentioned, then the 15 items will stand alone in the mind of anyone who may underestimate the evidence being obtained.

Interactions with Independent Auditors

Now that the COSO has clarified the underlying 17 Principles as a focus in controls evaluation, there will be a shift in the documentation of companies and auditors to reflect this refinement. Those auditors and entities already following the 20 principles outlined in the 2006 COSO *Smaller Public Company* report will still have to cope with the new principles and the changed principles. Ideally entities and their auditors would be coordinated in making this shift, but the SEC has always maintained that auditors cannot dictate to clients how they should make their assessment, so there will continue to be a real barrier to the efficiency of alignment of auditor and company assessments. The positive aspect of this is that the independent approaches of the entity and the auditor might provide more opportunities to identify risks, control deficiencies, and issues. The downside is, of course, the need to map COSO to the audit tools and to the management assessment tools. While this could be quite confusing and obscure rather than detecting issues, the enumeration of the 17 Principles will likely be helpful in the long run in establishing a consistent basis for assessment, even if details still need to be mapped.

While outright collaboration of auditor and entity on controls classification and testing may not be viewed as appropriate, it would be wasteful to not engage in some dialogue to get the respective parties on the same page in 2014 and beyond. Those entities and auditors using control objectives and just the five components may experience the most adjustment to the 17 Principles approach. However, it may not be that difficult to make a one-time mapping of the detailed current control objectives to the new Framework. It is recommended that in this mapping process, the 2013 COSO Framework published guidance that illustrates various examples and approaches be reviewed to ensure as much consistency as practical with the thought process behind the revised Framework. Entities and auditors aligning their tools as closely as practical with the revised Framework may find this mostly accomplishes the desired synchronization and does so for a broad base of clients.

As previously mentioned, public companies need to gather evidence supporting their assertions. Auditors may leverage some testing of others, such as internal audit or consultants (other than in highly judgmental areas), that is objective and sufficient for controls reliance or for auditor reporting. Auditor testing to establish the competence of the audit work performed and evidence obtained by others is expected. Nonpublic entities may still want to test controls for their own purposes even if not publicly reporting on internal controls. Audit efficiencies are often possible when entity controls are demonstrated to be effective. Thus, even in the nonpublic sector, management testing may yield benefits in improved operations and audit costs.

Under AS No. 5, the independent auditor was granted more leeway in using the results of management's tests in determining the sample sizes required of the auditor when supporting his or her controls opinion. One large certified public accounting (CPA) firm uses a chart of multiple testing scenarios where the extent and result of management testing is related directly to the level of required auditor testing to achieve high assurance. So if management tests a key control at a level of 50 items and finds no exceptions, the auditor might perform a small additional sample on this important control, or even limit the auditor testing to a walk-through. If the company tested the control only 10 times, the sampling by the auditor would revert back to the firm general policy of testing, say, 45 items for high assurance. In higher-risk and highly judgmental areas, independent auditor testing at a high assurance level would generally always be expected.

Minimizing company testing may have the unintended consequence of increasing audit effort and fees and flirting with the risk the auditor may conclude that company testing was insufficient for supporting management's assertion. It also makes it more likely the auditor will identify the control deficiencies. As mentioned previously, that can be costly in terms of timing of the discovery and inability to remediate in a timely manner.

By the way, testing reliance is not a two-way street. The company cannot rely on the work of the independent auditor for making its assertion. COSO defines internal control in such a way that the independent auditor is not part of the system of internal control. Management's responsibility to establish and maintain internal controls must stand on its own. SEC guidance requires management of public companies, and not the auditor, to support its assessment and assertion regarding the effectiveness of controls over financial reporting.

To be clear, the independent auditor will still need to perform some tests on client controls where even the most perfect assessment and testing was performed by the company. In certain judgmental areas, such as assessing the control environment, the review of the controls over significant estimates, and where judgment indicates additional confirmation of the results may be warranted, the auditor should be relying more on his or her observations and judgments in these areas. But to the extent that the company process is robust, it will pay dividends in the first and future years by reducing audit effort, providing a evidential basis for lowering risk assessments in an area, and making for easier testing and assessments in future years.

What is often inexplicable is the discovery of an out-of-control process years later that should have been detectible by entity or auditor procedures, had the controls over the process been adequately tested. Such discoveries raise questions that you do not want to have raised, particularly when regulators point out issues.

Unfortunately, close collaboration with the auditor on the details of performing assessment and testing procedures to support the controls assertion can quickly turn into risks to the independence requirements. Companies and auditors should be mindful of the overarching importance of not breaching that requirement and invalidating the audit opinion.

GATHERING INFORMATION

Types of Evidence

Evidence is obtained by companies to support an assertion of control effectiveness. The auditor obtains evidence to support the opinion on the financial statements and, when required, the opinion on the effectiveness of internal controls.

Evidence comes in many forms and can be strong or weak. Much evidence regarding controls will come from sources inside the entity, despite the perceived higher reliability of evidence when it can be obtained from independent outside sources. When external information can be obtained, it can be very useful in corroborating (or not[8]) information available from within the entity. For example, analyst reports, business publications, and research reports may touch on issues of top management quality or experience and style of operations, important elements in the control environment assessment.

Procedures to obtain evidence that entities and auditors need include:

- Inspection of documents.
- Observation of procedures.
- External confirmations (when possible).
- Recalculations.
- Reperformance of control procedures.
- Inquiry.

In some cases, analytical procedures and benchmark statistics may provide limited information about controls, but these procedures are more often used for verifying reported amounts in financial statements. The precision of these procedures is usually too coarse to provide positive assurance regarding controls operation.

Among the evidence procedures, inquiry is often considered to be the weakest form of evidence. In auditing, inquiry alone is generally considered insufficient evidence in support of an explanation. Whenever possible, inquiry is usually always accompanied by at least one other source of evidence supporting the results of the inquiry. In some cases, where it is difficult to obtain other evidence (e.g., the intent of management), multiple inquiries of different individuals with knowledge of management strategy may strengthen the evidence, but some other confirming evidence still should be sought by the auditors, such as past experience and track record with management representations.

---

[8] Contradictory evidence needs to be addressed by analysis, additional testing, or other means, and any impact on the testing strategy needs to be documented and reflected in the strategy of the engagement.

Audit standards indicate certain conditions that point to sources of more reliable audit evidence:

- Information from independent or external sources
- When related controls are found to be strong
- Information obtained directly by the auditor
- Documentary evidence rather than oral evidence
- Examination of original documents rather than copies

These considerations should be applied by entities and auditors when assessing the appropriateness and sufficiency of audit evidence obtained.

There is an expectation that entity documents used in the audit and evidence-gathering process will be complete and accurate. A common expectation is the direct tie-in of the document or schedule being examined or used to select test items to the official books and records of the entity. This cannot be simply assumed without some evidence. There are lots of examples of tainted reports and information being produced to hide fraudulent activity or just erroneous data leading to bad management decisions. Testing key documents to confirm the attributes of accuracy and completeness can also be leveraged/referenced to the conclusions in the information and communication component, where the accuracy of internal data is also part of that analysis (Principles 13–15).

Base Level—"Functioning" and Walk-throughs

All audits, including public audits, expect that the controls that are described in the documentation are to be confirmed as actually in operation, and are not just controls that sound like they should be in place. Entities should be the first line of defense to verify that the controls are as described before testing begins to avoid false starts and wasted time by all. It continues to be amazing what you learn when asking employees what they actually do and how they deal with issues that arise versus what is written in the controls documentation (often prepared some time ago and when different individuals were performing the control). As in physics, all systems seem to deteriorate or morph into other shapes over time. It is no different in accounting.

A common way to confirm your understanding of control design and documentation accuracy is to perform a walk-through (aka walkthrough). A company is not required to perform walk-through procedures; however, it is in management's best interests to do so to avoid inefficiencies that may arise in testing and confusion when auditors oversee or try to rely on company documentation and testing.

A walk-through is a procedure in which you trace a transaction from its origin through the company's information processing system all the way to its reporting in the financial statements. Although inquiries of company personnel are a major component, a walk-through is more than just an inquiry. Think of a walk-through as:

- *Corroborative inquiry*, in which you ask questions of client personnel and then obtain corroborating evidence to support their answers.

- *A test of one*, in which you take a single transaction and perform detailed procedures or observations to verify the operation of the controls for processing that transaction.

The walk-through can help you evaluate the effectiveness of the design of internal controls surrounding the processing of each transaction or performance of the monitoring function. While performing your walk-through, you also may often obtain some limited evidence about the operating effectiveness of the controls (like a sample of one item). Walk-through procedures should continue to be relevant as long as there are no significant changes to the information-processing stream. When significant changes do occur, you should update your walk-through to confirm your understanding of the new processing and control procedures. Walk-throughs are also suggested periodically to confirm that changes have not occurred in the operation of a control.

A common misunderstanding regarding walk-throughs relates to *what* is being walked through. It is easy to be distracted by the complexity of transaction processing and wind up following the trail of the transaction or document through the system to its summarization and posting to the books and records. Even today, a great deal of walk-through documentation seems to lack of any discussion of controls. However, a walk-through in the context we are discussing is supposed to be a walk-through of the controls, not the paper or electronic process. The focus should be on the control points and how each control point handled the transaction as it passed through. Did the control operate as described? Is there documented evidence the control operated?

Some transactions, say, electronic-processed transactions, may not always indicate whether the transaction was processed through the control point. Information technology (IT) auditors might trace transactions through systems to gather evidence that transactions were processed through the controls, as described. Systems can also be modified to provide a positive indication when an electronic transaction is processed through a control point or to provide positive evidence that a transaction was authorized by the appropriate person before it was further processed. Just because a transaction was processed correctly does not imply the controls that were supposed to be in place were applied to that transaction. It is a continuing challenge to ensure control points are evidenced in manual and electronic systems. While the initial COSO Framework indicated that a lack of evidence of a control operation did not mean the control did not operate, the revised Framework indicates that regulators may require evidence of control operation, and such evidence may need to be added to existing systems to meet the regulator requirements. Evidence of control operation helps everyone to perform the most efficient procedures and not having to seek evidence through expensive means.

Planning the Walk-through

Walk-throughs are not simple tasks when performed properly, and time is necessary up front to design the walk-through to achieve the objective in the most efficient manner.

- Plan on performing the walk-through for each key area and transaction stream where reliance is planned or as required for attestation.

- Identify cycles (sales cycle, purchasing cycle) or groups of related controls to test using the same transaction. This minimizes the number of separate procedures and helps the evaluator to see the overall integration and quality of the control design.
- Your walk-through should encompass the entire scope of the transaction stream, including the controls surrounding the transaction's:
  - Initiation;
  - Authorization;
  - Accurate and complete recording in the company's books and records; and
  - Summarization and reporting in the financial statements or in the financial statement footnotes.
- It is typical to start your walk-through at the initiation of the transaction and work forward toward the summarization in the financial accounts. The AICPA also accepts other forms of walk-throughs (e.g., backward tracing). The PCAOB only accepts the more common cradle-to-grave walk-through.
- As part of your walk-through, you should evaluate whether there is adequate segregation of duties.

Because some activities in a company affect several different financial account balances, you should consider this when planning the walk-through. For example, cash disbursements affect not only cash balances but also interact with accounts payable, employee reimbursements, capital expenditures, and payroll. The use of transaction cycles and business processes in defining logical documentation, walk-throughs, and testing units will help you identify these shared activities. Where efficient, plans to streamline procedures can provide benefits. The most common accounts with shared activities include:

- Cash receipts.
- Cash disbursements.
- Payroll.

For example, you should plan on walking through and testing the shared function in cash disbursements only once, not several times for each different processing stream that might include cash disbursements.

When making inquiries you should consider the following suggestions.

- Make inquiries of the people who actually perform control procedures and process information as part of their daily job requirements. Don't limit your inquiries to those who supervise or review the process or are otherwise a step or two removed from actually performing the work. Talk to people in operations, outside of management and outside of the accounting department.
  - Design your inquiries to obtain information about the person's understanding of:
    - What is required by the company's prescribed procedures and controls.
    - Whether the procedures are performed as described and on a timely basis.

- Ask questions to identify any specific situations (which may occur regularly) in which personnel do not perform the control procedures as described in the company's internal control documentation. Have employees been asked to make exceptions?
- When speaking to employees: Do they seem to know what they are doing and how it relates to the overall control process? Do they know how to handle exceptions and when to follow up? Document your observations.
- Consider conducting some inquiries over time regarding control environment and company policy issues with a focus group rather than only in one-on-one interviews.

When obtaining supporting, corroborating information, you can support answers received to your inquiries by:

- Asking the individual to demonstrate the performance of the procedure being described.
- Using the same documents and IT (live data) that company personnel use to perform the procedures.
- Asking other individuals to describe their understanding of the previous and succeeding processing or control activities.

Additional guidance on walk-through interviews is provided in Chapter 9 on questionnaires and interviews and its appendix.

Documentation of Walk-throughs

Walk-throughs are sometimes not approached with the respect they deserve. Consequently, their documentation rarely receives the scrutiny it deserves. Real gems can be identified in walk-throughs, if only they would be scrutinized by attentive reviewers.

A SAD STORY

A junior staff auditor was assigned to perform a walk-through of a commercial loan application process. She had no prior work experience with the client. After the walk-throughs were completed, she was not further assigned to the engagement. She dutifully noted on the provided checklist that the loan being walked through was for less than the appraised value of the property, and a recent collateral appraisal was in the loan file.

Unfortunately, a few details were not communicated to this staff, and issues were never identified in any reviews of the documentation.

The company's policy called for the loan to be *no more than half* the appraised value of the property. Company policy also called for an appraisal performed independently by a company-approved appraiser. The appraisal also had to be for the property in its current state, not considering any proposed improvements

(continued)

(*continued*)

resulting from the loan. These policies were important to the accounting policies of the firm, which did not provide for loan loss reserves because of the "low risk of loss" when following their underwriting procedures.

The walk-through documentation failed to note the loan in the *one* loan transaction selected for the walk-through was for 90% of the appraised value, in violation of policy. The appraisal in the file was from a developer (not an approved company appraiser) who was appraising the value of the project at its completion, therefore violating two company policies.

Had these issues been identified in the walk-through, it might also have been discovered that management had ordered policy in this case (and in others) to be overridden to meet their desire to own the property, anticipating likely borrower default.

Despite the "lucky" identification of this transaction for the walk-through, failing to attach importance to the walk-through process and treat it seriously snatched defeat from the jaws of victory. Issues arose with defaulted loans in future periods that would lead to the demise of the company and some sanctions and jail time for senior executives. Auditors also experienced significant grief and financial loss in that process.

There are no prescribed formats for walk-through documentation. While a popular format, wordy narratives often include a lot of process discussion that can obscure the controls focus the walk-through is meant to address. Forms and matrices can be designed to be more succinct regarding the walk-through control points. An example is provided in Chapter 13 of this text of a sample form for documenting a walk-through.

Over time, and by piecing together some elements from the PCAOB discussion of walk-throughs, there are a number of quality points that can be used to evaluate walk-throughs. While not exhaustive, the list is a step in the right direction. Interestingly, there is little discussion of walk-throughs or their documentation in the AICPA Standards. The AICPA Audit Guide *Assessing and Responding to Audit Risk in a Financial Statement Audit* does contain several examples of walk-throughs using a matrix/form approach as part of the case study in that guide.

- The walk-through document ideally should link to any inherent or fraud risks identified in the area to alert the performer and reviewer of concerns.
- The document ideally should clearly link the control points back to the controls documentation. The assertions being addressed should be clear.
- If there are IT-related components to the walk-through, they should ideally be identified. If there are known deficiencies in IT related to the walk-through, they should be identified in advance.
- It should be clear who performed the procedure, when it was performed, who was interviewed, whether the employee appeared to understand the control and their role, and what evidence was obtained.

- Any suggested additional procedures or open issues as a result of the walk-through should be documented.
- The conclusion should be clear.

As noted, the walk-through should not be a mindless task or one disconnected from the important engagement risks and entity policies. It requires careful planning, execution, and supervision, as does any other element in the controls assessment or audit process. It is not a low-risk training tool for inexperienced staff to perform with little background information, oversight, and coaching.

An all-too-common problem with existing walk-throughs is that they include a lot of the *process* in the documentation, and sometimes the controls (the focus of the walk-through) receive little or no attention. For this reason, it may be best to separate the process narratives and flowcharts from the controls walk-through documentation because it is the controls walk-throughs that need to be performed periodically, even if the process does not change. By creating two documents, the walk-through can cross reference the narrative and be a shorter and more focused document that clearly focuses on the controls. In lectures, I use a redacted example from a real walk-through of payroll. I challenge participants to identify *any* controls that are noted, technology that was employed, inherent risks for the area, or even the person interviewed or the interviewer and date of the procedure. They are still looking.

A well-thought-out walk-through can gather evidence not only for specific transactional controls but that is helpful to supporting the entity-level control environment principles and fraud issues. For example, when asking an individual about the control procedures he or she performs, you could expand the inquiries to include these issues. Examples of inquiries that go beyond understanding activity-level control procedures include:

- If changes to your procedures were required, how would they be communicated? (control environment)
- What kind of on-the-job or formal classroom training do you receive? Do you find it helpful? (competence)
- Has management asked you for special treatment of any items being processed? (management override and the control environment)
- If any problems or errors that you can't fix are identified, do you ever get the impression that they are ignored without being adequately addressed? (control environment, monitoring)
- Have you had to communicate issues to higher-level management in the past year? Can you give me an example? What happened as a result of the report? (control environment, monitoring)

As an epilogue to this topic, please note that deficient walk-through documentation is a commonly cited peer review and inspection comment. Lack of controls focus and lack of documentation of the controls examined, evidence reviewed, and conclusions reached are common deficiencies. Following the guidance in this section and in the provided sample form will assist you in preparing a useful, compliant, and efficient walkthrough.

TESTING AND SAMPLING

Top-Down Concept

The financial impact of the initial implementation of PCAOB AS No. 2 in 2004 brought a backlash of criticism of the costs and inefficiency of the company requirements and audit processes. It was a confusing period since neither companies nor auditors had been previously trained in complying with COSO, Sarbanes-Oxley (SOX), Section 404, or the accompanying SEC or PCAOB rules. Independence concerns inhibited most entity-auditor communications, and there were no standardized tools for the documentation and testing of controls as envisioned in SOX and under the COSO Framework. It was a nearly perfect storm: aggressive regulation by a new agency of a new audit requirement involving untrained companies and untrained auditors under strong time pressure. To add insult to injury, in the year of implementation, many additional companies were unexpectedly swept into becoming accelerated filers because of a midyear tick upward in the stock market. Requests for a one-year deferral for these new, unsuspecting accelerated filers was surprisingly denied by the SEC. Whereas established accelerated filers had a longer period to get ready for SOX, these victims of a jump in stock values (and capitalization, which defined accelerated filer status) had less than six months to start and complete their process and have their auditors also complete their required process.

A potential remedy was suggested by the PCAOB to the alleged overkill testing in the early period of SOX implementation. The top-down concept urged the early consideration of key controls issues, such as the control environment and common shared controls (e.g., entity-level controls), across the entity. Considering these controls early would identify potential showstoppers that could arise later in the process and be difficult or impossible to remediate before year-end and thus lead to adverse opinions on controls and public material weakness disclosures.

Indeed, the concept did hold a lot of common sense and help companies and practitioners better understand how to better implement an efficient process. Such guidance today still has relevance for entities and auditors, as some areas remain more difficult to remediate at year-end and can have major impacts on other controls if assessed and tested only late in the process. Of course, the concept would have been most useful had it been circulated during the initial documentation and testing year. Once controls are documented for the first time and a better understanding of the testing process is obtained, the top-down concept becomes fairly easy and natural to discover by alert companies and auditors.

In addition to the suggested control environment issues and common, shared (entity wide) controls, I would also add information technology general controls (ITGCs) (Principle 11) and any related information and communication controls in that component, as weaknesses in security or access or new systems problems from these areas can invalidate controls tests already performed in various financial areas and create havoc late in the reporting year.

Additionally, the efficiency in administration and testing of entity-level (e.g., controls in common and shared) controls have encouraged more entities to build such controls into their overall structure. Such directions reduce entity complexity and increase audit efficiency.

Test Timing

It becomes important for all participants in controls documentation and testing to be clear regarding their objectives and requirements. For nonpublic engagements, the minimum requirement is currently to assess the adequacy of the internal controls and obtain some evidence the described controls are in operation (i.e., functioning). Thus, it may be possible to stop after documentation and a walk-through for these entities. While no time period is specified for making this assessment, the likely intended time frame is one that is representative of the year. The decision on timing is best documented as part of the project.

When nonpublic companies and auditors are relying on controls to reduce audit procedures and audit costs, the tests performed to verify the functioning of the controls need to be representative of the period of reliance. Thus, samples of control operations are often drawn from the entire period under examination. Populations from which the samples are selected should be defined as all control operations within the year. It may be impractical to await the last transactions of the year to test controls, so auditors frequently perform interim audit procedures at an earlier date, say autumn, for year-end clients. Clearly, the earlier these interim tests are performed, the more effort is needed to roll the controls conclusions through to year-end. One way to structure the testing is to:

- Calculate the required sample size using an estimate of the number of year end transactions (e.g., 22 sample items[9] for an estimated yearly population of, say, 1,000).
- Perform a portion of the control tests based on the transactions to the date of the test (e.g., for 900 completed transactions, sample 20 items).
- Perform the remaining tests at or near year-end (e.g., test the 2 remaining sample items).

When the period between testing controls and year-end is short, then inquiry regarding control changes and maybe a walk-through or observation of continued controls operation can be sufficient. Unfortunately, the failure of auditors to adequately extend tests to year-end is a common inspection deficiency cited by the PCAOB and is also noted in peer reviews for nonpublic entities.

Issues with the Reporting Date for Internal Controls Opinions

Public companies face similar challenges in testing when seeking audit cost reductions as a result of effective controls. The tests need to cover the entire period, and practical

---

[9] Based on 90% confidence (assurance) and a 10% tolerable deviation rate from a large population.

issues such as new or changed controls during the period may call for separate tests of the pre- and postchange controls for reliance and effectiveness.

However, attestations of controls effectiveness (e.g., required of public companies) are based on the condition of the controls at a point in time. The attestations of companies and auditors regarding controls are made "as of " a specific date, namely the ending balance sheet date. As such, the tests supporting the attestation need to be performed in such a way to demonstrate that at the report date, the controls were functioning. This leads companies and auditors to want to test controls close to the report date. This disconnect between testing for reliance on controls throughout the period and the need to have strong evidence of controls effectiveness at the reporting date has led public companies to different testing strategies. In some cases, some entities test controls throughout the period and test with more emphasis near the reporting date (e.g., for a target sample of 22 total sample items, they might test 4 items each of the first three quarters and test 10 items near the report date). In some cases, the target sample size is increased so that more meaningful tests can be performed each quarter and at year-end. This helps support both reliance on controls and the attestation. Other entities may test controls in the last quarter of the year to meet the attestation requirement. This leaves auditors without a basis for controls reliance throughout the year and may require them to test earlier-performed controls as a basis for reliance. In all cases, when the period of testing does not encompass all transactions during the year, then some documentation action (e.g., inquiry, inspection, reperformance, etc.) is expected in order to close the testing gap to the report date.

With interim testing, a unique issue for entities can arise. Suppose you are doing testing in several periods as the year progresses, but you meet or exceed the number of exceptions you allow for the entire test period earlier in the year. Do you increase the amount of testing planned or perhaps look early into the cause and potential remediation of the problem? In most cases the wise action is to evaluate the deficiencies and, if remediation is indicated, do it. No sense waiting until the year is over to find you failed to get high assurance and cannot remediate the control since no time is left. Also, auditor reliance on the control will be limited in any period which is *not* remediated, so you get a double whammy from waiting. Be proactive and address any issues identified as early as practical.

If you think the early-discovered deviation was an aberration, you may wish to double the original sample size and consider the findings of the original plus expanded sample. Sampling theory supports using something like the doubling factor. Adding "a few" more items to the original sample contributes little to overcoming the original finding and is likely to mislead the assessor.

We are today clearly aware that when testing occurs late in the year, the opportunity for public companies to remediate identified control deficiencies decreases.[10]

---

[10] Bedard and Graham, *Accounting Review*, 2011 (previously cited) and L. Graham and J. Bedard, "The Influence of Auditor and Client Section 404 Processes on Remediation of Internal Control Deficiencies at All Levels of Severity," *Auditing: A Journal of Practice and Theory* (November 2013).

This argues for earlier assessment and testing when possible to identify and correct serious deficiencies and avoid adverse opinions and public disclosures of weaknesses. Nevertheless, certain controlled accounting processes, such as the consolidation process and the tax accrual, are performed after the year-end date and may not be able to be tested in advance of their performance as easily as revenue and expense transaction streams.

From the early implementation of SOX, regulators have touted the synergy of required controls tests and potential reductions in substantive audit procedures to help offset the costs of SOX Implementation. The different test timings of the two objectives continue to be an impediment to realizing all of these hypothetical synergies.

AUDITOR **ALERT**

A frequent concern of inspectors and peer reviewers is the performance of early tests on internal controls without effective or sufficient follow-up to extend the test results to the year-end. The greater the gap between the testing date and the end of the period, the more evidence is expected to be gathered regarding the operation of controls in that gap period, whether for financial reporting or reporting on the effectiveness of internal controls. Simple inquiry and observation are usually sufficient to close only a very small time gap.

Related Financial Statement Areas

Financial statements have related elements. This has been described in the past in terms of cycles, which describe a process rather than focus on a single trial balance caption. For example, the sales cycle includes the order process through to the cash collection process. The accounts receivable generated are also an intermediate step in cash collection. Similarly, the payments and procurement cycles involve multiple accounts and control relationships. The risk associated with false sales or uncollectible sales is embodied in the lack of cash collection. That risk is mostly addressed through the work performed on receivables, such as the aging of receivables, confirmation of the obligations, and so on. Some auditors refer to the issue of related financial statement areas as a holistic approach. To others this is just inherent in their thinking about financial data.

In my view, it is helpful to think about related financial statement areas when assessing and documenting and testing controls and identifying what can go wrong. This will also help in prompting better documentation of the basis for audit decisions about the procedures performed and evaluating the evidence obtained. While perhaps not foolproof, such thought and documentation does not leave the wide ambiguity associated with cryptic documentation.

EXAMPLE

Sample of 25 sales selected for existence testing.

Better

Cash receipt controls were tested effective (X-ref). Accounts receivable were aged, confirmed, and valued, and controls were tested to be effective (X-ref). Because existence risk for sales would be reflected in issues in these two areas, only a small amount of evidence is needed to supplement the existence evidence. Risk = 50%, tolerable 3%, expected = 0, resulting in a sample of 25 items.

Alternatively

Because existence risk for sales would be reflected in issues in cash receipts or accounts payable controls and accounts, limited evidence was needed to supplement the existence assertion based on the results of tests in these areas (X-ref). Risk = 50%, tolerable 3%, expected = 0, resulting in a sample of 25 items.

Sampling and Sample Sizes

Much discussion and debate surrounds the issue of sample size. More attention than it deserves is given to this important but not all-encompassing detail. The subject of sampling itself is surrounded by confusion and lack of very specific guidance and expectations for professional training. In the decades preceding, sampling was deemphasized, as its effectiveness in identifying error and fraud was debated. However, in more recent times, we have identified the fallacy of this argument and placed some constraints around the practices that weakened sampling as a tool (e.g., excusing deficiencies as isolated, failing to project sample results, failing to use supportable sample sizes). In recent years, the AICPA Auditing Standards have sought to tighten the guidance but still not prespecify rigid parameters for auditors.

Sample size is simply a relationship between certain parameters. It is the extent of testing required to meet those parameters when sampling without bias. The parameters for controls tests (attribute samples) are:

- Risk.
- Tolerable deviation rate.
- Expected deviation rate.
- Population size.

Risk is the allowable risk that the true population condition will not be revealed by the sample. In terms of the most serious risk, it is that the auditor will accept the functioning of a control when the true population deviation rate exceeds the tolerable rate specified. If my tolerable threshold is 10%, the *risk* is that the sample will not detect that the true population rate exceeds that, and therefore you will get a false reading and false assurance. In statistical terms, the complement of the risk[11] is the *confidence level* of the test. Guidance regarding risk in the AICPA Audit and Accounting Guide on Sampling (AAG-S) indicates for reliance on controls (or for attesting to the controls effectiveness), a high assurance (confidence) or low risk, say, 90% confidence (or above), is usually supportable. When would higher risk levels (lower confidence levels) be acceptable?

- When less than high reliance is placed on controls
- When other tests of the control (e.g., regulators) have been performed and had a good result
- When testing the accuracy of the tests of others like internal auditors (tests of tests)

While the general public seems wedded to expecting 95% levels of confidence due to some sort of pervasive groupthink, there is nothing magical about that specific confidence level. Certainly when critical controls are heavily relied on to provide significant evidence, levels of 95% or more may be used. When a 25% to 30% increase in sample size is associated with a few additional percentage points of confidence, it does cause pause to the wide use of 95% confidence levels. In auditing financial statements, some substantive procedures must be applied to each significant audit area, so often the 90% assurance level will overall be sufficient to place high reliance on controls. When attestations regarding controls are not the objective, confidence levels of, say, 50% or more can be used to size the degree of reliance on controls with the levels supported by the testing.

Tolerable deviation rate is the rate of deviation that would change your decision about relying on the controls. This is a judgment, and for some controls, it might be lower than for other controls. The AAG-S suggests that for reliance on controls, a deviation threshold of 10% or less is commonly used. While a 10% deviation rate may sound high, not all deviations will result in financial misstatement, so a control failure may not equate to a financial consequence. It also is pretty impractical to expect any control (unless computerized) to be 100% effective. Finally, a control is something that operates over a process, and having a control in place is a lot more assuring than relying solely on the 100% operation of an uncontrolled process and the proven inconsistency of human performance. From that perspective, controls help maintain consistent and accurate processing throughout the period. If designed properly, they reduce risks of error or fraud more effectively than random tests of the accounting data could likely discover.

Expected deviation rate is an allowance for a deviation to appear in the sample without the sample failing to meet the objective. It needs to be a lesser rate than the tolerable rate, or there is no sense in performing the test, and a sample size cannot be determined to meet that condition. Allowing for some level of deviation increases the sample size, so sometimes this parameter is bypassed to get to a lower sample size. That can be a false economy when deviations might appear since failing the test (more deviations were

---

[11] The complement means that when risk is 10%, then confidence is 90%. When risk is 30%, then confidence is 70%. Risk and confidence add to 100%.

found than were planned for) may cause reduced reliance on an acceptable control or cause the sample size to be increased to attempt to show the acceptability of the control. The AAG-S suggests the doubling of the original sample size to overcome an unexpected deviation. Adding just a few extra items does not dilute the sample result sufficiently for the purpose. The more costly aspect of this is the additional selection, documentation gathering, and unplanned time and delay required to increase the sample size, sometimes resulting in similar result as the first sample. When to allow for deviations has a linkage to where one might get an estimate of the deviation rate—a common question. Here are some indicators to when and clues as to how to estimate this parameter:

- When prior tests of this control revealed deviations
- When audit substantive tests previously identified financial misstatements related to this control area
- When the expectation of zero exceptions is based solely on the strength of the control design without prior experience of testing the control.

In many cases it will be efficient to reduce the expected deviation rate after a period of good testing results, so a realistic or slightly conservative estimate (e.g., 1% to 2%) might be a good starting point. Note that a high rate of expected deviation (e.g., over 5%) might indicate the need to remediate the control and not just increase testing levels.

Deviations are not just a numeric. Deviations need to be examined to determine the nature and cause of the deviation. Sometimes deviations reveal issues that transcend the number that were identified in the sample. These are some examples of such reasons that may have more serious impacts on the assessment than the sample numbers may imply:

- Indications of management override of controls
- Indications of fraud or deliberate control failure
- Systematic errors (e.g., computer glitches), which are likely to occur in many other transactions of a similar nature

Population size is a factor here, but a far less important one than most people think. This is the first "parameter" many people name when asked for a factor that influences sample size. Once we are dealing with larger populations of controls (e.g., over 500 items[12]), the population size often has a negligible effect on the resulting sample size. That assumes the parameters of tolerable and expected deviation are expressed in percentage terms. The AAG-S has, in Chapter 3, illustrations of how sample size responds to diminishing population size as well as changes in the expected deviation rate for a given situation. Tables and formulas for determining sample size often assume a large population. To deal with smaller populations, the AAG-S has suggested small population guidance based on practice input to more standardize higher reliance

---

[12] While different sources cite different "large population" sizes, the point at which sample sizes change appreciably changes depending on the other parameters. Once populations are over 2,000 instances, it is safe to assume population size will not impact the sample size.

TABLE 8.1 Infrequently Operating Controls

Control Frequency and Population Size	Sample Size
Quarterly (4)	2
Monthly (12)	2–4
Semimonthly (24)	3–8
Weekly (52)	5–9

Source: AICPA, AAG-S, Chapter 3.

testing of these infrequent controls. When populations fall between 52 instances and a large population calculation, 10% of the population has been suggested by some sampling guidance for Office of Management and Budget (OMB) A-133 engagements as an estimate of a supportable sample size for high assurance. These guidelines do not anticipate expected deviations, since any identified deviation in a small population is likely to indicate ineffective controls. (See Table 8.1.)

Appendix 8A illustrates the determination of sample sizes using various methods, including a computer program application example. Before playing with the sample size methods, it is important to understand the inputs and the guidelines around the sample size guidance.

Determining the sufficiency of your tests is affected by a number of factors. Table 8.2 lists these factors and indicates how they will affect the extent of your tests.

TABLE 8.2 Factors Determining the Extent of Tests

Effect on the Extent of Tests		
Factor to Consider	Increase Number of Tests	Decrease Number of Tests
How frequently the control procedure is performed	Procedure performed often (e.g., multiple times daily)	Procedure performed occasionally (e.g., once a month)
Importance of control	Important control (e.g., high reliance on this control, control addresses multiple assertions or it is a period-end detective control)	Less important control
Degree of judgment required to perform the control	High degree of judgment	Low degree of judgment
Complexity of control procedure	Relatively complex control procedure	Relatively simple control procedure
Level of competence of the person performing the control procedure	Highly competent	Less competent

These factors are generally reflected in the sampling plan by considering them when setting the risk parameter in testing plans.

Sample Sizes for Computerized Controls

A special consideration (benefit) generally exists for controls that are programmed into the computer system. These controls generally relate to transaction controls and controls that operate frequently. Sometimes these controls are called application controls. For example, a control that might be in place could be a three-way match among a sale, relief of inventory, and the invoice and receivable posting (or cash receipt). In other cases such controls might simply identify unusually large transactions for a second level of authorization and review. Thus the automated portion of a control could identify any anomalies for further (e.g., manual) follow-up and resolution. To test that this whole control identifies exceptions, it often need not be tested by a representative sample of items, but if it is identified to operate properly based on one or two instances, that may be sufficient to establish the control's effective periodic operation. The prerequisite to this guidance is that effective ITGCs be in place, since failure of those controls could negate the assumed consistent effective operation of the automated control.

The accompanying manual process cannot be assumed to be accurate without testing, so a sample of exceptions and resolutions will often be necessary to ensure the effective operation of the overall control and process. The efficiency of built-in controls is encouraging more entities to build controls into the computer systems when possible, to reduce manpower and streamline operations.

Although not often thought of as software, spreadsheets serve important roles in accounting systems in some entities and lack of controls over that software can be damaging. Entities need to consider how spreadsheets and used in their accounting processes and how the spreadsheets are developed, controlled, and maintained. A very thoughtful white paper was produced over a decade ago by PricewaterhouseCoopers on the use and control of spreadsheets in the accounting process. Additional reading on this topic and suggestions for establishing controls over spreadsheets integral to financial reporting and be found in various publications, but this article can be very informative on the issues and risks:

http://seeseven.squarespace.com/storage/external-and-analyst-research/PwC%20The%20Use%20of%20Spreadsheets%20Considerations%20for%20Section%20404%20of%20the%20Sarbanes%20Oxley%20Act.PDF

 NONSAMPLING SITUATIONS

While a lot is said about sample sizes and controls, many controls cannot be assessed or tested by using sampling techniques. For example, the important issue of segregation of duties that pervades all the controls components, transactional controls, and the computer environment needs to be considered through analysis (do individuals hold duties that could cause a circumvention of controls or allow the initiation, processing, and approval of transactions without oversight?). Controls from the control environment and risk assessment components are often the result of analysis and inquiries, and sampling may have limited application. When assessing whether the right tone at the top exists in an organization, the examination of the code of conduct itself would not give rise to a sample application. However, when establishing that employees have completed the required annual attestation to the policy, sampling may be employed unless the number of employees is small enough to perform a census (examine all). When establishing the competency of the governance and audit committee, sampling may not be a logical method. Assessments of the adequacy of ITGCs will often call for informed judgments based on inquiries and observations and may not utilize sampling principles. Sampling may be appropriate when verifying computer log entries or verifying password access in larger organizations.

Each principle and the means for gathering evidence regarding that principle will need to be examined and the best methods for accumulating evidence determined. Frequently operating, transactional controls are most likely to be best tested with a sample.

CONFUSION OF SAMPLE SIZE GUIDANCE IN PRACTICE TODAY

Confusion has arisen since 2009 over the sample sizes that can be used to test internal controls, when sampling is appropriate. The confusion is the conjunction with the application of the guidance in the AICPA *Government Auditing Standards and Circular A-133 Audits* guide[13] for Circular A-133 audits to tests of internal controls over financial reporting. This guidance sets out required high-assurance minimum sample sizes of 25, 40, and 60 items for testing controls over compliance with laws and regulations. Underlying the sample sizes are a number of inherent risk criteria identified in the OMB A-133 guidance that drive these testing levels. For example, new federal programs, recovery act programs, high volume or complexity in transaction processing, and so on, will indicate that the larger sample size (60) should be used for testing an important control. The guidance states that these sample sizes do not need to consider expected control deviations, and there is no requirement to modify the samples to allow for deviations or extend samples when deviations are found. The results of these tests then drive specific substantive compliance test sample sizes. The objectives of the OMB and Government Accountability Office (GAO) in having these guidelines differs from the purpose of testing and relying on financial statement controls.

While 25, 40, and 60 are potential sample sizes, so is any other number. AAG-S applies to controls tests over financial reporting performed under AICPA standards. Both PCAOB and AICPA standards indicate that risk, tolerable deviation, and expected deviation rates (and population size) lead to sample sizes. As the AAG-S explains, high controls assurance is generally considered to be attained with 90% or more assurance and

---

[13] American Institute of Certified Public Accountants, Audit Guide: *Government Auditing Standards* and Circular A-133 Audits, AICPA, 2014 Available through www.cpa2biz.com.

10% or less tolerable deviation rates. Tables and formulas are presented in the guide to illustrate sample sizes that meet the sampler's criteria and consideration of expected deviations. While attestations of internal control effectiveness expect a high level of testing assurance, when auditors are just leveraging the testing work of internal auditors or regulators or external consultants, testing levels less than "high assurance" are often sufficient to the purpose. AICPA audits do not *require* high assurance on tests of controls but permit a continuum (low to high) of reliance, depending on the quality of the control and extent to which it was tested. Thus an auditor only wishing a 50% assurance regarding controls might only test seven items (tolerable rate of 10%) if no deviations were expected to support that level of controls reliance. In practice, very critical controls, such as controls over revenue recognition, may sometimes be designed at 95% or more levels of confidence and 1% or less of tolerable deviation, resulting in high-reliance sample sizes of hundreds of items. Thus, the strategy or purpose of the controls test determines the parameters for sampling, and those parameters drive the sample size. Documentation of the parameters should support the sample size chosen for various tests.

Caution is urged when the 25-40-60 sample sizes are suggested, since that may be an indication that inappropriate guidance is being applied to controls over financial reporting, when the guidance is not designed for that purpose.

INFORMATION TECHNOLOGY GENERAL CONTROLS

Principle 11 addresses the COSO ITGC expectations: "selects and develops general controls over technology." Assessing the effectiveness of ITGCs is often performed by or in conjunction with IT specialists, particularly for more complex computer environments. This does not preclude the participation and collaboration of other company project team members and general practice auditors. In fact, an integrated team approach is more likely to lead to an effective response to any issues identified and may help direct an efficient evaluation by the IT professionals. Some IT specialists are more attuned than others to the audit and controls evaluation team needs for the audit reliance and/or SOX assessment. The involvement of IT specialists is recommended when:

- Systems and operations are more complex and involve home-grown software.
- Technologies employed in the business are more advanced or are new.
- The entity is highly reliant on systems for operations and accounting functions (e.g., e-commerce).
- There is much data sharing between applications.
- Little audit evidence is produced to demonstrate the application of automated controls.

A number of the IT benchmark standards for systems evaluation (e.g., COBIT[14]) may set a very high theoretical "ideal" that is likely to be beyond the project team needs.

---

[14] COBIT 5 is a framework for developing, implementing, monitoring, and improving IT governance and management practices. The framework is published by the IT Governance Institute (ITGI) and the Information Systems Audit and Control Association (ISACA).

A more targeted tool is available from www.isaca.org entitled *IT Control Objectives for Sarbanes-Oxley*, 2nd edition. However, even this tool may exceed what is needed to meet the principle effectively and efficiently. However, these resources may be helpful in understanding the general nature of the systems issues.

Different literature may identify either four or five elements of ITGCs. The common elements often include:

- Access and security.
- Systems modifications.
- New systems development.
- Operations.

Another potential element is the IT organization and IT "environment." Some have placed this element as a subset of the overall control environment since the two are indeed highly correlated in systems-dependent enterprises. Under all these elements, an assessment should be made whether segregation of duties issues could arise with IT personnel or in interactions of IT personnel with other employees. In smaller IT environments, issues such as incompatible functions and segregation of duties issues are more common, and management needs to identify monitoring procedures to detect and correct problems as a result of this condition.

The reason ITGCs are singled out for attention and are good candidates for early attention when following the top-down guidance is that deficiencies in these controls can have a pervasive impact on other programs and the processing of accounting data. The theory is that while these overarching controls do not directly cause financial data processing error, they can permit it to happen.

Gathering evidence to support effective ITGCs requires consideration of each of the elements and assessing the extent to which they impact the processing of financial information in the entity. While all audits (AICPA, GAO, PCAOB) need to consider the design of the ITGCs in an organization, when reliance is placed on the computer systems and attestations are publicly made about controls effectiveness, a greater-than-basic level of understanding and evidence that these elements are consistently functioning effectively is required.

 ## TESTING SECURITY AND ACCESS

A very important element is security and access controls. These controls should restrict access to transaction processing programs and databases to only those persons authorized to have access. These controls can be exercised at a network or a program (application) level, or both. Failure to protect databases and programs from unauthorized access and changes can nullify the results of other tests performed to validate the data content. Some procedures used to assess and test security and access include:

- Inquiries and corroborating evidence regarding unauthorized access or network intrusions.

- Recent tests of system penetration or security adequacy by internal or external specialists.
- An analysis of the physical and password accessibility of the servers and workstations to unauthorized persons during or after business hours.
- A mapping of the network, showing the programs used and the controls over authorized access.
- A matrix of personnel and programs, identifying access permissions, including the access or programmers and other systems personnel while performing their duties.
- Identification of network and program password protections. Some systems control application program access at the network level, others may control access at the program level, and some may control access at both or some combination of the two.
- Review and testing of the policy regarding passwords and required periodic changes. A policy should be in effect regarding adding and deleting authorized users of programs (new employees and terminated employees). Passwords should be changed periodically and may be set to meet certain external standards (e.g., *ISO/IEC 27001:2005 > Information technology > Security techniques > Information security management systems > Requirements*).
- Many systems have the capacity to create running logs of system or application access and functions. In most cases these logs should be enabled, to assist in identifying any unauthorized access or changes to data or programs.
- While programmers, vendors, and others may be granted temporary access to systems and applications under revision or development, once programs are tested and functioning, care should be taken to remove that access.

Entities today face severe state and federal financial penalties for the failure to protect personal information from hackers and data thieves. Even apart from possible distortions of accounting data, unauthorized access can create contingent and real financial liabilities when employee data is compromised. Revised AICPA audit standards now require auditors to be proactive in ensuring that laws and regulations are not violated. This heightened responsibility makes it necessary for entities to ensure documented controls are in place to prevent or detect violations.

Testing Program Modifications

There comes a time when programs and systems need to be modified to meet additional regulatory requirements or business needs. Historically many programs were written specifically to address the needs of the entity at the time of the computerization and were modified as needed. When changes were required, programmers modified the program and it was put back on line. How that process of change and implementation occurred often determined whether it was a successful change. Best practices, including written change specifications, extensive testing before the program was made "live," and gathering user feedback at various stages in the change process, became the controls that benchmarked an effective change process. With some packaged systems there are fewer opportunities to modify the underlying program operations, but the same principles can apply when activating or deactivating modules or features or functions that may be part of the accompanying software toolkit. Clear objectives and a quality testing plan can mitigate the risks that financial statement errors will be introduced into the process. Interestingly, if the entity has not undergone any program changes in the period, then this ITGC is not relevant. A forward-thinking organization, though, should consider having a controlled process plan available for when this does occur. Some procedures relating to this element include:

- Identification of any program changes affecting financial reporting information during the period.
- Examination and testing of the controls over the changes—user specifications, preservation of existing data, documentation of program changes, testing plans, user feedback, and evidence of effective testing and implementation.
- Identification of any corrective changes necessary after implementation that may indicate controls ineffectiveness. Note that just a lack of corrective changes does not imply a well-controlled implementation process, as controls might not exist.

Testing New System Development and Implementation

Similar to the issues associated with program changes, new systems/program implementation is just at a grander scale. For example: Replacing legacy (home grown) software with packaged or enterprise software can be a daunting process with consequences. However, continuing to maintain home-grown software despite technology and operating system changes can be even more expensive and risk-laden. If not a managed process, a bad experience can lead to data loss and financial loss. Many organizations, including the government, are transitioning to commercial software and abandoning homegrown software that has become difficult to maintain. The quality and flexibility of commercial software continues to improve. If a company has skipped several updates, even upgrades to later versions of simpler software (e.g., QuickBooks, Peachtree) can create risks that the data may not transfer properly. Changing to a different software raises the risks associated with data transfer or information loss, requiring even more careful testing.

Many of the benchmarks for effective control of this process are similar to the ones for program modifications:

- Specifications are documented for the functionality and performance of the new system.
- Timing of the change is considered relative to the entity business cycle.
- Mapping the data elements to be transferred to the new system before it will resume on-line operations. Overall, there should be a map of data that flows or might flow between systems as part of the systems documentation, so that whenever a program change or new system is implemented, the data flows affected can be identified in advance.
- Backup and recovery plans in case the implementation fails.
- Identification of the program changes affecting financial reporting information during the period.

- Robust testing of the software and transferred data before it goes live.
- Gathering user feedback and evidence of effective implementation as part of the testing process and after the system goes live.
- Identification of any corrective changes necessary after implementation that may indicate controls ineffectiveness. Note that a lack of corrective changes does not imply a well-controlled implementation process, as controls over the process might not exist.

TRUE **STORY**

A major corporation decided to replace its legacy inventory and receivables system in part of the country with well-known commercial enterprise software. To save money, the organization identified several of its top IT professionals to attend three days of training on implementation. While the training was more of an orientation course than a how-to, the techs set out anyway to make the conversion.

Not only was the system implementation unsuccessful, but in the process there was a corruption of the data and a material amount of receivables information was lost. At the end of the year, accountants were challenged to determine if there should be losses recorded, since the information and systems had not been restored at that point. It was decided not to record estimated losses since it seemed improbable that the data was not recoverable.

Unfortunately, the company and its auditors were under challenge in this time period in a class action shareholder suit alleging misstated financial statements. The missing data was material to that allegation, and its treatment in the financials was important.

In the end, significant losses due to the systems issue were recorded in the following year. A saving grace for the company and its auditors was an astute audit committee action, which, when faced with the dilemma of the accounting issue, solicited a written report from an independent, large auditing firm confirming the judgments made in the financial statements.

The company and its auditors nevertheless paid a stiff price trying to avoid professional installation consulting expenses. This situation brings to mind the Ben Franklin quote: "Penny wise and pound foolish."

Testing Operations

Over time, the operations aspects of ITGCs have changed importance. Today some primary functions relating to this area include: maintenance of software and hardware acquisition, meeting user needs and issues through the help desk or some alternative, and backup and disaster recovery functions. When mainframe computers were the primary computing tool, the sequencing of various batch processing functions (e.g., sales, receipts, etc.) was an important element of effective operations. This no longer is a major concern since batch processing is rarely practiced. Of course, there are exceptions to every rule, and the individual entity situation drives the issue the relevance of controls. Some controls commonly associated with operations will include:

▪ Controls to ensure the policies and procedures for hardware and software acquisition and upgrades and maintenance are followed.
▪ Effective and timely resolution of user problems and issues.
▪ Controls to ensure the monitoring of any open issues for resolution or reporting of deficiencies that could impair financial reporting.
▪ Ensuring that timely backup procedures are performed, including the proper maintenance of software and backups if needed. Some entities may require that images of software platforms be retained so that past information can be accessed and read or printed as potentially needed for regulatory or commercial purposes.
▪ A disaster recovery plan. Events like 9/11, Hurricanes Katrina and Sandy, and other incidents prove the importance of creative thinking in designing these plans.

BEST-LAID **PLANS**

On 9/11 a high-tech computer service business in a World Trade Center building that tracked hardware and software licenses for many businesses had a sophisticated backup and recovery operation that still failed to be effective. The backup and recovery site was located in the other World Trade Center building that also collapsed in the attack. What were the chances?

Further Thoughts on Testing ITGCs

For the most part, ITGC tests will involve inquiry and observation and some examination of evidence. Sampling may be used in some situations, and that may depend on the size of the operation and number of systems and personnel involved. For example, when testing the accuracy of the matrix of personnel and programs for permitted access, one could think of the matrix as a group of cells, a selection of which could be tested to ensure access is or is not permitted as indicated in the matrix. In a log of "issues" calls, a sample could be selected to ensure timely and adequate resolution and that issues that should have been reported regarding hardware or software operation were carried to appropriate levels in the organization.

Obviously, user changes or new systems implementation cannot be tested in periods when they do not occur. Therefore, deficiencies in these controls cannot be identified except through current issues that can be traced back to prior periods. For the most part, absence of these activities makes direct testing impossible, even if policies and controls are described to be applicable during such activities. In various guidance, it has been noted that disaster recovery plans need not be directly tested for SOX if they seem adequate, but of course a dry run of the procedures to ensure completeness and feasibility is a wise investment. Similarly, material weaknesses in disaster recovery could not be identified in a period where disaster recovery was not employed.

Some IT professionals question such guidance and believe that in the absence of seeing these controls working, plans can be assessed sufficiently for feasibility to reliably identify material weaknesses. Different auditors may reach different conclusions regarding this issue from their perspective when performing financial statement audits. Audits of internal control are directed to follow the guidance on severity assessment. Best practice says that a good recovery plan is advisable in all cases, whether implemented and tested or not.

Sample Size Tutorial

THE SAMPLE SIZE determination approaches described in this appendix assume that a representative sample of controls will be selected. By *representative*, it is meant that the selection is made without bias, not that the sample will result in a mini-version of the population in all respects. Random selection procedures are considered to be appropriate for this purpose. Other selection approaches, such as haphazard selection, that simulate random selection or systematic sampling (e.g., every *n*th item) are often used by the nonstatistical sampler and those without access to sample selection software.

Recent sampling guidance has reinforced the linkage between the sampling parameters (e.g., risk, tolerable, expected) that have been long established in professional standards and computed statistical sample sizes. American Institute of Certified Public Accountants (AICPA) AU-C No. 530, *Audit Sampling*, paragraph A.14, states:

> An auditor who applies nonstatistical sampling exercises professional judgment to relate the same factors used in statistical sampling in determining the appropriate sample size. Ordinarily, this would result in a sample size comparable with the sample size resulting from an efficient and effectively designed statistical sample, considering the same sampling parameters.

In practice, the Public Company Accounting Oversight Board (PCAOB) also seems to embrace this guidance, as tables and other practice aids seem to be in common use when they assess the adequacy of sample sizes.

Unless we are among the privileged who were born with an embedded chip in our heads for calculating probabilities, most mortals need to reference some decision aids to estimate sample sizes that meet our specifications. However, over time and with experience, many professionals can estimate sample sizes similar to the tables or formulas without formal reference to these aids. In this appendix, several aids are described.

Different sample size estimation approaches may result in slightly different sample sizes even when the same sample parameters are used. These differences are usually negligible and should not be a matter of concern. The sampling police will not be visiting you to discuss sample sizes of 59 versus 60 items. Challenges will arise when 10 items are sampled and the sampling parameters suggest 22 or so items should be examined.

SAMPLE SIZE FORMULA

It is not always practical to have computer programs or extensive tables close at hand when determining sample sizes for planning purposes. Sample sizes can be roughly estimated using a few factors and a simple formula.

For situations where more precision in the sample size determination process is desirable (e.g., when designing the sample to allow for some level of expected deviation, or when the population is small), tables or computer programs can be used to determine more precise sample sizes.

A simple formula composed of two key sampling parameters—confidence level and tolerable deviation rate—can provide a rough estimate of a sample size (assuming zero exceptions) from a large population.

$$N = F/T$$

where

N is the sample size.
F is the confidence level factor from the next table.
T is the tolerable % (deviation rate or misstatement) expressed as a percentage of the population.

Factors

Confidence Level	99	95	90	87	80	75	63	50
Factor (F)	4.61	3.00	2.31	2.00	1.61	1.39	1.00	.70

Source: Adapted from AICPA *Audit Sampling* Guide, 2014 ed., Appendix C.2.

Example—Test of Controls
Check Authorizations: 3,000
Tolerable Deviations: 300 (10% rate)
Confidence: 90%
$N = F/T$
$N = 2.31/.10$
$N = 23$

The formula is based on attributes sampling theory and assumes no deviations will be found. To allow for a low level of deviation in the sample, double the computed sample size or use a more refined tool, such as a table or computer program, to determine the sample size.

The formula assumes the use of a random selection where each population item is given an equal chance of selection.

The formula assumes a large population (over 1, 000 control operations). It will be overly conservative (the sample size will be excessive) when used in smaller populations.

To consider expected deviation rates when determining sample size, a computer program such as IDEA can be used to determine precise attribute sample sizes for a full range of confidence levels, tolerable deviation rates, expected deviation rates and population sizes.[1] In addition, the AAG-S has tables that can provide sample size guidance at the 90% and 95% confidence levels (Tables A-1 and A-2).

 ## DECISION RULE FOR RESULTS

If no deviations are found in the sample, the sample achieved the planned-for level of reliance. However, if a deviation is identified in the sample, since none was planned for, then the test fails to provide the planned-for level assurance. In nonpublic engagements and when attestations regarding controls effectiveness are not relevant, an option is to reduce or eliminate reliance on the control depending on how many deviations were identified. When attestation is still sought although the test failed, adding additional sample items to the first sample is also possible. If the first sample was for 45 items (90% confidence, 5% tolerable), an additional 45 items with no deviations is suggested to support reliance on the control. Adding just a few additional items to the original sample is a meaningless procedure and does not support control effectiveness. When results reveal many deviations, a first step is to make sure the test person understood the control and what to look for, but then it may be prudent to have the control remediated (redesigned and personnel trained in its performance) and retested after remediation. A remediated control will not affect attestation at a later date but will preclude reliance on that control for financial reporting purposes in the period when it was ineffective.

 ## USING A TABLE TO DETERMINE SAMPLE SIZES

In general:

1. Select a table appropriate for the confidence level (100% − Risk%) desired. The AICPA guide has tables for 90% and 95% assurance. Tables in other publications, such as *Montgomery's Auditing*,[2] may include many other confidence levels.
2. Locate the sample size where the tolerable and expected rates intersect within the table. The number in parentheses in the table is the number of expected deviations than can be tolerated.

---

[1] See www.audimation.com.
[2] V. O'Reilly, P. McDonnell, B. Winograd, J. Gerson, and H. Jaenicke. *Montgomery's Auditing,* 12th ed. (New York: John Wiley & Sons, 1998).

TABLE 8A.1 Sample Size Table: 90 Percent Confidence/Reliability[3]

Expected Rate	Tolerable Rate										
	2%	3%	4%	5%	6%	7%	8%	9%	10%	15%	20%
0.00%	114(0)	76(0)	57(0)	45(0)	38(0)	32(0)	28(0)	25(0)	22(0)	15(0)	11(0)
.50	194(1)	129(1)	96(1)	**77(1)**	64(1)	55(1)	48(1)	42(1)	38(1)	25(1)	18(1)
1.00	*	176(2)	96(1)	77(1)	64(1)	55(1)	48(1)	42(1)	38(1)	25(1)	18(1)
1.25	*	221(3)	132(2)	77(1)	64(1)	55(1)	48(1)	42(1)	38(1)	25(1)	18(1)
1.50	*	*	132(2)	105(2)	64(1)	55(1)	48(1)	42(1)	38(1)	25(1)	18(1)
1.75	*	*	166(3)	105(2)	88(21)	55(1)	48(1)	42(1)	38(1)	25(1)	18(1)
2.00	*	*	198(4)	132(3)	88(2)	75(2)	48(1)	42(1)	38(1)	25(1)	18(1)
2.25	*	*	*	132(3)	88(2)	75(2)	65(2)	42(1)	38(2)	25(1)	18(1)
2.50	*	*	*	158(4)	110(3)	75(2)	65(2)	58(2)	38(2)	25(1)	18(1)
2.75	*	*	*	209(6)	132(4)	94(3)	65(2)	58(2)	52(2)	25(1)	18(1)
3.00	*	*	*	*	132(4)	94(3)	65(2)	58(2)	52(2)	25(1)	18(1)

Example

Determine an appropriate substantive sample size for a sample requiring 90% confidence, a tolerable deviation rate of 5%, and an expected deviation rate of .5%.

The highlighted sample size is 77 items. The sample can tolerate 1 deviation of a noncritical nature and still meet the 90% assurance being sought.

A similar decision rule to that previously mentioned is followed for table-based sample sizes. If the planning criteria are met, then the sample is assumed to support the planned-for confidence level/risk level. If not, then the test fails, and similar options may exist regarding the next steps.

In some cases, the expected deviation rate is very hard to estimate (a new control, first test of a control, recently remediated control, etc.). In such cases, a formal two-stage sample may result in a valid conclusion at the most economical cost. In a two-stage sampling the sampling can be stopped (and the sample result "passes") if after the first stage no deviations are found. If a deviation is found, the test continues to an additional number of items. When two deviations are found, the overall plan "fails," and it is recommended that the underlying process be fixed before further sampling. For example, a two-stage sequential sampling plan (see Table 8A.2) is described in *Montgomery's Auditing* and the AICPA guide for a 90% confidence level. Other tables at different confidence levels are also shown in *Montgomery's Auditing*.

---

[3] Adapted from AAG, *Audit Sampling* (AICPA, 2014) Table A-2, page 133. An asterisk (*) indicates an impractical sample size for general audit situations due to the close proximity of the tolerable and expected rates. In such situations the use of software to compute a more accurate sample size is recommended.

TABLE 8A.2 Two-Stage Sequential Sampling Plan

Tolerable Rate	Initial Sample Size	Second-Stage Sample Size
10	23	29
9	26	30
8	30	30
7	35	32
6	41	38
5	51	39
4	64	49
3	89	56
2	133	87

COMPUTER-DETERMINED SAMPLE SIZES

Today the use of computer-assisted audit tools (CAATS) by internal and external auditors is common. Such programs may have functions to generate sample sizes based on supplied parameters, including population size estimates. ACL and IDEA are two common tools with such capabilities. IDEA[4] has granted permission to illustrate its program in this volume.

Suppose there were a population of 800 control operations and you wished a 90% assurance that the control would not fail to operate more than 5% of the time. No exceptions were expected. Using IDEA, you would identify the program that generates attribute sample sizes under the **Analysis** tab, and complete the input screen as shown in Figure 8A.1. The computed sample size is 43 items.

Some additional information is observable from this output that is not evident from the tables. If 1 deviation is found (see the row under 1 Deviation in the output), the achieved confidence from the test is shown to be 66%, which is less than designed. But such information may help assess you what level of reliance might still be placed on this control for financial reporting purposes even though for the attestation of controls effectiveness purposes, this lower level of assurance might not be acceptable. An additional benefit of the computer analysis is the ability to test the impact of different parameters, such as population size, on the computed sample size. This function can be most useful when population sizes are between small and large, and when less than high levels of assurance (e.g., less than 90%) are sought. For example: Would the sample size change if the true population size was 1200 instances rather than my estimated 800 instances?

---

[4] IDEA Data Analysis Software V9 2013. CaseWare IDEA, Inc. Toronto, Canada, www.caseware-idea.com/fsh.asp. See also www.audimation.com.

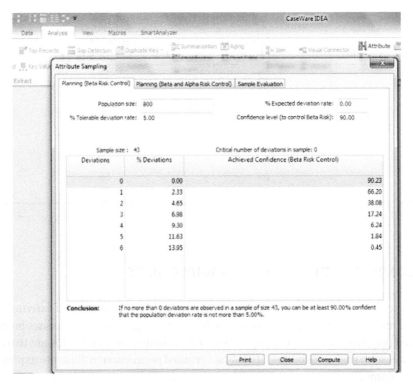

FIGURE 8A.1 IDEA Sample Size Determination

  CAUTIONS ABOUT DEVIATIONS

Care needs to be taken that when "accepting" a control deviation, even when it is planned for, the deviation does not represent qualitative characteristics that indicate a serious issue, such as a fraud, or a systematic error that is likely to be repeated throughout the population of controls under certain conditions. Seemingly infrequent fraudulent transactions are not to be overlooked due to their serious nature. You may only have identified the proverbial tip of the iceberg.

The old concept of excusing an isolated exception found in a sample result has pretty much disappeared from reputable sampling practice because, more often than not, the selection of a representative sample of items did indeed select a "representative" exception of some sort. Even if the exception seems to be explainable, there could be other deviations in the population with different explanations. Recall that it is the incidence of deviation that is of interest when selecting an unbiased sample, not the exact cause or nature of the deviation. It may be tempting to dismiss identified deviations, but it is a dangerous practice in the real world. Don't fool yourself here.

9

Developing Questionnaires and Conducting Interviews

T HE TOPICS OF developing questionnaires and conducting interviews are not standard academic or certified public accounting (CPA) firm training topics for accountants and auditors. Prior to Sarbanes-Oxley (SOX), many financial audits were conducted primarily by substantive procedures that tested balances and transaction streams with direct tests. The requirements of SOX for public companies and a reinvigorated set of American Institute of Certified Public Accountants (AICPA) risk standards required companies and auditors to look at broader controls issues on all audits, including the control environment. As a result, information not previously directly gathered needs to be evidenced in the controls documentation of both entities and auditors. In addition, the continued improvement in controls of public and nonpublic companies and governments have made the reliance on effective internal controls a plausible and efficient strategy for many more audits than ever before. Management benefits from effective systems of internal controls by experiencing fewer fire drills and surprises and by opening the door to more efficient audits.

Sometimes "difficult" and sensitive inquiries and assessments must be made during this process. For example, it is not easy to openly acknowledge the chief executive officer (CEO) is an overbearing and abrasive executive when it was that person's initiative that founded the company; similarly, it is difficult to assess that the controller is not qualified to address the complex accounting issues the entity faces. But when management style interferes with effective governance or competence in financial reporting or borders on intimidation and management override, the issue is important to the control environment assessment. Sidestepping these issues has risk implications for entities and auditors. Cases have been launched against CPA firms for failing to pass along to governance issues of control weaknesses the CPA firm was well aware of. In a number of cases, top leadership changes in corporate offices has been attributed to the focus on responsible and ethical leadership brought about by the new controls and governance emphasis in the business environment. Some "leaders" simply knew their style would not result in a passing grade.

Management of public companies is required to have support for their assertion regarding the effectiveness of the internal controls. Securities and Exchange Commission (SEC) Release No. 33-8809 states:

> Management's assessment must be supported by evidential matter that provides reasonable support for its assessment. …
>
> Reasonable support for an assessment would include the basis for management's assessment, including documentation of the methods and procedures it utilizes to gather and evaluate evidence. (p. 31)

Similarly, auditors of public companies are required to have evidence to support their opinion regarding the effectiveness of internal controls. Even entities and auditors not in the public company environment, but still seeking an audit, are expected to have evidence regarding the implementation and effectiveness of internal controls. COSO reminds us that the responsibility for establishing effective controls lies with management and not the auditors. That goes for nonpublic entities also. Testing and evidence gathering are critical to supporting the assertions that the controls are effective.

When we talk about tests supporting controls effectiveness, we invoke thoughts of sampling and examining entity documentation supporting transactions. Indeed, sampling is a primary testing procedure when evaluating the effectiveness of a control activity, such as the approval of a credit sale or an expenditure. Often the nature of the control itself will suggest a test. If the stated control is that employees annually review and sign that they have read and understood the code of conduct, then a sample of employees could be drawn to ensure the signatures were obtained and the employees stated that they comprehended the policy. Sampling and evidence gathering were also addressed in Chapter 8 of this book.

However, gathering evidence regarding many control environment, risk assessment and monitoring principles may not involve sampling as a test since there may not be a population of examples from which a sample can be drawn. For example, how would you evidence the effectiveness of the board and governance structure? Often such information is gathered from reading meeting minutes, attending meetings, observing behavior and actions, and reviewing the qualifications of board members. The full gamut of evidence gathering may be considered in the process of supporting the effectiveness of the control—observation, inquiry, examination of specific documents, and so on.

What is often overlooked is the evidence gathered every day by every person on the entity project or audit team that supports the controls environment assessment. While a daily journal of observations would be overkill, a summary paragraph or two from project team and audit team members of their periodic observations and any noted direct evidence of effective (or ineffective) controls monitoring (e.g., management questioning the lack of timely bank reconciliations) can add considerable evidence to the information gathered by direct inquiries and questionnaires.

While more of an art than a science, there are some principles and considerations to developing questionnaires and conducting interviews that can be employed by project and audit staff.

SURVEYS OF EMPLOYEES

Surveys can be an effective way of collecting documentary information. In particular, surveys are often used to evaluate whether an entity's culture and personnel policies create an environment that enables the effective functioning of activity-level controls. In other words, a company's written code of conduct or personnel policies, by their mere existence, will not be sufficient to support an assertion about these control environment examples. In order to determine whether the policies are operating effectively, feedback from employees is most useful. For most entities, that information will be gathered most efficiently through a survey. (See Figure 9.1 for common problems with surveys.)

Whom and How Many to Survey

The reliability and validity of the survey results are directly related to the survey techniques, whom you survey, and how many responses you receive. For the purposes of your assessment, whether you use formal random selection procedures for identifying respondents or use less formal methods (provided you try to avoid bias in the selection process), the method should not matter. Nonstatistical sampling methods and qualitative analysis of the results will usually suffice.

Some common problems with surveys, which will reduce their reliability, include:
- Questionnaire is too long or hard to read.
- Questions are difficult to answer because:
  - Language is unclear or ambiguous.
  - More than one question is being asked.
  - Respondents do not have information available to answer question (e.g., asking the wrong person).
- Choices in multiple-choice questions are incomplete, hard to interpret, or not mutually exclusive.
- There may be bias in framing the questions that suggests or prompts an answer.
- Directions or transitions between sections of the survey are hard to follow.
- Respondents may be reluctant to provide written answers to sensitive questions. This can also be a response to autocratic management and a culture of fear of reprisal.

FIGURE 9.1 Common Problems with Surveys

However, in order to ensure the most reliable and valid results, you should design the survey in a way that incorporates some main concepts underlying statistical sampling methods, including:

- *The more respondents, the more reliable the results.* If it is feasible, ask for responses from a reasonable proportion (e.g., 5%–10%) of the employees.
- *Stratified samples yield better results.* If the entity has several divisions or locations, make sure that your survey includes employees from these different segments. You also should try to obtain results from different levels of employees within the organization, from top management on down. Include operating and administrative personnel in surveys of the control environment
- *To be valid, a sample should be representative of the population. Representative* is defined in terms of a lack of bias in selection. *Representative* does not mean that each subgroup at each location has to be sampled in proportion to the totals. The survey can be varied to include other groups and locations over time. When entities take surveys and report results, independent audit evidence could include a few overlapping responses to verify management assessments, and look at other groups and locations to confirm the assessment.
- *Think twice before knowingly excluding a group from the population.* Your engagement is limited to testing the effectiveness of internal control over financial reporting. However, it would be a mistake to limit your survey about corporate culture and personnel policies only to those individuals directly involved in the financial reporting process. Current fraud and risk assessment guidance suggests that operations and sales personnel can provide insight into issues of financial reporting significance (e.g., budget stresses and management interference in business practices). Operational and administrative personnel can provide valuable insights into the operating effectiveness of several components of the entity's internal control. For example, sales personnel may relate excessive management pressure to meet aggressive sales targets. That could signal risks of period-end cutoff control failures or channel-stuffing or using bill-and-hold sales to boost sales in the current period.

Determining whether you have received enough responses to your survey to draw a valid conclusion is a matter of judgment, but as a control procedure, the extent of controls sampling guidance can help guide the minimum extent of testing to reach valid conclusions. More evidence may be needed when exceptions are noted or expected in the survey responses. For example: When a disgruntled employee is surveyed in a small sample, the result stands out and will need further investigation and likely call for more evidence. Significant issues arising from the survey usually call for an investigation and resolution anyway, which can take time. For example, in the course of a litigation case against the company and its auditors, it was noted by the plaintiff that an employee had made a fraud accusation against the company. On further review, it was determined that the company's audit committee was alerted to this accusation, and they hired independent counsel to look into the matter. In the end, it was concluded that the accusation was baseless. That example of the responsible handling of the situation neutralized the (baseless) assertion that fraud risks were ignored by the company and its auditors.

When and How Often

Most of the tests you will perform will have to consider their timing. Perform the tests too far in advance of the entity's reporting date, and you run the risk that the tests will need to be updated or reperformed. If you test too close to the reporting date, you have little or no time to take corrective action if the results identify a deficiency or a weakness.

Surveys can also take a long time. Even when management provides support and sets deadlines, survey responses are rarely all completed timely and when due. Individuals need time to respond, and if they do not respond, you will need time to follow up and obtain responses. The evaluation of survey results, especially if they include open-ended, written responses, can also be time consuming.

Additionally, you should consider the nature of the subject matter of the survey, which often addresses the entity's culture and the effectiveness of its personnel policies. Both of these typically change slowly over time. Thus, in most instances, your biggest risk would be in performing your tests too late to take corrective action, *not* in performing them early and having the results subject to dramatic change.

If you do perform a survey well in advance of the entity's reporting date, you should consider resurveying later in the reporting period if:

- The entity makes significant changes to its policies or takes corrective action for identified control environment weaknesses.
- Other significant events occur that could affect the entity's culture or effectiveness of its personnel policies. For example, unanticipated layoffs can alter employees' perceptions about the entity's culture.

Update the earlier evidence by observation, inquiry, or asking a sample of respondents if their responses would differ if the questions were asked today.

Testing the Survey

Plan on pilot testing your survey. By pilot testing and making necessary corrections to the survey, you will increase response rates and create more reliable and valid results. In her book *How to Conduct Surveys*, Arlene Fink provides suggestions for pilot testing a survey:[1]

- *Pilot test in segments.* For example, you may want to start by testing just the instructions or the wording of a few questions or one section. Is the question clear? Can it be answered by the person being surveyed? Is there a need to provide a comment area where the employee can clarify, explain, or provide examples to support the assessment?

---

[1] Arlene Fink, *How to Conduct Surveys: A Step by Step Guide*, 4th ed. (Thousand Oaks, CA: Sage, 2008).

- *Test the administrative details.* If the survey is relatively simple, such as a paper-based survey that is filled out and mailed back to you, this test may not be that crucial. However, if the administration of the survey is more complex, such as an online survey, testing the delivery mechanism (e.g., Web-based surveys) in advance will be more important to make sure the respondents can work the delivery technology.
- *Informal testing can work just fine.* The whole point of pilot testing is to identify weaknesses in either the survey questions or the way the survey is delivered that can affect the reliability of its results. That objective may be accomplished in a relatively informal fashion, such as by showing the questions to several prospective respondents and asking them if they could respond.
- *Focus on the clarity of the questions and the general format of the survey.* These issues may indicate that the survey is unreliable or otherwise needs revision:
  - Failure to answer questions
  - Several different types of answers provided to the same question
  - Comments written in the space provided or in the margin
- If you expect your survey will result in a range of responses, then be sure that your pilot test allows for responses from both ends of the range.

Data Analysis and Reporting Results

When planning your survey, give some thought to how you will analyze and interpret the data and report your conclusions to management. For example, a report to management on a survey of employees about the company's culture may read:

> We sent a survey to all of the company's 750 employees asking for their feedback on the company's culture and climate for ethical behavior. Four hundred of those surveys were returned to us. Approximately 60% of those who responded were not even aware that the company has a code of conduct, which is posted on the company intranet and reproduced in the employee handbook. Only 15% of respondents had read the code. However, of those who read the code, nearly 80% agreed with the statement: "The company's code of conduct helps me identify unacceptable business practices."
>
> The response to this survey question, combined with our own reading of the company's code of conduct, led us to conclude that, as written, the code could contribute toward creating a control environment that is conducive to the effective operation of activity-level controls. However, in order to be effective, the company should take steps to ensure that more employees are aware of the code's existence and familiar with its contents.

So did the survey support or not support the effectiveness of the control objective? Even the conclusion is confusing. Potential effectiveness is not effectiveness. The response rate was low, and the exception rate for those not having read the code was high. This response would not lead to a conclusion of effective implementation of the code. When designing your survey, if you cannot anticipate how you will analyze the data and set criteria to be able to report your conclusions, then you should reconsider the survey design. Establish some advance criteria, based on expectations and preliminary inquiries against which to evaluate the results.

Writing Your Own Survey Questions

You should modify any sample survey to meet the needs of your specific entity or engagement. Fink offers this advice for writing survey questions:

- *Each question should be meaningful to respondents.* If you introduce questions that have no obvious purpose (e.g., demographic information), you may need to provide some explanation to the respondent why you are asking the question.
- *Use Standard English.* Avoid specialized words, such as "entity-level controls," or even "COSO" whose definition is not readily known, particularly when the survey will go to operations and administrative people. Legal terms such as "fraud" are generally not understood by respondents nor are the names of fraud schemes, such as kiting or skimming.
- *Make questions concrete: Questions should be as close to the respondent's personal experience as possible.* For example, the question "Is management ethical?" is very abstract. A more concrete question that addresses the same issue would be "Has your supervisor ever asked you to take action that appears unacceptable under the company's code of conduct?" Alternatively, in a more general way: "Has your supervisor ever asked you to take action that has made you feel uncomfortable?"
- *Avoid biased words and phrases.*
- *Avoid questions that are simply unanswerable because they are predicated on an incorrect premise.* A common example is "When did you stop beating your spouse?" One that I like in the context of testimony is the question "Are you or are you not a pathological liar?" Those questions boggle the mind.
- *Each question should have just one thought.* For example, a respondent could be confused by the question "Are the activities of the company's employees and board of directors consistent with the company's ethical values?" What if the respondent believes that the actions of board members are consistent with the ethical values but those of the employees are not? How should he or she respond? To avoid confusion, the question should be split into two, one that asks about the board and a second that asks about employees.

While best practice indicates that bias in survey questions can taint the survey results, there is some evidence that the wording of questions sometimes can help the respondent's recall of facts. For example, a questionnaire asking recall about the existence of certain audit risks in an entity they audited was completed by engagement audit seniors and managers. This experiment involved a number of audit teams and engagements and different CPA firms. The questionnaire was manipulated between the managers and seniors so that they would alternatively receive the two different versions of the questionnaire (to neutralize the difference between the two levels of respondents). Across the groups, it was shown that questions that focused directly on risks in the "negative" frame (e.g., "there are instances of management ignoring control deficiencies brought to their attention") were more effective than neutral or positively worded questions (e.g., "management responds appropriately to control deficiencies brought to their attention") in eliciting more specific recall of engagement facts and risks. As a result, some major CPA firms started to use more pointed, negative-framed questions in their surveys to facilitate recall and deeper thought. The positive and negative wording also may have focused more attention on the question being asked, in lieu of having each question only framed in one way.[2] In sum, building some variety in the format and structure of the questions can encourage more effective, detailed responses and avoid the risk of mechanical just checking the box for each answer.

Few questionnaires provided by outside vendors or even industry groups will be appropriate for every entity and circumstance. It is worthwhile to review and customize these instruments before dissemination. When questions do not meet the nature of the business (e.g., questions regarding inventories in a service business or government agency), the result can be low response rates and confusing responses when respondents try to answer these questions. Even CPA firms need to tailor their tools to specific audit client circumstances since rarely does one size fit all in questionnaires.

 ## CONDUCTING INTERVIEWS

The skill of interviewing is an art, and you will conduct more effective interviews through practice and through further training. Watching others conduct successful interviews will also help you to build skills. However, executives and politicians are warned to watch for loaded questions from press reporters. An effective interview is not designed to trip up the respondent or trigger a confession but to gather reliable information that relates to the control issue being studied. So, the "interviews" most familiar to you from the news media you may not be the best models to follow.

Interviewing will generally be used to:

- Obtain your understanding of the procedures and controls that employees perform.
- Obtain information regarding what other evidence exists to support the five components of internal control.
- Gain evidence of consensus regarding the overall control environment. Control environment evidence is often gathered from management and employees through surveys, focus groups, or direct interviews.

In some cases, the information being sought through the interview process is qualitative, such as the tone at the top. Such responses do not generally lend themselves to quantitative measurement, but certainly observations of the tone are evident in the

---

[2] Lynford Graham and Jean Bedard, "Fraud Risk and Audit Planning," *International Journal of Auditing* 7, No. 1 (2003): 55–70; and Jean C. Bedard and Lynford Graham, "The Effects of Risk Orientation, Underlying Risk, and Client Experience on Risk Factor Identification and Audit Test Planning," *Auditing: A Journal of Practice and Theory* (Fall 2002): 39–56.

auditor's, internal auditor's, or evaluator's daily activity on site. When other evidence is not practical to obtain, such observations of the evaluator are certainly appropriate to support inquiry responses. However, some questions in a questionnaire may include a scale of agreement (e.g., 1 = disagree, 10 = agree) with a statement like "Management sets a positive ethical tone to operations." Such questions can create opportunities to identify anomalies and also provide a quantitative rating of overall impressions. In general, more senior executives are likely to be interviewed as opposed to completing a written survey. In addition to the more personal touch of an interview, astute interviewers who are observant sometimes can obtain more than the specific answer. The respondent avoiding answering a clear question, unclear and rambling responses, physical clues to stress, and the like can all lead to important follow-up situations.

For some tasks, inquiry will provide a principal (and not the only) source of evidence regarding some internal controls. Inquiry may be a principal source of evidence in assessing the effectiveness of the governance group (e.g., board and audit committee) or whether ethics policies have been well implemented. Thus, a procedure that is often combined with inquiry regarding the more qualitative information about internal controls is observation. Your team's on-site observations can also provide corroborating or disconfirming evidence that should also be considered when drawing conclusions.

The auditor will want to assess any evidence the entity has gathered about the control environment. Sometimes reviewing those procedures will help auditors reduce their audit effort or design other tests that do not duplicate the efforts of management to document their design, implementation, and compliance with the COSO Principles. Nevertheless, it is hard to envision a circumstance where the auditor will reach a more favorable conclusion from applying his or her tests than the one reached by management in documenting and assessing their own controls. Human behavior often suggests a more favorable result when grading your own paper.

Examples of Where Interviews Are Used

Oral communication is an important element of documenting and assessing internal controls over financial reporting. Some common areas where interviews will be used to gather evidence include:

- Walk-throughs—confirming documented procedures with employees performing the controls.
- Tone at the top and other control environment principles, objectives, and attributes.
- Antifraud program awareness, implementation, and effectiveness.
- Ethics policies and employee awareness.
- Personnel policies covering ethical issues and laws protecting workers.
- Possible evidence of management override of established controls. The AICPA published a study that identified management override as the "Achilles' Heel of Fraud Prevention." This report can be obtained at the AICPA site: www.aicpa.org/audcommctr/download/achilles_heel.pdf
- Review of the password and security policies and the process for their implementation and periodic change.

- Information systems reports and databases and how they relate to the overall business objectives and COSO Principles.
- The receipt of relevant, timely, and accurate information used in the employee functions or in the executive management of the business.
- The proper functioning of the computer systems and appropriate response times for resolving reported issues.
- Monitoring and supervision practices.

Wherever there is objective evidence available, make it a practice to review and cite that as part of your assessment process. Inquiry alone is weak evidence. When asking questions, a common follow-up is: Can you think of an example?, which can often lead to other evidence.

Remember that the overall purpose of your inquiries is to gather evidence about the effectiveness of specific controls. Your primary purpose is *not* to gather information about what the policy is; you should be able to gather that information mostly through reading existing, relevant documentation. If there are corporate ethics and code of conduct policies you wish to inquire about, read them first to assess their content for potential effectiveness as well as for developing a basis for the questions in the interviews. Consider their potential effectiveness as they are written. In larger entities, the human resources (HR) function may keep records of employees completing any required ethics or code of conduct policy review. Examine these records (consider sampling if the population is large) for completeness and inquire about how exceptions are handled. Are the records, policies, and interview results consistent? If so, document this. Together, your various procedures contribute to the evidence supporting your overall assessment regarding an attribute or characteristic.

Planning and Strategy for Interviews

Planning for interviews is essential. Consider up front when and where interviews will be needed to support your assessments. Often, but not always, entities share many common elements of the control environment, so it may be possible to gather a small amount of information from a broad number of locations to support some of the overall control environment objectives (e.g., integrity, oversight, structure). However, in some entities, a few locations, branches, or segments may be very different in culture and nature from the entity as a whole. If so, and if the location is part of the core of the business, you may need to apply sufficient tests and perform separate, sufficient inquiries at that location to be able to conclude that the control environment design and implementation are acceptable at that location.

When management or internal audit is visiting remote locations, consider doubling up the purpose of the visit so that separate trips are not necessary for different purposes. When procedures are performed early in the year, consider how you will update or confirm your earlier assessments. Generally this is performed by inquiry and some evidence of continuity of the controls operation. For example, cycle counts of inventory may be performed at different locations at different times of the year. Independent auditors often observe some of these counts. When on site for the counts, management and/or the auditors may be able to gather other information useful to the controls assessment purpose.

Consider having alternative ways of getting at the information for your assessment. If last year you used primarily written surveys, you may wish to rely more on interviews or focus group discussions another year. Targeting the same people every year also does not demonstrate objectivity, so share the wealth. If you are aware that internal audit will likely use group interviews, then maybe the independent auditor will use a survey of issues to be more effective and less invasive, and vice versa. It is desirable to vary the mode of information gathering to keep the process from becoming stale. Just going through the motions every year is a time-wasting exercise, and the entity often receives little or no constructive feedback in the process.

Be candid in discussing any issues raised in management's interview and questionnaire process with your auditors and identifying any actions you have taken in response to things that were brought to your attention. This shows that the process is meaningful to you and avoids nasty shocks when the auditor later (sometimes too late) identifies these issues as part of (or after) the audit. Shared information works two ways and helps build a trusting relationship. Auditors of public entities are required to share controls issues identified by the auditors with management on a timely basis. The SEC anticipates management will do the same.

Focus Groups

Focus groups (group interviews) can be complex to conduct, due to group dynamics, but can also be very revealing and provide multiple responses for a given investment in interviewer (called a moderator) time. For example, it usually takes a few minutes to get a group to open up, and it may be may be difficult to keep the conversation on track to ensure that the important points are fully covered and all participants have a chance to contribute. There may also be a reluctance to discuss highly sensitive issues or provide strongly negative information while in a group. A sensitive and experienced moderator will understand when to circle back later to address touchy issues or whether to address them at all. When using focus groups, I suggest using a mix of focus groups and direct interviews to get the best out of both procedures—with and without the group dynamics. Some marketing research firms have trained focus group facilitators who can maximize the time spent in the session and garner worthwhile observations and feedback. Selection of an appropriate facilitator would include inquiries regarding business acumen and experience.

Corporate and country cultures can be important considerations in evaluating responses during interviews. In certain country cultures, one might be very reluctant to question any person in authority, even in the face of overwhelming evidence of a problem. When interviewing people from other cultures, nonverbal cues can be confusing, as a head movement back and forth that would ordinarily indicate a negative response may indicate "I agree," or "I am following you." This was very unnerving when I experienced it in a classroom lecture situation. Be alert to such situations and factor this into your analysis. Some corporate cultures are more relaxed and conversation is encouraged; in others, formal memos (and even e-mails between persons in adjoining workstations) are the desired means of communication. These factors can impact the information that is communicated and the way it is communicated in an interview or in a group session.

Tips for an Effective and Efficient Interview

- Do your homework before the interview. Know the information you wish to gather and other relevant information regarding the topic.
- Make sure the interview is conducted by the right person. A new junior accountant should not be put on the spot to conduct an interview with the chief financial officer (CFO). In some cases, hiring an experienced third-party interviewer can facilitate the discussion.
- Interviewing is not everybody's bag, so do not expect that college or life experience has taught the skill of how to have a worthwhile conversation or conduct a fruitful interview. The stereotypical accountant is an introvert, but there are certainly exceptions. In addition, the digital age has reduced the level of personal interactions that might otherwise occur. Social media may increase communication but not personal interaction. Over time, most people can learn to improve their skills, and there are courses and development programs that can help refine such skills.
- Don't get this task tied up with fraud-focused interrogation skills. The last thing that you want to do is give the impression you are conducting an interrogation of a suspect. You may stumble across some salient information, but you should not feel empowered to ratchet up the conversation into something you would expect to see on TV. There are good interrogator courses out there for that sort of investigation, but that is not the immediate purpose here. You want to obtain information quickly and efficiently and have the on-your-feet skills to be able to follow up on leads and comments without becoming a blunderbuss.
- You may identify some surprising information in the course of an interview, and it will be tempting to run off in a new direction based on that. There is a judgment call here. In general, remember your main purpose for the interview and be sure to complete the planned purpose of the interview. You may be able to circle around at the end to probe that "surprise" a little more. Again, you are not a fraud examiner, and it may be important to relay the information to supervisors and let them handle next steps. A risk here is that perpetrators who become wary of an investigation can destroy evidence that would have been a valuable lead had a careful and thoughtful investigation been conducted.

Interview Process

Unless you just have a quick question or two, try to arrange a time when the person being interviewed is not hassled. It's a good idea to start the interview by introducing yourself (if you are not known to the person) and noting the purpose of the interview.

Early on in the interview, start by asking some short factual questions and mix those with a few open-ended or opinion questions to put the respondent at ease.

- How long have you been with the company?
- How long have you been in your current position?
- Describe for me some of your daily responsibilities.

Pay attention to nonverbal cues. Come back to an area later in the interview with some open-ended questions if something comes to your attention, such as an obvious shift in demeanor or attitude when you mentioned the boss's son. "How long have you been working with Joe? Do you work together on some projects?"

With nonaccounting personnel, avoid technical terms that relate to accounting and auditing (e.g., SAS, FASB) and alarming wording ("We are required by our regulator to assess our internal controls … "). Sometimes respondents will not understand the context in which the question is being asked. Be prepared to restate the question and clarify or explain. However, the question that is being posed should still be asked. Don't be led into asking a different question or accepting an answer to a different question. Sometimes an apparent inability to understand a question that seems clear means that the respondent would rather not answer the question as it is posed.

Whenever possible, make the questions "personal" ("Have *you* ever become aware of an instance where … ? "How do *you* think the company would respond if they became aware of an instance where … ?"). Respondents often have a difficult time speaking for the company ("How would the company respond if … ?").

Be prepared for the unexpected. Follow up, and gather enough information so that matter can be pursued later if necessary ("Sure, I was asked to override the normal procedures … lots of times … but I refused."). Ask:

- What happened when you refused?
- Did they say why they asked you to do that?
- When was the last time?
- Are you aware of others that have been asked?

Listen carefully. If you are so busy writing notes or thinking about the next question, you will miss the current answer. A slight pause to formulate the next question is not a bad thing. Don't rush.

One of the most alarming and distracting things you can do is to start to scribble or type furiously when the respondent is speaking. The use of recording devices can also unnerve respondents and diminish the effectiveness of the interview. Trying to type notes on a portable computer during the interview can be distracting. Learn to take notes by jotting down a few key words on a small pad next to the questions and fill in the details *after* the interview ends. Leave yourself time to do this after the interview while your memory is fresh, not later in the day or the next day. That means that when several interviews are conducted, a buffer between them is desirable when possible to organize your notes and flesh them out.

Ask for information rather than prompt with an answer. For example:

- How would I know by looking at this that you have performed the reconciliation? versus Do you then initial the invoice?
- Start with: Are you aware of whether the company has an antifraud policy? versus Did you take the required refresher course this year on the company's antifraud policy?

When the interview is completed, thank the participant for his or her time and ask if you can follow up later if there are further questions. You may need to ask for the telephone extension or other contact information.

Corroborate other responses and observations to identify any issues or inconsistencies in responses. Experienced interviewers sometimes ask a few similar (not exactly the same, to avoid respondent annoyance) questions over the course of an interview to ensure that consistent answers are received on important issues.

Examples of Setting the Scope of Interview Procedures

Of course, when the purpose of the documentation is limited to design and some evidence implementation, such as can be the case with nonpublic company audits, less extensive direct interviewing or surveying is necessary. You can probably get a pretty good sense of the situation through observations and some limited inquiries. However, when the scope of the documentation is for the entity and/or the auditor to report on controls, more evidence is needed to support the assertion regarding controls effectiveness, and for that circumstance sampling principles and more extensive evidence gathering may be needed. The remainder of this section discusses some design considerations when management plans to report on controls.

Reporting on Controls

Consider the nature of the inquiry, and identify a potential population of respondents. When the scope of the inquiry includes the company as a whole (e.g., awareness and acceptance of the corporate ethics policy), evidence should be gathered from a variety of personnel groups including production and sales personnel, administrative personnel, and management. While not necessarily covering all groups in any one year, the sample should include a variety of personnel groups and may study some groups more intently some years than others.

The extent of testing (sample size) is a difficult concept to operationalize in this context. Examples of determining the extent of required procedures when assessing the awareness and understanding of the company code of conduct and code of ethics by employees are presented next.

Example 1: Company A is composed of a single plant in one location. It is a public company and makes an assertion regarding the effectiveness of its internal controls. HR instructs all new employees on the company code of conduct and ethics and requires an annual confirmation by existing employees that they have read and understand its provisions. The total number of employees is 5,000. Documentation of compliance with the policy is available in HR.

- The code should be reviewed for content and understandability.
- The company has tested its records of policy compliance by 30 interviews of 10 minutes each and also through a short company-wide e-mail survey. Confirmations in these 30 employees' files were examined. No exceptions were identified.
- Toward the end of each interview, an open-ended question was asked about the employee's awareness of any risks or instances of fraud.

Example 2: Company B comprises one manufacturing and distribution location with 20 employees. Many of the employees have been with the company for more than 10 years. It is a private company. The company is profitable, and its employees seem fairly compensated and appear dedicated to the company and long-term service. Top management comprises two individuals. This year the company drafted and circulated an ethics policy and posted it in a common location. The policy was reviewed at an all-hands meeting. The audit strategy followed by the independent auditor places some, but not high, reliance on internal control when auditing the financial statements.

This entity does not need to make a public controls assertion, but COSO suggests it still should have some evidence that it has implemented the code of conduct and ethics policy as part of its control environment. To this objective, the minutes of the all-hands meeting, the policies discussed and handed out, and the list of attendees were maintained. The auditor reviewed the policies for content and observed their posting in a prominent location. The auditor selected two employees (10% of employees) and one member of management to interview and confirm the meeting discussion and awareness of the policies. This was considered sufficient for the company and the auditor to meet their objectives.

Follow-up

There will be instances when some follow-up will be necessary. Often issues and comments can be clarified by a simple phone call, but if significant additional information is needed, schedule a follow-up meeting.

Remember that a *strong* suspicion of fraud or evidence of fraud should be communicated within the organization to a level above the suspected person involved, and it may call for a timely communication to the entity's governance body. Your organization may need to consult with legal advice to clarify what next steps to take. Most organizations have legal advisors or in-house counsel who may be helpful. Management or the governance body may engage independent, trained, forensic investigators to examine a suspected fraud situation more closely. Employees, and even CPAs, are not generally trained as fraud examiners, and important evidence can be altered or destroyed in a short time if employees believe that they have been targeted for investigation. Don't play detective. Time and proper action is of the essence if fraud is active.

Inquiries Supporting Walk-throughs

Your goal in gathering evidence is to determine whether the stated controls are functioning as intended. To accomplish this objective, you will need to consider:

- *Whom to ask.* In many instances, several people may be involved in the controls covered by a single walk-through. Plan on making inquiries of several people involved in the process. By gaining multiple perspectives, you will increase the effectiveness of the procedure. By asking a similar question or two of two different persons, you can get corroboration of what has been communicated. If the trade-off is available, try to talk to more people with fewer questions than just a few people with a long series of questions. Most frauds and misconduct are discovered through tips from employees. Just having any sort of conversation can evoke disclosures that may lead to important revelations.
- *What to ask.* Ask questions that will allow you to evaluate whether the described procedure and control is being followed regularly and if it is effective. A list of sample questions is provided later in the appendix to this chapter that may be helpful when gathering your thoughts. Assess whether employees are likely to understand the concepts of assertions like completeness and existence and formulate questions that do not rely on technical or unfamiliar terms.
- *Ask for specific examples. You should know the stated policy already.* Ask if the interviewee can provide some recent examples that illustrate that the control is working.
- *What to look for.* As an inquiry technique, it often is helpful to ask objective questions first to break the ice. Questions like "How long have you been in this role?" can be good lead-ins. Next, you might ask, "What process do you follow to … ?" While the literal answer to the question is important (e.g., "First we … then we … "), you also need to evaluate the qualitative, subjective aspects of the response. For example, based on the way the respondent answers the question "What is the procedure for … ?" consider whether:
  - The control seems well defined as opposed to ad hoc.
  - The respondent understands the control at a level that is appropriate, given his or her responsibilities for implementing or monitoring the control.
  - The person's attitude about his or her role and the value of the control is appropriate. Does the person think the control is effective? Is it valuable or more trouble than it's worth?

Discussing Entity-Level Controls with Management

Inquiries of management regarding the effectiveness of the control environment and entity-level controls are fundamentally the same as inquiries you make in other professional contexts. However, recognize that some of the questions that you are asking may be sensitive. You will rely on the techniques and interpersonal skills you have developed throughout your professional career to conduct the interviews required at this level. Be sure to choose the right person to conduct the interview. Junior staff are not a good match to interview senior executives. The interviewer needs sufficient stature to elicit serious responses and be able to follow up as needed in the situation. As noted previously, a couple of principles can be applied to make these discussions more productive and valuable.

1. *Ask more than one person.* For inquiries to be a reliable source of evidence about the effectiveness of controls, you should conduct interviews with more than one person. This may be especially important in discussing issues with management, since there are fewer potential respondents and management should be on the same page as to the issues being discussed. When several different people tell you the same story, you become more confident that the evidence you have gathered is more reliable. However, be sure to ask if concrete examples can be cited of what is being communicated and what you could look at that would reflect that (e.g., " … implemented an enhanced monitoring policy this year, and here is the schedule of the procedures and persons responsible for following through the various elements of the policy").
2. *Ask factual questions first.* This strategy will help:
   - Put the respondent at ease. (People usually are more comfortable describing facts than offering an opinion.)
   - Establish a factual basis for asking additional questions. An example would be: "I see you have hired additional production staff recently."

Once you establish the facts, you can then probe deeper to understand the respondent's attitudes, opinions, or interpretations of those facts.

Other tips you should consider include:

- *Start a new topic with open-ended questions.* Try to get the respondent talking so he or she will be in the frame of mind to volunteer information. (Example: "Tell me a little about your new marketing plan and how it is expected to affect sales and production.")
- *Don't tip your hand.* Before performing the interview, you should have prepared thoroughly, for example, by reading the client's documents related to the policy. You also may have interviewed one or more other people about the same subject. It is important that you get an unbiased answer from the person you are interviewing. Avoid prefacing questions with information that could lead to a biased or predetermined answer, such as "Your code of conduct states … " or "Other people I have talked to say … "
- *Nonverbal cues matter.* A study by the Institute of Internal Auditors (IIA)[3] concluded that only 7% of a message communicated in an interview is conveyed through what is said. Thirty-eight percent of the message is conveyed by word emphasis and tone, and 55% is conveyed through nonverbal cues. Be mindful of your presentation and the body language and the nonverbal cues of the respondent.

---

[3] J. W. Harmeyer, S. P. Golden, and G. E. Summers, *Conducting Internal Audit Interviews* (Altamonte Springs, FL: Institute of Internal Auditors Research Foundation, 1994). Cited in Canadian Institute of Chartered Accountants, *Audit Enquiry: Seeking More Reliable Evidence from Audit Enquiry* (Toronto: CICA, 2000).

■ *Debrief with other team members.* Research[4] indicates that the effectiveness of inquiries can be improved when the information about interviews is shared among audit team members. Through the comments and questions received from others, you will be able to identify pertinent information gathered and recognize the importance of things that otherwise might have been overlooked or forgotten. Care needs to be taken that staff conducting controls walk-throughs are informed of inherent risks that relate to those walk-throughs, issues of IT that are relevant, and any potential fraud risks relating to the area.

■ *This is not an interrogation.* It is best to step back and remember this is not a police investigation and you are not seeking a confession. Many good opportunities to identify and remediate fraud situations have been ruined by a bumbling Inspector Clouseau investigation that spontaneously sprang from an information-gathering exercise.

■ *Don't take too many notes and become a distraction.* During the interview, you should focus on making sure that you are receiving all the information you need to make your evaluation. You might consider making short, abbreviated notes during the conversation and then writing more detail immediately after the interview is over.

 MANAGEMENT INQUIRIES: SAMPLE QUESTIONS

Most of the sample questions in Figure 9.2 are relatively objective and focus on actions taken by management. They are intended as a way to introduce the subject matter in

---

Commitment to Integrity and Ethics (Principle 1)

1. What was the process followed to develop the company's code of conduct?
2. Has the code been revised and updated? How often does that happen?
3. What was the main reason for developing the code?
   a. Has that objective been fully met?
      ■ Yes. How can you tell?
      ■ No. What major barriers did you encounter along the way?
4. If management becomes aware of an allegation of unacceptable behavior, what is the process for investigating the matter?
   a. Can you give me a recent example?
5. Has the board identified compensation policies or other incentives that may motivate unethical behavior by employees?
   ■ Yes. What are they? How do you monitor these policies for possible unintended consequences?
   ■ No. What criteria are considered when setting incentive policies and programs?

FIGURE 9.2 *(continued)*

---

[4] Ibid.

6. Have you become aware of any significant control deficiencies in the last year?
   a. How did you become aware?
   b. What action was taken?
   c. (public companies) Did this affect your SOX Section 302 certification?
   d. Did the deficiency need to be disclosed in a filing (or to a regulator)? If not, why not?
7. Do you receive all the business information needed to perform your job effectively[1]?
   ▪ Yes. Is it reliable? Timely?
   ▪ No. What seems to be the problem?
8. Does the governance group periodically discuss the company's culture and tone at the top and how these affect the overall effectiveness of controls?
   ▪ Yes. How is this assessment made? Is the assessment available for review?
   ▪ No. What prevents you from doing so?

Establishes Structure, Authority and Responsibility (Principle 3)

1. How did management determine the overall organizational structure for the company?
   a. When was the last time the structure was reviewed for continued relevance and effectiveness?
   b. How could you determine that the structure is effective?
   c. How are internal control and financial reporting problems that are internally identified handled within the company's organizational structure?
2. Is there a process used to determine which responsibilities should be delegated to upper management or lower levels? Can you describe that process for me?
   a. How do you ensure that responsibility and authority are sufficient for management or staff to be successful in their position?
3. How do you ensure that incompatible functions such as initiating a purchase and approving payments are not vested in the same individual?
4. Once management decides to pursue a certain strategy (such as your . . . .), what is the process for determining the human resource needs required to implement the strategy? Consider:
   ▪ Number of people needed
   ▪ Required skills
   ▪ Experience level
   ▪ Training
5. What is the process for determining the resources that are necessary for employees to perform their responsibilities effectively? Resources include:
   ▪ Training
   ▪ Budget/funding
   ▪ Personnel
   ▪ Supervision and feedback
6. Who in executive management oversees the Information Technology function? Is there evidence that they oversee the issues and operations of the IT function?

FIGURE 9.2 (*continued*)

Identification of Risk: Selection of Accounting Principles (Principle 6)

1. What is the process used by management to:
   a. Identify emerging accounting issues or other circumstances or events that may require a consideration of new accounting policies?
   b. Identify the accounting policies described as "critical" in the entity's 10K?
   c. Choose appropriate accounting policies?
2. Are there currently any accounting principle issues that have not been resolved to everyone's satisfaction?
3. Describe any conversations management and the board has had recently regarding the quality of the entity's accounting principles. What actions did the board take as a result of those discussions?
4. How does management view the concept of materiality? Whom does the entity consider its primary financial statement user(s)?

Identifies and Analyzes Risk (Principle 7)

1. Describe the process used to identify the risks reported in the company's most recent Form 10K.
   a. Who is involved in the process?
   b. What criteria are used to determine the risks to report?
   c. Are there risks that were not reported? Why was it decided not to report them?
2. How does the company decide how to manage or mitigate the identified risks?
3. Is a rating or severity assessment made for identified risks? Who makes this assessment? Is it reviewed or communicated by anyone?
4. How is the board of directors or governance group involved in the risk identification and management process?
5. What recent concerns and issues have been raised about the risks facing the entity?
6. In the past year, what new risks has the company encountered?
   ▪ When did management recognize these risks? What triggered the awareness?
   ▪ How did the company respond?

Assesses Fraud Risk (Antifraud Programs and Controls) (Principle 8)[2]

1. In what ways is the entity vulnerable to fraud?
   Consider:
   a. Employee defalcation
   b. Fraudulent financial reporting
   c. Theft
2. Have there been any recent discoveries of fraud in the organization? If so, what was done? How was the issue identified?
3. Is there a process followed if a fraud is alleged or suspected? Is the process written or described? Is it communicated, and if so to whom? Does the audit committee get involved? At what point?

FIGURE 9.2 *(continued)*

4. What steps does management take to mitigate the risk of fraud within the entity? For example, consider:
   a. Hiring and promotion policies
   b. Training
   c. Investigation and resolution (including disciplinary action) of alleged incidents of fraud
   d. Anonymous hotline for incident reporting, vulnerabilities assessment by Certified Fraud Examiner, whistleblower protection policy, etc.

Deploys controls (Period-End Financial Reporting Processes-Partial Principle 12)

1. Are there written procedures governing the year-end close process, development of estimates and consolidations?
2. Who is responsible for this process and how is it monitored or controlled?
3. How is the accounting for unusual, non-routine transactions handled? Were there examples of these types of transactions in the past year?
   a. What was the motivation behind these transactions? Do they relate to the entity's strategic plan? Do they affect the forecasted financial results?
   b. At what point in the process does management receive input on the accounting treatment of these transactions?
   c. What factors do management and the board consider when reviewing and approving these transactions?
4. What process does the entity follow for making its most significant accounting estimates? What are the most sensitive or high risk estimates?
   a. Is this a formal or informal process?
   b. How is information relating to the underlying assumptions gathered?
   c. How do you know the information used in the estimation is reliable?
   d. What factors are considered when making significant assumptions about the estimate?
   e. Are there circumstances where outside expertise is usually employed when making the estimate? What procedures and controls are in place to ensure the competence of the hired expert resource?
   f. How are senior management and the board involved in the review and approval of significant estimates? In the company's most recent financial reporting cycle, what were the most significant issues raised regarding the estimates?

Monitoring (Principles 16 and 17)

1. What specific responsibilities do you have to monitor the continuing operations of controls?
2. Has your responsibility for monitoring changed in the last year? If so, what prompted the change?
   a. Change in business
   b. Change in regulation
   c. Routine change in order to vary the controls monitored

FIGURE 9.2 (*continued*)

3. Do you use any benchmarks or rules of thumb to assess the effectiveness of the controls operations? Are there metrics that are helpful in assessing the continuity of some controls?
4. How might you be alerted if a control became ineffective other than during your periodic review of that control?
5. How do you document your reviews?
6. What oversight is provided to ensure that outsourced functions (e.g., payroll, benefits administration, IT support) have adequate controls for your reliance on their performance?
7. Is there any linkage or coordination between your monitoring activities and your internal audit activities?
8. Are you using any tools or checklists to guide and document your monitoring activities?
9. How are control deficiencies communicated with the management group? Can you give some examples of recent issues and how they were communicated and resolved?
10. How can you be sure the issues are adequately resolved?
11. In your view is the monitoring program effective? What in your view is the weakest link in that program?

FIGURE 9.2 Sample Questions.

[1]This also is a reflection on the Information and Communication COSO component.
[2]Note: Independent auditors are expected to make extensive fraud inquiries of management and other personnel based on the specific requirements of SAS 99 (public companies) or AU-C 240 (AICPA) *Consideration of Fraud in a Financial Statement Audit*. These questions are not a census of those requirements.

a relatively nonthreatening way. Follow-up questions should be asked to develop an impression of the respondent's awareness, understanding, and attitude toward the subject. Since follow-up questions will depend primarily on the responses the individual gives to the initial question, the samples include only a limited number of follow-up questions.

Sample Practice Aids

THIS APPENDIX CONTAINS several practice aids that will help you in designing employee surveys and structure interviews related to the operating effectiveness of entity-wide controls. Included are:

- Sample Letter to Employees in Advance of Employee Survey
- Sample Employee Survey of Corporate Culture and Personnel Policies
- Guidance on the Evaluation of Employee Survey Results
- Sample Inquiries for Walk-throughs and Transaction Controls

SAMPLE LETTER TO EMPLOYEES IN ADVANCE OF EMPLOYEE SURVEY

Dear ___:

We annually review and report on the policies and procedures we use to manage and control our company. The scope of this review is quite broad and includes evaluating not just individual tasks you perform in your daily work assignments but also the environment in which you perform those assignments.

To help us perform our review, we are conducting a survey of all [a sample of ...] employees to obtain their observations about the way in which they perceive our company is managed.

You will be receiving this survey within the next two weeks. We have tried hard to balance our need for comprehensive feedback with everyone's desire to keep the survey as short as possible. We believe we have reached a suitable balance.

I urge you to complete this survey and return it as soon as possible to _____. Your prompt attention to this matter is important, not only because it will allow us to comply with certain reporting requirements, but also because it will help us to continually improve our management practices. All individual responses to the questionnaire will be kept strictly confidential.

/s/Chief Executive Officer

Notes

- This letter should be sent out a week or two in advance of sending the actual employee survey. The purpose of the letter is to prepare employees for the survey's arrival and to encourage them to complete it as soon as possible.
- If not sending the survey to all employees, then the letter should explain how the individual employee was selected—for example, "We are sending the survey to 10% of all our employees and management. Your name has been selected at random by the vendor we are using to conduct the survey."
- To convey a proper sense of urgency and importance to the completion of the survey, the letter should be signed by a member of senior management, such as the president or the chief executive officer (CEO).
- To provide confidentiality, the survey could be sent to a neutral third party that will compile and summarize the results. If this is the case, you may want to mention this in the letter.

 ## SAMPLE EMPLOYEE SURVEY OF CORPORATE CULTURE AND PERSONNEL POLICIES

Suppose a company is required to review and report on internal controls, including the policies and procedures used to manage and control the company. The scope of this review is broad and includes an evaluation of the overall environment in which individual employees perform their assigned responsibilities.

The most effective responses are provided when individual results will be kept confidential and responses will be available to management only in summary form. If confidentiality is intended, it should be clearly communicated to potential respondents and respected when analyzing the results.

Web-based surveys are common today, and many vendors are available to provide assistance in the design of the Web interface and summarization of the survey. Mail surveys can be cumbersome and expensive for large entities, but are more practical in smaller organizations.

The purpose of the sample survey that follows is to obtain input from employees to help management assess Principles 1 and 4. The sample employee survey focuses on points of awareness and attitudes regarding two control environment topics: company culture and human resource policies. As discussed before, management is in the best position to answer certain pointed questions about the development of policy and procedures, but employees need to be aware of the policy and be able to refer to it should the need arise. The questionnaire illustrated here is a mixture of some factual questions and some opinion questions. Some questions are worded in the "negative" frame to encourage careful reading and consideration of all the questions. To create a custom questionnaire, you can develop questions relevant to the entity based on the relevant principles, approaches, and examples from the COSO Framework volume, *A Compendium of Approaches and Examples*.

Strategies to avoid painfully long questionnaires that diminish response rates include having several versions of the questionnaire that ask only some of the questions, with some overlapping sections or questions to assess continuity and validity.

Sample Employee Survey

Instructions

You have been selected at random to participate in this confidential survey. Management will receive the survey responses only in summarized form. The identification number on this survey is used only by the survey company to log completed responses and to send reminders for surveys not received.

- As indicated on the form, provide a yes or no response or assign a numeric value to each of the 5 possible responses: for example, "strongly agree" = 5 and "strongly disagree" = 1.
- Feel free to add comments or examples to support your ratings. Please do not include any personal identifying information in your responses.
- [Due date information and return address]

Ethical Values (Principle 1)	Yes/No	1–5 Value Scale	Comments, Examples
1. I have read the company's code of conduct.			
2. The company's code of conduct helps me identify unacceptable business practices			
3. If I observe unacceptable behavior on the job and report it to a member of the management team, I believe that the matter will be investigated and resolved appropriately on a timely basis.			
4. I believe that people who demonstrate a commitment to high ethical standards of behavior are valued and will be rewarded (e.g., through compensation or advancement).			

(continued)

Ethical Values (Principle 1)	Yes/No	1–5 Value Scale	Comments, Examples
5. I believe that people who act in an unethical manner will be punished (e.g., through diminished compensation, lack of advancement, or termination).			
6. In the last year, I have been asked by someone senior to me to take action that I considered to possibly be unethical or contrary to stated policies.			
7. I believe that in the past year, someone else in the company has been asked by someone senior to them to take action that would be considered unacceptable.			
8. For the most part, company employees act in an ethical manner.			
9. For the most part, company management acts in an ethical manner.			
10. There is an effective process in place for reporting violations of company policies, regulations, or laws.			

Competence (Principle 4)
1. My job responsibilities have been clearly communicated to me.
2. The criteria for assessing my performance have been communicated to me.
3. The feedback I receive on my performance is fair and balanced and helps me to improve and succeed.
4. The information I need to do my job well is available when I need it. The information is complete, accurate, and timely.
5. The training I receive helps me do a better job.
6. I have been delegated the decision-making authority necessary to effectively perform my job.
7. For the most part, I have been provided with the resources necessary to perform my job effectively, including time, budget, and supervision.
8. For the most part, compensation and promotion policies seem to be fair.

GUIDANCE ON THE EVALUATION OF EMPLOYEE SURVEY RESULTS

The example employee survey focuses on two entity-level control objectives: company culture and personnel policies. It is designed to gather information about the effectiveness of each of these elements of the control environment. Unless the survey responses are summarized and properly analyzed and responded to, the survey time will have been wasted.

First of all, it is unlikely that all of the survey responses will be properly and promptly completed. Some responses may clearly be inappropriate or may stem from corrupted electronic data. Careful consideration should be given to just ignoring improperly completed surveys. In some tainted environments, deliberate attempts to subvert the efforts of the surveys may occur. Tabulate the nonusable responses on a whole questionnaire and on a by-question basis. There may be hidden information value in such responses even though they do not address the survey purpose. Patterns of nonresponse may call for follow-up procedures.

Tabular information about the survey could include:

- Number of surveys distributed and number returned.
- Number of fully, partially, and unusable responses.
- Functional departments included in the survey.
- Employee levels surveyed (e.g., General Service [GS] grades, salary ranges, etc.).
- Locations surveyed.

Try to be sensitive not to summarize the data in a way that a particular respondent can be clearly identified (e.g., a one-person sales office in a particular location). Presumably most surveys already were stratified for some of these characteristics before they were distributed, so information on these characteristics may not need to be collected from respondents. If you need to add this information to the survey, be sensitive that the respondent may feel this information may be used to identify them. Use very broad categories.

Question responses should be tabulated by question. For yes/no responses, a provision may be needed for unusable responses to the question. The total number of question responses should agree with either the number of responses received or the number of surveys sent. Responses to the scaling exercise can be summarized by computing an average or using statistical measures such as mean, median, and mode or by using a bar chart to show the number of responses for ratings 1 to 5. Again, a provision needs to be made for reporting unusable responses. Survey designers can benefit from reviewing the questions where nonresponses are more regularly noted to improve questionnaire design in future questionnaires.

If there are numerous comments and examples provided in the responses, these might need to be summarized separately (by question) from the more objective summary data to make the review of the information less distracting and cumbersome to review.

Some important aspects of the review of the responses include:

- Did the respondents seem to understand the task?
- Do the responses (including comments) generally support the related principle? Responses can trigger information about the awareness of policy and procedures as well as employee attitudes on a variety of topics and levels.

- Are there outlier responses and comments or examples that need to be considered further? Disconfirming evidence cannot be ignored. Serious accusations and issues may need to be further investigated through independent counsel. Note that a decision to try to identify an individual respondent could destroy any trust that management will hold the results as confidential. In such cases, some entities have launched broad investigations to address the issue and still preserve confidence.

When several versions of the questionnaire are used, thought needs to be given in advance to the most useful way to tabulate the results. Generally this will still result in a by-question analysis under the relevant principle.

While the purpose of the survey was to obtain a snapshot view, it would be a shame for management to not consider ways to enhance awareness or create more positive attitudes based on the responses received. Such actions would also be confirming evidence that management is responsive to identified issues and problems if the need for corrective action was implied by the responses.

Additional investigation is sometimes required to determine the root cause of an issue. For example, if a number of responses point to insensitive management attitudes during routine oversight, it may be that some managers are simply unaware of how their actions affect employees, or it could be that they are overburdened with other responsibilities (lack of resources), which causes them to devote less time than is necessary to effective supervision. If the behavior of managers needs to change, the company should consider one or more of these changes:

- Formal training
- Informal coaching or mentoring of managers
- Changes to the way the company provides incentives to its employees
- Allocation of additional resources where necessary

Ignoring poor interpersonal skills on the part of management or supervisory staff generally results in higher employee turnover, which is costly.

Low scores in any one area by itself may indicate a material weakness in the system of internal control. For example, employees with significant control responsibilities for financial reporting must have a clear knowledge of their responsibilities if the control procedures are to be effective.

However, it is possible that weaknesses identified as a result of the responses to this survey may be compensated for by other controls. For example, close supervision or redundant control procedures that address the same control objective may adequately compensate for a lack of employee understanding of a particular control procedure. Just do not be too quick to wipe away the problem without some evidence that the compensating or redundant procedure really works. And why should the issue continue when communications, training, and education often resolve the issue? Fix the problem.

While not a focus of the sample questionnaire, accounting department staff might receive a number of questions focused on controls over financial reporting and controls over certain processes, such as the year-end close process. A common weakness in smaller companies is a weakness in the controllership and senior accounting officer positions. These issues can be overcome with more support, training, and supervision of the accounting functions. However, such weaknesses have very serious implications for financial reporting and are identified as such by auditing standards. Better that the entity identify the potential deficiency and begin a remediation program than the independent auditor reach this conclusion.

In response to identified possible control weaknesses, you should modify your assessment approach by:

- Revising the control to become effective. (Do this first.)
- Expanding the scope of internal and external auditor direct testing of the data in the area affected by the control problem for the period before the control procedure was fixed to identify any errors introduced into the system.
- Testing to ensure the remediated control is effective.

 ## SAMPLE INQUIRIES FOR WALK-THROUGHS AND TRANSACTION CONTROLS

These sample questions may assist you in structuring the walk-through interview or to support other evidence regarding the effective implementation of a transaction control. Watch carefully for disconfirming information, personnel who may have new duties, and indications of problems or issues that arose during the period. Be prepared to ask for additional information and follow up on significant issues identified. This is a wonderful opportunity to gather control environment confirming or disconfirming information, as you are often one on one with a nonmanagement person.

For Design Effectiveness
- What documents or electronic files are necessary for you to perform your job? From whom do you receive this information? How do you access the electronic information?
- Is the information you use normally available to you timely and accurate? Have you encountered any problems with the information in the past year?
- In what ways do you add to, combine, manipulate, or change the data you receive?
- What happens to a file or document when you're finished with it?
- How to you indicate you have performed your function? Can I tell by looking at something?
- When you discover errors, how do they get corrected?
- What checks do you perform on the information you use to make sure it's accurate?
- How would you know that you received all the transactions you should receive? How do you make sure that you process everything you receive and that some transactions don't accidentally get dropped from the process?
- When you're processing the information, what steps do you take to make sure that no errors are introduced into the system? What controls are built into the system itself?

- Are any preapprovals necessary or other types of documentation required before you process a transaction/perform your function? How do you know that the transactions presented to you for processing are valid ones?

For Operating Effectiveness

Your inquiries of operating effectiveness should be directed toward gathering information about two broad areas: the consistency with which the control procedure was applied and the qualifications of the person who performed the control. Ask if there have been problems or issues, and how they were resolved. You also should consider asking employees for their opinion about the operating effectiveness of controls. As with any sample, the questions here may not be relevant for all walk-throughs in all types of entities. The questions need to be customized to be relevant for different entities and circumstances.

For Consistency

- Do you encounter situations where company policies or procedures do not exist or are unclear? How often do you encounter these situations?
    - If you encountered a situation or transaction for which no clear policy existed, what would you do? Can you describe an instance where this happened and what you did? How frequent are such transactions?
- If you were in charge of designing policies and procedures, what changes would you make to improve their effectiveness and efficiency?
- When is it okay to not follow written policies exactly? Have you been asked to not follow policy? Who asked you to do this?
- If there are others in the company with the same job functions as yours, do you think they perform the job in the same way? If differences exist, what are they? What causes these differences?
- Have you performed the procedures since the last annual evaluation of internal control effectiveness? Who took your place if you were not available to perform the procedures?
- Have there been any changes to the procedures since the last annual evaluation of internal control effectiveness?

Qualifications of Personnel

- Do you feel adequately trained and the training updated to be able to perform your duties?
    - If you had to design training for a new person for your position, what topics would you be sure to include? How did you learn these things? How long did it take you to learn them? What else would you like to be trained in that would help you do your job better?
    - Is training or education relevant to your duties available to you? Have you taken advantage of this? If not, why not?
- Incompatible responsibilities exist when one individual is in a position where he or she must both process data (e.g., prepare invoices or post the general ledger) *and*

check his or her own work for errors *and* no one checks the individual's work. Have you observed situations like that in your department?

- Suppose that someone was inclined to deliberately create an error in the reporting process, for example, by introducing a fictitious or unauthorized transaction. How could they do it without getting caught?
- Which company assets are most vulnerable to employee theft? How could these assets "disappear" without someone finding out?
- Do you feel your coworkers and supervisors are qualified and trained to perform their responsibilities well?

Assessment of Effectiveness

- Overall, how effective is your job (area of responsibility) at preventing or detecting and correcting errors that might occur?
- Consider the overall reliability of your system of processes and controls. If you had to give it a letter grade, what grade would you give it? Do you have recommendations you would make to improve the system?
- Have you brought issues and problems to the attention of your supervisor or management? What happened as a result of the communication?
- Suppose that you leave the company, and shortly after you leave, you learn that there was a major error in the company's financial statements relating to your division/location. What do you think might be the source of the error? Why would it not have been detected?

CHAPTER TEN

Assessing the Severity of Identified Controls Deficiencies

 IT'S INEVITABLE

In the process of assessing and testing controls, you are likely to encounter deficiencies in the design or operating effectiveness of the controls. For example, an important control objective might not be addressed or might be only partially addressed by the control that is in place. If you do not have a control over the selection of vendors for fulfilling various service needs, you might run the risk that business could be diverted to a vendor who will share some overbillings with the accountant or business manager directing the business to it. In addition, even if the control is designed properly, unless it operates effectively, it is deficient. For example, you might find through the auditor's procedures or through customer returns and complaints that your controls failed and led (or could have led) to substantive errors on the financial statements, even though your tests showed that the controls seemed adequate and to be working. This happens in all sorts of entities, including governments and nonprofits.

Finding control deficiencies is not a rare event. Most businesses have some if the assessment is done competently and fairly. Little public data about deficiencies and their rates of occurrence is available. The reported material weaknesses of public companies are only the tip of the iceberg when it comes to the total deficiencies found. Since deficiencies of less severity than a material weakness or deficiencies remediated prior to the year-end are not reported, we see only a fraction of the deficiencies discovered in the period. One study examined all the deficiencies identified by entities and auditors for a two-year period involving 76 engagements and 44 entities.[1] The study revealed that 3,990 deficiencies were identified. The study involved accelerated filer public companies with revenues of less than $1 billion and not in a specialized industry. One might think that public companies of this nature would be pretty well controlled, but there were a wide range of findings in these companies. One engagement identified over 200 deficiencies in a single-year period. One can just imagine the deficiency conditions of smaller, nonpublic entities.

An odd aspect of controls assessment is that finding errors in the financial statements generally implies a control failure of some sort, but not finding a substantive error in the financial data *does not* imply the controls are working (or even exist). This oddity is caused by the fact that even in the absence of any real controls, the processes may be performed by individuals who are honest, competent, and diligent. Thus, even though what we call controls may be lacking, correct financial data and reports can be produced. As mentioned previously, the "could" factor drives the severity of a deficiency. In assessing the severity of control deficiencies, you need to look beyond the amount of any actual misstatements associated with the deficiency and assess the likelihood and magnitude of potential deficiencies that could result from the misstatement. This has been a difficult concept to communicate to entities and auditors. In the aforementioned study, more severe deficiencies seemed to be assessed when an actual misstatement of some magnitude was identified. This bias toward linking severe control deficiencies only with misstatements is important to recognize and consider in rating the severity of control deficiencies.

Only automated controls (controls implemented using computerized processes) should be expected to operate the same way each time. We humans have our ups and downs and sometimes fail to give each detail the attention it deserves, so manual controls generally are considered more risky and less reliable. The upside and downside of automated controls is that they will operate exactly as programmed. If programmed incorrectly, they will be consistently ineffective. Also, when unusual situations arise (transactions may be unique or require special considerations), automated controls may not perform as you would want, depending on how the function is programmed. Computers are generally not able to exercise judgment (expert systems try to emulate judgments, but such systems are not commonly employed in accounting systems).

Expect to encounter some deficiencies when undertaking to document and test internal controls. A survey by Ernst & Young in 2005 noted that 25% of companies with over $5 billion in sales remediated over 500 controls in their first year of assessing and reporting on the effectiveness of their internal controls.[2] Recall that these were considered among the largest and most well-controlled entities in the world, many with significant internal audit staffs. In prior years, their auditors may have actually relied on their internal controls for audit assurance, but a closer scrutiny revealed quite a few holes. The application of the controls framework based on COSO concepts, while

---

[1] Bedard, J., and L. Graham. 2011. Detection and severity classification of Sarbanes-Oxley Section 404 internal control deficiencies. The Accounting Review 86 (3): 825–855

[2] Ernst & Young, "Emerging Trends in Internal Controls: Fourth Survey and Industry Insights" (September 2005).

not new, was certainly performed with greater depth and structure under the rigorous Public Company Accounting Oversight Board (PCAOB) Auditing Standard (AS) No. 2, *An Audit of Internal Control over Financial Reporting Performed in Conjunction with an Audit of Financial Statements.*

As attributed to Yogi Berra, "It's amazing what you see when you look."

The fact that deficiencies and weaknesses in controls are identified does not make the entity a bad business entity, and the identification of a deficiency does not mean that the entity messed up. Do not attach a moral label to the issue at the outset. If issues are identified and the entity refuses to make adjustments, then it is okay to flog it in shame. Let's look at the worst thing that can happen here. Suppose you are an audited entity. Even if you have weaknesses in controls, as long as your auditor can gather the information necessary to audit the financial statements, you can still receive a "clean" (unmodified) audit opinion on the financial statements.

However, under reinvigorated auditing standards on communications regarding internal control, auditors should communicate significant deficiencies and material weaknesses in controls to management and those charged with governance (e.g., owners, boards, township committees, etc.) in writing.[3]

The frauds and financial statement misstatements found in private, not-for-profit, and government entities over the years can be traced directly to the ineffectiveness of controls design and operation. This was the genesis of the Sarbanes-Oxley (SOX) Act of 2002 that followed the colossal frauds at Enron, WorldCom, and others. For the most part, this required auditor communication to the entity creates a clear record of the issues auditors and management and owners discussed so that later finger-pointing about who told who what is less subjective. The auditor does not share this communication with third parties in private companies, and unlike when an entity voluntarily chooses to or is required to report on internal controls, the communication is not part of the financial statements. Over time, it is possible that venture capitalists, entities that award grants and contracts, regulators, and other third parties may ask companies about these communications, but right now is the time is right to fix the issues. Indeed, it seems likely that in a few years, governments and agencies may have to report on internal controls as a measure of their stewardship of public funds.

Additionally, the private entity seeking someday to go public or attract a suitor (buyer) might use a report on effective internal controls as an indicator of value that can provide a competitive advantage in the marketplace. Some private entities, such as charities, may hire auditors to perform an attestation on the effectiveness of their internal controls, and that auditor report on internal controls (currently under AT No. 501 of the AICPA auditing standards) can be published with the financial statements and communicated to potential investors.

Various levels of deficiencies have been identified in controls writings. In order of decreasing severity, they are:

- Material weaknesses.
- Significant deficiencies.

---

[3] Public company standards require this, and nonpublic engagements under American Institute of Certified Public Accountants (AICPA) Standards require this also under AU-C Section No. 260. Additionally, the Securities and Exchange Commission (SEC) and PCAOB require public company unremediated material weaknesses to be reported to the public.

- Deficiencies.
- Exceptions.

The good news is that many issues encountered in the assessment, testing, and monitoring of controls are simple to identify and assess as to severity. There is no need to go through a tortured assessment of likelihood and magnitude and follow a step-by-step process in thinking through the classification. For example, if there is no identified control to ensure that credit sales will be collectible, and such sales are voluminous (such as with a retail operation where consumer credit sales are common), then the deficiency quickly rises to the level of a material weakness. If a company does not have the technical resources to account properly for its transactions under generally accepted accounting principles (GAAP) and prepare financial statements, that also is a pretty easy call. However, at the margins, the need for following a structured approach to assessing the severity of the deficiency becomes more evident.

Many managers and auditors note that after they follow a more structured decision process a few times, the calls and judgments are easier to make. The simple process of building experience will assist you over time in making consistent judgments. Experience has been successfully gained and disseminated in organizations by having a few individuals initially act as a filter for all deficiencies identified. At a certain point they can leverage some of their understanding and experience to others. Sharing their thought processes will also help auditors and companies reach supported shared conclusions.

Unfortunately, studies of early management internal control deficiency assessments in public companies are not encouraging. Besides not even identifying over 70% of the deficiencies found after auditors made their assessments, public companies underrated the more severe deficiencies (when they were found) over 70% of the time. While some specific factors may have contributed to the poor showing, such as the newness of the legislation and focus on controls, lack of assessment guidance directed at companies, and the inability to collaborate with independent auditors during this process, there may also have been a tendency to simply undergrade the deficiencies. After all, it was not long into grade school that we were no longer being asked to grade our own quizzes and tests. Why is this so different?

If management is committed to changing the processes and meeting the controls performance expectations when deficiencies are identified, the need to precisely rate such deficiencies also declines, since change and correction are likely to follow shortly. When management is more cost–benefit focused or is reluctant to make changes, the assessment process can be more important as it will help prioritize what deficiencies will need to be corrected.

ALIGNMENT OF PUBLIC AND PRIVATE COMPANY STANDARDS FOR ASSESSING DEFICIENCY SEVERITY

One saving grace in this process of severity assessment is the alignment of the various regulators and auditing standards setters of many of the criteria used to assess the severity of control deficiencies. This has been purposeful, to reduce confusion and cope with a rather vague set of definitions and standards to begin with. Examples from public company SEC, PCAOB, and AICPA guidance can be considered when assessing your deficiencies. However, be alert that it may be necessary to follow the thought process underlying guidance directed to you when explaining your reasoning for a rating.

In my view, the COSO guidance remains at a very conceptual level when it comes to this very important practical step of evaluating deficiencies. COSO only identifies the categories of deficiency and major deficiency and provides little discussion of a methodology or approach to rating severity. Most of the guidance on assessing severity comes from the regulators and audit standard setters. However, to encourage some consistency in assessments, we discuss the examples and available guidance.

CONTROL DEFICIENCIES AND DEFINITIONS

COSO indicates that an unremediated major weakness (or an aggregation of lesser deficiencies to create a material weakness) in a principle or component precludes assessing the system of internal control as effective. This has special meaning for public companies whose managements have a responsibility to publicly report on the system of internal controls. For accelerated filers, auditors are required to make their own assessment and separately report on internal controls. The following excerpt from SEC Release No. 33-8810 relates to specific SEC guidance for public companies.

> Management may not disclose that it has assessed ICFR [internal control over financial reporting] as effective if one or more deficiencies in ICFR are determined to be a material weakness. As part of the evaluation of ICFR, management considers whether each deficiency, individually or in combination, is a material weakness as of the end of the fiscal year. (p. 34)

Deficiencies in internal control can arise in two ways:[4]

1. *Design deficiency.* A design deficiency exists when either:
   - A control that is necessary to achieve a control objective does not exist.
   - An existing control is not properly designed so that, even if the control operated as designed, the control objective would not be met.
2. *Operating deficiency.* An operating deficiency exists when either:
   - A properly designed control is not reliably operating as designed.
   - The person performing the procedure does not possess the necessary authority or qualifications to perform the control effectively.

---

[4] As stated in SEC Release No. 33-8810: "A deficiency in the design of ICFR exists when (a) necessary controls are missing or (b) existing controls are not properly designed so that, even if the control operates as designed, the financial reporting risks would not be addressed" (p. 15). "If management determines that the operation of the control is not effective, a deficiency exists that must be evaluated to determine whether it is a material weakness" (p. 30).

FIGURE 10.1   Internal Control Deficiencies

Note that the 2013 COSO Framework tees up these concepts under the headings of *present* and *functioning*, but this has not yet replaced the terms *design* and *operating* in most internal controls literature or in the auditing standards at the date of this publication.

As indicated in Figure 10.1, internal control deficiencies range from inconsequential to a material weakness. Note that the levels of deficiency are placed in a continuum.

An issue is where one should draw the lines between severity classes; that is, at what point is a deficiency no longer inconsequential, and when does a significant deficiency become a material weakness?

When an assessment reveals that control deficiencies exist as of year-end, the severity of those control deficiencies must be evaluated. If a public company, this assessment may affect its public reporting responsibility. If a nonpublic entity, the severity defines which control deficiencies must be communicated to governance and management.

However, it is a best practice to assess the severity of a deficiency as soon as possible. This permits the early identification of issues that need to be addressed and may accelerate the remediation process and lessen the risk of error or fraud affecting the financial statements. When control deficiencies are outstanding, auditors cannot rely on the associated controls in performing their audit procedures. That may mean more costly auditor procedures may need to be performed later in the year, driving up audit costs. Early attention to the correction of identified deficiencies is a goal of the current focus on controls. Public companies need to be alert to weaknesses that may be identified during the year, as Section 302 certifications in quarterly filings are expected to consider such findings during the year.

The definition of a material weakness is aligned in SEC, PCAOB, and AICPA guidance. The term *reasonable possibility* is an important one and has a history. Quoting the PCAOB AS No. 5:

> A *material weakness* is a deficiency, or a combination of deficiencies, in internal control over financial reporting, such that there is a *reasonable possibility* that a material misstatement of the company's annual or interim financial statements will not be prevented or detected on a timely basis.
>
> Note: There is a *reasonable possibility* of an event, as used in this standard, when the likelihood of the event is either "reasonably possible" or "probable," as those terms are used in Financial Accounting Standards Board Statement [FASB] No. 5, *Accounting for Contingencies* . . . . (paragraph A7).[5]

---

[5] Now re-codified under the new Accounting Standards Codification in Financial Accounting Standards Board (FASB) Accounting Standards Codification (ASC) 450.

An issue arose where many companies and auditors believed that the original definition of the term *material weakness* in the earlier standards biased deficiency assessments toward more severe assessments—and more material weaknesses. The original definitions used the phrase *more than remote* (possibility) to express the thought we today have replaced with *reasonable possibility*. In defining this level, the explanation points the reader to the use of this terminology in existing accounting literature.

The irony is that when you compare these definitions to FASB usage, the concepts expressed in Statement No. 5, *Accounting for Contingencies*, they do not say anything different. The lower threshold in the accounting standard is "remote," and the next level in the scale is "reasonable possibility," so "*more* than remote" is the same as "reasonable possibility." It is not clear that the change in definition had any effect on the assessment of deficiencies, but the kinder and gentler language has attained greater acceptance.

Assessing the Likelihood and Significance of Possible Misstatement

For the purposes of evaluating the severity of control deficiencies, the key terms in this definition are:

- *Reasonable possibility*. Means that you have to assess the *likelihood* that a financial misstatement will result from a control failure
- *Material*. Means that you should assess the *potential amount* of the misstatement that could result from the control failure

It's important to note that under this definition, the severity of a deficiency does *not* depend on whether a financial statement misstatement *actually occurred*. Rather, it depends on the likelihood that an event *could* happen, namely, whether there is a reasonable possibility (more than a remote chance) that the company's control will fail to prevent or detect and correct a material misstatement.

When assessing likelihood and significance, consider these points. Likelihood is the chance that the deficiency could result in a financial statement misstatement. When assessing likelihood, you may consider:

- The nature of the financial statement accounts, disclosures, and assertions involved (e.g., suspense accounts and related party transactions involve greater risk).
- The susceptibility of the related assets or liability to loss or fraud (i.e., greater susceptibility increases risk).
- The subjectivity, complexity, or extent of judgment required to determine the amount involved (i.e., greater subjectivity, complexity, or judgment, such as that related to an accounting estimate, increases risk).
- The interaction or relationship of the control with other controls (i.e., the interdependence or redundancy of the control).
- The interaction of the deficiencies (e.g., when evaluating a combination of two or more deficiencies, whether the deficiencies could affect the same financial statement accounts and assertions).
- The possible future consequences of the deficiency.

If you did a good job of risk assessment and scoping, many of these issues will already have been considered regarding the control before getting to the evaluation of an identified deficiency.

The last point is interesting, though. It says that you need to consider future consequences. Some examples of future situations to consider could be that the deficiency is in a part of the business that is expected to grow larger in future periods, and what may be a less severe deficiency today might have much bigger implications in the near future. Another situation to watch for is that in a high-income year, the materiality threshold might be higher now, but it may be much lower when misstatements from the control deficiency are identified.

Some companies and auditors find that many of these suggested considerations also involve materiality (the second criterion). The real focus of the term *likelihood* is the probability that if a misstatement or error were introduced, the controls might not catch it. Materiality is an elusive accounting concept all by itself. To try to project it into future periods and different circumstances is not easy.

When material misstatement is identified during the course of an audit, that discovery seems to be obvious evidence of some material control failure and a 100% probability that the existing controls did not catch it. An important control that is missing (a design deficiency) also has a 100% likelihood of missing the error, since the control does not exist. When deviations appear in a controls test, then the possible deviation rate (the "upper limit" in statistical terms at a high level of confidence) relates to the likelihood criteria. (Appendix 10B to this chapter illustrates how to compute this limit.) Remember that the criteria are based on the *possible* misstatement; any actual misstatement is not the only factor to be considered.

Significance relates to the magnitude of potential misstatements resulting from the deficiency. When assessing significance, consider:

- The financial statement amounts or total of transactions exposed to the deficiency.
- The volume of activity in the account balance or class of transactions exposed to the deficiency that has occurred in the current period or that is expected in future periods.

When evaluating the significance of a potential misstatement, the maximum amount that an account balance or total transaction could be overstated generally is the recorded amount, while understatements could be larger. For example, consider the risks related to the amount of cash reported on the company's balance sheet. If that amount was $10,000, then:

- The magnitude of the misstatement that could result from the company's *overstatement* of its cash balances is, at most, $10,000. That is, the company's cash balance is zero, but it has reported $10,000.
- The magnitude of the misstatement relating to the company's *understatement* of its cash balances could be much larger than its reported balance. Suppose that the company's true cash balances were $50,000, but $40,000 was omitted from the

financial statements by "accident." In that case, the magnitude of the misstatement was $40,000, which is much greater than the reported account balance itself of $10,000.

Thus, the account balance provides some information about the potential significance of the misstatement that could result from a control failure, but that balance, by itself, may not give you the complete picture of the risks and magnitude of misstatement associated with the account in an understatement situation.

By understanding the transaction cycles and business processes, you can better assess the volume of dollars flowing through the control point that is deficient and thus "at risk" regarding control failure. Accounts that process trivial amounts would not trigger the materiality criteria, but if the risk assessment was correct, that control might have been scoped out of the assessment from the outset.

The likelihood and magnitude criteria may be difficult to implement in assessing the severity of some control deficiencies—for example, the control environment. A deficiency related to the effectiveness of the governance function (the board of directors and the audit committee) is generally assessed on the facts and circumstances of the deficiency. Pervasive and entity-level control deficiencies will often involve mega-material amounts and often involve design deficiencies, so the matter quickly moves up the ladder to a material weakness. The issue is whether there exist compensating (or monitoring) controls that can mitigate the problem.

For example, a strong and effective board may compensate for some deficiency in the audit committee composition when assessing severity, but the issue should still be addressed and scheduled for correction.

Special Deficiencies that May Be Material Weaknesses

Auditing standards draw attention to certain control deficiencies, suggesting that they may indicate a deficiency in internal control, which may be a material weakness. The initial PCAOB/AICPA standards presumed these "special" conditions were at least a significant deficiency and a strong indicator of a material weakness. We call these "special deficiencies" to identify them as we work through the book.

The current, softer SEC guidance in Release No. 33-8810 reads:

Management should evaluate whether the following situations indicate a deficiency in ICFR exists and, if so, whether it represents a material weakness:

- Identification of fraud, whether or not material, on the part of senior management;
- Restatement of previously issued financial statements to reflect the correction of a material misstatement;
- Identification of a material misstatement of the financial statements in the current period in circumstances that indicate the misstatement would not have been detected by the company's ICFR; and

- Ineffective oversight of the company's external financial reporting and internal control over financial reporting by the company's audit committee. (p. 37)[6]

The PCAOB guidance (paragraph 69) is a bit less polite and states: "Indicators of material weaknesses in internal control over financial reporting include … " The current AICPA guidance in AU-C Section 265 is similarly direct: "Indicators of material weaknesses in internal control include … " While there is wiggle room to not classify such situations as material weaknesses, few successful arguments can be raised against such a classification.

You are required to assess all control deficiencies to determine whether they are material weaknesses. However, the fact that these conditions are singled out is a reason to pay very special attention to them. As a practical matter, if these deficiencies exist at your company as of the reporting date, and if you somehow determine that they are not material weaknesses, you should document your rationale and be prepared to fully explain your reasoning to the independent auditors and possibly the regulators.

Significant Deficiencies

A significant deficiency is a broad category of deficiencies that includes material weaknesses and somewhat lesser deficiencies. Stated another way, material weaknesses are a more severe classification of significant deficiencies. While operationally of limited practical importance, this distinction does make a difference in communications with third parties, so it helps to know the relationship of the concepts. Its definition is even more amorphous than material weakness.

> A *significant deficiency* is a deficiency, or a combination of deficiencies, in internal control over financial reporting that is less severe than a material weakness, yet important enough to merit attention by those responsible for oversight of the company's financial reporting.[7]

While that is a fairly imprecise concept, it can be further refined in practice. Early SOX implementation guidance used by the major firms and published for company and auditor use initially set a somewhat arbitrary significance level of 20% of materiality as a threshold to distinguish "just" deficiencies from significant deficiencies. If the materiality test of a deficiency indicates the "at risk" dollars were less than material and more than 20% of materiality, then it was a candidate for significant deficiency status. While some firms no longer use this threshold, it is important to remember that COSO and the standards ask that you consider the aggregation of deficiencies in determining whether there might be a material weakness. How many related significant deficiencies might

---

[6] Similar wording is used in AICPA AU-C Section No. 265.

[7] PCAOB AS No. 5, paragraph A11, and also AU-C No. 265, *Communicating Internal Control Matters*, paragraph 7. The AICPA references "governance."

constitute a material weakness if they existed in the same component, principle, line of business, or account in the financial statements?

Would you call a deficiency that you assessed could have an impact of 90% of materiality a significant deficiency? Most would. How about 50%? Many would also call this a significant deficiency since just a couple of these significant deficiencies in concert could create exposure to a material misstatement if they occurred in the same account, balance, or other logical grouping, such as COSO component. Since there is no authoritative threshold to rely on, it may be helpful to develop some internal criteria for assessment, and document the thought process behind your assessments of individual deficiencies. Such a policy also helps to create more internal consistency in assessments within the project team.

A practice that has been in use by some firms and companies for assessing the severity of operating deficiencies arising from tests of control activities is based on approximating the potential monetary misstatement associated with the sample result and incidence of control deficiencies identified from the test. This procedure is described in Appendix 10A to this chapter. It is also illustrated in the AICPA Audit and Accounting Guide (AAG) *Audit Sampling* (2008, 2012, and 2014 editions[8]).

When Is a Material Weakness Not a Material Weakness?

The reasoning behind deficiency assessment as it relates to the information technology (IT) general controls (e.g., security and access, changes in systems, new systems development and operations) is different. The rationale for this difference is that IT general controls (ITGCs; unlike the applications and programmed procedures) do not cause misstatement themselves but may allow for irregular or ineffective operation of the application controls over which they operate.

Deficiencies in the underlying computer applications and programmed control procedures are assessed for severity like any manual control, but ITGC deficiencies are theoretically different. They are only assessed as significant deficiencies (or material weaknesses) if they have impacted the quality of the underlying applications. Recent trends have resulted in more ITGC deficiencies classified as significant deficiency or material weakness even in the absence of application deficiencies. While this makes sense in some situations (e.g., deficiencies in security and access), this continues to be an evolving area of practice. A conservative approach would recognize the severely deficient ITGCs. Since ITGC now is a specific principle under COSO 2013, it seems logical that a material weakness in ITGC would preclude the assessment of effective internal controls under COSO. This would be a major change.

The organization might have the worst new systems implementation approach in the world, but if it had no new systems implemented in the current period or if any failures of the underlying applications cannot be traced to the ITGC deficiency, then the otherwise material weakness in the ITGCs is not identified as a deficiency in that year. When systems changes do occur during a period (common in complex entities), then the concept is relevant and evaluated. Generally, poor processes eventually yield

---

[8] Sections 3.85 to 3.95 in the 2012 and 2014 editions. This guidance was also released in the 2008 revision of the AICPA AAG (Guide) *Audit Sampling*.

poor results. The key here is that the underlying automated process may need to be tested sufficiently to detect an operating effectiveness problem if it exists. If there are deficiencies in the underlying application controls that are related to the ITGC issue, the severity of those deficiencies determines the minimum severity ranking of the observed ITGC deficiency. Quite frankly, IT professionals often have difficulty with this conclusion, as it seems to denigrate the importance of ITGCs, to which COSO now assigns a specific principle. However, this is how many firms and companies had viewed such issues under SOX and other auditing standards.

A situation that really requires further thought is a severe ITGC deficiency in access and security controls. If the proverbial barn door is wide open, how can that risk be classified as just a deficiency, even if there has been no apparent compromise or loss? In such circumstances, it may be possible for unauthorized persons to commit mischief in the system and then cover their tracks to escape detection. Such problems may be more closely related to potential misstatements in the financial statements and very hard to detect in underlying applications. It is best to fix that problem if it exists right away rather than debate the severity of the classification. The blessing here is that security deficiencies are usually pretty easy to remediate, and that is also the best answer. This is one of those issues your COSO project team may want to discuss with your IT staff and also with your independent auditors.

Further muddying the waters surrounding this approach to ITGC severity classification is that the 2013 COSO Framework identifies effective ITGC controls as a principle (Principle 11) that must be satisfied to consider controls over financial reporting to be effective. The author suggests the reconsideration and refinement of the current conditional premise surrounding the security and access ITGCs to recognize poor security as a material weakness, as consistent with the definition of a material weakness.

Deficiencies and Exceptions

Exceptions or *deviations* are findings from tests that do not even rise to the level of deficiencies but are simply findings that need to be considered, as they might, in combination with other exceptions, indicate deficiencies. For example, in documenting a control, suppose there were some points in the documentation that were inaccurate or not complete, but not to the point of being misleading or wrong. Suppose in the controls testing process you found that certain data fields, other than the financial data fields you were focusing on, had missing or inaccurate information, but such issues did not affect the data you were working with or your ability to verify the reported transaction information. Those might be exceptions. While not major issues, sloppy documentation and record keeping in general could indicate a more serious issue and should not be ignored or underassessed.

Deficiencies are control issues (more than exceptions), but not at the significant deficiency level. Deficiencies lie in the broad area between exceptions and significant deficiencies. They cover a wide continuum of combinations of likelihood and magnitude (amounts at risk). In many projects, distinctions between exceptions and deficiencies are not very important except when a large number of them seem to cluster around components, principles, accounts, and the like. Then it may help to separate the lesser from the greater issues to consider the required aggregation issue.

In my view, the most critical distinction that needs to be made by entities and auditors is between deficiencies and significant deficiencies. This threshold distinguishes between those issues that will be clearly discussed with and likely addressed by management and those that may not be. While uncorrected material weaknesses are critical to public companies because they will be reported to shareholders, significant deficiencies are, by SEC regulation, to be corrected or they will become material weaknesses at some point. Therefore, the more severe deficiencies are going to be addressed. This was where company assessments were shown to fall short, as 70% of the time, companies underassessed the severity of significant deficiencies in the early implementation period of SOX. One might also assess there to be a control environment weakness in an entity refusing to address or correct known significant deficiencies. Why would management and the board ignore such issues?

Compensating Controls

Suppose a control deficiency meets the likelihood criterion (there is a reasonable possibility that misstatement could slip through) and the materiality criterion (a material amount is "exposed" to the deficiency); then the deficiency is a potential material weakness. However, further considerations will determine whether it will be finally assessed as a material weakness. The initial criteria of likelihood and magnitude do not create an "automatic" classification. There are a few get-out-of-jail cards (in the Monopoly sense) that can mitigate or lessen the severity of the assessment.

Before concluding on severity, you should consider the effect of any compensating controls that are identified. The guidance by the SEC in SEC Release No. 33-8810 is clear in this regard:

> Management should evaluate the effect of compensating controls when determining whether a control deficiency or combination of deficiencies is a material weakness. Compensating controls are controls that serve to accomplish the objective of another control that did not function properly, helping to reduce risk to an acceptable level. (p. 37)

Note that a *compensating control* is one that is designed to achieve the same control objective as a missing or ineffective control. For example, the company may have an ineffective control related to verifying that a vendor is on the approved vendor list before ordering merchandise or services. That is, a risk exists that some expenses may not be valid, and the control to prevent this error is poorly designed or not operating effectively. However, the objective review of all the documentation for expenses over $500 by a supervisor before payment is sent may somewhat "compensate" for the ineffective preventive control or reduce the severity of an otherwise material weakness to a lesser level.

The existence of a strong compensating control can sometimes fully mitigate the risk of misstatement and therefore was probably another choice for initially testing and relying on the control. To have a full mitigating effect on the relative magnitude of a missing or ineffective control, the compensating control (in the example, the reconciliation) should operate at a level of effectiveness and precision that would prevent or detect a misstatement that was more than inconsequential. In reality, there are few of these, despite their frequent citation when controls clearly fail.

The sources of compensating controls are varied, but to seek a compensating control, there are some places one might consider first:

- Tests of internal audit performed as a routine part of their audit responsibilities.

    There may be a duplicate or redundant control. Sometimes there is a manual control that performs the same function as an automated control, such as checking that the customer credit limit has not been exceeded when accepting a new order. Unfortunately, efficiency experts over the years have driven many of these redundant procedures out of existence. Also, look farther down the line and see if a later control might also detect the problem the earlier control might miss. The example here would be the final review of the support for the expenditure before the check is sent. In some cases it will be most efficient to seek out controls that operate later in the process and have this overview quality that verify many attributes before the transaction is approved or accepted.
- Monitoring controls may partially or fully mitigate the deficiency.

You should be prepared to support your conclusion that the compensating control effectively mitigates the risk posed by the missing or ineffective control. To support your conclusion, you should evaluate the design of the compensating control and test it or observe it in operation to verify its operating effectiveness. Of course, misstatements that have slipped through this compensating control in the past are indicators of the ineffectiveness of the compensating control and need to be considered before relying on the newly identified "compensating" control.

In early SOX experience, the most often cited compensating control was a monitoring control. Monitoring was so often the "well" that was gone to as to why a weakness was not really a weakness that in 2009 COSO released separate guidance on monitoring, reiterating how the concept might and often might not mitigate detailed deficiencies in the controls. Unfortunately, before then, company sophistication regarding monitoring was in its early stages, and estimates of the precision of some monitoring procedures were greatly exaggerated. The 2009 COSO guidance on monitoring was designed to increase understanding of the component. Further, the compensating control was rarely sought out and documented when the various detailed controls were documented, so when the detailed control failed by design or by performance, the hunt began to find the compensating or mitigating control. This sometimes resulted in rationalization regarding the significance of any deficiency in the absence of identified misstatements traced to the control deficiency. Compensating controls should be able to be identified in advance from a good understanding of the accounting procedures and controls. If documented (even if not tested), it is more likely they will be readily and correctly identified when needed.

In most instances, there are no real compensating controls in place that are truly precise enough in operation to be able to replace lower-level controls or fully reduce material weaknesses to simple deficiencies. This was true with respect to accelerated filers, and it seems reasonable that it would be even more so in smaller public companies and other entities. However, there might be structures that can mitigate the severity of a deficiency, so the concept still has relevance.

While the literature is encouraging in terms of describing this concept, do not be too excited about this being a nearby rescue boat in all the rough seas you will encounter.

"Prudent Official" Test

Before making a final determination about the severity of a control deficiency, your final step should be the "prudent official" test. That is, if you determine that the control deficiency is or is not a material weakness, then the auditor (and SEC) guidance directs you to step back from your assessment and consider whether a prudent official would agree with your determination.

Ask yourself this question: Would a prudent official, having the same knowledge of facts and circumstances that I have, conclude that this control deficiency (or combination of deficiencies) was (less than) a material weakness?

If the answer is no, then you should reconsider the severity of the deficiency. This "gate" supposedly swings in both directions, and in some cases it may be appropriate not to assess an apparently severe deficiency as severe. As tempting as this may sound, there are few instances where valid arguments have been crafted to downgrade a severe deficiency based on the prudent official test. Readers are encouraged to submit to the author examples of successful arguments to this point so they can be shared in a future edition.

Think of this prudent official test as a reality check, one final, objective look at your assessment to see if it makes sense. One of the examples sometimes posed is whether reading the facts and circumstances of the issue in the newspaper would cause a reasonable businessperson to agree with your conclusion regarding the severity of a control deficiency. If you identified 35 deficiencies and errors in a sample of 58 items and concluded that the balance and the controls were fine because each one of the deficiencies had a different "reason," then you probably could not pass a prudent official test—the answer is simply implausible. An incident like that once made the front page of the *Wall Street Journal*, column one. The company was in bankruptcy and litigation. Even the nonaccountant reporter did not think that the audit judgment made any sense.

A Framework for Assessing the Severity of Deficiencies

In 2004, amid the sorting out of the public company requirements, an implementation task force was formed from the larger certified public accounting (CPA) firms plus an academic member. A major problem with the implementation of the severity definitions was that companies and auditors seemed unable to apply consistent judgments. An inherent limitation with conceptual guidance and definitions is that once the documentation, control design assessments, and tests of controls are complete, assessing the severity of the identified deficiencies is more of an art than a science. Both companies and auditors found it hard to dollarize the implications of control deficiencies, particularly when misstatements of amounts were not associated with control deficiencies or control failures. Additionally, when company reporting and auditor inspections motivate the players in the process to reach different conclusions, clashes can result. The author recalls a late-night call with board members of a public company who wanted to argue the classification of each of over 100 significant deficiencies and material weaknesses identified during the audit. The end result was still an adverse opinion on internal controls.

Entities and auditors with the same information could reach different conclusions regarding the severity of a deficiency, particularly when the deficiency is on the margin between one category and another. However, the assessment process was never intended to be a subjective, random guess, or decided on the basis of the strength of personalities and debating skills. There should be principles and reasoning approaches that can lead reasonable people to reach a similar conclusion about a given situation.

It was in this spirit that the implementation task force created a document, *A Framework for Evaluating Control Exceptions and Deficiencies*, which was posted to the Web sites of the major firms and organizations such as the AICPA for wide dissemination. While not endorsed or required by the PCAOB or AICPA, it was referred to in speeches as being *a way* to meet the concepts in the standard, which was a sufficient-enough blessing to encourage many companies and auditors to follow its principles. The document was produced in three progressive releases; the third and final release in the cumulative series was December 20, 2004, rather late in the process for 2004 annual reports. That document is updated to 2013 context/terminology in Appendix 10A for current user reference.

While public company guidance may seem irrelevant to those entities operating in nonpublic company markets, to unify concepts and terms, the AICPA has tried to avoid creating nuance-level differences in the implementation of private company and public company deficiency definitions. After all, the genesis of the current public company guidance was guidance and definitions developed for all companies (public and private) years ago and adopted first by the AICPA, and it has been in supposed use for a long time in audit practice. The COSO Framework has not been as explicit in how to assess the severity of identified deficiencies as the auditing guidance in this area, so that is the reason for the focus on the auditing literature regarding this issue. SOX requirements for all public companies to report on internal control heightened the need for companies and auditors to share a common vision of how to assess the severity of identified deficiencies. Companies, in particular, were unfamiliar with the concepts; and thus the need for broad communication of the guidance.

The pioneers in 2004 (including the author) laid the general groundwork for how to assess the deficiencies, and that is the perspective taken in this book. The Framework may be most helpful to those assuming responsibility for the severity assessment in their entities or for testing the current methods of determining severity. Discussions continue between entities and auditors over the assignment of severity to specific deficiencies. Many of those discussions are simply unnecessary.

KEY FACTORS WHEN ASSESSING THE SEVERITY OF A DEFICIENCY

Before getting further into the mechanics of assessing deficiencies in design and operation, we should take a bird's-eye view of the factors and characteristics that can affect your assessment. These variables include the:

- Purpose and level of the control.
- Objectives and timing.
- Potential likelihood and magnitude of the misstatement.
- Business characteristics and risk environment.

Gaining familiarity with these factors will help you to work through the assessment process and over time will help you to build the judgment necessary to assess control deficiencies more consistently. These factors should be considered by entities and auditors alike and may assist in discussing any differences in opinion that may arise in assessing the severity of a deficiency.

Purpose and Level of the Control

Before severity can be assessed, deficiencies need to be considered in the context of the purpose and level of the control. Controls that are strictly related to operations are not the focus of financial reporting. For example, controls over stocking levels in a retail operation may be ineffective, resulting in lost sales or excess inventory. The lost sales aspect would not have a financial reporting implication, but the excess inventory, if it might lead to spoiled or damaged or unsalable goods, might have a financial consequence and affect the valuation assertion for the inventory. If assessing inventory spoilage or damage was already included somewhere in the financial reporting cycle procedures, then the lack of an effective ordering and restocking control might be of negligible consequence, even though it might have a consequence to the business as a whole.

Recall that the COSO Framework identifies three components of internal control:

1. Operations.
2. Financial reporting.
3. Compliance with regulation.

Our primary focus is on financial reporting controls, but care needs to be taken in excluding processes that have overlaps and financial implications. In many cases, the lack of a process and controls to capture risks associated with regulatory issues, such as environmental and pollution laws, would be a deficiency. A company that is in a highly regulated industry that fails to have an effective regulatory compliance monitoring function is likely to be assessed with a material weakness. A lack of awareness and controls to prevent or detect violation of labor laws relates to the human resource function and would generally be scoped into an assessment of a deficiency of some magnitude where management plans to report publicly on the controls effectiveness. In cases where the controls are tangential to financial reporting, entities should be prepared to demonstrate how processes and controls are in place to capture information that might be relevant to the financial statement amounts or disclosures (e.g., a potential risk or liability). Today numerous laws restrict or prohibit trade with certain countries (e.g., conflict minerals restrictions) must be adhered to or serious penalties may be assessed. Controls over compliance with such laws are certainly "in scope" for entities with any transactions covered under these laws.

In controls theory, some controls are by their nature controls that other controls rely on. For example, if a computer report is generated that shows unmatched orders and shipments for later manual reconciliation, the effectiveness of the manual control is dependent on the effectiveness of the computerized (automated) control. Similarly, if automated computer processes are dependent on the integrity of the access control and security to the computer files and programs, ineffective security can trump the otherwise apparently effective underlying application control. As a final example, if management is prone to override controls when it is convenient for them to do so, then all the underlying accounting system controls are potentially compromised. This implied hierarchy of controls is an element to be considered in the assessment of deficiencies. Obviously, a related control or process that is out of control can have significant implications for other controls. A poor *control environment* can poison the entire system and can rarely be compensated for by lower-level controls. A chief financial officer (CFO) who commits a theft affects a controls assessment more than a clerk who lifts some petty cash or steals office supplies. Pervasive system access and security weaknesses have more severe consequences than deficiencies in a payroll process, where employees are likely to notice and report errors such as underpayments. So the concept of both underlying and overarching controls helps position the control and provides clues to how severe a deficiency in that control might be.

Objectives and Timing

Many using this book to better understand controls are not intending to report publicly on internal controls anytime soon. Nevertheless, there is not a lower standard by which controls are assessed or deficiencies measured for smaller or for nonpublic entities. Your overall objectives can still impact your approach to the analysis and the severity and implications of some identified deficiencies.

Let's say you or a consultant under your direction embarked on a controls assessment assignment early in the New Year as an exercise in identifying opportunities to improve controls, as you know improvements are probably necessary. The severity of any deficiencies identified from this exercise may not require as much detailed analysis as if they had been discovered late in the period or during the audit. Since the intention of the early project is to correct all major issues, the concern is just to ensure that all potentially significant deficiencies and weaknesses are promptly corrected. Those that you choose not to correct because they are insignificant should only be ones that cannot come back and bite you later on. Thus, the safe way is to plan to correct just about everything that is identified.

Early experience with SOX paints a rather dismal picture of correcting deficiencies. Most (76% in 2004 and 70% in 2005) of the deficiencies identified in a 2004–2005 study of 76 audit engagements remained unremediated at the end of the year that they were identified.[9] Data limitations did not permit the tracing of specific deficiencies into future periods to determine when, if ever, the lesser deficiencies were corrected

---

[9] L. Graham and J. Bedard, "The Influence of Auditor and Client Section 404 Processes on Remediation of Internal Control Deficiencies at All Levels of Severity," *Auditing: A Journal of Practice and Theory* (2013).

(remediated). The study identifies some of the factors underlying the remediation rates, noting that late discovery is an important determinant in whether remediation occurs. Other studies that only were able to observe publicly reported material weaknesses report higher remediation rates, but this is to be expected since only material weaknesses were studied. One factor that could have influenced the findings is that in the early years of SOX implementation, there was so much going on and often so late in the year that remediation in the period of discovery was just not practical unless it prevented a public report of ineffective internal controls.

In general, if deficiencies are identified during the year, care needs to be taken both by management and the auditor that transactions which were processed but not effectively controlled were nevertheless still correctly processed and accounted for. This requires some additional monitoring and testing of those transactions. Auditors cannot rely on controls during periods of ineffectiveness, so significant deficiencies and material weaknesses will generally result in more audit testing of transactions and balances and less reliance on controls in those areas. This usually translates into higher audit costs. For purposes of this assessment, the severity of the deficiency is more important, as it will dictate an appropriate audit response to the issue.

An anomaly arises if the entity's purpose is to publicly report on controls. In public companies and in some required government entity controls reports, reports relate to controls "as of" the specific reporting date: the ending date of the balance sheet. Entities that are not public follow the guidance in AICPA's current Attestation Standard (AT) No. 501 when reporting on controls;[10] it permits reports to cover controls either within a period or as of a reporting date. When reporting on controls within a period, a weakness identified and corrected in that period would still be reported, even if it was remediated and tested to be effective by the end of the year. When reporting as of a date, past remediations, if effective, would not be included in the report, and a clean opinion could be issued. This has important implications for those publicly reporting on controls or seeking an auditor opinion on the effectiveness of controls. The reporting period or reporting date selected can affect the importance of the assessment of a deficiency and determine whether the deficiency will impair your ability to attest to the effectiveness of your controls.

In addition, in the ITGC area, the as-of date for reporting on controls has another peculiar wrinkle for deficiency assessment. If a deficiency in, say, change control procedures or new systems development procedures exists, the practice convention has arisen that the severity of the deficiency is initially dictated by the severity of any deficiency in the underlying controls identified as of the reporting date. Say, for example, it is found that the sales processing system has been incorrectly generating sales and receivables because of reference to an incorrect data table, and this deficiency can be traced to a defective change control process (ITGC) earlier in the year. If the deficiency in the sales system is deemed a material weakness, the ITGC deficiency would also be identified as a material weakness. Had the same deficient change control process not

---

[10] As this book goes to press, the AICPA is proposing an auditing standard, like PCAOB AS No. 5, for reporting on internal controls in conjunction with a financial statement audit. That standard, if issued, could modify the guidance in AT Nos. 501 and 101 for attesting to controls.

resulted in any known application-level deficiencies, the same deficient ITGC might be simply a deficiency for purposes of the as-of internal controls report, but its severity for financial reporting reliance purposes would be assessed separately. Thus, auditors might be obliged to conduct substantive tests on the underlying data to place reliance on that data for financial reporting even though the ITGC was not a material weakness for controls assessment and reporting purposes. This was not an intuitive conclusion for many IT professionals but is based on the general view that ITGC deficiencies do not *create* misstatements but open the door to misstatements, and the underlying computer systems and processing controls are the front line in ensuring proper accounting. This factor can be a point of confusion during discussions of the supposed synergy that exists between an audit of financial statements and the reporting on the effectiveness of internal controls. With effective ITGC necessary to satisfy Principle 11 in the 2013 COSO Framework revision, there should be no doubt that the ITGC issue is decided when the 2013 Framework is followed.

Potential Likelihood and Magnitude of the Misstatement

AICPA and PCAOB literature clearly indicate the important role of the potential likelihood and magnitude of misstatement. The term *likelihood* relates to the chance that a misstatement might be caused by the deficiency. Generally, if you are at the stage of assessing the severity of a deficiency, you have already met the likelihood threshold. A deficiency in design of an important control (the attribute or objective cannot be met because the design of the control is insufficient to do so) passes this test right away, since there is no control in place and the "could" factor indicates that misstatement is not controlled. For example, when there is no control that specifically ensures the GAAP classification of revenues, this would usually result in a material weakness due to "design" (the control is not "present"). When the deficiency is identified as a result of observations or failed tests of the control, the deviation rate observed can be a strong indicator of the likelihood that misstatement could occur. If a test is designed at a minimum sample size and expects no deviations, then finding one or more deviations generally means that the test cannot support the desired conclusion at the level of assurance desired. The result fails the likelihood threshold, and the assessment moves on to estimate the possible magnitude of the deficiency. To clarify this, AICPA guidance specifically states that identifying more deviations in a sample than planned for results in a deficiency.

Chapter 8 addressed the sampling and testing considerations inherent in assessing the operating effectiveness of controls and includes guidance on extending tests when initial ones are inconclusive or provide less assurance than desired. For reference regarding the likelihood issue, you may wish to look at Figure 10.2.

When assessing the magnitude, the volume of control dollars (gross dollar exposure) that could be affected by the control deficiency is estimated. For example, if the system fails to add proper shipping charges to a certain type of sales, then the gross exposure can be estimated by the potential misstatement of the shipping charges on the total volume of affected sales. When important controls fail when tested, the volume of transactions that pass through that control point generally will cause the magnitude of the deficiency to be significant or material.

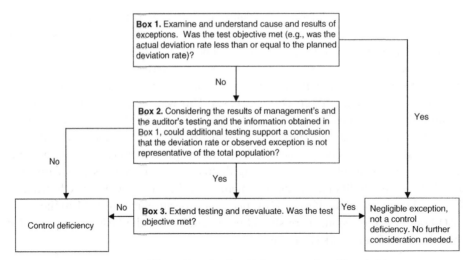

Individual boxes should be read in conjunction with the corresponding guiding principles.

FIGURE 10.2 Chart 1. Evaluating Exceptions Found in the Testing of Operating Effectiveness

Before determining the severity of the deficiency, you should consider if there are other controls, including monitoring controls, that might compensate for or mitigate the ineffective control and limit the magnitude of the deficiency to something less than materiality. Be alert that rationalization may play a part when assessing whether another control might be effective in identifying a misstatement if the detailed control is defective. As previously noted, the overuse of the concept that monitoring would detect misstatements in such circumstances led COSO to issue 2009 guidance on what monitoring might realistically be expected to identify. Entities need evidence to support the assertion that monitoring is an effective compensating control, and not just armchair hypothetical assertions.

Finally, you need to step back from the situation and apply a reasonable person test (e.g., the prudent official test) to the misstatement. Does your assessment pass the sniff test if the circumstances were revealed in the newspaper the next day? Is it a believable conclusion, considering the contortions you underwent to draw it?

For most control activities, magnitude assessments follow the guidance in Figure 10.3. This exhibit will be used later on when illustrating the assessment of a few example deficiencies.

Business Characteristics and Risk Environment

Consider the business as a whole and the relative risks and importance of the function exhibiting the deficiency when assessing the severity of a deficiency. You may also consider this factor as a component of the likelihood assessment, but some prefer to ensure it is at least clearly articulated during the assessment process. Suppose your business was highly dependent on specific company intellectual property and knowledge contained

Step 1: Determine whether a significant deficiency exists.

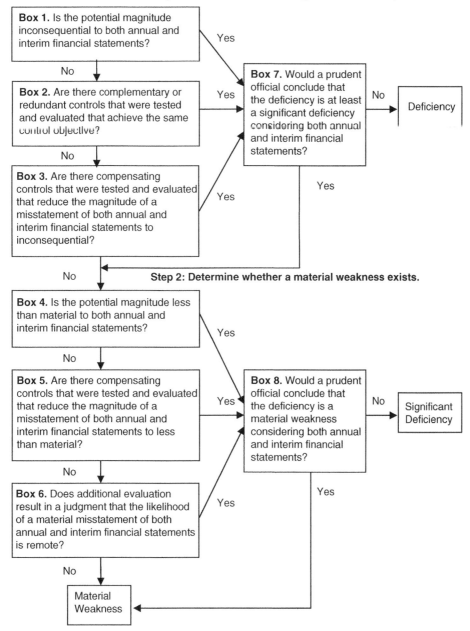

Individual boxes should be read in conjunction with the corresponding guiding principles.

FIGURE 10.3   Chart 2. Evaluating Process/Transaction-Level Control Deficiencies

within your systems. You might expect you would be very concerned about the theft or corruption of that data and would have industrial-strength security and Internet firewall protection. A community service organization also needs security and intruder protection, but to the same degree? Of course not, but if it holds important donor list or personal data in its systems, maybe the organization should rethink its exposure to loss and fines should such data be stolen.

Suppose that passwords are in place, but password security is simple (e.g., five-character minimum), and passwords are not changed several times a year, as is generally recommended. Although that situation would be a deficiency to both entities, it might be much more severe for the intellectual property risk entity than for the community service organization. The importance of the data and the risk of industrial espionage and even political espionage heighten the severity of the deficiency in one environment versus the other. Do not generalize that smaller companies have a lesser standard to fulfill. It is just that the underlying risks might be lower and the amounts and things at risk might not attract the most sophisticated of fraudsters and hackers. Relying on their organization as a lesser target for protection is a poor defense mechanism and not a "control" to place reliance on. There are plenty of examples of not-for-profit, religious organization, and government program frauds that were supported by loose controls. However unattractive you think you might be as a target for a fraud, there are lots of opportunists who will take you on and exploit any opportunity you provide. In fact, charities and religious organizations are frequent targets because they are often so vulnerable and trusting and unfamiliar with security measures.

Because governments often control so much money, they are frequent targets of fraudsters through a variety of scams. However, according to the statistics, in recent years, government controls awareness has reduced the instances and magnitude of government frauds. Actually, as cited before, the 2012 survey on occupational fraud noted that the median reported fraud in private companies was actually larger than for public companies and almost twice the median fraud amount for governments.

As another example, suppose a business is paperless, and all transactions and documents are stored in electronic form and images. Timely data backups, disaster planning, and off-site storage issues would be more critical to this type of business than many others due to its reliance on systems and data. The quality of the ITGC should be correspondingly high.

 ## CONDITIONS INDICATING CONTROL DEFICIENCIES

The auditing community standards literature defines a number of issues and situations that should be considered deficiencies of some level of severity.[11] The final assessment of the severity is dependent on judgment, as there are degrees of deficiency.

Table 10.1 contains examples of more severe deficiencies.

---

[11] Note: There is a *reasonable possibility* of an event, as used in the definitions of *material weakness* and *significant deficiency*, when the likelihood of the event is either "reasonably possible" or "probable," as those terms are used in Financial Accounting Standards Board Statement No. 5, *Accounting for Contingencies* (FAS No. 5).

TABLE 10.1 Examples of More Severe Deficiencies

Entity *accounting expertise* insufficient to effectively select and apply the appropriate GAAP accounting principles to the transactions of the entity.

A lack of *antifraud programs and controls*, and awareness of fraud risks.

A lack of controls over *nonroutine and nonsystematic* transactions.

Insufficiently designed controls over the *period-end closing process* and preparation of the financial reports. This includes the calculation and recording of periodic adjustments such as depreciation and amortization expenses, fair value measurements as required by GAAP (in accounting for changes in some investment holdings and for testing impairment of asset values), and the provision for accrued expenses, allowances, and reserves.

Lack of *oversight* of the entity's internal control over financial reporting by those charged with governance.

Restatement of previously issued financial statements to reflect past accounting errors. A restatement to reflect changes in accounting principles to comply with a new accounting standard or a voluntary change from one GAAP to another would not indicate a deficiency.

The auditor's discovery of a *material misstatement* or an aggregate of misstatements that were material in the financial statements for the period under audit, including misstatements of estimates and accruals. These would be considered material misstatements even if the entity corrected these items identified by the auditor. Because the auditor is not considered an element of internal control of the entity, it is the entity's responsibility to prepare GAAP financial statements and disclosures.

An ineffective *internal audit* function in larger and more complex entities where the monitoring and risk assessment functions are important to the entity.

For regulated entities, an ineffective *regulatory compliance function* that could have a material effect on the reliability of financial reporting. For example, if the issuance of additional debt instruments is essential for the continued financial viability of an entity, and regulators may prohibit such issuances due to failing other regulatory requirements, disclosures and possibly accruals might be necessary to reflect the circumstances. An attitude of contempt or indifference toward regulatory requirements might also indicate a more general control environment deficiency.

Identification of any magnitude of *fraud on the part of senior management* and officials. Senior management includes owners, the senior financial and accounting officers, and so on. The reason for this concern is the possible implications on the control environment and the existence of evidence that such behavior exists in this management group. This issue includes, but is not limited to, deliberately overstated requests for "expense" reimbursements and the use of entity funds for items or services of a personal nature without recording compensation expense.

An attitude on the part of management or those charged with governance that creates *indifference* to correcting known significant deficiencies or material weaknesses in internal controls.

An *ineffective control environment*. Since the control environment sets the tone of the organization, an ineffective control environment is unlikely to be overcome by controls at the more detailed level. Of particular concern in smaller entities is the existence or risk of management override of controls, where management or owners instruct employees to perform actions outside the normal operating procedures (e.g., make payments without adequate documentation or invoice support).

In-House Accounting Expertise

Smaller entities have particular problems in securing at a reasonable cost the accounting expertise and experience necessary to properly account for all transactions and prepare the financial statements. Not every entity can afford the level of in-house expertise necessary to handle unusual situations, perform the tax accrual (i.e., creation of tax expense and deferred tax amounts when the tax and financial records are not in sync), and close the books and make appropriate accruals and draft financial statements. The inability to perform these functions is considered an internal control deficiency that may be severe enough (e.g., a significant deficiency or a material weakness) to require communication to management and those charged with governance every year. While preparing financial statements for clients is clearly addressed by the restrictive SEC independence guidance for public company auditors, the previous guidance for AICPA engagements has been less restrictive, recognizing the limitations of many clients to perform this function.

Under previous AICPA rules, the independent auditor can assist clients in making adjustments and preparing the financial statements and disclosures, but he or she still needs to identify if the reason for performing such services is due to the entity's lack of resources to perform these financial accounting functions. When a deficiency is deemed to exist, the auditor needs to assess its severity and communicate with management or those charged with governance when the deficiency is a significant deficiency or a material weakness.

For AICPA audits for years beginning after December 15, 2014, the professional ethics Section 101-3 is scheduled to be clarified such that cash-to-accrual conversions and preparation of the financial statements are clearly defined as nonattest services and could impair auditor independence under certain circumstances. Be alert for numerous questions and answers forthcoming about this tightened standard as the implementation date approaches. The rule was tightened to agree with the previously tightened independence requirements set forth by the Government Accountability Office (GAO) for audits governed by government auditing standards.

A practical way to address this issue for nonpublic entities may be to upgrade the skill sets of the accounting staff to include the knowledge and techniques necessary to perform some of these functions. Another alternative some have found to be cost effective is to hire another accountant on a consulting basis to perform these basic functions and to prepare the books, records, and financial statements for the external auditor review. Often consulting accountant fees will be less than those otherwise charged by an independent auditor for the same service. Some entities have actually reduced total costs by securing timely consulting advice and minimizing independent auditor costs. However, the preparing accountant needs to be aware of all the information necessary to prepare the statements and footnotes, or deficiencies will be identified and assessed by auditors reviewing the work performed when omissions are identified.

Other Deficiencies

Other deficiencies in either the design or operation of controls may be identified by management through testing or the monitoring function, or they may be implied by customer complaints and special allowances or returns or misstated financial statement amounts. These deficiencies can range in judgment from trivial to material, depending on the facts and circumstances. Judgment and consideration of qualitative factors are necessary in assessing severity. Many of the operating deficiencies in control activities and ITGCs would be run through the deficiency framework charts to assist in assessing the severity. Table 10.2 presents some deficiencies that might be encountered.

Inadequate Documentation

While documenting company controls has been a requirement of public companies for many years, lack of adequate controls documentation is still a common deficiency. Without good controls documentation, it may be difficult to identify the controls that exist and the gaps that should be identified and corrected. It may be difficult for management to monitor controls that are not documented and to create consistency in processing and controls over time, when entity accounting staff retire or change. Most people can relate to the parlor game where a joke or phrase is passed via oral communication from person to person, and the beginning and ending communications often are found to be quite different. The same can happen with oral policies and procedures: They will migrate and morph over time and circumstances, often becoming something quite unintended.

At a certain level, the total lack of documentation of processes and controls may render your controls data unauditable/unreviewable and the preparation of financial statements and disclosures impossible. Your certified public accountant may refuse to undertake an engagement that includes reporting on controls under such circumstances.

Many people believe that a robust accounting and procedures manual is a minimum threshold for documenting *control activities*. To the extent practical, the manual should also address *control environment* issues, *monitoring* (e.g., what and by whom), and the standard management reports that are to be generated (and when and to whom). Some accounting manuals include these topics:

- Procedures and controls over the main revenues and expenses (including payroll) of the entity
- Measures to protect the personal data of employees
- The bank and investment accounts, and authorized persons to sign checks or direct investments in those accounts
- Measures to safeguard entity assets
- Insurance information
- Bonding information regarding accounting or cash-handling employees
- IT policies and procedures
- Templates for reports to be generated periodically
- Financial statement and disclosure examples
- Statements of ethical values or codes of conduct and antifraud programs and controls
- Harassment and whistleblower policies and procedures

When controls are documented and monitored in accordance with the COSO Framework format discussed in this book, the amount of independent auditor time

TABLE 10.2 Design and Operating Deficiencies

Design Deficiencies

▪ Inadequate design of internal control over a *significant account or process*, including the preparation of the financial statements.
▪ Inadequate *documentation* of internal control (all five components).
▪ Insufficient attention to creating the proper *control environment*—for example, tone at the top, lack of ethics statements, fraud consciousness, or communication of values.
▪ Inadequate *segregation of duties* within a significant account or process.
▪ Absent or inadequate physical controls over the *safeguarding of assets* from loss or theft (e.g., "shrink" in the retail industry). If an entity has excellent accounting controls to identify any physical loss before the financial statements are prepared, that may be an adequate compensating control to mitigate the financial reporting weakness, but management should assess the risks and costs of failing to implement preventive measures to mitigate losses.
▪ Inadequate attention to the design of *IT general controls* (e.g., security and access, change controls, new system implementations, and operating issues) and accounting-related software *application controls* that may prevent the information system from processing authorized transactions as needed for financial reporting and monitoring needs.
▪ Employees or management who lack the *qualifications and training* to apply GAAP in recording transactions or the skills and knowledge to prepare the financial statements and footnotes.
▪ Ineffective design or documentation of the *monitoring* function.

Operating Deficiencies

▪ Observed deficiencies in the *performance of controls* over a significant account or process. This may be observed from a failure to perform a control, such as a bank reconciliation or the failure to adequately follow up on exceptions that should be investigated or as a result of a financial statement error that would imply a control failure. Recall that the absence of financial statement deficiencies is not an indicator that controls are operating effectively, but the identification of misstatements is a valid indicator that controls may have not operated effectively.
▪ Failures of *safeguarding controls* to prevent loss from damage or theft that are not timely detected by financial accounting controls and properly reported in the financial statements and communicated to management.
▪ Failures of the *reports* and other information and communication components to provide timely, accurate, and relevant information to the appropriate levels of personnel and management to enable them to perform their management functions and monitor operations and related financial data. Flooding management or auditors with irrelevant information that obscures relevant information is as much a deficiency as failing to provide adequate information.
▪ The identification of more deficiencies than planned for in a test of internal controls.*

*This issue has implications for sample planning. The frequent design of samples without any allowance for expected deviations when deviations are possible can result in inefficient testing (extending testing later) and many "failed" controls tests.

necessary to obtain and understand of internal controls is reduced, resulting in audit savings for the entity.

Not-for-profit entities are facing increasing scrutiny from the Internal Revenue Service for keeping adequate books and records to support their tax status and their reported Form 990 or Form 990A. States such as California have enacted statutes, such as the Nonprofit Integrity Act of 2004, which call for audits and public disclosure of the financial statements and other requirements for not-for-profits with over $2 million in gross revenues. There is increasing pressure at various levels for more accountability in these organizations, and numerous federal, state, and local committees are discussing the imposition of SOX-like legislation to raise the organizations' accountability to the public. Be mindful of any such legislation that relates to your entity.

Government entities should also note that in the development of the AICPA Attestation Standard for reporting on internal controls, GAO task force participants expressed the intention of imposing internal control reporting requirements on government entities at some point in time, perhaps starting with reports on the design of controls and ultimately resulting in reporting on both the design and operating effectiveness of controls. Smaller banks have been reporting on their internal controls for some years and continue to do so under the revised auditing guidance in the AICPA's Attestation Standard AT No. 501.

Inadequate Evidence of Controls Performance

A source of misunderstanding and potential friction arises when the independent auditor is unable to see any evidence that the control operated or the monitoring occurred. COSO conceptually accepts the premise that controls could operate but not inherently leave evidence of their operation. Auditors unfortunately are uncomfortable with this concept, as there is no evidence they can rely on that the control procedure or oversight was performed. In such cases, auditors may need to make additional observations of the control being performed, reperform more examples of the control operation, and perform extended inquiries to be satisfied the control exists and is in use. That costs auditors time, which costs entities money. The 2013 COSO Framework addresses this by simply noting the entity may be required by regulators or others (e.g., auditors) to document such activities.

In many cases, a simple method can be devised to indicate the performance of a task, but people often resist such measures, however simple and cost effective they may be. Initialing and dating a bank reconciliation (or use of a stamp to do so) can serve as attestation of its performance by the authorized person and can also be used to indicate its review by a member of management as a part of the monitoring process. In some cases, the stamp or signature may not be evidence of anything, since the "documentation" may be false. Testing, observation, and inquiry should be used to support the signature or documentation as evidence that can be relied on. Alternatively, lists of tasks, such as some of the scheduled monitoring functions, can be documented quickly and easily that the task was performed, and by whom and when. While auditors generally will test that the list or form is accurate, it is simpler and cheaper to audit this form to establish its reliability than to establish that the individual controls are in place by other means.

Weaknesses over Time

Over time, one might think that entities might learn more about the nature and causes of material internal control weaknesses, and thus there is a tendency for many types of weaknesses to be far less prevalent. Laurence Gordon and Amanda Wilford made an academic study of the proportion of different material weakness deficiency types as disclosed over time by public companies.[12] What emerges from that study is that while some material weaknesses do shift in importance over time, the proportion of these material weaknesses still remain rather similar. Gordon and Wilford do find "statistical" significance in the shifts of some of the types, but that simply means there is more variation in the measure than can be attributed to chance. Overall, from a broader perspective, the proportions remain similar. While some comfort might be taken from the decline in the segregation of duties and restatement types of weaknesses, it is disturbing to see increases in ethical, journal entry, year-end adjustments, and senior management types of weaknesses. Perhaps some of these observed increases are due to better detection procedures and refinements of analyses over time. Nevertheless, most types seem to be rather "sticky" in proportion over time. Table 10.3 is derived from that research and shows the remarkable similarity in the makeup of deficiencies, despite the passage of time and increasing experience. Are we really learning from prior experience?

TABLE 10.3   Consistency of Material Weakness Deficiencies over Time

Type	Percentage of Firms Nov 2004–Jan 2006	Percentage of Firms, Feb 2006–2009
Accounting documentation, policy, procedure	93.3	99.4
Accounting personnel resources and competency/training	42.9	49.5
Ethical or compliance issues with personnel	1.4	7.8
Ineffective regulatory compliance issues	.7	1.4
Information technology, software, security, and access issues	17.4	19.2
Journal entry control issues	8.9	10.8
Material and/or numerous auditor/year-end adjustments	51.8	60.1
Nonroutine transaction control issues	15.6	19.1
Restatement or non-reliance of company filings	52.5	42.5
SAB 108 adjustments noted	0.0	0.5
Segregations of duties/design of controls (personnel)	17.7	12.0
Senior management competency, tone, or reliability issues	1.8	7.2
Untimely or inadequate account reconciliations	30.5	22.7
Total Observations	**287**	**752**

[12] L. Gordon and A. Wilford. "An Analysis of Multiple Consecutive Years of Material Weaknesses in Internal Control," *Accounting Review* 87, No. 6.

EXAMPLES OF EVALUATING THE SEVERITY OF DEFICIENCIES

Manual Control Deficiencies

During your monitoring of controls over sales, suppose you note a number of instances where credit sales were accepted from customers who were not preapproved, as they were supposed to be in accordance with the documented controls. Further inquiry does not reveal a reason for these exceptions. Since the preapproval of customers is considered to be an important control for your organization to prevent losses, the incidence of the findings is a concern. Whether sampling controls or monitoring, when the incidence found of unexpected deviations exceeds expectations, the likelihood criteria (see Figure 10A.1 in Appendix 10A) are generally met. Next the review turns to the magnitude of the potential misstatement.

Following the general structure of Figure 10A.2 in Appendix 10A, the gross credit sales annually "exposed" is $1,000,000 and financial statement materiality is assessed to be $10,000. A second review of all transactions over $2,000 is tested and seems to be working, and this is considered to be a partial compensating control that limits the risk of a material misstatement being caused by this control deficiency. Further, sales monitoring at an even higher level might prevent a single material transaction from escaping scrutiny.

Based on this information, plus considering any qualitative factors and stepping back to consider how a reasonable person (e.g., prudent official) might view the deficiency, management concludes that the compensating control limits the risk that failure of the lower-level control will lead to a material misstatement. However, management is unable to conclude that the controls are working well enough to limit the misstatements to an inconsequential level.[13] Thus, this control is considered a significant deficiency based on the fact that the deficiency could lead to misstatement of more than an inconsequential amount.

If total credit sales (as a component of all sales, including cash sales) were less than material to the overall operations, this deficiency might be assessed at just a deficiency, since there would be a low risk that the control deficiency could lead to a material misstatement.

Automated Control Deficiencies

Deficiencies in automated controls that are considered key in achieving a control objective are generally found to be deficiencies in design, as automated (computerized) controls should operate consistently when in a proper ITGC environment. However, automated controls can be programmed to process transactions from different sources differently, so exceptions need to be investigated to determine the reasons and the conditions under which the control will not perform as desired.

---

[13] See AU No. 325, *Communications about Control Deficiencies in an Audit of Financial Statements,* or AU-C No. 265.

If the control failure is due to a design deficiency (e.g., the control was not pro-grammed to be performed with a certain class of transactions, such as credit sales), the magnitude of the possible deficiency needs to be considered. If the control is important to achieving a control objective or attribute, and the stream of dollars exposed to the con-trol deficiency is more than material, the initial assessment is likely to result in a material weakness assessment, and any compensating or complementary or monitoring controls that might serve to limit the deficiency would then be considered.

A benefit of an automated control (e.g., sales order prices are checked against an approved sales price database listing) is that it often needs to be tested only once or a few times for operating effectiveness when ITGCs are assessed as effective, as an automated control should perform consistently. Despite the "theory" of a single test, on critical con-trols it is often a practical decision of entities and auditors to observe the control in operation at a couple of points in the period to provide extra assurance of effectiveness without busting the budget.

Some controls are actually combinations of automated and manual procedures. For example, an automated control may select payments that do not exactly match approved invoices for a manual reconciliation. In such cases, both the automated and manual controls need to operate effectively in order for the overall control to be effective. The automated portion of the control might need to be tested only one or a few times, since automated controls generally operate consistently in an effective ITGC environment. However, to reach the same conclusion on the manual control, more instances are gen-erally examined since deficiencies in the manual process portion can lead to instances where the control does not function effectively due to inconsistency in human processes. In most cases, the combination control is assessed as a unit, as both phases need to be effective.

If the manual portion of the control fails often enough to meet the likelihood test, then the magnitude of the potential deficiency needs to be examined. Suppose manage-ment wanted to use an *upper limit methodology* (as described in Appendix 10B to this chapter) to assess magnitude. If one unplanned-for manual procedure deviation was found in 45 control instances examined, then the observed deviation rate is 2.2%. Using statistical sampling tables or computer programs at a 90% ("high") level of confidence, the upper limit on the error rate can be determined to be approximately 8.4%. If 8.4% of the population of $1,000,000 is misstated, the corresponding monetary limit on the amount would be $84,000. This method of quantifying the deficiency amount helps to relate the test findings to the materiality criteria but rests on assumptions about the relationship between the incidence of control failures and the dollar amounts. People who are assessing the severity of deficiencies can use either the upper limit approach or the approach that considers compensating and monitoring controls; however, both methods should not be applied to the same deviation since they are both approaches to quantifying the possible magnitude, but they do not work together in reducing the true magnitude.[14]

---

[14] When the likelihood of misstatement is assessed as negligible, then the assessment process can assign an *exception* level to any deviation instances.

IT General Control Deficiencies

As previously noted, ITGC deficiencies do not *cause* misstatements, but lax ITGCs may *permit* misstatements to occur in the underlying applications or data.

A failure to implement any passwords to limit access to programs or data at the network or accounting software level is generally assessed as a material weakness by auditors just in terms of an ITGC issue. If anyone can access the software and initiate transactions, such as to schedule payments or change data files, perhaps to divert funds, then the entity is highly exposed to fraud risk. A unique aspect of this deficiency is the ability of talented fraudsters to cover their tracks after making changes to the accounts or data. In many smaller entities where passwords are used, often they are taped to writing surfaces, inside drawers, or monitors. The appearance of any protection whatsoever is misleading. The blessing here is that such poor practices can be easily remediated. From a financial auditing standpoint, it would be foolhardy on the part of the auditor to not respond to this ITGC issue by increasing testing levels of all accounts and disclosures to respond to the possible fraud risk and to ensure that the reported amounts are fairly stated.

While smaller entities should change passwords periodically and use appropriate firewall protection for network connections to the Internet, it is not anticipated that one size fits all regarding security. Some cost–benefit considerations will enter into the equation of whether the designed protection is adequate for the assessed risk.

Failure to restrict access to programs and data can expose a company to unauthorized, fraudulent activity. Deliberate management manipulations of files and programs in the case of the *SEC v. Livent* (see www.sec.gov/litigation/litreleases/lr16022.txt) show the importance of security and access controls and the risk associated with this element of ITGCs.

In the *Livent* case, the lack of auditor attention to controls (including IT) opened the door to a management record-keeping fraud involving misdirecting the costs of projects to under budget or incomplete projects in order to hide impending losses in other projects. The complexity of the scheme required the fraudster managers to keep track of the true state of affairs so that payments would still be made on time. Unrestricted access to the accounting system was necessary to create the doctored records from the real records. Programs were written to help keep track of the true and bogus records and to transfer costs for the "auditor" books and restore then for the "real" books and records. Cost transfers are also a fertile technique for making inappropriate charges to certain government supplier contracts to maximize the overall entity returns on government projects.

Many smaller and less complex entities use packaged software that has few user options to customize processing logic. In such cases, the absence of a change control process may not be relevant, since the underlying software may not allow user-requested changes. Also, in the absence of implementing new software, the ITGCs relating to new system development and implementation are probably not relevant to many businesses, and deficiencies in the procedures would not result in a significant or material ITGC deficiency finding.

Failure to perform timely backups or failure to monitor and evaluate systems issues, while often easy to fix, could cause serious issues and should be assessed as to severity and reported to management.

Failures in the ITGC controls may preclude auditors from relying on automated controls as an audit strategy and may raise the costs of audits because of the need to perform extensive substantive detail procedures.

As mentioned, entities reporting on internal controls "as of" a date may not assess some ITGC deficiencies as significant deficiencies or material weaknesses if the underlying application controls can be shown to be effective at the as-of date. Figure 10.4 reflects this thinking as it was prepared to be used in conjunction with public company reporting on internal controls using the as-of assumption. However, the implementation of Principle 11 of the 2013 COSO Framework revision is not reflected in following Figure 10.4. In this case, a stand-alone decision should be made on the effectiveness of ITGC deficiencies based on their severity.

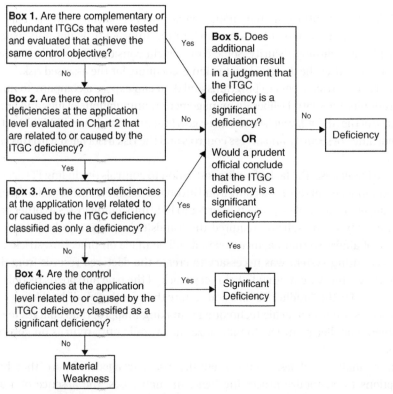

Individual boxes should be read in conjunction with the corresponding guiding principles.

FIGURE 10.4   Chart 3. Evaluating Information Technology General Control Deficiencies

Aggregating Deficiencies

If an entity identifies numerous significant deficiencies in controls over revenue and these deficiencies affect primarily the existence assertion, consideration should be given as to whether, in combination, the control deficiencies constitute a material weakness since they are concentrated in the revenue account and the existence assertion.

If the same number of significant deficiencies were spread out to the accounts, assertions, and COSO components, in the aggregate they might not be considered a material weakness.

In some cases where many, many deficiencies of less-than-material-weakness severity are identified across many accounts, disclosures, and assertions, it may be appropriate to assess this "carnival" as a material weakness when viewed from the perspective of the prudent official. One of the engagements in the 77-engagement 2011 Bedard–Graham study identified over 200 deficiencies of various magnitudes in the examination of controls. Anecdotally and in other surveys of deficiencies, other public engagement examinations reported that over 500 deficiencies were found when controls were examined more closely than before.[15]

The 2013 COSO Framework tries to tie together related control deficiencies in a way not previously emphasized in the COSO guidance. For example, deficiencies in the information and communication systems (e.g., timeliness and accuracy of reports) can have a negative impact on managing the business (control environment and risk assessment) and monitoring (e.g., identifying anomalies for follow-up) as well as control activities (e.g., providing adequate data for developing estimates and allowances for various purposes). In another example, failure to effectively control the purchasing process may introduce a previously unidentified fraud risk that needs to be considered in the overall controls structure and audit plan. More than ever before, entities and auditors are being challenged to link and relate control deficiencies and consider how they might relate to other controls, principles and components. This is very consistent with the expectation that entities will implement the controls in an integrated way rather than viewing the individual components, principles, and controls as mini-stovepipes that stand alone.

 ## OVERALL ASSESSMENT

A conclusion that internal controls are ineffective will arise (1) when a material weakness exists in any COSO component or (2) in one of the 17 Principles or (3) when the controls are not implemented in an integrated fashion in the entity. This is a refinement of previous guidance by COSO. The aggregation of numerous deficiencies in a COSO

---

[15] See SEC Staff Accounting Bulletin Topic 1 M2, *Immaterial Misstatements that Are Intentional*, for further discussion about the level of detail and degree of assurance that would satisfy prudent officials in the conduct of their own affairs.

component, account, or process or in an assertion could preclude you or your auditor from concluding that internal controls were effective (akin to death by a thousand small cuts). You should examine any identified deficiencies from different perspectives before concluding that controls are effective. Suppose that a particular remote location was poorly controlled as a business unit. Then all the transactions processed through that unit could be exposed to those poor controls, and the aggregate exposure to the entity could be more significant than the relative asset or income base might indicate. An example could be a remotely located sales subsidiary that services international sales transactions.

Like some professional examinations, you need to get passing grades on all parts of the COSO examination in order to pass with an effective controls assessment. No piecemeal or except-for opinions can be directed to the partial effectiveness of internal controls. This fact reinforces the overarching concept of the integrated nature of controls. The weakest link defines the strength of the chain.

Additional examples of deficiency assessments from the auditor perspective are illustrated in the AICPA's 2014 AA-Guide, *Assessing and Responding to Audit Risk in a Financial Statement Audit*.

APPENDIX 10A

A Framework for Evaluating Control Exceptions and Deficiencies

VERSION 3, DECEMBER 20, 2004

Adapted and revised for 2013 by Lynford Graham, coauthor of the original framework in 2004.

INTRODUCTION AND PURPOSE

This paper outlines a suggested framework for evaluating exceptions and deficiencies resulting from the evaluation of a company's internal control over financial reporting. Issuers and auditors may find this framework useful.

This paper should be read in conjunction with the auditing standards (e.g., PCAOB Auditing Standard No. 5, *An Audit of Internal Control Over Financial Reporting Performed in Conjunction with an Audit of Financial Statements*, and AU-C Section 265, *Communicating Internal Control Related Matters Identified in an Audit*), especially the definitions in paragraphs 8 through 10, the section on evaluating deficiencies, the examples of significant deficiencies and material weaknesses in Section D, and the Background and Basis for Conclusions in Section E. The framework is not a substitute for the COSO Framework and other relevant professional literature.

The framework was originally developed by representatives of the following nine firms:

1. BDO Seidman LLP
2. Crowe Chizek and Company LLC
3. Deloitte & Touche LLP
4. Ernst & Young LLP
5. Grant Thornton LLP
6. Harbinger PLC
7. KPMG LLP
8. McGladrey & Pullen LLP
9. PricewaterhouseCoopers LLP

In addition, William F. Messier, Jr., Professor, Georgia State University, also contributed to the development of the framework.

This framework reflects their views on a framework consistent with their understanding.

The framework represents a thought process that will still require significant judgment. The objective of the framework is to assist knowledgeable and experienced individuals in evaluating deficiencies in a consistent manner. The mere mechanical application of this framework will not, in and of itself, necessarily lead to an appropriate conclusion. Because of the need to apply judgment and to consider and weigh quantitative and qualitative factors, different individuals evaluating similar fact patterns may reach different conclusions.

The framework recognizes the requirement to consider likelihood and magnitude in evaluating deficiencies. It also recognizes that the maximum amount that an account balance or total of transactions can be overstated is generally the recorded amount. However, the recorded amount is not a limitation on the amount of potential understatement, and the risk of misstatement might be different for the maximum possible misstatement than for lesser possible amounts.

The framework applies these concepts through the evaluation of a combination of magnitude and likelihood. Because of the wide variety of control types, population characteristics, and test exception implications, the group did not undertake to develop a purely quantitative model. Instead, the framework considers quantitative and qualitative factors.

This paper does not address the determination of materiality. This paper recognizes that the same conceptual definition of materiality that applies to financial reporting applies to information on internal control over financial reporting, including the relevance of both quantitative and qualitative considerations:

- The quantitative considerations are essentially the same as in an audit of financial statements and relate to whether misstatements that would not be prevented or detected by internal control over financial reporting, individually or collectively, have a quantitatively material effect on the financial statements.

▪ The qualitative considerations apply to evaluating materiality with respect to the financial statements and to additional factors that relate to the perceived needs of reasonable persons who will rely on the information.

GUIDING PRINCIPLES

The principles set forth below correspond to the box numbers on the appropriate charts included in this paper.

The evaluation of individual exceptions and deficiencies is an iterative process. Although this paper depicts the evaluation process as a linear progression, it may be appropriate at any point in the process to return to and reconsider any previous step based on new information.

In applying the framework, the following should be considered in determining which chart(s) to use for evaluating individual exceptions and deficiencies:

▪ Chart 1 is used to evaluate and determine whether an exception noted in performing tests of operating effectiveness represents a control deficiency.

▪ Chart 2 is used to evaluate and classify control deficiencies in manual or automated controls that are directly related to achieving relevant financial statement assertions.

▪ Chart 3 is used to evaluate and classify deficiencies in ITGCs that are intended to support the continued effective operation of controls related to one or more relevant financial statement assertions. If an application control deficiency is related to or caused by an ITGC deficiency, the application control deficiency is evaluated using Chart 2 and the ITGC deficiency is evaluated using Chart 3. Note: this relates to the 1992 COSO Framework environment, relevant at the time of the publication.

▪ Chart 4 is used to evaluate and classify control deficiencies in pervasive controls other than ITGCs. Such control deficiencies generally do not directly result in a misstatement. However, they may contribute to the likelihood of a misstatement at the process level.

After evaluating and classifying individual deficiencies, consideration should be given to the aggregation of the deficiencies using the guiding principles outlined in "Consider and Evaluate Deficiencies in the Aggregate" below.

Evaluating Exceptions Found in the Testing of Operating Effectiveness (Chart 1)

General

The testing of controls generally relates to significant processes and major classes of transactions for relevant financial statement assertions related to significant accounts and disclosures. Therefore, the underlying assumption is that all exceptions/deficiencies resulting from the testing must be evaluated because they relate to accounts and disclosures that are material to the financial statements taken as a whole.

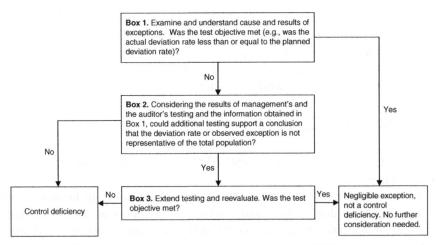

Individual boxes should be read in conjunction with the corresponding guiding principles.

FIGURE 10A.1 Chart 1. Evaluating Exceptions Found in the Testing of Operating Effectiveness

The purpose of tests of controls is to achieve a high level of assurance that the controls are operating effectively. Therefore, the sample sizes used to test controls should provide that level of comfort. In cases in which samples are selected using a statistically based approach, sample sizes for frequently operating manual controls that result in less than a 90% level of confidence that the upper limit deviation rate does not exceed 10% typically would not provide a high level of assurance. (Refer to the AICPA Audit and Accounting Guide, *Audit Sampling*.)

The magnitude of a control deficiency (i.e., deficiency, significant deficiency, or material weakness) is evaluated based on the impact of known and/or potential misstatements on annual and interim financial statements.

While some of the concepts discussed in this paper relate to statistical sampling, the framework does not require the use of statistical sampling. A statistical sample is (1) selected on a random or other basis that is representative of the population and (2) evaluated statistically. In tests of internal controls, it may be impractical to select samples randomly, but they should be selected in an unbiased manner.

Box 1. All exceptions should be evaluated quantitatively and qualitatively. A thorough understanding of the cause of the exception is important in evaluating whether a test exception represents a control deficiency. This evaluation should consider the potential implications with regard to the effectiveness of other controls (e.g., the company's ITGCs and other COSO components).

In concluding whether the test objective was met, considerations include:

- The deviation rate in relation to the frequency of performance of the control (e.g., absent extending the test, there is a presumption that an exception in a control that operates less frequently than daily is a control deficiency).
- Qualitative factors, including exceptions that are determined to be systematic and recurring or that relate to the four specific factors outlined in the standards.

▪ Whether the exception is known to have resulted in a financial statement misstatement (e.g., there is a presumption that an exception that results in a financial statement misstatement in excess of the level of precision at which the control is designed to operate is a control deficiency).

A control objective may be achieved by a single control or a combination of controls. A test of controls may be designed to test a single control that alone achieves the control objective or a number of individual controls that together achieve the control objective.

Box 2. If the test objective is not met, consideration should be given to whether additional testing could support a conclusion that the deviation rate is not representative of the total population. For example, if observed exceptions result in a nonnegligible deviation rate, then the test objective initially is not met. In a test designed to allow for finding one or more deviations, the test objective is not met if the actual number of deviations found exceeds the number of deviations allowed for in the plan.

Box 3. If the test objective initially is not met, then there are two options:

▪ If the observed exceptions and resulting nonnegligible deviation rate are not believed to be representative of the population (e.g., because of sampling error), the test may be extended and reevaluated.
▪ If the observed exceptions and resulting nonnegligible deviation rate are believed to be representative of the population, the exceptions are considered to be a control deficiency and its significance is assessed.

Evaluating Process/Transaction-Level Control Deficiencies (Chart 2)

Step 1. Determine Whether a Significant Deficiency Exists

Box 1. When evaluating deficiencies, potential magnitude (inconsequential, more than inconsequential, or material) is based on the potential effect on both annual and interim financial statements. The potential magnitude of a misstatement of annual or interim financial statements of not more than inconsequential results in the deficient control being classified as only a deficiency, absent any qualitative factors. Potential magnitude of misstatement may be based on gross exposure, adjusted exposure, or other appropriate methods that consider the likelihood of misstatement.

Boxes 2 and 3. If there are controls that effectively mitigate a control deficiency, it is classified as only a deficiency, absent any qualitative factors. Such controls include:

▪ Complementary or redundant controls that achieve the same control objective.
▪ Compensating controls that operate at a level of precision that would result in the prevention or detection of a more than inconsequential misstatement of annual or interim financial statements.

Boxes 1, 2, and 3 should be considered separately. Adjusted exposure should not be reduced by the quantitative impact of the compensating and complementary or redundant controls.

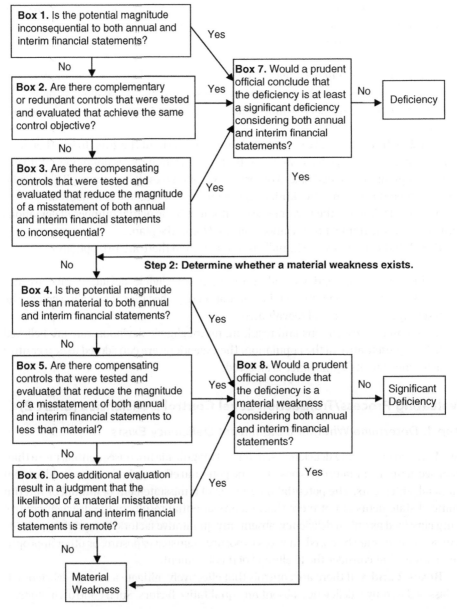

FIGURE 10A.2 Chart 2. Evaluating Process/Transaction–Level Control Deficiencies

Box 3. An unmitigated deficient control that results in a control objective not being met related to a significant account or disclosure generally results in a more than remote likelihood of a more than inconsequential misstatement of annual or interim financial statements and, therefore, is at least a significant deficiency.

Step 2. Determine Whether a Material Weakness Exists

Box 4. The potential magnitude of a misstatement of annual or interim financial statements that is less than material results in the deficient control being classified as only a significant deficiency, absent any qualitative factors. Potential magnitude may be based on gross exposure, adjusted exposure, or other appropriate methods that consider the likelihood of misstatement.

Box 5. Compensating controls that operate at a level of precision that would result in the prevention or detection of a material misstatement of annual or interim financial statements may support a conclusion that the deficiency is not a material weakness.[1]

Box 6. In evaluating likelihood and magnitude, related factors include but are not limited to the following:

- The nature of the financial statement accounts, disclosures, and assertions involved; for example, suspense accounts and related party transactions involve greater risk.
- The susceptibility of the related assets or liability to loss or fraud; that is, greater susceptibility increases risk.
- The subjectivity, complexity, or extent of judgment required to determine the amount involved; that is, greater subjectivity, complexity, or judgment, like that related to an accounting estimate, increases risk.
- The cause and frequency of known or detected exceptions in the operating effectiveness of a control; for example, a control with an observed nonnegligible deviation rate is a deficiency.
- The interaction or relationship with other controls; that is, the interdependence or redundancy of controls.
- The possible future consequences of the deficiency.
- An indication of increased risk evidenced by a history of misstatements, including misstatements identified in the current year.
- The adjusted exposure in relation to overall materiality. This framework recognizes that in evaluating deficiencies, the risk of misstatement might be different for the maximum possible misstatement than for lesser possible amounts.

As a result of this additional evaluation, determine whether the likelihood of a material misstatement to both the annual and interim financial statements is remote. In extremely rare circumstances, this additional evaluation could result in a judgment that the likelihood of a more than inconsequential misstatement to both the annual and interim financial statements is remote.

---

[1] It has been identified in practice that truly compensating or redundant controls are rare. If the compensating or redundant control did not identify a financial issue resulting from a control deficiency, the compensating or redundant control is probably not effective.

Boxes 7 and 8. When determining the classification of a deficiency, consider the level of detail and degree of assurance that would satisfy prudent officials[2] in the conduct of their own affairs that they have reasonable assurance that transactions are recorded as necessary to permit the preparation of financial statements in conformity with generally accepted accounting principles. If the auditor determines that the deficiency would prevent prudent officials in the conduct of their own affairs from concluding that they have reasonable assurance, then the auditor should deem the deficiency to be at least a significant deficiency. Having determined in this manner that a deficiency represents a significant deficiency, the auditor must further evaluate the deficiency to determine whether individually, or in combination with other deficiencies, the deficiency is a material weakness.

Additional Considerations Related to Misstatements Identified

A greater than de minimis misstatement of annual or interim financial statements identified by management or by the auditor during a test of controls or during a substantive test is ordinarily indicative of a deficiency in the design and/or operating effectiveness of a control, which is evaluated as follows:

- The design and/or operating deficiency(ies) that did not prevent or detect the misstatement should be identified and evaluated based on Chart 2—Evaluating Process/Transaction-Level Control Deficiencies—applying the following:
  - A known or likely (including projected) misstatement that is inconsequential to annual or interim financial statements is at least a deficiency
  - A known or likely (including projected) misstatement that is more than inconsequential to annual or interim financial statements is an indicator of a potential significant deficiency
  - A known or likely (including projected) misstatement that is material to annual or interim financial statements, or is associated with one of the four listed conditions in the standards is at least a significant deficiency

The implications on the effectiveness of other controls, particularly compensating controls, also should be considered.

Evaluating ITGC Deficiencies (Chart 3)

General. Deficiencies in ITGCs are evaluated in relation to their effect on application controls.

- ITGC deficiencies do not directly result in misstatements.
- Misstatements may result from ineffective application controls.

---

[2] This terminology has origins in the Securities and Exchange Commission (SEC) literature but has been widely adopted as it applies to "stepping back" to assess how a business person would view the controls.

There are three situations in which an ITGC deficiency can/should rise to the level of a material weakness:

- An application control deficiency related to or caused by an ITGC deficiency is classified as a material weakness
- The pervasiveness and significance of an ITGC deficiency leads to a conclusion that there is a material weakness in the company's control environment
- An ITGC deficiency classified as a significant deficiency remains uncorrected after some reasonable period of time

In evaluating the effect of an ITGC deficiency on the continued effective operation of application controls, it is not necessary to contemplate the likelihood that an effective application control could in a subsequent year become ineffective because of the deficient ITGC.

Relationship between ITGCs and application controls. An understanding of the relationship among applications relevant to internal control over financial reporting, the related application controls, and ITGCs is necessary to appropriately evaluate ITGC deficiencies. ITGCs may affect the continued effective operation of application controls. For example, an effective security administration function supports the continued effective functioning of application controls that restrict access. As another example, effective program change controls support the continued effective operation of programmed application controls, such as a three-way match. ITGCs also may serve as controls at the application level. For example, ITGCs may directly achieve the control objective of restricting access and thereby prevent initiation of unauthorized transactions.

Similarly, ITGC deficiencies may adversely affect the continued effective functioning of application controls; in the absence of application controls, ITGC deficiencies also may represent control deficiencies for one or more relevant assertions.

Evaluating ITGC deficiencies. All ITGC deficiencies are evaluated using Chart 3 (under the 1992 COSO framework). Additionally, if an ITGC deficiency also represents a deficiency at the application level because it directly relates to an assertion, the ITGC deficiency also is evaluated using Chart 2. In all cases, an ITGC deficiency is considered in combination with application controls to determine whether the combined effect of the ITGC deficiency and any application control deficiencies is a deficiency, significant deficiency, or material weakness.

Box 1. Controls that effectively mitigate a control deficiency result in the deficiency being classified as only a deficiency, absent any qualitative factors. Such controls include complementary or redundant controls that achieve the same control objective. An ITGC deficiency identified as a result of an application control deficiency indicates that other ITGCs could not have achieved the same control objective as the deficient ITGC.

Box 2. If no deficiencies are identified at the application level (as evaluated in Chart 2), the ITGC deficiency could be classified as only a deficiency.

Boxes 3 and 4. If there is a control deficiency at the application level related to or caused by an ITGC deficiency, the ITGC deficiency is evaluated in combination with

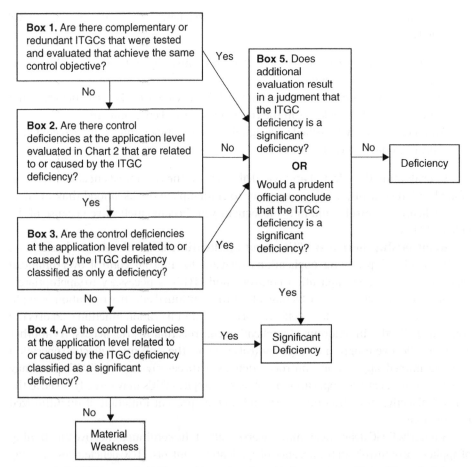

Individual boxes should be read in conjunction with the corresponding guiding principles.

FIGURE 10A.3   Chart 3. Evaluating Information Technology General Control (ITGC) Deficiencies

the deficiency in the underlying application control and generally is classified consistent with the application control deficiency, that is:

- A material weakness in an application control related to or caused by an ITGC deficiency indicates that the ITGC deficiency also is a material weakness.
- A significant deficiency in an application control related to or caused by an ITGC deficiency indicates that the ITGC deficiency also is a significant deficiency.
- An application control deficiency (that is only a deficiency) related to or caused by an ITGC deficiency generally indicates that the ITGC deficiency is only a deficiency.

Box 5. Notwithstanding the guiding principles relating to Boxes 7.2, the classification of an ITGC deficiency(ies) should consider factors including but not limited to the following:

- The nature and significance of the deficiency; for example, does the deficiency relate to a single area in the program development process or is the entire process deficient?
- The pervasiveness of the deficiency to applications and data, including:
  - The extent to which controls related to significant accounts and underlying business processes are affected by the ITGC deficiency
  - The number of application controls that are related to the ITGC deficiency
  - The number of control deficiencies at the application level that are related to or caused by the ITGC deficiency
- The complexity of the company's systems environment and the likelihood that the deficiency could adversely affect application controls
- The relative proximity of the control to applications and data
- Whether an ITGC deficiency relates to applications or data for accounts or disclosures that are susceptible to loss or fraud
- The cause and frequency of known or detected exceptions in the operating effectiveness of an ITGC; for example, (1) a control with an observed nonnegligible deviation rate, (2) an observed exception that is inconsistent with the expected effective operation of the ITGC, or (3) a deliberate failure to apply a control.
- An indication of increased risk evidenced by a history of misstatements relating to applications affected by the ITGC deficiency, including misstatements in the current year

When determining the classification of a deficiency, consider the aforementioned prudent official guidance.

Additional Consideration

ITGCs support the proper and consistent operation of automated application controls. Therefore, consideration should be given to the nature, timing, and extent of the testing of related application controls affected by, or manual controls dependent on, the deficient ITGC.

Evaluating Control Deficiencies in Pervasive Controls Other than ITGC (Chart 4)

General. Deficiencies in pervasive controls like control environment issues may not directly result in a misstatement. However, they may contribute to the likelihood of a misstatement at the process level. Accordingly, evaluation of a deficiency in a pervasive control other than ITGC is based on the likelihood that such deficiency would contribute

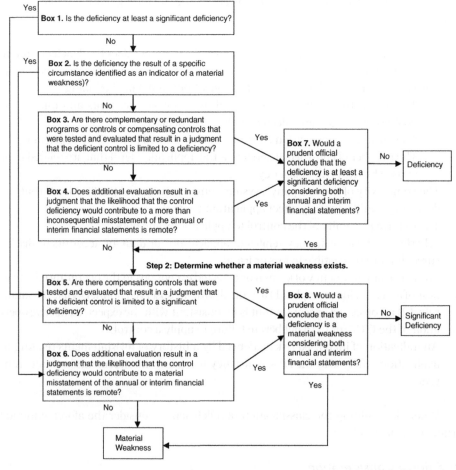

FIGURE 10A.4 Chart 4. Evaluating Control Deficiencies in Pervasive Controls Other than ITGC

to circumstances that could result in a misstatement. Quantitative methods generally are not conducive to evaluating such deficiencies.

Step 1. Determine Whether a Significant Deficiency Exists

Boxes 1 and 2. A deficiency of the character of the four "special deficiencies" often results in deficiencies being at least a significant deficiency. The circumstances in which an evaluation would lead to the deficiency not being classified as at least a significant deficiency are rare.

Box 3. Certain controls could result in a judgment that the deficient control is limited to a deficiency and classified as only a deficiency, considering qualitative factors. Such controls include:

- Complementary or redundant programs or controls.
- Compensating controls within the same or another component (e.g., monitoring).

Box 4. A deficiency with a reasonably possible likelihood that the deficiency could contribute to a more than inconsequential misstatement is a significant deficiency. Such judgment considers an evaluation of factors such as:

- The pervasiveness of the deficiency across the entity.
- The relative significance of the deficient control to the component.
- An indication of increased risks of error (evidenced by a history of misstatement).
- An increased susceptibility to fraud (including the risk of management override).
- The cause and frequency of known or detected exceptions for the operating effectiveness of a control.
- The possible future consequences of the deficiency.

Step 2. Determine Whether a Material Weakness Exists

Box 5. The evaluation of certain controls could result in a judgment that the deficient control is limited to a significant deficiency and classified as such, considering qualitative factors, including those associated with the "special deficiencies." Such controls include compensating controls within the same or another component.

Box 6. A deficiency with a reasonably possible likelihood that the deficiency would contribute to a material misstatement is a material weakness. Such judgment considers an evaluation of factors such as:

- The pervasiveness of the deficiency across the entity.
- The relative significance of the deficient control to the component.
- An indication of increased risks of error (evidenced by a history of misstatement).
- An increased susceptibility to fraud (including the risk of management override).
- The cause and frequency of known or detected exceptions for the operating effectiveness of a control.
- The possible future consequences of the deficiency.

Boxes 7 and 8. When determining the classification of a deficiency, consider the previously described prudent official test.

Consider and Evaluate Deficiencies in the Aggregate

Deficiencies are considered in the aggregate by significant account balance, disclosure, and COSO component to determine whether they collectively result in significant deficiencies or material weaknesses. Aggregation of control activities deficiencies by significant account balance and disclosure is necessary since the existence of multiple control deficiencies related to a specific account balance or disclosure increases the likelihood of misstatement. Aggregation by the control environment, risk assessment, information and communication, and monitoring components of COSO is more difficult and judgmental. For example, unrelated control deficiencies relating to design ineffectiveness in other COSO components could lead to the conclusion that a significant deficiency or material weakness in the risk assessment component exists. Similarly, unrelated control deficiencies in other COSO components could lead to a conclusion that a significant deficiency or material weakness in the control environment or monitoring component exists. The COSO Framework released in 2013 emphasizes that control issues identified in one principle can also reflect on another principle, and these relationships should also be considered in the aggregation process.

 TERMINOLOGY

Adjusted exposure—gross exposure (see below) multiplied by the upper limit deviation rate.

Application controls—automated control procedures (e.g., calculations, posting to accounts, generation of reports, edits, control routines, etc.) or manual controls that are dependent on information technology (IT) (e.g., the review by an inventory manager of an exception report when the exception report is generated by IT). When IT is used to initiate, authorize, record, process, or report transactions or other financial data for inclusion in financial statements, the systems and programs may include controls related to the corresponding assertions for significant accounts or disclosures or may be critical to the effective functioning of manual controls that depend on IT.

Compensating controls—controls that operate at a level of precision that would result in the prevention or detection of a misstatement that was more than inconsequential or material, as applicable, to annual or interim financial statements. The level of precision should be established considering the possibility of further undetected misstatements.

Complementary controls—controls that function together to achieve the same control objective.

Control deficiency—a deficiency in the design or operation of a control that does not allow management or employees, in the normal course of performing their assigned functions, to prevent or detect misstatements on a timely basis.

- A deficiency in design exists when (a) a control necessary to meet the control objective is missing or (b) an existing control is not properly designed so that, even if it operates as designed, the control objective is not always met.
- A deficiency in operation exists when a properly designed control does not operate as designed, or when the person performing the control does not possess the necessary authority or qualifications to perform the control effectively.

Control objective—the objective(s) related to internal control over financial reporting to achieve the assertions that underlie a company's financial statements.

Gross exposure—a worst-case estimate of the magnitude of amounts or transactions exposed to the deficiency with regard to annual or interim financial statements, without regard to the upper-limit deviation rate or likelihood of misstatement, and before considering complementary, redundant, or compensating controls. Factors affecting gross exposure include:

- The annual or interim financial statement amounts or total transactions exposed to the deficiency.
- The volume of activity in the account balance or class of transactions exposed to the deficiency that has occurred in the current annual or interim period or that is expected in future periods.

Inconsequential—

- Potential misstatements equal to or greater than a threshold (e.g., 20%) of overall annual or interim financial statement materiality are presumed to be more than inconsequential.
- Potential misstatements less than some threshold of overall annual or interim financial statement materiality may be concluded to be more than inconsequential as a result of the consideration of qualitative factors.

Information technology general controls (ITGCs)—policies and procedures that relate to many applications and support the effective functioning of application controls by helping to ensure the continued proper operation of information systems. This includes four[3] basic IT areas that are relevant to internal control over financial reporting:

- Program development.
- Program changes.
- Computer operations.
- Access to programs and data.

Material weakness—a deficiency, or a combination of deficiencies, in internal control, such that there is a reasonable possibility that a material misstatement of the entity's financial statements will not be prevented, or detected and corrected, on a timely basis. (See AU-C Section 265 and PCAOB AS No. 5.)

Pervasive controls other than ITGC—the general programs and controls within the control environment, risk assessment, monitoring, and information and communication, including portions of the financial reporting process, that have a pervasive impact on controls at the process, transaction, or application level.

---

[3] Some sources identify a fifth element relating to the organization structure of the IT function.

Potential misstatement—an estimate of the misstatement that could result from a deficiency with a more than remote likelihood of occurrence.

Redundant controls—controls that achieve the same control objective.

Remote likelihood—the chance of the future event or events occurring is slight.

Significant deficiency—a deficiency, or a combination of deficiencies, in internal control that is less severe than a material weakness yet important enough to merit attention by those charged with governance (AU-C Section 265 and PCAOB AS No. 5).

Test objective—the design of the test of a control activity to determine whether the control is operating as designed, giving consideration to:

- The nature of the control and the definition of an exception.
- The frequency with which the control operates.
- The desired level of assurance in combination with the reliability of the control; for example, whether the control is designed to achieve the control objective alone or in combination with other controls.
- The number of exceptions expected.

Upper limit deviation rate—the statistically derived estimate of the deviation rate based on the sample results, for which there is a remote likelihood that the true deviation rate in the population exceeds this rate (refer to AICPA AA-G *Audit Sampling*).

Assessing the Potential Magnitude of a Control Deficiency

I N ASSESSING the severity of a deficiency in a controls operation, calculating the upper limit on the deviation rate is one way to assist in classifying the deficiency as simply a deficiency, a significant deficiency, or a material weakness.

The following is a possible approach to quantifying the potential magnitude of exposure to misstatement based on deviation rates in the control tests. Qualitative factors, such as whether the deficiency arose from management override or fraud, should also be considered when assessing the severity of a deficiency.

When the auditor identifies control deviations in a sample, deficiencies are implied in the design or operating effectiveness of the control. In a sample that is planned such that some deviations may appear in the sample result and the sample objectives (in terms of confidence and tolerable rate) will still be achieved, the sample will meet the desired criteria as long as the deviations do not exceed the rate used in planning. When the deviation rate in the sample exceeds the expected deviation rate used in planning, an approach that may be used to quantify the likelihood and magnitude of the observed rate or deviation is described below. The prudent official step would still be applied to the result from this procedure.

If, in a sample of 30 control operations, one deviation is found, but the sample was planned to allow for no deviations, then the "likelihood" criterion of deficiency evaluation is met (assuming the auditor decides not to extend the test). Alternatively, in a sample of 60 control operations where an allowance for one deviation *was* expected and considered in determining the sample size, one deviation found in the sample would generally indicate that the likelihood criterion has not been met since the sample size is still sufficient to conclude the tolerable deviation rate is not exceeded.

A limit on the magnitude of a deficiency may be developed based on an assumption that the upper limit on the deviation rate can be used to roughly estimate the proportion of dollars exposed to the control deviation. This estimate may, along with consideration of other quantitative and qualitative factors, assist the auditor in assessing the severity of a deficiency.

 EXAMPLE FACTS

In a sample of 30 manual control operations from a population of 5,000 control operations, one deviation was identified. The sample was designed with an expectation that zero deviations would be found.

One deviation in a sample of 30 is a rate of 3.3 percent. A statistically based upper limit on the deviation rate at a specified confidence level (e.g., 90%) can be estimated using software, tables (as illustrated in the following section), or formulas. That upper limit relates to the criterion of tolerable deviation rate that was used in planning the sample.

Calculate the Upper Limit in Percent

The following illustrates the use of Table A.4 in Appendix A of the AICPA AAG, *Audit Sampling* (AICPA, 2014). A portion of that table appears as Table 10B.1 in this appendix. Results may also be obtained using software with statistical functions such as the program IDEA (www.audimation.com).

1. Locate the sample size (30) along the left column.
2. Locate the number of deviations (1) along the top row.
3. Identify the intersection in the body of the table—this is the upper limit (12.4%).

Relate the Upper Limit to the Magnitude of Exposure

The following illustrates how to relate the upper limit to the magnitude of monetary exposure:

1. The gross exposure of the dollars processed through this control is $4,000,000.
2. The upper limit on the control deviations, based on the sample result, is 12.4%.
3. The adjusted exposure is $496,000 (12.4% × $4,000,000).
4. The $496,000 potential indicated exposure can be compared to materiality. This may assist the auditor in evaluating the severity of the control deficiency.

Care should be taken when interpreting these results. The results are based on a presumption that the rate of deviation in the sample can be equated to monetary misstatement. Due to the imperfect relationship between control deficiencies and misstatements, the small sample sizes often used for controls tests, and the variability in dollar

TABLE 10B.1   Upper Limit on Deviation Rates at 90% Confidence

Sample Size	Actual Number of Deviations Found							
	0	1	2	3	4	5	6	7
20	10.9	18.1	24.5	30.5	36.1	41.5	46.8	51.9
25	8.8	14.7	20.0	24.9	29.5	34.0	38.4	42.6
30	7.4	12.4	16.8	21.0	24.9	28.8	32.5	36.2
35	6.4	10.7	14.5	18.2	21.6	24.9	28.2	31.4
40	5.6	9.4	12.8	16.0	19.0	22.0	24.9	27.7
45	5.0	8.4	11.4	14.3	17.0	19.7	22.3	24.8
50	4.6	7.6	10.3	12.9	15.4	17.8	20.2	22.5
55	4.2	6.9	9.4	11.8	14.1	16.3	18.4	20.5
60	3.8	6.4	8.7	10.8	12.9	15.0	16.9	18.9

value between different items in the population, the technique is not a substitute for the direct testing of the account or balance for misstatement, but it is an approximation procedure than can be more objective than alternative methods.

- The body of the table presents the upper limits as percentages.
- The table assumes a large population (e.g., the sample size is a negligible proportion of the population).
- Different tables are required when other confidence levels are appropriate for the analysis.

Notes: When the compensating controls are not independent from the control examined, applying the upper limit calculation *and* the compensating controls approach together might take double credit for mitigating the deficiency, as these approaches are both means to estimate the extent of possible deviation from the observed sample result.

CHAPTER ELEVEN

Reporting Requirements

P UBLIC AND NONPUBLIC entities diverge when it comes to publicly disclosing the effectiveness of internal control over financial reporting and material weaknesses. Only public entities are required to publicly report on internal controls effectiveness and disclose material weaknesses. Nonpublic entities may be required by regulatory requirements to report on controls over compliance with laws and regulations or on internal controls as defined in specific regulations.[1] In addition, lenders, venture capitalists, or absentee owners may require such reports. Of course, such entities may voluntarily report on internal control and can have an auditor issue an opinion on the entity's internal control.

The Government Accountability Office (GAO) has indicated that it may require some form of internal controls reporting for entities under its audit jurisdiction in the future.

 ## NONPUBLIC ENTITY REPORTING

While not required to report on internal controls unless required by a regulator or a covenant, private entities and other nonpublic entities can obtain an auditor's opinion on the effectiveness of their internal controls over financial reporting (ICFR). That report would be accompanied by management's assertion about the effectiveness of

---

[1] For example, for nonfiler banks: Section 112 of the Federal Deposit Insurance Corporation Improvement Act (FDICIA) (Section 36 of the Federal Deposit Insurance Act, 12.U.S.C. 1831m), and its implementing regulation, 12 CFR Part 363.

controls, similar to the reporting model for public companies, and would be issued under a newly revised Statement on Standards for Attestation Engagements (SSAE) No. 15, *An Examination of an Entity's Internal Control over Financial Reporting that Is Integrated with an Audit of Its Financial Statements.*[2] In general, SSAE No. 15 converges the standards practitioners use for reporting on a nonpublic entity's internal control with Public Company Accounting Oversight Board (PCAOB) Auditing Standards (AS) No. 5, *An Audit of Internal Control that Is Integrated with an Audit of Financial Statements.* The SSAE No. 15 report would cover both the design and operating effectiveness of internal controls. An entity desiring a report on just the design of the system of internal controls without the testing of those controls would receive that report under the guidance in AT section 101, *Attest Engagements.* An illustrative report from AT No. 501 (in effect at the time of this writing) is provided in the appendix to this chapter.

Why would an entity voluntarily report on internal controls? While not common, there can be good reasons to do so. Not-for-profit entities compete with each other for funds. Given some of the unfortunate stories regarding the use of funds at some well-known charities, such as the United Way and Red Cross, entities may wish to raise (or redeem) their profile with potential contributors by providing such a report. If the public perceives that the report gives them confidence in the organization's use of funds, the attestation has value even though the reports may not directly address all of the issues of how funds are spent by the entity. As more governmental units require some level of attestation regarding controls, will the absence of such a statement accompanying the financial statements of other entities be perceived as a negative?

In some cases, experiments in voluntary reporting on internal controls have resulted in a suspension of the project. Too often, the energy to initiate the voluntary project is later diminished by further questions regarding the value of the effort—when the scope and costs are clearer, by the resources available to document and assess and test the controls, and by the magnitude of control deficiencies identified during the first phases. A common tactic is to put the assessment on hold until the identified issues to this point are remediated. Without the public company mandate to report, this sidetrack often stalls the project indefinitely, despite the value it brought in identifying serious deficiencies. For example, an entity like a university or a hospital is complex, comprised of groups of semiautonomous units without dedicated resources devoted to controls procedures and monitoring. Underestimating the scope and effort to do a project in such an environment is more the rule than the exception.

Governance of nonpublic entities will receive communications from their auditor about control deficiencies that are significant deficiencies and material weaknesses that were identified in the course of the audit. These communications are designed for internal communication. Regulators, lenders, or other parties may have an interest in such matters, but the auditor communication is with the entity.

---

[2] SSAE No. 15 is planned to supersede extant American Institute of Certified Public Accountants (AICPA) AT section 501, *Reporting on an Entity's Internal Control Over Financial Reporting.* At the time of this writing this SSAE may be elevated to a SAS.

PUBLIC COMPANY ANNUAL AND QUARTERLY REPORTING REQUIREMENTS

When, as a result of management's testing and evaluation process, it determines that no material weaknesses in internal control exist as of year-end, management may conclude that internal control is effective. If one or more material weaknesses do exist at year-end, then management is precluded from stating that internal control is effective. According to Securities and Exchange Commission (SEC) Release No. 33-8810: "Management is not permitted to conclude that ICFR is effective if there are one or more material weaknesses in ICFR" (p. 6).

Figure 11.1 provides an example management report. Rather than example reports, the SEC guidelines list the expected contents of the report. (See SEC Releases No. 33-8238 and 34-47986 as modified August 28, 2008. The original effective date of the original release was August 2003.) Thus, while companies have some discretion over the details of their reports, most management reports are similar in wording, as adventuresome experimentation is not encouraged by being in a regulated environment. You may wish to view some recent reports filed with the SEC by various companies to see variations in presentation and wording; however, the independent auditor will review this report carefully to ensure that the disclosures are not misleading.

The next-to-last paragraph of the example report states management's conclusion about internal control. The SEC has stated that management must state whether internal control is functioning effectively. Negative assurance, in which management states,

AMERICAN EXPRESS COMPANY
MANAGEMENT'S REPORT ON INTERNAL CONTROL OVER FINANCIAL REPORTING

MANAGEMENT'S REPORT ON INTERNAL CONTROL OVER FINANCIAL REPORTING

The management of the Company is responsible for establishing and maintaining adequate internal control over financial reporting.

The Company's internal control over financial reporting is a process designed to provide reasonable assurance regarding the reliability of financial reporting and the preparation of financial statements for external purposes in accordance with GAAP in the United States of America, and includes those policies and procedures that:

- Pertain to the maintenance of records that, in reasonable detail, accurately and fairly reflect the transactions and dispositions of the assets of the Company;

- Provide reasonable assurance that transactions are recorded as necessary to permit preparation of financial statements in accordance with GAAP, and that receipts and expenditures of the Company are being made only in accordance with authorizations of management and directors of the Company; and

- Provide reasonable assurance regarding prevention or timely detection of unauthorized acquisition, use or disposition of the Company's assets that could have a material effect on the financial statements.

Because of its inherent limitations, internal control over financial reporting may not prevent or detect misstatements. Also, projections of any evaluation of effectiveness to future periods are subject to the risk that controls may become inadequate because of changes in conditions, or that the degree of compliance with the policies or procedures may deteriorate.

The Company's management assessed the effectiveness of the Company's internal control over financial reporting as of December 31, 2012. In making this assessment, the Company's management used the criteria set forth by the Committee of Sponsoring Organizations of the Treadway Commission (COSO) in *Internal Control — Integrated Framework.*

Based on management's assessment and those criteria, we conclude that, as of December 31, 2012, the Company's internal control over financial reporting is effective.

PricewaterhouseCoopers LLP, the Company's independent registered public accounting firm, has issued an attestation report appearing on the following page on the effectiveness of the Company's internal control over financial reporting as of December 31, 2012.

FIGURE 11.1 Example of Management's Statement on Internal Control over Financial Reporting

"Nothing has come to our attention that would lead us to believe that internal control was not functioning effectively," is not acceptable.[3]

For reports issued for periods ending after December 15, 2014, companies will be expected to identify whether they are using the original 1992 Framework or the revised (2013) Framework. While transition issues continue to be considered as this book is being updated, the Chief Accountant of the SEC, Paul Beswick, CPA, has stated in speeches that the SEC may question reports that continue to use the 1992 Framework for their assessment. Since the revised Framework will have been released over 18 months before, the expectation is that sufficient time has passed for most entities to implement the revised Framework.

Management should state its assessment in an unqualified manner, that is, without qualification or exception. For example, management should not state that internal control is effective "except for" certain material weaknesses.

Similarly, management's report may not include a "scope restriction," stating that it was unable to assess certain aspects of its internal control and that its report is limited only to those aspects it was able to assess.

For example, suppose that an entity uses an outside service organization to process certain transactions. Normally, the service organization would provide a Service Organization Controls (SOC) 1, Type 2 *Service Organizations* report, which would serve as the basis for management's assessment of the relevant controls of the provider. But what if the service organization did not provide such a report? Going further, suppose it would not grant management or the auditors access to review their controls. Would it be permissible for management simply to state this in its report and conclude only on other elements of internal control?

No, this type of reporting is not allowed. In this situation, management must determine whether its inability to assess controls maintained by the service organization is significant enough to conclude in its report that internal control is not effective. The SEC's position has been that companies need to include in their contracts for outside services a "right to audit" to avoid such scope limitations. According to SEC Release No. 33-8810: "The Commission's disclosure requirements state that management's annual report on ICFR must include a statement as to whether or not ICFR is effective and do not permit management to issue a report on ICFR with a scope limitation" (p. 41).

There can be very legitimate reasons why scope may be limited. In an unusual situation, an important manufacturing and processing facility was closed due to local civil unrest. The facility was locked and patrolled by heavily armed guards because of the fungible nature of the inventory and processed materials. Access could not be obtained by either company management or the auditors. Nobody volunteered to test the threat that "the guns are loaded." In situations like this, the SEC staff have encouraged registrants to consult with them in advance. Because the failure to file or the failure to adhere to the reporting requirements is subject to sanctions and fines, it is in the company's best interest to consult with the SEC on unusual situations as soon as possible.

---

[3] See footnote 62 to the SEC's final rule "Management's Reports on Internal Control over Financial Reporting and Certification of Disclosure in Exchange Act Periodic Reports (release numbers 33-8238 and 34-47986 as modified August 28, 2008).

Management's Report When a Material Weakness Exists at Year-End

When a material weakness exists at year-end, management is required to report that internal control is not effective as of year-end. Figure 11.2 provides an example of management's internal control report when a material weakness exists at year-end.

In addition to the fact that one or more material weaknesses were identified, information should be disclosed regarding the nature of the weakness. Practice varies regarding the level of detail and commentary surrounding the disclosure, and again, some research into the practices of other publicly reporting companies with similar issues and discussions with SEC counsel may be helpful in thinking through what you should be disclosing. In SEC Release No. 33-8810, the SEC states the purpose of these disclosures: "The goal underlying all disclosure in this area is to provide an investor with disclosure and analysis that goes beyond describing the mere existence of a material weakness" (p. 39).

Recently the SEC has expressed concern that the level of detail provided in some reports regarding the nature of the material weaknesses has been less than expected. While no specific parameters are specified so far, the SEC may inquire of companies when disclosures are insufficiently detailed to identify whether the weakness disclosure is related to a prior material weakness that continues to exist or is a new issue. Clarifying the disclosure will reduce unnecessary inquiries that waste SEC and company time.

[*Introductory paragraph. See* Exhibit 11.1]

[*Optional inherent limitations paragraph.* See Exhibit 11.1]

A material weakness in internal control is a significant deficiency or an aggregation of significant deficiencies that preclude the entity's internal control from providing reasonable assurance that material misstatements in the financial statements will be prevented or detected on a timely basis by employees in the normal course of performing their assigned functions. A significant deficiency is an internal control deficiency in a significant control or an aggregation of such deficiencies that could result in a misstatement of the financial statements that is more than inconsequential.

The management of XYZ has assessed the effectiveness of the company's internal control over financial reporting as of December 31, 20XX, and this assessment identified the following material weakness in the company's internal control over financial reporting:

[*Describe the material weakness*]

To make our assessment of internal control over financial reporting, we used the criteria described in *Internal Control—Integrated Framework (date)*, issued by the Committee of Sponsoring Organizations of the Treadway Commission. We believe that our assessment of the company's internal control over financial reporting met those criteria.

Our independent auditors have issued an attestation report on our assessment of the company's internal control over financial reporting. You can find this report on page xx.

FIGURE 11.2 Example of Management's Report on Internal Control over Financial Reporting When a Weakness Is Disclosed

Because material weaknesses identified in one period need to be remediated as soon as possible, but are expected to be remediated within a year, this situation relates to a potential SEC enforcement issue.

It is sometimes difficult, for example, for readers and academic researchers to identify whether a material weakness noted in a prior-year report remains in the current report or if the prior weakness was remediated and a related weakness in the same general area (e.g., sales) was identified and is now being reported for the first time. When researching remediation rates between periods, assumptions need to be made regarding whether similar-sounding weaknesses are continuations or new issues. Because researchers are unable to query management on this issue, the assumptions they make may be faulty and the research conclusions incorrect. Such a situation can be harmful to the user and harmful to policy makers who may consult research to assess the effectiveness of existing policy.

As-Of Reporting Implications

The SEC rules require management to report on the effectiveness of internal control *as of* a point in time rather than during a given period. This distinction is important for several reasons, including:

- *Extent of testing.* Reporting on controls at a point in time may require testing of controls with an emphasis on the period closer to year-end. Unfortunately, for the auditor to utilize information from the tests of controls in reducing the extent of other tests, those control conclusions need to be useful throughout the period of reliance. In populations with limited activity, testing near year-end may also involve sampling from very small populations, and thus some of the sample sizes for this specific purpose will be smaller than if the tests covered the entire reporting period. This issue is discussed further in Chapter 8, Evidence and Testing.
- *Correction of deficiencies.* Early testing is more conducive to the identification and correction of deficiencies. This is because the *correction of a deficiency early* in the reporting period may allow management to redesign and retest the control and conclude that internal control is functioning effectively *at the end of the period.* For example, suppose the company identified a material weakness during the first quarter of its fiscal year, and it took *immediate corrective action.* That corrective action would still require disclosure in the entity's first-quarter 10-Q and Section 302 certification, since it would indicate a change in internal control that would have a material effect on internal control. Going forward, assuming that the corrective actions were successful, the company and the auditor may be able to conclude that controls are effective at subsequent reporting dates. When the auditor is able to conclude the controls are effective over the reporting period, often less audit work is required and thus audit efficiencies can result.

It seems clear that without the ability to remediate material weaknesses during the period and still report that controls are effective at year-end, the rate of ineffective control opinions would greatly exceed the "ineffective" rates observed.

For management to conclude that an identified control deficiency has been remediated successfully, the corrected control must be in place and operating effectively for a period of time that is sufficient to draw a reliable conclusion about its effectiveness. It should also be remembered that the independent auditor will likely want to test this control, given the risk associated with its prior status as a material weakness. That can also add some additional lead time to the time constraints. Change does not always imply that the control is now effective. In some cases, changes in controls may fix one aspect of deficient operation but create unexpected problems in other areas affected by the control. Testing or other evidence is required to confirm that the change has remediated the control. Furthermore, when a material weakness is the product of the aggregation of significant deficiencies and other deficiencies, it may take extra time to design a number of fixes to related deficiencies.

Determining what constitutes a "sufficient period of time" will require management and the auditor to exercise judgment. Matters to be considered when making this determination include:

- *Nature of the control objective.* The nature of the control objective being addressed should be considered. For example, some control objectives are transaction oriented and narrowly focused, and have a direct effect on the financial statements. A review of vendor invoices for payment or a revenue recognition control may be sufficiently precise and frequent in operation to detect improvements or changes in controls fairly easily. Other control objectives may be control environment–oriented and affect the entity broadly, and have only an indirect effect on the financial statements. Management's tone at the top and the entity's hiring and training practices are examples of these types of controls. It may be more difficult to immediately confirm that the changes have resulted in improvement.

  In general, because of their indirect effect on the financial statements and their ability to influence the effectiveness of other controls, corrections to environment-oriented controls should be in place and operating effectively for a much *longer* period of time than corrections to controls that are more transactions based. That is, it will take you longer to determine whether a change in management's attitude is having its desired effect on internal control performance than it will to determine whether a new account reconciliation procedure is being performed properly.

- *Nature of the correction.* Some corrections may be programmed into the entity's information processing system. For example, to correct a control deficiency, the entity may change its system to correct a flaw in data processing or generate a better exception report. Assuming that the entity has effective information technology (IT) general controls, a computer application should perform the same task consistently for an indefinite period of time. The change to correct a processing flaw might be quick and easy to confirm. Thus, this correction may need to be operational only for a relatively short period of time before you can draw a reliable conclusion about its effectiveness.

  In contrast, a *person* must investigate and properly resolve the items identified in an exception report. Unlike a computer application, the performance of an individual often varies. For this reason, a correction that involves human performance (rather than a computer system) should be operating effectively for a relatively longer period of time before a reliable conclusion is reached.

■ *Frequency of the corrected control procedure.* Some control procedures are performed frequently (e.g., the authentication of credit card information for all online customers who purchase goods). Other procedures are performed less frequently (e.g., account reconciliations between the subsidiary and general ledgers). When control procedures are performed frequently, less time is needed for you to have enough evidence to draw a reliable conclusion about the remediation. For a credit card authorization, the control procedure may be performed thousands of times in just a few days. If an account reconciliation is performed only once a month, however, the control may need to be in place for more than a month before you would have evidence to conclude on its effectiveness.

Ultimately, taking steps to correct a control deficiency and then waiting a certain amount of time is not sufficient for management to conclude that the deficiency no longer exists. New controls must be tested, and the evidence from these tests must be sufficient to enable management (and the auditor) to reach a conclusion about their effectiveness. When program adjustments are made in computerized systems, IT general controls over changes in programs include testing the program before accepting it as functioning. These test results can also be considered when assessing the effectiveness of the remediation.

REPORTING ON MANAGEMENT'S RESPONSIBILITIES FOR INTERNAL CONTROL

Although not required, many companies include other management statements relating to internal control in their annual reports to shareholders. Typically, these statements are located in close proximity to the company's financial statements. These optional statements may or may not be designed to comply with Sarbanes-Oxley (SOX) reporting requirements. Care should be taken that any additional disclosures are not confused with the required reporting on internal control. Indeed, if statements are made that are potentially misleading or incomplete, auditors are advised to specifically disclaim association with these statements. Wordings of additional commentary on internal controls effectiveness or other assertions included in the management discussion and analysis (MD&A) section or elsewhere should be carefully reviewed with your auditor in advance. The SEC requirements identify the elements of the company report that must be present but stop short of providing examples of specific reports in the desire to have companies draft presentations that are most informative to their shareholders.

In 1994, COSO presented model guidelines on the preparation of internal control reports to shareholders. These guidelines attempt to achieve a balance between two competing needs: conformity and flexibility. Management may also wish to report on:

- Plans concerning possible future business changes and related changes in controls.
- Statements regarding management's remediation of controls.
- Other matters.

The independent auditor will consider whether any of the other disclosures might be confusing or misleading regarding the internal control requirements. If so, the auditor may have to note the issue in his or her report if a change is not made. Note point (d) in this list of potential auditor report modifications from paragraph C1 in PCAOB AS No. 5.

The auditor should modify his or her report if any of the following conditions exist:

a. Elements of management's annual report on internal control are incomplete or improperly presented.
b. There is a restriction on the scope of the engagement.
c. The auditor decides to refer to the report of other auditors as the basis, in part, for the auditor's own report.
d. There is other information contained in management's annual report on internal control over financial reporting.
e. Management's annual certification pursuant to Section 302 of the Sarbanes-Oxley Act is misstated.

The auditor requirements regarding "additional" information provided by management regarding internal control are sufficiently clear. If management is unsure about any additional disclosures it wants to make, it should speak with its SEC counsel and its auditor in advance. From PCAOB AS No. 5:

C12. Management's Annual Report on Internal Control Over Financial Reporting Containing Additional Information. Management's annual report on internal control over financial reporting may contain information in addition to the elements described in paragraph 72 [the required elements] that are subject to the auditor's evaluation.

C13. If management's annual report on internal control over financial reporting could reasonably be viewed by users of the report as including such additional information, the auditor should disclaim an opinion on the information.

C14. If the auditor believes that management's additional information contains a material misstatement of fact, he or she should discuss the matter with management. If, after discussing the matter with management, the auditor concludes that a material misstatement of fact remains, the auditor should notify management and the audit committee, in writing, of the auditor's views concerning the information. AU sec. 317, Illegal Acts by Clients and Section 10A of the Securities Exchange Act of 1934 may also require the auditor to take additional action.

Note: If management makes the types of disclosures described in paragraph C12 outside its annual report on internal control over financial reporting and includes them elsewhere within its annual report on the company's financial statements, the auditor would not need to disclaim an opinion. However, in that situation, the auditor's responsibilities are the same as those described in this paragraph if the auditor believes that the additional information contains a material misstatement of fact.

Independent Auditor Reports on Internal Control

Auditors of accelerated filers can choose to issue a separate report on the audit of the financial statements and a report on their assessment of internal controls effectiveness, or they can issue a combined report (financial audit and internal controls). Such a combined report is illustrated in AS No. 5 and in Figure 11.3. If selected, the combined auditor report must contain all the required elements of the opinion on the financial statements and the opinion on internal controls. The complexity of presentation and

AMERICAN EXPRESS COMPANY
REPORT OF INDEPENDENT REGISTERED PUBLIC ACCOUNTING FIRM

REPORT OF INDEPENDENT REGISTERED PUBLIC ACCOUNTING FIRM

THE BOARD OF DIRECTORS AND SHAREHOLDERS OF AMERICAN EXPRESS COMPANY:

In our opinion, the accompanying consolidated balance sheets and the related consolidated statements of income, comprehensive income, cash flows and shareholders' equity present fairly, in all material respects, the financial position of American Express Company and its subsidiaries at December 31, 2012 and 2011, and the results of their operations and their cash flows for each of the years in the three-year period ended December 31, 2012, in conformity with accounting principles generally accepted in the United States of America. Also in our opinion, the Company maintained, in all material respects, effective internal control over financial reporting as of December 31, 2012, based on criteria established in *Internal Control — Integrated Framework* issued by the Committee of Sponsoring Organizations of the Treadway Commission (COSO). The Company's management is responsible for these financial statements, for maintaining effective internal control over financial reporting and for its assessment of the effectiveness of internal control over financial reporting, included in the accompanying Management's Report on Internal Control Over Financial Reporting. Our responsibility is to express opinions on these financial statements and on the Company's internal control over financial reporting based on our integrated audits. We conducted our audits in accordance with the standards of the Public Company Accounting Oversight Board (United States). Those standards require that we plan and perform the audits to obtain reasonable assurance about whether the financial statements are free of material misstatement and whether effective internal control over financial reporting was maintained in all material respects. Our audits of the financial statements included examining, on a test basis, evidence supporting the amounts and disclosures in the financial statements, assessing the accounting principles used and significant estimates made by management, and evaluating the overall financial statement presentation. Our audit of internal control over financial reporting included obtaining an understanding of internal control over financial reporting, assessing the risk that a material weakness exists, and testing and

evaluating the design and operating effectiveness of internal control based on the assessed risk. Our audits also included performing such other procedures as we considered necessary in the circumstances. We believe that our audits provide a reasonable basis for our opinions.

A company's internal control over financial reporting is a process designed to provide reasonable assurance regarding the reliability of financial reporting and the preparation of financial statements for external purposes in accordance with generally accepted accounting principles. A company's internal control over financial reporting includes those policies and procedures that (i) pertain to the maintenance of records that, in reasonable detail, accurately and fairly reflect the transactions and dispositions of the assets of the company; (ii) provide reasonable assurance that transactions are recorded as necessary to permit preparation of financial statements in accordance with generally accepted accounting principles, and that receipts and expenditures of the company are being made only in accordance with authorizations of management and directors of the company; and (iii) provide reasonable assurance regarding prevention or timely detection of unauthorized acquisition, use, or disposition of the company's assets that could have a material effect on the financial statements.

Because of its inherent limitations, internal control over financial reporting may not prevent or detect misstatements. Also, projections of any evaluation of effectiveness to future periods are subject to the risk that controls may become inadequate because of changes in conditions, or that the degree of compliance with the policies or procedures may deteriorate.

PricewaterhouseCoopers LLP

New York, New York
February 22, 2013

FIGURE 11.3 Example of Combined Opinion on Financial Statements and Internal Controls

communication in a combined report has made the separate reporting option an overwhelming favorite. However, the option still exists to issue a combined report, and some reports are issued this way.

The auditor will date the audit opinion on internal controls as of the same date he or she uses to date the financial statement audit report. The auditor cannot date these opinions until all the evidence necessary to issue both the audit reports has been obtained. The implication of this is that the auditor will need to request updated information from the company regarding internal controls to cover any additional information learned in the period between the as-of date (the date of the balance sheet) and the date in which the auditor dates his or her audit report. Thus the door remains open in this period to a risk that additional weaknesses will be identified, but because the reporting date has passed, such deficiencies cannot be remediated, and the auditor would have to conclude that internal control was ineffective as of the reporting date.

 REQUIRED COMPANY AND AUDITOR COMMUNICATIONS

In addition to reporting requirements over internal control, public companies should be mindful of the required communications between companies and auditors and the reciprocal communication requirements between the auditors and management and the audit committee.

The concept embedded in the integrated audit is that the controls audit supports and enhances the audit of the financial statements. When internal controls of the company are effective, the auditor can reduce the extent of other tests of the books and records. If these controls are effective only at the reporting date and not throughout the year, the auditor cannot rely on the controls for any period and area the controls were ineffective. Thus, it is very important that the auditor be informed of any important findings and issues relating to controls as the work of management progresses so he or she can consider the implications for the financial statement audit. At a minimum, significant deficiencies and material weaknesses need to be communicated. If the severity assessment of the deficiency is not clear or a determination is not made, it is better to be on the safe side and communicate the deficiency. If a timely communication is not made, further inefficiencies can occur in the audit process. According to SEC Release No. 33-8810:

> Pursuant to Exchange Act Rules 13a-14 and 15d-14 [17 CFR 240.13a-14 and 240.15d-14], management discloses to the auditors and to the audit committee of the board of directors (or persons fulfilling the equivalent function) all material weaknesses and significant deficiencies in the design or operation of internal controls which could adversely affect the issuer's ability to record, process, summarize and report financial data. (p. 34)

The auditor will also seek out information from other sources that might provide important information about the design and performance of internal controls. The audit committee and the SOX project team should also be in the loop on any such information. At a minimum the auditor will inquire about such matters at the end of the audit, but that may not be timely information and may hold up the required filings if such late-discovered information affects the sufficiency of evidence gathered in the audit. According to AS No. 5, paragraph-94:

> To obtain additional information about whether changes have occurred that might affect the effectiveness of the company's internal control over financial reporting and, therefore, the auditor's report, the auditor should inquire about and examine, for this subsequent period, the following—
>
> - Relevant internal audit (or similar functions, such as loan review in a financial institution) reports issued during the subsequent period,
> - Independent auditor reports (if other than the auditor's) of deficiencies in internal control,
> - Regulatory agency reports on the company's internal control over financial reporting, and
> - Information about the effectiveness of the company's internal control over financial reporting obtained through other engagements.

A key representation of management will be that management has disclosed significant control matters to the auditor of which the company was aware. The underlined paragraphs of AS No. 5, paragraph 75 are of specific importance with respect to communications:

> In an audit of internal control over financial reporting, the auditor should obtain written representations from management—
>
> a. Acknowledging management's responsibility for establishing and maintaining effective internal control over financial reporting;
> b. Stating that management has performed an evaluation and made an assessment of the effectiveness of the company's internal control over financial reporting and specifying the control criteria;
> c. Stating that management did not use the auditor's procedures performed during the audits of internal control over financial reporting or the financial statements as part of the basis for management's assessment of the effectiveness of internal control over financial reporting;
> d. Stating management's conclusion, as set forth in its assessment, about the effectiveness of the company's internal control over financial reporting based on the control criteria as of a specified date;
> e. Stating that management has disclosed to the auditor all deficiencies in the design or operation of internal control over financial reporting identified as part of management's evaluation, including separately disclosing to the auditor all such deficiencies that it believes to be significant deficiencies or material weaknesses in internal control over financial reporting;
> f. Describing any fraud resulting in a material misstatement to the company's financial statements and any other fraud that does not result in a material misstatement to the company's financial statements but involves senior management or management or other employees who have a significant role in the company's internal control over financial reporting;

g. Stating whether control deficiencies identified and communicated to the audit committee during previous engagements pursuant to paragraphs 77 and 79 have been resolved, and specifically identifying any that have not; and stating whether there were, subsequent to the date being reported on, any changes in internal control over financial reporting or other factors that might significantly affect internal control over financial reporting, including any corrective actions taken by management with regard to significant deficiencies and material weaknesses.

The auditor also has reciprocal communication responsibilities to management and the audit committee regarding their internal control findings. Again, timely communication is helpful in coordinating the overall efforts to improve internal controls. The requirements of AS No. 5 are clear:

[paragraph 78] The auditor must communicate, in writing, to management and the audit committee all material weaknesses identified during the audit. The written communication should be made prior to the issuance of the auditor's report on internal control over financial reporting.

[paragraph 80] The auditor also should consider whether there are any deficiencies, or combinations of deficiencies, that have been identified during the audit that are significant deficiencies and must communicate such deficiencies, in writing, to the audit committee.

[paragraph 81] The auditor also should communicate to management, in writing, all deficiencies in internal control over financial reporting (i.e., those deficiencies in internal control over financial reporting that are of a lesser magnitude than material weaknesses) identified during the audit and inform the audit committee when such a communication has been made. When making this communication, it is not necessary for the auditor to repeat information about such deficiencies that has been included in previously issued written communications, whether those communications were made by the auditor, internal auditors, or others within the organization.

REPORTING THE REMEDIATION OF WEAKNESSES

When weaknesses are identified in the formal annual 10-K report to the shareholders, the expectation is that the company will remediate the deficiency as soon as possible. In fact, significant deficiencies are also expected to be corrected as soon as possible, but earlier than the next annual reporting period. Issues that continue to be unremediated should be reflected in the required quarterly Section 302 certification and may need to be disclosed in quarterly 10-Q reports. Questions may be raised when such deficiencies are not remediated in a timely manner, and there may be implications regarding the effectiveness of governance or the control environment when issues remain unresolved.

Companies may make disclosures regarding the remediation of deficiencies but auditors cannot be associated with such statements unless the procedures in PCAOB AS No. 4, *Reporting on Whether a Previously Reported Material Weakness Continues to*

Exist are followed. There is no requirement for companies to contract for this service. This statement was created to fill the perceived need for auditor attestation on the remediation, to support a management assertion to the marketplace that a weakness has been remediated, but this has not been widely applied. Cost is often cited as a reason not to request auditor reporting on remediations. Such reports have been rare since the standard was issued.

In the circumstance where the company is contemplating seeking auditor confirmation of a remediation assertion on an interim basis before the next annual reporting period, the provisions and requirements of PCAOB Standard No. 4 should be consulted and reviewed with the auditor in advance.

 ## COORDINATING WITH THE INDEPENDENT AUDITORS AND LEGAL COUNSEL

Independent Auditors

Before presenting your management reports to the independent auditor, you should review the contents of the report(s), including:

- Completeness and whether the contents satisfy the SEC reporting requirements.
- The presentation of any material that is not required or could be misunderstood.
- Report language.
- Definition of "significant deficiency" and "material weakness" provided by the most current auditing standards.
- Disclosure of material weaknesses that exist at the reporting date.
- The nonreporting of material weaknesses that existed and were reported at an interim period but have subsequently been remediated.

While it was clearly understood when SOX was implemented, due to time passing and players changing, companies sometimes still forget that every auditor adjustment and correction to company-prepared financial statements is evidence of a company control deficiency of some magnitude. As a result, the extra effort associated with careful preparation of the financials and disclosures is an effective and efficient activity. This also includes careful documentation of any assumptions and computations is reaching estimates or fair values, a common area of documentation and process failures.

Legal Counsel

It is recommended that the entity's SEC counsel should also be involved in the drafting process to ensure that the resulting report(s) meet the SEC reporting requirements without exposing the entity or the individuals signing the reports to unnecessary legal risk. Counsel will often have updated checklists that can be used to ensure compliance with various disclosure regulations.

Illustrative AICPA Report on Internal Controls

S IMILAR TO THE reports used by public companies, the illustrative report that follows is for situations where the auditor is opining on the financial statements. It provides similar assurance and cautions to readers regarding the effectiveness of the system of internal control over financial reporting and references management's assertion on internal control. The illustrative report is for a clean opinion. AT 501 and Statement on Standards for Attestation Engagements (SSAE) No. 15 provide examples of disclaimer and adverse opinions. This report is from AT No. 501.[1]

Independent Auditor's Report

[Introductory paragraph]

We have examined SAMPLE Company's internal control over financial reporting as of December 31, 20XX, based on (e.g., *2013 Internal Control—Integrated Framework* issued by the Committee of Sponsoring Organizations of the Treadway Commission [COSO]). SAMPLE Company's management is responsible for maintaining effective internal control over financial reporting and for its assertion about the effectiveness of internal control over financial reporting, included in the accompanying [identify management's report]. Our responsibility is to express an opinion on SAMPLE Company's internal control over financial reporting based on our examination.

[Scope paragraph]

We conducted our examination in accordance with attestation standards established by the American Institute of Certified Public Accountants. Those standards require that we plan and perform the examination to obtain reasonable assurance

---

[1] At the time of this writing the AICPA was about to expose an SAS to replace AT 501. Readers should check the status of this proposed standard if it is relevant to their engagement.

about whether effective internal control over financial reporting was maintained in all material respects. Our examination included obtaining an understanding of internal control over financial reporting, assessing the risk that a material weakness exists, and testing and evaluating the design and operating effectiveness of internal control based on the assessed risk. Our examination also included performing such other procedures as we considered necessary in the circumstances. We believe that our examination provides a reasonable basis for our opinion.

[Definition paragraph]

An entity's internal control over financial reporting is a process effected by those charged with governance, management, and other personnel, designed to provide reasonable assurance regarding the preparation of reliable financial statements in accordance with (e.g., accounting principles generally accepted in the United States of America). An entity's internal control over financial reporting includes those policies and procedures that (1) pertain to the maintenance of records that, in reasonable detail, accurately and fairly reflect the transactions and dispositions of the assets of the entity; (2) provide reasonable assurance that transactions are recorded as necessary to permit preparation of financial statements in accordance with [e.g., accounting principles generally accepted in the United States of America], and that receipts and expenditures of the entity are being made only in accordance with authorizations of management and those charged with governance; and (3) provide reasonable assurance regarding prevention, or timely detection and correction of unauthorized acquisition, use, or disposition of the entity's assets that could have a material effect on the financial statements.

[Inherent limitations paragraph]

Because of its inherent limitations, internal control over financial reporting may not prevent or detect and correct misstatements. Also, projections of any evaluation of effectiveness to future periods are subject to the risk that controls may become inadequate because of changes in conditions, or that the degree of compliance with the policies or procedures may deteriorate.

[Opinion paragraph]

In our opinion, SAMPLE Company maintained, in all material respects, effective internal control over financial reporting as of December 31, 20XX, based on [e.g., the aforementioned COSO Framework].

[Audit of financial statements paragraph]

We also have audited, in accordance with auditing standards generally accepted in the United States of America, the [identify the financial statements] of SAMPLE Company and our report dated [date of report, which should be the same as the date of the report on the examination of internal control], which expressed [e.g., an unqualified opinion].

[Signature]

[Date]

CHAPTER TWELVE

Project Management and Tools Assessment Design

THE REVISION OF the Framework provides an excellent opportunity to assess the efficiency and effectiveness of any assessment approach used previously. In addition, first-time Securities and Exchange Commission (SEC) filers and first-time auditees will also need to perform their initial project. This chapter reviews some of the basics of project organizational structure and tools selection. As it is likely that a COSO assessment will be a continuing annual event, it is worthwhile to give up-front consideration to the maintainability of any approach taken. As an auditor, you will encounter a number of different COSO approaches taken by your clients, so it is particularly important you be well versed in the COSO concepts and have flexible tools to cope with diversity in approaches.

We now have a decade of experience in learning and applying COSO to financial reporting. There is no need to assume that everyone is at the starting line and have to experience all of the "learning opportunities" of your predecessors. This work is dedicated to helping you benefit from what others have found works and does not work. There will be changes to any prior approach, so why not make the best of it and try to do a more efficient and effective project?

 PROJECT MANAGEMENT

For those public companies and auditors who started assessing controls under the Sarbanes-Oxley (SOX) Act in 2004 and those private companies and their auditors that have been responding to the mandate in the American Institute of Certified Public Accountants (AICPA) Risk Assessment Standards from 2007, it is likely that the people

318

who initiated that project are not directing that project in the same role today. In fact, in periodic seminars I do for state certified public accountant (CPA) societies, trade groups, and entities, there are more startled expressions coming out of that training than after the 2002 period, when everything was new. In the beginning we were all learning, and new information was not unexpected. In some ways the complete learning experience deadened our reactions to new information and the emerging standards and clarifications of that early period. In some cases we are in the second to fourth set of team members. Like the proverbial story that gets told around the circle, the COSO story tends to morph and change as it is told. Fewer individuals are reading the requirements directly; they are relying on what they have been told or what they infer from reading prior documentation. The internal control assessment process has taken on a certain maturity in some organizations and does not command the level and quality of resources once devoted to it.

What that leaves open is a risk of complacency and going through the motions to complete the controls assessment task. We have lessened the losses from public company frauds due to greater diligence and fraud awareness and have mitigated the trend of increasing financial statement restatements, which was also a motivation for imposing the controls requirements on business. But fraud and restatements continue, so we have only been partially successful in performing our requirements. The Dodd-Frank Act in 2010 permanently suspended the need for independent auditors to report separately on client internal controls, so the oversight that proved so valuable to accelerated filers in their initial implementations will not be there for smaller public companies.

Deterioration in quality and performance is the general rule without a periodic stimulus to refocus efforts and assess the efficiency and effectiveness of procedures and processes. The 2013 revision of the COSO Framework can be such a stimulus to ensure that the effort expended is worthwhile.

STRUCTURING THE PROJECT TEAM

You will want to perform your work as effectively and efficiently as possible. To accomplish this, you will need to create a project team with the required skills, knowledge, and experience to achieve the engagement objectives. The work of each team member will need to be defined and coordinated with other members.

Establishing Responsibilities and Lines of Reporting

COSO Principle 3 focuses on reporting lines, and appropriate authorities and responsibilities in the pursuit of objectives from an entity control environment perspective. That issue is relevant to the COSO project too. If a continuing project, is the project organization still properly aligned, or has time weakened the structure or competence of those performing the tasks? The penalties for chief executive officers (CEOs) and chief financial officers (CFOs) who sign false Section 302 and Section 404 certifications have not diminished.

The project team should have the responsibility for overseeing and coordinating all of the activities relating to the evaluation of and reporting on the effectiveness of the entity's internal control. As a condition for assuming this responsibility, the team should have the authority to conduct the evaluation in a way that is appropriate given the nature, size, and complexity of the organization. That requires sufficient seniority in the organization to command timely cooperation and instill sufficient seriousness into the tasks.

For example, one way a project team for evaluating internal control could fit into an entity's overall financial reporting structure is by reporting to the disclosure committee. Alternatively, the engagement team could report directly to the CEO and CFO, who are responsible for certifying the periodic effectiveness of the entity's internal control.

However the lines of reporting are configured, you should be sure that the project team reports to one of the senior committees or executives at the entity in order to emphasize that:

- The successful completion of the evaluation is important for the entity.
- Communications and requests from the engagement team should be given a high priority.

Project Team Members

The project team should be comprised of individuals with the knowledge, skills, and authority within the entity to oversee a successful engagement. Collectively, the group should have a high-level knowledge of the entity's operations and strategies and obtain and allocate the necessary resources. The project team usually consists of key operating personnel, technical information technology (IT) specialists, and one or more testing and evaluation teams.

Internal auditors (IAs) are often a valuable resource in helping an entity assess the effectiveness of internal control. In general, internal audit can provide assistance in two different ways.

1. *Use of work product.* The work that IAs perform as part of their normal, routine responsibilities may provide you with:
   - Documentation about the design of many aspects of internal control.
   - Evidence to support the effectiveness of the design, operations, or both of specific controls.

   Auditing Standard (AS) No. 5 is considerably more flexible than AS No. 2 was in allowing auditors to rely on the work product of IAs when assessed to be objective, tested, and shown to be competent.

   Over time, the work programs and procedures of IAs can be aligned such that they are accomplishing their internal mission and assisting in the SOX documentation and assessment process as a regular aspect of their responsibilities. In the long run, many companies are maintaining their annual SOX update responsibilities through internal audit once the initial project team has completed the first round of documentation and assessment and temporary consultants are phased out of the project. In smaller entities, IAs may be unable to devote the time to be a major resource in the project, and without additional hiring may be relegated to higher risk or more sensitive assessments and overseeing the work of production and administrative staff that are sharing project responsibilities.

2. *Project team member or supervisor.* The internal auditor can be a member of the project team, working under the direct supervision of the engagement team leader to perform procedures designed specifically to comply with the SOX internal control reporting requirements. In some cases, the lead technical resource and day-to-day leader under the project "owner" may be the head IA or a designee.

Because of the inherent overlap of some of the tasks charged to a typical internal audit function and the SOX objectives, IAs are a natural fit as team members and leaders in the SOX controls assessment project. With some additional orientation to the COSO Framework and components like the control environment and monitoring, and the SOX requirements, IAs, given their knowledge of the company, can often be "ready to go" before other people can be trained and oriented in the company to participate in the project.

As project team members, IAs may provide assistance in any number of areas, including:

- Enhancing the understanding of entity operations, significant risks, and controls.
- Knowledge of the people in the organization who will need to cooperate with the SOX project team.
- Providing insight or a preliminary analysis on the relative strengths and weaknesses of each component of internal control.
- Providing internal technical expertise in areas such as IT auditing.
- Assisting in the design or testing of controls.

Operations and Accounting Personnel

Operating and accounting personnel from the entity's major business segments or activities can be a part of the SOX project team. These individuals can contribute their in-depth understanding of various entity operations, the business risks of various activities, and existing controls. Having these individuals on the project team will also help establish important communication channels between the team and entity employees who will be responsible for providing information to the team or implementing its recommendations. It will also serve to raise the controls knowledge and awareness of these employees, perhaps assisting in their training and organization.

One caution in this regard is that self-assessment of controls functions is fully acceptable for completing the required company SOX tasks, but independent auditors may not be able to rely on self-assessments when the persons performing the assessment might not be considered objective in their work. Assessing the controls effectiveness of your own department is viewed with some skepticism, since objectivity may not be maintained (akin to grading your own exams in school). This may be one reason that research has shown that entities often fail to identify deficiencies with their internal procedures and often underrate their severity when they do find them.

For maximum efficiency, when internal personnel are utilized on the SOX project team, consideration should be given to how the project assignments are made so that the assessments can be relied on to the maximum extent possible by the independent auditor.

Public Company Accounting Oversight Board (PCAOB) AS No. 5 is abundantly clear on this point:

> [paragraph18] The auditor should assess the competence and objectivity of the persons whose work the auditor plans to use to determine the extent to which the auditor may use their work. The higher the degree of competence and objectivity, the greater use the auditor may make of the work. The auditor should apply paragraphs .09 through .11 of AU sec. 322 to assess the competence and objectivity of internal auditors. The auditor should apply the principles underlying those paragraphs to assess the competence and objectivity of persons other than internal auditors whose work the auditor plans to use.
>
> Note: For purposes of using the work of others, competence means the attainment and maintenance of a level of understanding and knowledge that enables that person to perform ably the tasks assigned to them, and objectivity means the ability to perform those tasks impartially and with intellectual honesty. To assess competence, the auditor should evaluate factors about the person's qualifications and ability to perform the work the auditor plans to use. To assess objectivity, the auditor should evaluate whether factors are present that either inhibit or promote a person's ability to perform with the necessary degree of objectivity the work the auditor plans to use.
>
> Note: The auditor should not use the work of persons who have a low degree of objectivity, regardless of their level of competence. Likewise, the auditor should not use the work of persons who have a low level of competence regardless of their degree of objectivity. Personnel whose core function is to serve as a testing or compliance authority at the company, such as internal auditors, normally are expected to have greater competence and objectivity in performing the type of work that will be useful to the auditor.

While worded differently, the AICPA Standards voice similar expectations when auditors consider the work of others in determining their scope of procedures. Entities seeking to minimize audit costs will also assemble relevant information supporting the objectivity and competence questions in advance, as part of the company project.

Technical Specialists

The project team is likely to need certain technical expertise in order to meet its objectives successfully. In some industries, it is typical for entities to establish certain quality control groups; for example, financial institutions will have a credit review committee whose responsibilities include setting underwriting criteria and ensuring that the entity's lending practices conform to those criteria. Individuals with this type of expertise can be invaluable to project teams seeking to understand an entity's operations and internal control structure.

If fair valuations play an important role in financial reporting (and today they often do), having a valuation specialist available to the team may be critical in evaluating the appraisal and valuation processes and controls over tests of impairment or the valuation of monetary assets and liabilities and investments that are accounted for at fair value. Tax accrual has been shown to be an area of struggle for many entities, and specialty assistance is often needed in order for entities to prepare the tax accrual and expense allocations. Controls over this process have proven to be vexing. Pre-SOX, the tax accrual was often performed by tax specialists from the independent auditor's firm or prepared in some collaborative way. Such practices are no longer allowed in public companies due to toughened independence rules.

IT specialists may often be required since most entities are heavy users of IT to enable key business activities and process significant transactions. The presence of one or more of the next conditions may indicate that a high degree of IT expertise is needed on your engagement:

- The entity has significant e-commerce activity.
- Data is shared extensively between computer applications.
- The entity uses emerging technologies (e.g., cloud computing or cloud storage).

It is anticipated that IT expertise will be required on most projects that involve complex systems and networks. An IT specialist is essential for helping the project team:

- Identify risks related to these IT systems.
- Document and test IT general controls (COSO Principle 11) and application (e.g., transaction processing software) controls.
- Design, implement, and remediate missing or deficient IT controls, if any.
- Monitor the continued effectiveness of IT general and application controls.

The Information Technology Governance Institute (ITGI) and the Information Systems Audit and Control Association (ISACA) have published *IT Control Objectives for Sarbanes-Oxley (2006)*, which provides guidance to IT auditors who assist management in the testing and evaluation of internal control. This practice aid is discussed further in Chapter 8, Evidence and Testing. In addressing the planning for these projects, the authors of the document note:

> To meet the demands of Sarbanes-Oxley, most organizations will require a change in culture. More likely than not, enhancements to IT systems and processes will be required, most notably in the design, documentation and evaluation of IT controls. Because the cost of noncompliance can be devastating to an organization, it is crucial to adopt a proactive approach and take on the challenge early.[1]

---

[1] This report can be downloaded at: www.theiia.org/chapters/pubdocs/135/ITGI_Spreadsheet.pdf

As a first step toward planning the IT component of the project, the document recommends that:

- Management and the project leader should obtain an understanding of the risks inherent in IT systems and the effect these risks have on the project. These risks are often very entity-specific, so broad generalizations about the risks are not often effective.
- IT management should obtain an understanding of the financial reporting process and its supporting systems.
- The Chief Information Officer should have advanced knowledge of the types of IT controls necessary to support reliable financial information processing.

Testing and Evaluation Teams

Depending on the size and complexity of the entity, the project team itself may conduct the testing and evaluation of internal controls. Alternatively, it may act in more of a supervisory capacity and delegate the performance of the procedures to one or more testing and evaluation teams. If the engagement requires the use of multiple project teams, steps should be taken to ensure the consistency and quality of the procedures performed. For example, training on the evaluation process and control documentation tools may be required.

One practice that has been shown to be efficient to implement is to have the documentation and testing performed by the same team members. Because of their familiarity with the controls and functions, the documentation team is "ready to go" on completion of the documentation and assessment that the design is sufficient to meet the control objectives. Training the documentation team in testing methods is generally more efficient than having dedicated testing teams learn the controls and procedures associated with each of the controls areas and types of controls they test. The efficiency can be further enhanced when the project is oriented around logical transaction cycles (e.g., Sales to Receipts or Purchases to Payments) rather than compartmentalized by accounts. The separation of design and testing seems to have been an outgrowth of the early SOX requirements that separately discussed these two phases. Additionally, early SOX implementers often sought independent auditor assistance in performing some of the testing procedures required, but independence requirements effectively limited independent auditor involvement to that of scribes in the documentation process. The lack of familiarity with COSO may have also contributed to segregating the functions, as specialist consulting teams were formed to focus on the documentation and design assessments, while IAs and others focused on testing the controls. With the benefit of hindsight and experience, more integrated documentation and testing is being planned.

One caution is that sometimes another set of eyes can be helpful in ensuring the quality of the assessments and procedures. With a combined documentation and testing team, that second perspective is not there. Effective and close supervision of each phase of the assessment process can help close the gap between the possible quality risks and the economic advantage of having independent teams perform the procedures.

TOOLS ASSESSMENT DESIGN

While no specific tools or format for documentation is specified by COSO, the AICPA, or PCAOB, we have had enough experience with different approaches in different environments to make informed suggestions regarding approaches with a good track record of success. The 2006 COSO guidance for smaller public companies took a step forward in providing some template examples. The 2013 revised Framework also has provided a number of template examples.

Unfortunately, a dominant software solution to the COSO documentation and testing process never clearly emerged in the initial period of COSO implementation. The market was fragmented between auditors and companies and between large and small entities. Industry and lines of business differences required entities to perform a fair amount of customization in their initial implementations. Once auditors and entities set their initial approach, inertia made changing less attractive. Negative attitudes about the task on the part of business and the constant efforts to overthrow the requirements made it hard to make further investments in the face of possible suspension of the requirements.

Today it seems unlikely the COSO requirements for all entities will be further suspended or watered down, despite periodic business complaints and efforts to dismantle the legislation. In addition, the 17 Principles and further commentary, examples, and approaches to the controls concepts add more structure to controls assessment and make it easier to develop tools around that structure. As the revised Framework consists of more mature guidance, we can also anticipate fewer tweaks, twists, and changes that can raise havoc with computer programs that are tuned to a specific task. Nevertheless, it would take bold thinking to reintroduce a software solution when the market did not respond to prior offerings.

There can be benefits of designing the documentation approach and tools to be used beyond an efficiency goal. Entities that automate business processes analysis will need to make advance decisions about how the tool should be configured and deployed. Making these decisions will require management to consider carefully the processes it puts in place, the information resources people need to perform their assigned task, and how controls are monitored and exceptions handled. All of these considerations will add further definition to the project and improve its effectiveness.

There are two basic types of tools you may wish to consider for your SOX project. The decisions about these need not be finalized at the commencement of the assessment but should be decided on early in the project. One type of tool you may wish to consider is project management software. This is scheduling software that helps link the scoping conclusions, calendar dates, and resources available to do the actual project work. Familiar to consultants and many project managers, these tools can help organize complex projects and identify impossible completion objectives in advance, allowing for revisions during the planning phase rather than in real time. The larger and more complex the entity, the more valuable this type of tool may be. With respect to which tool to select, it seems that the most important success criterion is that the project members using it are familiar with the tool and like it. You might consider looking at Microsoft's Project Management tool if you do not have another alternative. Some higher-end software solutions tailored to compliance projects may have front-end modules integrated with the elements of the software that serve as project management software. If you go in that direction, the issue may be whether the included software is sufficient for the task and whether some of the known project phases relating to a SOX engagement have been preloaded into a template for convenience. Stand-alone project management software is the most common software of this type in use by smaller companies.

The second type of tool is one you will need to decide on sooner or later. This is the tool that provides the general format for your COSO Framework documentation of the controls. The remainder of this section is devoted to that critical decision.

FEATURES OF A GOOD TOOLS SOLUTION

We can learn from the software features present in some early COSO software efforts some project issues we need to consider in the absence of an identified software solution to handle all of these for us. Today, the common solutions in entities and audit firms still revolve around Word and Excel documents, which have the capacity to address some of the issues identified in this section in the hands of skilled individuals. The power of inertia and the pain of developing and implementing better solutions have kept firms on this path. As a reminder, Word and Excel meet the definitions of software, although they are highly user adaptable. As more advanced functions are built into these basic user-friendly tools, there is a point where the direct development of special-purpose software might be easier and more effective.

Let's consider some specifications of what an effective solution might look like. From there you can decide what features and functions should be built-in and which ones may need to be compensated for by other procedures in your application. The discussion can also serve as a benchmark to assess various commercial or in-house developed tools to support the COSO assessment process.

Security and Access

COSO assessment projects are generally complex and require a team of individuals to accomplish the task. It is common to find various members working on various pieces of the project at the same time. A permissions function in programmed software can be helpful in restricting access and function, as defined by project management. Who will have access to which elements of the project to evolve and modify the elements to meet specific entity needs? How do you restrict access to just those modules and functions that an individual needs to perform their tasks? If reviewers are used for quality purposes, can they both review and comment and also change the documentation? Can anyone with access to the documents just sign off that the module or section has been reviewed? When projects are archived for review at some future point, how do you protect them from accidental or deliberate modification?

Flexibility and Adaptability

The Framework was designed to apply to all types of entities: public, private, governmental, large and small, and in all industries. This implies that customization must be the rule and not the exception. While greater structure in the 2013 Framework assists to define some boundaries, the accounts involved, risks, and controls employed will all differ. An approach needs to accommodate such a need, and the user will need to be able to make modifications to the default structure without extensive special (e.g., programming) skills. Word and Excel perform well on this attribute, as a large number of people have basic skills in using these tools.

Network Compatible

Experience shows that project teams from larger applications need tools that can shared, often implying the use of networks. The concept of the COSO project resting in a single file that is in a single location or is passed around between team members as a whole is an impractical model in many situations. Audit teams in particular are likely to need multiple access to modules and pieces of the systems. Some software designs allow for modules to be assigned and then locked while being worked on so that data conflicts do not occur in real time. As the new Framework stresses the interactions between principles and technology, conflicts may become more common. For example, suppose a defect in software access and security is identified for the in-house payroll system. The defect affects the IT assessment but also affects the payroll assessment. With IT identifying the issue and another project member working on control activities including payroll, there can be conflicts in reporting the deficiency and its implications. Work in payroll should not be signed off until the deficiency is assessed as it relates to the payroll application. With multiple accesses come the issue of data conflict and how to resolve it. When modules are updated to a master version in a computerized environment, conflicts are identified and resolved. In the absence of an electronic solution, care needs to be taken so that data conflicts are not overlooked, leading to conflicting documentation and errors in assessment.

Easy Interface

Screen design is an art and a science. A poorly designed user interface leads to errors in performance. Simplicity in presentation, the placement of elements on a screen, and ensuring the right tools to work with the screen are accessible to the user are all important considerations. Whether using a matrix, form, flowchart, or narrative format, the careless placement of the data fields on the screen will create inefficiency and likely contribute to errors. Testing screen design before implementation is worth the effort. Often the developers are not subject matter experts and may not be able to distinguish which information gathering is likely to take place first or last, and they may not understand how data flows or may be repeated/copied in the overall system.

One-Write Capability

As one reviews the COSO examples and sample forms for reporting deficiencies, it becomes pretty clear that deficiency issues—for example, reported at the transaction or entity level—may be repeated in several of the summary processes supporting the final overall assessment. In the absence of a software link that replicates the text as suggested through the assessment summary screens, a manual cut-and-paste or some other mechanism should exist to ensure the consistency and accuracy of information repeated within the system. Other functions that can benefit from a one-write capability are the assertions to be used on transactional control activities and certain other components. As common elements, these selected assertions need to be populated widely in the system to appropriate modules.

Contextual Help Screens

Forms and matrices are wonderful tools to assist with documenting internal controls, but until users have experience and training in using the tools, questions may arise linked to how the information will be used by the system, in the assessment process, or what specific information is being sought to complete the information-gathering task. Context-sensitive help screens can give specific guidance to reduce data entry errors or remind users of specific COSO, audit, or SEC guidance on that point. Contextual guidance can also be helpful to remind users of software features that can be used in certain portions of the form, such as cut-and-paste, delete, and so on. While these features may often be known when using Word or Excel, if special features have been added to the common functions (e.g., locking the module to prevent others from changing data while the module is being worked on by another user), the user can use Help to understand how to apply them.

Cross Referencing and Linking

An important feature of a "system," as opposed to a series of documents or spreadsheets, is the ability to link (hyperlink) portions of the work papers together. As an aid to navigation through the work papers, the insertion of frequent cross references and direct links aid in, for example, ensuring the risks link to the control activities or to other procedures that might address the identified risk. Deficiencies can be related to other deficiencies more easily when cross references are used generously. Conclusions or other documentation can be supported by cross references to evidence or a narrative rather than forcing a repetition of the same information within the system. Users can also benefit and gain understanding from a system with predefined common linkages that can be programmed into the work papers. The failure to relate documents can lead to broken links, such as risks that are not addressed or findings that do not seem to be considered later in summarizing the conclusions by assertion, account, or component.

Status Indicators and Warnings

When a complex assessment is performed, a common risk when updating information is that a previously completed work paper will fail to be updated in the current period.

In the absence of the ability to read performance and reviewer sign-offs and reset them for the current period after archiving a past project, this becomes a manual tracking process. When data is changed after a work paper is reviewed, how will you be sure the work paper gets reviewed again? Warnings are a common feature of software systems. When numerical data is requested, what happens when text is inserted? Can edit checks be used to identify unusually large or small amounts and warn users? Is the project manager able to ascertain the status of the project by module or unit?

Work Paper Discipline

While not rocket science, the failure to sign and date the performance of a procedure or update is a common mistake. In the heat of the moment, with distractions and budget pressures, intended actions may be forgotten. In addition, when specific elements of a decision are expected by standards, it is helpful for the work paper to prompt for that information. For example, when sampling, the standards call for the documentation of risk, tolerable deviation rate, expected deviation rate, and sometimes the general or actual population size. Do the walk-throughs identify who was spoken to, whether the respondent seemed knowledgeable and competent, the controls covered by the walk-through, and the relevant risks and IT components of the controls in the walk-through? Are these so well ingrained in daily practice that such prompts are unnecessary? Not by my observations over the years.

Backups and Recovery

Good IT discipline includes a periodic backup of the data and a recovery plan if the unexpected happens. There is nothing unique about this issue as it relates to COSO or SOX, but the consequences of the loss of data are directly related to the importance of the COSO project to the entity. In a SOX compliance situation, regulatory penalties could be assessed if data is not available to support the required assessments by management and the auditor. In addition, if the entity lost its project data, the auditor of any entity would not have a basis to assess that work and rely on it to reduce procedures or offset documentation with client files. Another aspect of data loss is covered in the next list under "Archiving capability."

Additional Criteria

In addition, other software or tools should have certain characteristics to enhance their effectiveness and project efficiency. These features have been proven helpful though the experiences of entities and auditors addressing COSO compliance.

- ∎ *Migration of forms.* A feature of some internal controls documentation software that has significant value for audit practice is the annual closing of the auditor project file; retention of the customization of accounts, assertions, and other permanent project characteristics; and erasure of preparer and reviewer sign-offs and a reset of the status module to indicate the base new period files to be used in the next year. This feature is sometimes called a rollover, as the past-period file is transformed into the next-period starting file. This action is performed before or in conjunction with the creation of a permanent read-only archive of the past data file. To minimize the loss of the data that might be helpful and even relevant to the next period, some data fields are tagged to carry forward certain (e.g., narrative) information. A quality control feature helpful here is forcing the retained prior-year text or data to be confirmed or edited in the next year before the work paper can be signed off by the preparer. This prevents accidental acceptance of the possibly outdated documentation.

▪ *Archiving capability.* Audit requirements or state law may indicate the required period for data retention to support financial statements and business transactions. In brief, the AICPA indicates a minimum retention period of five years. For public companies, the PCAOB requires and minimum retention period of seven years. Other regulated entities operating under General Accountability Office (GAO) (Yellow Book) standards need to identify any other retention rules pertaining to these audits. State laws can extend the general minimums required, so each audit and entity needs to consider the appropriate retention period for the entity.

The principle reason for data retention from an audit and financial reporting perspective is the peer review and inspection requirements of the audit regulators. The AICPA peer-reviews applicable engagements on a three-year cycle. Audits are selected from that period, and quality assessments are made. Penalties are assessed if a CPA or firm fails to meet standards. In some cases the firm can be barred from audit practice. PCAOB inspections relate only to public company engagements. Larger CPA firms with many public clients are examined annually. Failure to correct deficiencies identified can result in public disclosure of the issues and loss of privilege to audit public companies. The interconnectivity of auditor and entity COSO requirements and reliance on entity records for the performance of audit procedures connects the auditor and entity when considering record retention requirements.

Rules directed to auditors may also have relevance to the entities they audit. Suppose the entity retains certain journals and supporting records for five years, but the auditor is required to keep records for seven years. In this case, the auditor cannot count on the data used in the audit to be accessible during the period of his or her required retention. This may cause the auditor to retain additional information to demonstrate the procedures that were performed, evidence that was examined, and conclusions that were reached. That retention may add cost to the audit. What is retained and for how long is a discussion that should occur between the entity and the auditor. The continuously declining cost of electronic data storage usually mitigates the cost issue for electronic data. However, many data elements still exist in physical form, and they do carry a cost of either digitization or retention.

An excellent software solution would be to close the COSO project file; gather all attachments, scans, charts, Word, and Excel documents; and create a CD or zip file that is in read-only form. This prevents accidental modification of the completed file by persons opening the file later for review, inspection, or as called for by a subpoena. Auditing standards limit the modification of an audit file after a point (e.g., the documentation completion date which should be 45 [e.g., PCAOB] to 60 days [e.g., AICPA] after the release of the audit report). Entities may also benefit from annually closing and archiving the COSO file to identify specifically the evidence and situation relevant to the audit period. Keeping an "open" and continuous file may create a risk that a file will not contain the information that is needed to understand a past circumstance or matter. Entities may wish to discuss with their in-house counsel the value of annual "snapshots" of project files such as the COSO project. A good electronic archiving solution permits the file to be read without the use of special software. It also preserves the ability to navigate through the project in order to facilitate the review.

Because of the continuing advance of software platforms and computer configurations, consideration should also be given to any potential software issues if a file needs to be opened, say, seven or more years hence. To address this risk, some CPA firms also archive an image of the standard platform of software distributed to the audit practice during an audit year.

Be alert for new software announcements for products designed for controls documentation, as additional entities in both the public and nonpublic marketplace are seeking tools for controls documentation and assessment, and additional product offerings may follow this demand. If you are considering a vendor product, some important considerations are:

- The vendor's reputation, experience, and accounting/COSO expertise.
- COSO-specific orientation versus a general-purpose shell.
- Ability to import and export data or attach documents from other applications like Word and Excel, Visio, and Adobe PDF files.
- Report generation capabilities. One software product used for controls documentation and assessment does not have the ability to print, which can be a significant issue to some.
- Maintenance and upgrades. Is the vendor committed to maintaining and enhancing the product?
- Service and support. Is there a mechanism available to have software questions answered or problems solved by the vendor?

VALUE OF A PILOT PROJECT

Whether preparing for an assessment for the first time or modifying an existing approach for greater compliance and efficiency, you should consider field testing your proposed approach. To do so before launching all boats with the full project or revision provides an opportunity to identify glitches and opportunities to enhance the process as applied to your specific engagement situation. This is one way for the core project team to gain experience without significant risk or wasting time and resources. The pilot project team should try to complete a piece of the documentation and assessment in advance of tackling the more complex subject areas. In first-time assessments, the group will likely understand better the personal attributes and skills that will be needed in order to form a highly effective project team. You can read this book and other materials until you become blind, but nothing substitutes for a driving lesson behind the wheel. It helps when your first driving experience is not at rush hour in downtown Manhattan.

I suggest including these individuals on the pilot project team:

- The most senior accounting officer: the CFO, treasurer, or the like. This person may likely be the ultimate "owner" of the bigger project.
- The most senior IT person: the chief information officer (CIO), the head of IT.
- The person in charge of the department or function selected to be the pilot project.
- A staff person who is likely to be asked to participate in the creation of the documentation, such as an IA or accounting staff.

Too large a pilot group will likely lessen its effectiveness. In smaller entities, two to three people may be all that are needed or available. However, if the plan is to leverage some documentation and testing tasks to operations personnel or temporary hires, the project team should include such a resource in order to assist in identifying the training needs for the project.

Selecting an area for the pilot project need not be difficult. Pick a "containable" project, and not one involving multiple processes in multiple locations. If there are six different ways to sell your product (e.g., cash sales, credit sales, Internet sales, electronic data interchange [EDI], etc.) and you use different systems for sales in each market or location, then pass on the revenue cycle for this phase or choose only one of the revenue streams. Selecting one of the control activities or only one component of internal control may be a good project base, as these are the elements most associated with "controls" and are not as highly judgmental in assessment as some of the other components, such as the control environment and risk assessment components. Payroll is usually a pretty well organized and centralized function, but sometimes that area is mostly controlled by the use of a service organization, which is a complication. Cash disbursements are often pretty well understood, organized, and controlled and can be an effective pilot project. When different types of cash disbursements are handled differently, depending on the type of invoice (e.g., routine utility bills, contractor payments, purchases, expense reimbursements), you might carve out one or two of these processes for the pilot, unless the processes share many elements that make them more alike than different.

Use the pilot project to gain an understanding of COSO and how it needs to be adapted to your organization. Familiarize yourself with some of the COSO terms so that the project team is communicating with a common vocabulary. Nothing creates chaos in a project as quickly as the use of inconsistent terminology between team members for the same activity or element. Accepting different terms for the same concept will create a Tower of Babel that will cause the efficiency of your project to suffer. Since COSO and auditing standards use different terminology, decide up front the terms you will use (probably the SEC, and auditing standards terms) and stick to them until they become natural for all participants.

Plan on working through and adapting the assertions (or control objectives) in the pilot area to your organization. You should also plan to make an assessment of the

IT general controls and software application controls related to the pilot application. Some sample control objectives and related assertions are illustrated in Appendix 5A of this book.

When you have completed your pilot project, you will have findings and observations. If you have identified potential risks or deficiencies in the process, you may not be able to classify them immediately as to their severity. That is okay for the pilot project, as you may need the benefit of further guidance and experience before being able to conclude. However, you should communicate the nontrivial deficiencies to management and governance as required. If you conclude that controls need to be strengthened or remediated, then that action can begin.

Let's suppose you chose payroll as your pilot project. You might have identified that the payroll clerk has access to changing the personnel data used to prepare the payroll (e.g., pay rates, as authorized by human resources or management). While no issues indicated that anything was misstated, and there were no complaints, the fact is that the access to changing these records *could* create a problem in future periods that might be hard to detect. So the assessment is generally that such issues *are an indication of a failure* of the segregation of duties concept, and actions and procedures to reduce the risk should be taken. Sometimes such access is controlled by limiting the clerk to a read-only status for that data or by a control requiring specific review of rate changes in the master file.

Once the project familiarization process is over, plan to have a group debriefing with management to review:

- Things that went well.
- Learning experiences.
- Considerations when expanding the process, such as documenting all five components of internal control and their attributes.
- The role of IT and any issues identified.
- What training, orientation, and review will be necessary to ensure consistency in the performance of tasks across the entity.
- Views on the documentation process used and any documentation tools used in the pilot.
- The composition of the future project team.

Effectively employed, the pilot project can help you relate your scoping conclusions to estimates of the resources and time that will be needed to complete the assessment process.

Use the pilot as a compass in setting your course for the project. In the rush to begin the big project, sometimes the entire perspective of what is being done gets lost in the process.

I rather favor an exchange between Alice and the Cheshire Cat in Lewis Carroll's *Alice's Adventures in Wonderland*:

Alice: Would you tell me, please, which way I ought to go from here?
The Cat: That depends a good deal on where you want to get to.
Alice: I don't much care where.

The Cat: Then it doesn't much matter which way you go.
Alice: ... so long as I get somewhere.
The Cat: Oh, you're sure to do that, if only you walk long enough.

So it is important to set your compass first. "Aiming" should precede "firing," or the result can be rather disastrous. Companies need to understand the target, or hitting the target will be the result of luck and not planning.

COORDINATING WITH THE INDEPENDENT AUDITORS

It is in your best interest that you coordinate your project with the entity's independent auditors. Coordination is not collaboration and is not cooperation. There are rather severe consequences associated with failing to meet the independence requirements of the PCAOB and SEC. To be clear, auditors cannot direct or manage the entity SOX project. They cannot direct the company in the selection of SOX tools and processes. They cannot test the controls as a basis for the client's assertion regarding controls and then turn around and rely on those tests for their work. In any situation, the question needs to be asked: Are the auditors being put in a position where they are auditing their own work? If so, then independence is a potential issue.

Failure to be independent can cause the audit report to be withdrawn and the appointment of another independent auditor to reaudit the financial statements and the opinion on internal control. The seriousness and cost implication of this issue is obvious.

Since any consulting project related to internal control needs to be cleared by the audit committee in advance, such committees have often shown reluctance to allow contracting for any services that might encroach on the independence mandates. While a more relaxed regulatory environment now surrounds the audits of internal control, the concerns about independence are real and should be taken very seriously by companies and auditors.

The coordination process generally begins at the planning phase of the project and continues at each subsequent phase. Proper coordination between your team and the independent auditors will facilitate an effective and efficient audit. A lack of coordination with the auditors could result in a variety of negative, unforeseen consequences, including:

- Duplication of effort.
- Unnecessary reperformance of certain tests.
- Performance of additional tests or untimely expansion of the scope of the engagement.
- Misunderstandings relating to the definition or reporting of material weaknesses.

As a starting point for understanding the auditors' expectations related to your engagement, you should have a working knowledge of the standards the independent auditors are required to follow when auditing an entity's internal control. Various citations in this edition will help entities and auditors understand their mutual responsibilities; however, SOX team leadership may find it helpful to review AS No. 5 and any related PCAOB guides[2] in their entirety. These publications are available from the PCAOB Web site at www.pcaobus.org under the Standards section. You should discuss with the entity's independent auditors certain key planning decisions, including:

- The overall engagement process and approach.
- The scope of your project, including locations or business units to be included.
- Preliminary identification of significant controls.
- The nature of any internal control deficiencies noted by the auditors during their most recent audit of the entity's financial statements.
- Tentative conclusions about what will constitute a significant deficiency or material weakness.
- The nature and extent of the documentation of controls.
- The nature and extent of the documentation of tests of controls.

In addition to identifying any potential issues that can be addressed earlier rather than later, this also serves to orient the independent auditor to the quality of your process and assists him or her in assessing the competence with which it is being planned and performed.

Larger firms have published brochures and booklets that are helpful to their clients and the public in general in understanding SOX requirements and their views on the requirements and issues of implementation. While obviously the views of your auditors are of primary interest, a lot of good information can be obtained from the publications of other audit firms, so SOX technical materials on their Web sites can be another good source of guidance and perspective for individuals in project leadership positions.

During the early phases of the project, it may not be possible to synchronize with the auditors on all significant planning matters, and there is no requirement that you do so. Nevertheless, the conversations can be helpful to you in obtaining:

- A clear understanding of the issue(s) that need resolution.
- The additional information required to reach a resolution.
- An estimated time frame for the process to be completed and the issue(s) to be resolved.

One practical issue for smaller public company requirements is that a significant number of smaller public companies are audited by firms with only one or a few public clients. Anecdotally it was noted by the PCAOB in speeches that over 1,000 smaller public companies are audited by CPA firms with only one or two public clients. Thus, the experience of these auditor firms may not include extensive reporting on internal controls. The implication for companies is to take extra care in planning and scoping their

---

[2] http://pcaobus.org/Standards/Pages/Guidance.aspx. See Alert No. 11: Considerations for Audits of Internal Control Over Financial Reporting (October 24, 2013).

engagements and to understand that a nod from the independent auditor on scoping and project issues may not be the way things should be.

One particularly disastrous example was the impetuous but preemptive desire of one entity that was geographically dispersed with a diverse product line to document controls in 2003, before various public company and auditor guidance was issued and before the audit firm had developed tools and training on COSO. An informal, early nod from the audit engagement team led the company down a path of unnecessary and voluminous documentation that later needed to be recast to address controls more directly and relate them to COSO objectives. While well meaning in the context of what was known at the time, the gesture of "acceptance" later led to a strained client relationship. Do your own homework.

CHAPTER THIRTEEN

Illustrative Forms and Templates

THE COSO FRAMEWORK, as illustrated in the 1992 Framework document and the 2006 guidance, illustrated the use of a matrix format for aligning the control objectives (attributes) with the control procedures, assertions, and assessed risks associated with the control objective or attribute. The 2013 revision continues to illustrate matrices as a tool to gather information. In addition, the AICPA Audit Guide *Assessing and Responding to Audit Risk in a Financial Statement Audit* (editions 2006 to 2014) contains an extended example of documenting a case study using a matrix format.

Sometimes a form can be a more effective approach to documentation since the form can present information in a specific order for more efficient and effective data entry. However, the display of information for review and analysis that is already collected may warrant a different presentation to assist the reviewer in organizing and integrating the information for the principle, component, and overall assessments. Thus, there may be trade-offs between ease of data entry and ease of analysis that could be solved by formatting reports from a database that display the information most useful for the analysis task.

The next section is adapted from the matrices from the COSO and AICPA guidance. This presentation may help readers discern the changes in the guidance over time and gain insight and clues as to how to modify existing documentation and data entry methods to comply with the 2013 Framework guidance. The remainder of the chapter is devoted to illustrating some data entry forms /matrices that may be helpful in designing work papers for a COSO assessment.

HISTORICAL PERSPECTIVE

Most templates developed since the imposition of the Sarbanes-Oxley (SOX) requirements use matrices for documenting controls including the 2006 to 2014 American Institute of Certified Public Accountants AICPA audit guides, *Assessing and Responding to Audit Risk in a Financial Statement Audit*. For illustrative purposes, an example of a control matrix format is provided from the 1992 and 2006 COSO documents. (See Tables 13.1 and 13.2.) As you will note in the 2013 Framework, the principles and financial statement assertions become more prominent in the assessment documentation.

Over time, the financial focus of accounting and auditing applications transformed the O, F, C (operating, financial, compliance) box into a place for recording the relevant financial reporting assertions, as can be noted in the format illustrated in the 2006 COSO guidance (Table 13.2).

While slightly different in presentation, both formats provide a structure in which to document controls effectiveness that is clearly different from the narrative or flowchart approaches also used over the years to document business processes. Clearly, the suggested approach is not endorsing a yes/no mentality of a checklist, where the existence or the absence of a control has some implied implication for the assessment. Rather, the approaches illustrated take the view of assessing *how* the controls and procedures in place address the objectives, risks, and assertions.

When documenting processes and controls, complexities can arise that may complicate the use of longitudinal matrices. For example, how is information on outsourced

TABLE 13.1 1992 COSO *Internal Control—Integrated Framework*: Evaluation Tools (pp. 42 and 43)

Risk Assessment and Control Activities Worksheet
Activity:

		Risk Analysis				
Objectives	O, F, C	Risk Factors	Likelihood	Actions/ Control Activities/ Comments	Other Objectives Affected	Evaluation and Conclusion

Key to the Illustration

- *Control objectives* were to be identified in the left column.
- *O, F, C* referred to whether the control was Operating, Financial, or Compliance in nature. In the current reporting focus, only the controls with financial implications are of immediate interest.
- The *risk analysis* section was to contain an assessment of what could go wrong as well as the likelihood of that happening.
- *Actions/control activities/comments* was set out as a place to document the controls and processes that achieved the objective and also addressed the identified risks.
- *Other objectives affected* facilitated the documentation of controls with multiple dimensions and benefits.
- *Evaluation and conclusion* provided a space to summarize conclusions.

TABLE 13.2 2006 COSO *Internal Control over Financial Reporting*—Guidance for Smaller Public Companies (p. 48, Revenues)

Part I

Financial Statement Assertion	Risk	Process Level Control	Preventive/ Detective	Manual/ Automated
Occurrence-only valid orders are fulfilled (continued)	Unacceptable customers are added to the customer list	Changes must be appointed in writing by specified executive or supervisory employee	Preventive	Manual
	Customer list is inaccurate or incomplete	Periodic review of customer lists for accuracy and completeness	Detective	Manual
		Written chart of accounts containing a description of each account	Preventive	Manual
	Order processing circumvents established procedures	The company has established order processing policy and procedure manual and training routines	Preventive	Manual

Part II (p. 15)

Control activities principles	Summary of controls		Design effectiveness (fully met, partially met, not met)	Summary of evidence of control	Operating effectiveness regarding principles
	Entity level	Process level			

Key to the Illustration

Part I

▪ Financial statement assertion. The control objective/attribute and financial statement assertion are shown combined in the first column.
▪ Risk. "What can go wrong" is considered in the second column.
▪ Process level control. This is where one would document the controls and processes that achieved the objective and also addressed the identified risks.
▪ Preventative/detective. This aspect of the nature of the control is documented here.
▪ Manual/automated. This aspect of the nature of the control is documented here.

Part II

▪ Entity level. Those controls that operate across the entity are documented here.
▪ Process level. Those controls that relate to the detailed assessments such as for revenues and expenses appear here.
▪ Design effectiveness. The assessment of design effectiveness is stated here.
▪ Summary evidence of control. Results of tests or walkthroughs are documented here.
▪ Operating effectiveness regarding principles. An assessment of operating effectiveness goes here.

activities integrated? Should there be a separate column to document walk-throughs or sample tests? Users could continue to add columns to accommodate documenting sampling plans and results and various permutations and combinations of issues that could relate to a control, but then the format becomes unwieldy. Some SOX spreadsheet applications extend well into "double-letter" column headings when a column is reserved for each potential point of documentation. In addition, a columnar data entry form needs to be able to expand cells to wrap text that may exceed a few words. This can also complicate the potential visual advantage of the matrix data entry approach. Furthermore, when data is not arrayed in rows or columnar form and is arranged in sections of a page, the visual advantage of the matrix can be lost to distortions in the format due to wrapping text that expands the cells or the limited display of the text in a fixed-size cell.

2013 FRAMEWORK EXAMPLES

Another approach that achieves a similar data collection objective may be the use of a form with the same information gathered in a structured format. As noted, this format may not always be the best presentation of the data form analysis and integration, so a better solution can be the formatting of reports that display only the relevant data for the task (e.g., assessment of the deficiencies identified and their implications) with links back to the full data on each deficiency should that information be helpful to the review. Data arrayed in a fixed (e.g., columnar) format report may also be more easily sorted so that different perspectives on deficiencies (e.g., by assertion, by account, by principle, by component) can be facilitated. To accommodate the suggestions for data entry and report display or writing here, the project application might be best structured using a database as a data repository.

Flow of Work Papers

The flow of documentation should be clear to ensure that all issues identified are properly summarized in reaching conclusions. Disorganized work papers contribute to mistakes and are difficult to accurately review. The revised Framework illustrates how deficiencies identified at the entity or transaction level become summarized in a single document, classified by component and principle, for consideration during aggregate evaluation.

Sixteen of the 17 Principles associated with the five components (except for control activities) are likely to require a minimum of one form or matrix to assess the design and evaluate evidence regarding each principle. Deficiency issues arising from these assessments would be carried to the deficiency summary, where they would be considered with other deficiencies. However, in the control activities area, transaction controls over revenues, expenses, accruals, adjustments, and period-end procedures are likely to call for many individual forms to support the controls design and testing in order to conclude on Principle 12. Since information technology general controls (ITGCs) have a potential pervasive effect, deficiencies in these controls need to be considered with any identified computer application controls deficiencies that arise because of the ITGC deficiency to assess their severity and implications on financial reporting controls.

Some Illustrative Forms and Reports

One benchmark for developing information-gathering and reporting tools is the Framework examples themselves. In addition to making adjustments to prior illustrated formats in the 1992 and 2006 COSO guidance, this chapter illustrates how an information-gathering form can be used. Rather than re-creating existing narratives and flowcharts of processes, these forms assume that such documents can be referenced, linked, or electronically attached to the form and thus do not need to be recast. The illustrated forms here have a place to list and reference these related documents. This approach allows the COSO project team to focus on the design of controls and evidence of their effectiveness.

To begin, COSO project work papers should be uniquely identified so they can be identified to be archived at the close of the annual assessment process. Some entities may wish to use prefixes to identify the components (5) or principles (17) to aid in navigation and indexing. An index of all work papers in the project should be maintained. To end the form, the preparer and reviewer should sign off with the date of completion.

Principle-Based Information-Gathering Forms

Appendix 13A illustrates an information-gathering form that can be adapted to those principles where a single form (plus attachments) can be used to document the evidence supporting the effective functioning of the principle. Many of the 17 Principles can be addressed using this format. When the documentation becomes voluminous, subdividing the principle may be more efficient, such as with control activities. For example, when individual accounts or streams of transactions are assessed in connection with Principles 10 and 12, separate forms for each assessment or related accounts (e.g., the sales cycle of sales, receivables and cash may be warranted. In some cases, specific controls or the presence of certain documents will be important to demonstrating effectiveness, and they can still be recognized here. Some sample entries have been made in this work paper to illustrate how the documentation might look, but are incomplete regarding full satisfaction of the principle. Noting the points of focus here can help direct the attention of the project member to appropriate sources of evidence. The examples and approaches in the COSO supplementary guidance can provide further insight for the assessment. Note that the form often prompts that any specific fraud or inherent risks identified with this principle be referenced or identified here. This informs the staff about these issues as work on the principle proceeds. Experience has shown that staff working in risk areas have not always been aware of issues identified by others as part of the planning or risk assessment process. Note that the form also prompts for consideration of related principles that might be affected by an identified deficiency. A recommended practice is to consider this early on when a deficiency is identified and not wait until the summarization process to consider interactions. This is so that timely adjustments can be made to the planned work in other areas to respond to issues identified. Awaiting the end summarization process to consider related areas provides little ability to remediate the control deficiency, if necessary, or to consider effects on related areas.

Transaction-Based Forms

Another type of form may actually be more appropriate when addressing the many transaction-based controls under Principle 12, Deploys through policies and procedures. Receipts, expenditures, period-end consolidations, closings, adjustments, and disclosure controls may need to be separately addressed by account, transaction cycle, or some other approach, since controls over the completeness and valuation of these elements of financial statements differ, and aggregation under a single principle form or matrix would be too complex. Of course, the design here needs to ensure the completeness of addressing controls over all the relevant accounts, balances and disclosures.

Appendix 13B illustrates a form focused on controls over revenues and their recognition in either the cash (cash sales) or accounts receivable (credit sales) accounts. Here we are likely encounter a number of specific controls to address the various financial assertions in this process. In addition, it is likely that software or spreadsheets will be involved in transaction processes, and that is linked to the controls here. Later we illustrate a separate form to identify key information about financial accounting software programs and spreadsheets. The information gathered in that form may need only to be referenced here rather than repeated. Since the assessment of issues with software and spreadsheets may be addressed as a group and also may be performed by a specialist, addressing the same issues at the transaction level may be inefficient. Note that earlier it was suggested that IT general and application control considerations be one of the initial areas to be examined. That is so because risks and issues identified at the software level (e.g., poor security, outdated versions, untested modifications) have implications for the accuracy of accounts and transactions they relate to. These are the types of controls most appropriate for walk-throughs. A special walk-through form is illustrated later, and that form can be linked or referenced back to the form where the control is described and to other documents that fully describe the process.

When high reliance on a control is planned or required, sampling or other persuasive evidence is needed before concluding the controls are effective. A sampling form can be completed for each sample that documents the thought process and attached or referenced to the control process work paper. Since efficiently designed walk-throughs may cover several control processes and many controls, a single walk-through form may be associated with a number of controls and processes. If testing is not required due to an audit strategy to not rely on controls and where audit standards only require an assessment of the design of controls ("present"), then there is no need to complete this portion of the form. The walk-through or other evidence should suffice to establish the design of the control.

Walk-through Form

While the AICPA literature is supportive of walk-throughs to confirm the "presence" (design) of controls, the PCAOB elevates their importance. Indeed, the walk-through can be a very informative procedure, particularly when the plan is not to extensively test controls. However, all too often the task of the walk-through is not taken as seriously as it should be. When a junior member of the team is assigned this task, often he or she is not informed of important issues to be aware of. In addition to meeting the documentation expectations of the walk-through, Appendix 13C has suggested data entry on the form to identify inherent or fraud risks that might have been identified, say, in Component 2, Risk Assessment, that might be seen/observed/addressed during the walk-through. In addition, the person performing the task should be alert to the software and spreadsheets that might be utilized in the tasks examined. Employee feedback on those tools can confirm or refute other evidence about the effectiveness of the software or other tools employed.

TRUE **STORY**

In a case ultimately leading to a fraud and resulting bankruptcy, a junior staffer was assigned to do a single walk-through of a commercial loan approval process. Dutifully the person checked off that the loan was less than the appraised value of the property and that an appraisal was in the loan file.

In the legal case, it was noted that the one commercial loan that was examined violated a critical policy of the company since it was for 90% of the appraisal value of the property. Company policy was that the loan could not be for more than half of the appraised collateral value, and that policy was used to justify not making a provision for loan losses, even though this was a subprime lender. Another anomaly was that it was company policy that the appraisal had to be one the company ordered, and not a broker appraisal, and had to be for the property "as is," and not a valuation of the property as it was to be developed. Unfortunately, the checklist did not note these important points, and while the auditor had evidence of management override in her hands, she was not aware of it, nor was she aware of the critical management policies.

As later determined, management ordered that specific loan to be made despite policy (i.e., management override) in anticipation of the borrowers' default and the company taking possession of the collateral, which it valued even more highly than the inflated appraisal. Had the fraud been discovered early on, the company might not have slid into bankruptcy due to holding many unsalable properties as a result of poor management judgment.

The design of effective walk-throughs is not a simple activity. If every control or account has a separate walk-through assigned, a lot of staff time and documentation will be wasted. If a walk-through covers too many controls and accounts, then it becomes an unwieldy task that begs for mistakes and oversights to occur. It is important to balance depth and breadth in matching walk-throughs to controls. Some experimentation based on entity characteristics and specific areas (e.g., control activities, monitoring) is worthwhile.

Also, walk-throughs can be overly complex if a lot of the business process is included with the controls assessment. Flowcharts and narratives can be referenced, linked, or attached to walk-throughs to provide adequate background, but all too often the staff gets tangled in process descriptions and fails to focus on the purpose of the walk-through:

the controls. To identify gaps in controls, the assertions and the control procedures need to be clearly identified.

Automated (computer) controls are a special breed. If ITGCs are effective, then automated controls can be tested *and* walked through with a single transaction (or two). Automated controls are often tested by IT specialists through the computer or by other means, as discussed in Chapter 8 on evidence and testing. Even more importance is attached to the design of such walk-throughs, as they serve both as a confirmation of the design and as evidence supporting reliance. As more entities see the value in automated controls, they are being used more often.

Information Technology General Controls

Appendix 13D presents a simplified form to gather information on aspects of the ITGCs. A sophisticated environment would likely warrant a more extensive inquiry and assessment using a framework such as the one developed by the IT Governance Institute (www.itgi.org). Today, complex, diversely located entities may not have a single IT environment, and it may not be possible to cover most of an entity by looking at only one or even two IT environments. Different regions, countries, and product lines require an analysis of the software and support functions and how they map to the accounts and disclosures in the financial statement. While entities recognize that similar policies, hardware and software platforms, automated controls, and security features will simplify the assessment process, the fact that these features operate independently makes it difficult to extrapolate from one location to all the locations. Considerable time and analysis is required to assess the best strategy for assessing ITGC effectiveness in complex, multilocation entities. In general, separate evaluations of ITGCs are often necessary for adequate overall coverage of the ITGC issue across the entity. Specific deficiencies may need to be localized to the accounts and disclosures being serviced by the control environment examined.

The IT area is one where service organizations are often employed. The introduction some years ago of cloud computing and data storage added to the complexity of risk assessments for such outsourcing. While major issues have not yet arisen in the media regarding these services, some IT managers are wary of the security and access issues surrounding outsourcing these functions to the "cloud."

To be effective, Service Organization Control 1 and 2 reports need to be read, and any exceptions noted therein need to be considered as to how they relate to financial reporting matters. In addition, such reports need to be timely and often require management to at least inquire regarding controls in the period between the report date and the entity's financial year-end. COSO now states that the outsourcer needs to be mindful of the entity's ethical policies entity. How that proposal will play out in practice will take some time to see.

Software and Spreadsheets and Standing Data Files

While sometimes assessed in conjunction with ITGCs and sometimes assessed with the transaction and disclosure controls, somewhere in the process, an inventory and assessment of the software and spreadsheets used in the financial reporting process needs to be made. Appendix 13E provides a format for documenting and inventorying the basic software and spreadsheets and standing data files used and some important information regarding security, testing and automated controls that can be helpful to the assessment and analysis. When referenced to specific controls and walk-throughs, the form can help avoid duplicate (or conflicting) documentation. When multiple IT environments are identified, a version of this form may be associated with each identified environment.

While today the trend is to utilize commercial software for applications whenever possible, some entities continue to maintain legacy software systems. These systems may not be fully documented and tested, so benchmarking tests of the software are recommended to establish a basis for reliance going forward. This is usually a specialist task. If there is a risk that the software cannot be updated if specific personnel or skills are not available, that risk should be recognized in the risk assessment component and a plan to address the risk developed.

Sampling Form

While sometimes included as extended columns on specific controls matrices, additional columns, if they include all of the relevant documentation points, sometimes make the matrix unwieldy and difficult to review. A recommended alternative is to document sampling applications in a standard information-gathering form or matrix and attach/link/reference that worksheet to the associated control. Appendix 13F illustrates the points of documentation and helps structure the sample evaluation that needs to be made when sampling is applied.

Auditors often use judgment to determine sample sizes, but starting with Statement on Accounting Standards (SAS) No. 107, *Risk and Materiality*, the AICPA defined the status of nonstatistical sampling by indicating the sample size should be comparable to one from a well-designed statistical sample, even though a statistical calculation is not required. Thus, for most humans who find it difficult to weigh risk levels, tolerable and expected rates, and sample sizes in their heads to determine sample sizes, the formulas and tables in the AICPA Audit Guide *Audit Sampling* may be helpful in developing defendable sample sizes. In addition, the attribute sampling routines in audit software such as ACL and IDEA[1] can develop sample sizes for a wide range of population sizes, risks, and tolerable deviation rates. Entities and auditors may develop specific sample size guidance to meet the most common needs for testing. The recent challenges to poorly documented sample sizes by auditors, inspectors, and third parties makes it worthwhile to document the sampling application fully and the source of the sample size used.

Considerable additional sampling guidance is available in Chapter 8 and its appendix and also in the AICPA Audit Guide *Audit Sampling*. The AICPA offers an eight-hour continuing professional education course on audit sampling, and various

---

[1] By using the hypergeometric (exact) distribution in its calculations, the IDEA software (Audimation, Inc.) can make exact computations across the entire range of parameters specified.

vendors offer courses and seminars to enhance your understanding of this important audit tool and concept.

Deficiency Summary

The COSO guidance illustrates the use of a summary matrix to accumulate the deficiencies identified throughout the project. Such a summary is useful since the assessment team is expected to consider the deficiencies alone and in combination with other deficiencies when concluding on whether they might be a material weakness and whether ICFRs are effective. In addition, the new Framework stresses the interrelationship of deficiencies, requiring the assessment team to identify any related principles or controls that might be affected by a particular deficiency.

Since the judgment should consider deficiencies by principle, by component and assertion, and possibly any other perspective that might be appropriate, such as by financial statement account or disclosure or location, it may be helpful if the data when gathered could be sorted by these characteristics to simplify the assessment. Thus, data helpful to this purpose should be gathered for each deficiency identified. Appendix 13F illustrates the data gathering process in advance of the multidimensional assessment process that needs to take place. When an integrated software application is designed, a design feature would be to capture the deficiency and related information at the time the deficiency is identified and carry that data automatically to the summary where it can be tabulated in various ways.

While the COSO guidance illustrates a matrix approach for this summary, a columnar approach for the summary may be more practical to display and eventually resort the data as desired in the assessment process. For example, one might use an Excel spreadsheet to display the summary deficiency data. The illustrated form in Appendix 13F can easily be adapted to a columnar summary. Table 13.3 is an example of the headings of a columnar summary adapted from the form.

Component and Final Assessment

During the final assessment process, COSO indicates that all of the principles and all of the components need to be satisfied. As part of the summarization process, one summarization should be at the component level. The form in Appendix 13G illustrates the various data points that might be need to evaluate deficiencies identified for the control

TABLE 13.3 Deficiency Summary in Columnar Form

Defic. ID	Component	Principle	Description	Control Point	Severity	P?[2]	F?[3]	Related Principles

[2]Present? Auditing standards refer to this as *designed and implemented.*
[3]Functioning? Auditing Standards refer to this as *operating effectively.*

environment (CE) component. Here all of the deficiencies regarding the five principles of the CE would be presented. Only one deficiency (the one in the deficiency summary) is illustrated in Appendix 13G.

If the deficiency summaries were displayed in columnar form and sorted into specific components, this separate summary might not be needed, as it would just be one of the reports or views generated from the deficiencies summary. Indeed, when the number of deficiencies identified is in the range of 25 to 50 deficiencies or less, the overall effectiveness assessment can often be made from the deficiencies summary. Research has shown this range of numbers of deficiencies to be common for even larger entities. However, when large numbers of deficiencies are identified (e.g., 200), it may be more appropriate to perform a stepwise assessment, rolling up from the financial statement area to the principle level, then to the component level, and then to the overall assessment.

Appendix 13H displays the summary information that may be useful in making component and overall decisions.

Information-Gathering Form—Principle Focused

THIS APPENDIX PROVIDES suggested formatted work papers for documenting internal controls assessments and testing. It should be used in conjunction with Chapter 13 and the guidance and suggestions in prior chapters. Some data is included in the forms to illustrate the application. Illustrative engagement data is presented in italics to distinguish it from the form. You are also encouraged to consider the illustrative matrices provided in the 2013 COSO Framework's "Illustrative Tools for Assessing Effectiveness of a System of Internal Controls"[1] and develop practice aids that are most meaningful to you and your application(s).

 INFORMATION-GATHERING FORM—PRINCIPLE FOCUSED

Work Paper ID	COSO 4- 105

Component	Control Environment			
Principle	4. Commitment to Attract, Develop, and Retain Competent Individuals in Alignment with Objectives			
Points of Focus	▪ Establishing competence policies and practices ▪ Evaluating competence and addressing deficiencies ▪ Attracting, developing, and retaining competent employees (and contract workers from outsourcing companies) ▪ Planning for succession			
Associated Work Papers	COSO 100	COSO 103		
Assertions	All			

---

[1] The complete set of COSO's 2013 *Internal Control – Integrated Framework* can be ordered in paperback or electronic form from the AICPA's www.cpa2biz.com website.

List of Attachments to This Work Paper

Ref./Link	Attachment Description
HRP	*Entity policy regarding hiring, retention, and promotion*
Focus	*Focus group meeting minutes and summary*

Inherent or Fraud Risks Related to This Principle

X-Ref.	Inherent Risk or Fraud Risk

Evidence of Effectiveness	X-Ref.
1. *Policy is implemented and understood per focus group discussion with employees.* 2. *Discharge of poorly performing staff after counseling and further training.* 3. 4. 5.	*Focus* *HR Action 6-2*

Associated Software	
N/A	

Are Related ITGCs Effective?	*N/A*	Implications if No:

Were deficiencies identified as a result of evidence gathered? Yes/No_____ If yes:

Deficiency Description	Severity Assessment	Related Areas or Principles Affected	X-Ref. to Deficiency Summary

Is the evidence gathered sufficient to conclude with the desired level of assurance that this principle is functioning effectively?

Yes/No	If no, discuss implications.

Preparer	Date
Reviewer	Date

Information Gathering Form—Revenue

Work Paper ID	COSO 12-17

Component	Control Activities			
Principle	12. Deploys through Policies and Procedures			
Points of Focus	<ul><li>Establish policies and procedures to support deployment of management's directives</li><li>Establish responsibility and accountability for executing policies and procedures</li><li>Activities performed in a timely manner</li><li>Take corrective action</li><li>Use competent personnel</li><li>Reassess policies and procedures</li></ul>			
Description	*Controls in the process over revenue recognition and distribution to receivables or cash*			
Statement Captions	*Revenues* *Accounts Receivable* *Cash (Receipts from Sales)*			
Associated Work Papers	*COSO 327*	*COSO 329*	*COSO 330*	*COSO 331*
Assertions	*Existence, Completeness, Accuracy/Valuation (under GAAP)*			

List of Attachments to This Form

Ref./Link	Attachment Description

Key Control and Assertion	X-Ref.	Prev/Det	Auto/Manual
1. *Buyer is approved customer–E* 2. 3. 4. 5 …	CA - 65	*Prevent*	*Auto*
Associated Software			
1. *Customer Verification Process* 2. 3. 4. 5 …	IT - 23	*Prevent*	*Auto*

Are Related ITGCs Effective?	*Yes*	Implications if No:

Related Inherent/Fraud Risks	Description	X-Ref. to RA

Walk-through or Other Evidence	Control	X-Ref.	Comments/Findings	Deficiency X-Ref.
	1. *Buyer is approved customer–E* 2. 3. 4. 5.			

Controls Tests or N/A	X-Ref. to Testing Work Paper	Conclusion
1. *Buyer is approved customer–E* 2. 3. 4. 5.		1. *Effective*

Were deficiencies identified as a result of evidence gathered?
Yes/No_____. If yes:

Deficiency Description	Severity Assessment	Related Areas or Principles Affected	X-Ref. to Deficiency Summary

Is the evidence gathered sufficient to conclude with the desired level of assurance that this process is functioning effectively?

Yes/No	If no, discuss implications.

Preparer	Date
Reviewer	Date

Walk-through Documentation Form

Work Paper ID	COSO W-21

List of Attachments to This Work Paper

Ref./Link	Attachment Description
FC-P	Flowchart of payroll process

Brief Walk-through Description—Scope

Employee payroll

Controls Included in This Walk-through (X-Ref.)

P003	P005	P006	P007		

Inherent and Fraud Risks Relevant to This Area

X-Ref.	Inherent and Fraud Risks
	No specific risks

Persons Interviewed

Name	Date	Role/Function	Discussed

IT/Software or Spreadsheets Utilized in This Process

Software/Spreadsheets	How Used in Process	Evidence/Observations during Walk-through

Description of Walk-through Procedures and Evidence Examined

Do you have any concerns about the attitudes ability or training of employees in this process?

Yes/No	Comments

Do the controls descriptions in the documentation appear accurate, based on your walk-through experience?

Yes/No	Comments

Comments or Deficiencies Identified as a Result of the Walk-through	X-Ref.

Preparer	Date
Reviewer	Date

Information Technology General Controls Assessment Form

Work Paper ID	COSO IT-1

List of Attachments to This Work Paper

Ref./Link	Attachment Description
Org-IT	Org chart for IT department

 ## PART 1. IT CONTROL ENVIRONMENT

Considerations

Organizational structure and reporting relationships are appropriate.
IT has access to senior management and to governance.
IT personnel responsibilities are defined.
Duties are segregated to reduce the risk of fraud.
Authority has been appropriately delegated to achieve the assigned responsibilities.
IT staff and management have adequate knowledge and experience.
IT activities are monitored, tested and periodically reported to senior management.
IT strategic plans are aligned with the general business objectives.
Mechanisms are in place to identify and react to events arising from internal and external sources.

IT Environment Name and Location[2] _____

IT Environment Applies to the Following Locations/Divisions/Entire Entity

Other IT Locations Separately Evaluated (X-Ref.)

Relevant Financial Reporting Applications at This Location

Application	Software or Spreadsheet	Current Version in Use

Applicable WAN/LAN Networks re: Financial Applications

Any recent network audits? Results?

Organization Chart of IT Function—X-Ref. or describe persons, title, contact information

Reference or Linkage	Attachment

Comments

Hardware in Service

Hardware	Placed in Service	Operating System

---

[2] Complete a separate form for every independent IT environment of importance to the entity in financial reporting.

Any noted IT environment changes since last evaluation?

Service Organizations and Outsourcing[3]

Outsourced Functions—describe.

Are SOC 1/SOC 2 reports available for all outsourced functions? Identify the periods covered (frequency) and last report received.

SOC Report? (Y/N)	Latest Report (date)	Issues? (describe)

Assess the implications of any deficiencies noted in these reports on ICFRs. Carry deficiencies to the deficiencies summary.

Report	Implications	Reference in Deficiency Summary

Describe any actions taken by management to inquire or test or update the service organization reports. How does management ensure that the service organization is aware of and complies with the entity's ethical policies?

If service organization reports are not available, how does the entity obtain evidence of the presence and functioning (design and effectiveness) of controls at these service organizations?

Service Organization	Evidence

---

[3] Complete only if IT general controls or any elements thereof are outsourced.

Does the evidence support the presence and functioning of organizational general controls? (Y/N)

Comments

IT Environment Sign-offs

Preparer	Date
Reviewer	Date

 ## PART 2: ACCESS AND SECURITY GENERAL CONTROLS

Considerations:

> Adequate safeguards (including physical, such as temperature, fire, flood, power loss) are in place to prevent unauthorized access to of destruction of documents, records, and IT assets used in financial reporting applications.
> Intrusion protection from outside the entity (Internet, virtual private networks, intrusion detection, firewalls).
> Use of wireless network—policies and procedures.
> Access to accounting functions is properly segregated and assigned to individuals only "as needed and authorized" to perform their duties.
> Programmers are restricted from access to live systems (or actively monitored to detect and supervise such activity).

Do the access and security functions appear to be properly designed (present)?

Y/N	If No, Explain and Assess Implications

Evidence Examined and Tests Performed to Confirm Present and Functioning

Is access to financial applications and functions therein limited to those whose duties require access? Identify the evidence/tests supporting this.

Regarding the last system penetration tests performed on related networks:

- **When and by whom was the test conducted?** _____
- **What were the results and recommendations?**_____
- **Actions taken?**

Has the issue been settled/resolved? What evidence supports your answer?

```
[                                                              ]
```

Have there been any reported security breaches that could affect any financial-related applications? What were the financial systems implications of the breach?

```
[                                                              ]
```

Are "acceptable use" policies present and communicated to all system users? Are policies enforced? Describe the evidence gathered regarding these policies and effectiveness.

```
[                                                              ]
```

Were any deficiencies identified in this period relating to access and security?

```
[                                                              ]
```

If yes:
Describe the deficiency.

```
[                                                              ]
```

Assess the severity and impact on financial reporting.

```
[                                                              ]
```

Identify affected controls and components and carry to control deficiencies summary.

Controls Reference	Impact	Deficiency	Ref. to Deficiency Summary

```
[                                                              ]
```

Does the evidence support the presence and functioning of security and access general controls including maintaining appropriate segregation of duties in the IT function? Y/N.

```
[                                                              ]
```

Comments:

```
[                                                              ]
```

Security and Access Sign-offs

Preparer	Date
Reviewer	Date

PART 3: CHANGE CONTROLS AND NEW SYSTEMS DEVELOPMENT GENERAL CONTROLS

Considerations:

Controls over development or modification process	*Back-out plans*
Process for emergency changes and approvals	Monitoring by management
Approval and communication process from initiation	Segregation of duties (e.g., programming/ testing)
Hardware and software acquisition	*Outsourcing Issues*
Data security issues	Policy and procedures re: backups or copying company data or applications
Documenting system changes including where documentation is stored	Who, what, when, where?
Pre- and postimplementation testing and user training	Process for engaging outsourced services
	Monitoring of outsourced services
Developer access to systems during and after implementation	Review and update agreements with outsourcer

Were there any system or program changes or new systems implemented in the current fiscal period? Y/N.

If not, a relevant issue is whether prior deficiencies noted regarding this element might have also impacted current financial reporting. If so, describe the situation below and update the documentation on the deficiency. If not, you may skip to the conclusions.

Impact of Prior Financial-Related Systems or Program Issues on Current Financial Reporting

Changes/New in Current Period (List all.)

Evidence of controls over the changes/new systems? Describe.

Evidence of and results of testing before implementation?

User feedback and errors discovered after implementation of changes or new systems? Describe actions taken.

Were any deficiencies identified in this period relating to system changes/new systems implementation?

If yes, describe the deficiency.

Assess the impact on financial reporting programs or accounts.

Cross-reference to any related controls and components and carry to control deficiencies summary.

Controls ID	Control Description	Deficiency Summary

Does the evidence support the presence and functioning of change/new systems development general controls including the proper segregation of duties? Y/N.

Comments:

Systems Changes Sign-offs

Preparer	Date
Reviewer	Date

PART 4: OPERATIONS AND MAINTENANCE GENERAL CONTROLS

Considerations

Operating problems noted—feedback within and outside the entity Backup and restore procedures (including periodic testing) User competency/training regarding financial functions	Disaster plans and off-site backup storage Performance metrics or benchmarks applied Observations/tests of controls Third-party outsourcing of any functions (SOC reports obtained and reviewed)

Does the entity effectively maintain its systems with periodic updates and recommended program or system patches? Describe any policy regarding this and evidence the policy is followed. Assess the potential effectiveness of the policy.

Have there been any incidents in the current period attributable to or related to backup and recovery plans?

If so, describe the incident and the actual and potential implications of the incident on financial reporting.

Does the entity have a documented backup and disaster recovery policy? Identify or include/attach the policy in/to the documentation.

Does the entity test its backup/recovery plans? Y/N. Describe.

Does the processing system include any data that is batched and/or processed as a scheduled job? Y/N.

If yes, how does the entity ensure that batched files are updated in proper order?

Have there been any incidents due to improper sequencing of jobs/updates? Y/N.

If yes, describe the incident and what happened and any implications to financial reporting.

```
┌─────────────────────────────────────────────────────────────────┐
│                                                                 │
└─────────────────────────────────────────────────────────────────┘
```

Were any deficiencies identified in this period relating to system operations or maintenance? Y/N.

```
┌───────────────┐
│               │
└───────────────┘
```

If yes, describe the deficiency.

```
┌─────────────────────────────────────────────────────────────────┐
│                                                                 │
└─────────────────────────────────────────────────────────────────┘
```

Assess the severity and impact on financial reporting.

```
┌─────────────────────────────────────────────────────────────────┐
│                                                                 │
└─────────────────────────────────────────────────────────────────┘
```

Cross-reference to any related controls and components and carry to control deficiencies summary.

```
┌─────────────────────────────────────────────────────────────────┐
│                                                                 │
└─────────────────────────────────────────────────────────────────┘
```

Does the evidence support the presence and functioning of operations and maintenance general controls? Y/N.

```
┌───────────────┐
│               │
└───────────────┘
```

Operations and Maintenance Sign-offs

Preparer	Date
Reviewer	Date

Documentation of Financial Reporting Software and Spreadsheets

Work Paper ID	COSO SSD1

List of Attachments to This Work Paper

Ref./Link	Attachment Description
SSP-C	Spreadsheet Policy and Compliance Report

Software

Software Application	PP&E Software				
Current Version	Version 14.1				
Where Is Software Resident?	LAN 1				
Password Protection	Software level PW protection Access limited to J. Lohr and D. Jack per policy				

(continued)

Software (*continued*)

Entity Developed or Commercial?	*Commercial*				
Related Financial Accounts	*PP&E Depreciation Amortization*				
Walk-throughs Reliant on Software	*X-Ref. WT-PPE*				
Automated Controls in software	*Allowance rates and useful life guidelines updated annually*				
Tests of Automated Controls	*See X-Ref. PP-E test*				
If Entity Developed: Tests of legacy software functions and date	*N/A*				
If Commercial Software: Entity modifications and date	*None*				
Tests of Modifications and Date	*N/A*				
Reported Software Issues and Date	*None*				
Identified Software Deficiencies	*None*				

Spreadsheets

Spreadsheet	*Prepaid*				
Application Description	*Prepaid Insurance allocations*				

(continued)

Spreadsheets (*continued*)

Related Accounts and Controls	Prepaid Insurance Expense				
Implementation Date	January 2005				
Person(s) Responsible	J. Deers				
Modified in Current Period?	Yes				
Tested? Date?	Yes. See X-Ref. PP-I				
Reported Issues? Describe issue and implications.	None				
Are proper controls maintained over development, security, and modification of this spreadsheet?	See attached write-up of spreadsheet policies and compliance.				
Identified Spreadsheet Deficiencies	None				

Data Files

Standing Data Files	Payroll				
Application Description	Payroll rates and deductions				
Related Accounts and Controls	Payroll				
Resident Location	Network 1				
Security Applied?	Separate password controls for modification. Limited access for read-only viewing.				
Tested? Date?	Passwords assessed with other password tests. No exceptions. X-Ref.				

(continued)

Data Files (*continued*)

Modified Procedures in Current Period?	No				
Reported Issues? Describe issue and implications.	None				
Are proper controls maintained over development, security, and modification of this data file?	See attached write-up of policies and compliance.				
Identified Data File Deficiencies	None				

Preparer	Date
Reviewer	Date

Sampling Form for Tests of Controls[4]

Work Paper ID	COSO SAM 27

Control Being Sampled (ID)	X-Ref.

Control Description

Dual signature authorization on all checks issued over $5,000

Primary Assertion(s) Tested

Occurrence, Valuation

Description of the Population

Checks over $5,000

How Was Population Completeness Ensured?

Population extracted from all checks. Numerical sequence checked for completeness. Searched for multiple checks issued just below the threshold.

Description of the Test Procedure

Examine voucher package for authorized dual signatures.

---

[4] Form should be associated with each sample of controls.

Definition of an Exception

> *Failure to obtain dual signatures and no evidence of postissuance review or authorization.*

Method of Sample Selection

> *Haphazard selection*

Reliance (Assurance) Desired from Control[5]

> *High (e.g., 90%)*

Reliance Placed on Others' Testing[6]

> *N/A*

Is this control unusually important?[7] Explain if Yes.

> *No*

Sampling Parameters

| Confidence (1.0–risk)[8] | *90%* |

| Tolerable Deviation Rate | *10%* |

| Expected Deviation Rate | *0* |

| Population Size[9] | *5200* |

| Sample Size | *22* |

How was sample size determined?[10]

> *2014 AICPA Audit Sampling Guide Table A-1*

Sample Results

> *No deviations*

---

[5] Normally this will be high for a controls-based audit. However, for a financial statement audit, the range of responses could be from no to high reliance.

[6] If auditors or management are placing some reliance on testing performed by others, then the assurance/confidence from this test can be reduced (risk increased). Note that management cannot rely on auditor testing to reduce their testing levels.

[7] For example, a control over GAAP compliance of revenues may warrant more than usual levels of testing and higher confidence levels (e.g., 95%) and lesser tolerable deviation rates (e.g., 2%).

[8] Consider desired assurance, work of others relied on, and whether control is critical.

[9] For very small populations, use the small population sampling guidance in AICPA *Audit Sampling Guide*, 2014 ed. This parameter can be approximate for controls.

[10] Cite table, formula, or computer program used.

Assessment of Sample Results[11]

No deviations. Sample met criteria.

Deficiency Identified? Yes/No______No_
Severity Assessment

N/A

Noted in Deficiency Summary	X-Ref.
N/A	

Prepared By	Date
Reviewed By	Date

---

[11] AICPA notes that identifying more exceptions in the sample than planned for is a deficiency. See guidance for options if more exceptions are identified than planned for. Note that all sample deviations should be evaluated for qualitative issues (e.g., evidence of circumvention of controls, fraud) in making the assessment.

Summary of Internal Control Deficiencies

Work Paper ID	COSO Sum 1

Deficiency ID Number	CED 1.1
Component Affected	Control Environment
Principle Affected	Principle 1. Commitment to Integrity and Ethical Values
Deficiency Description	Incomplete documented annual employee review of ethics and integrity policy. Files were 76% complete, but with no negative comments.
Specific Control Point re Deficiency	Control CE—Control Point 1.46
Severity Considerations	Compensating controls: No ethics or integrity issues reported through the entity confidential hotline. No evidence of employee suits or other dissatisfaction noted.
Impact on Present	Limited
Impact on Functioning	Limited
Owner	Jack Herringer (HR)
Remediation Plan and Date	Complete files to be obtained by 12/20/20xx
Related Principle Deficiencies	CED 5.1

Prepared by		**Date**	
Reviewed by		**Date**	

Control Environment Component Evaluation Summary

Work Paper ID	COSO 657

Principle 1	Commitment to Integrity and Ethical Values
Present	Y
Functioning	Y
Control X-Ref.	CE-1.14
Deficiency Description	Incomplete documented annual employee review of ethics and integrity policy. Files were 76% complete, but with no negative comments.
Specific Control Point of Deficiency	Control CE—Control point 1.46
Compensating Controls	No ethics or integrity issues reported through the entity confidential hotline. No evidence of employee suits or other dissatisfaction noted.
Severity of Deficiency (D, SD, MW)	D
Related Principles	Principle 5: HR failed to follow up to obtain all statements.
Assigned Deficiency ID	CED: 1.1
Cross Reference Related Area Affected	CE: P5.1
Component Effectiveness	Effective

Prepared By	Date
Reviewed By	Date

CHAPTER FOURTEEN

Summing Up

T HE UPDATING OF the COSO Framework in 2013 provides a challenge to existing entity COSO assessments to migrate to the new principles and guidance as soon as possible. With that comes an opportunity to reassess the efficiency and effectiveness of what was previously done, with an eye toward more effective and efficient projects. Entities new to the controls assessment task will find more guidance and implementation hints available today than were available in the early years of COSO assessments. We have learned a great deal in the last decade about internal controls and internal controls theory.

In the period since the COSO Framework became the standard benchmark for assessing the effectiveness of internal controls over financial reporting, public companies have had concerns about the cost–benefits of the exercise. However, the cost to our capital markets and investors of rising numbers of restatements and dramatic frauds cries out for some regulation to stop these dangerous trends. Since implementation in the public company arena, we have seen a measurable decline in the median level of loss attributable to frauds and a decline in the median value of financial reporting frauds in public companies. In addition, the number of restatements of prior-period financial statements has leveled off. To what extent the self-assessment performed by smaller public companies is as effective in preventing financial misstatements and frauds compared to the dual reporting (i.e., management and the auditors) of accelerated filers is not reliably measured at this time, but expectations are that the self-assessments and management certifications do add quality to the financial reporting of these entities.

One blessing may be that while the COSO Framework is not cast in stone, the 2013 revisions provide hope that we may have reached a level of maturity in the guidance that will signal a long period of effectiveness. The Framework has now fully integrated the current business trends of outsourcing and information technology into its guidance. The experimentation with principles in the 2006 guidance has led to a refined set of principles and their full integration into the Framework. Investments in refining and improving approaches to compliance with the Framework are likely to have a long life.

As entities adjust their COSO compliance approaches, auditors will need to adapt their oversight of management's process and their assessment of internal controls to the approach taken by management, again a challenge. Change brings added cost, but if effective adjustments are made in many of the existing projects, any investment in making a change will likely be recouped early on and longer-term significant savings may actually result. The insights and guidance in this book are directed to helping entities and auditors identify and implement more effective approaches.

About the Author

LYNFORD GRAHAM IS a Certified Public Accountant with more than 30 years of public accounting experience in audit practice and in various national firm policy development groups. He is a visiting professor of accountancy and executive in residence at Bentley University in Waltham, MA. He currently maintains an active consultancy practice in statistical audit sampling, litigation support and audit methodologies, and develops numerous training seminars for conferences and Firms.

He was a partner and the national director of audit policy for BDO Seidman LLP, responsible for the development and implementation of audit policy, sampling training, and audit software. Dr. Graham was responsible for BDO Seidman's implementation of audits of internal control under PCAOB AS 2 and participated with professional groups in developing industry-wide guidance on audits of internal control. Prior to joining BDO Seidman LLP, Dr. Graham was an associate professor of accounting and information systems and a graduate faculty fellow at Rutgers University in Newark, NJ. Prior to that, he was a national accounting and SEC consulting partner for Coopers & Lybrand.

Dr. Graham is a member of the American Institute of Certified Public Accountants and a past member of the AICPA's Auditing Standards Board. He chaired the AICPA's Audit Risk Guide Task Force (Assessing and Responding to Audit Risk in a Financial Statement Audit) and its updates through 2014, and was the principal author and chair of the task force clearing the 2008–2014 revisions of the AICPA audit guide *Audit Sampling*. He is the author of several AICPA courses on technical subjects.

Throughout his career he has maintained an active profile in the academic as well as the business community. In 2002 he received the Distinguished Service Award of the Auditing Section of the AAA. His numerous academic and business publications span a variety of topical areas, including information systems, internal controls, expert systems, audit risk, audit planning, fraud, sampling, analytical procedures, audit judgment, and international accounting and auditing. The coauthored paper cited several times in this book (Bedard, J., and L. Graham. 2011. Detection and severity classification of Sarbanes-Oxley Section 404 internal control deficiencies. The Accounting Review 86 (3): 825–855) was awarded the AAA-Deloitte Wildman award Gold Medal in 2012.

Index

Printed and bound by CPI Group (UK) Ltd, Croydon, CR0 4YY

10/09/2024

14554095-0001